ABOUT THE AUTHOR

Trained in sportswriting at the *Baltimore News American*, Anne Janette Johnson has contributed to such sports publications as *Hotdogs, Heroes & Hooligans*, *The Olympic Factbook*, and *Professional Sports Team Histories*. She is an avid runner and hiker, and her other interests include birdwatching and genealogy. A graduate of the Johns Hopkins University, Anne lives in Haddonfield, New Jersey, with her husband and two daughters. She is working on a novel.

ALSO FROM VISIBLE INK PRESS

THE OLYMPIC FACTBOOK: A SPECTATOR'S GUIDE TO THE SUMMER GAMES. Licensed and sanctioned by the U.S. Olympic Committee, The *Olympic Factbook* brings Olympic events up close, from the lighting of the torch to the closing ceremonies. This companion to the Summer Games offers complete statistics and schedules, poignant human interest stories, and entertaining anecdotes, as well as highlights from previous Olympic competitions and medalists for all 28 Olympic sports. Edited by Rebecca Nelson and Marie J. MacNee, 6" x 9" paperback, 855 pages, 60 photos, ISBN 0-7876-0620-0.

GREAT
WOMEN
in
SPORTS

GREAT WOMEN in SPORTS

ANNE JANETTE JOHNSON

Foreword by
DONNA LOPIANO
Executive Director of the Women's Sports Foundation

DETROIT • NEW YORK • TORONTO

GREAT WOMEN IN SPORTS

Published by Visible Ink Press™
a division of Gale Research
835 Penobscot Building
Detroit, MI 48226-4094

Visible Ink Press™ is a trademark of Gale Research.

Most Visible Ink Press books are available at special quantity discounts when purchased in bulk by corporations, organizations, or groups. Customized printings, special imprints, messages, and excerpts can be produced to meet your needs. For more information, contact Special Markets Manager, Gale Research Inc., 835 Penobscot Bldg., Detroit, MI 48226. Or call 1-800-776-6265.

Art Director: Pamela A. E. Galbreath

Front cover photo of Martina Navratilova: AP/Wide World Photos. Front cover photo of Jackie Joyner-Kersee: © 1988 David Madison/Duomo Photography, Inc. Spine photo of Rebecca Lobo: AP/Wide World Photos. Back cover photo of Bonnie Blair: Reuters/Corbis-Bettman.

Library of Congress Cataloging-in-Publication Data

Johnson, Anne Janette, 1959-
    Great women in sports / Anne Janette Johnson
        p.   cm.
    Includes index.
    ISBN 0-7876-0873-4
    1. Women athletes—Biography.   I. Title.
  GV697.A1J64   1996
  796.092'2—dc20
  [B]   96-12428
                                                       CIP

To Cory Danielle Kram

CONTENTS

WHO PLAYS WHAT

INTRODUCTION

Hard work and high ambition. Those are the two driving character-istics of the great women athletes in this book. Many of these champions have sacrificed any semblance of a normal life to pursue their goals in the arenas of amateur and professional sports. They begin with talent, with supportive families and optimistic coaches. And then they work—every day, from before dawn until dark, pulled along by that vision of the Olympic medal stand, the LPGA championship, the U.S. Open singles title.

"Winning—it's better than breathing," says swimming champion Amy Van Dyken. She should know. She has suffered from asthma all her life.

"I dream of the Olympics," says figure skater Michelle Kwan. So does her family—they have spent an estimated $20,000 a year on her training.

"I like playing against men. It's a real test of my skills," says Manon Rheaume. She gets plenty of opportunity, tending goal in the National Hockey League.

Ask these champions: Is all the sacrifice worth it? Almost to a woman, they would answer with an emphatic *yes!* They become role models, sought after for their opinions, revered for their examples. Shoe companies, cereal makers, makeup manufacturers shower them with endorsement contracts. Wide-eyed kids beg for their autographs. They can even wind up on television, doing commentaries on the very events that made them famous. Greatness in sports today can bring fabulous wealth as well as fame.

There is a dark side, of course. The specter of injury looms. Eating disorders beckon those who must stay petite and slender. Domineering par-ents, with their lives tied up in their children's success, can make impossible demands.

"They turned me into some kind of circus animal," says former teenage track phenomenon Zola Budd Pieterse. *"I was plucked away from everything I loved and put in an environment where I as a person no longer counted."*

"I burned out—I'll say it," admits tennis star Jennifer Capriati. *"I really was not happy with myself, my tennis, my life, my parents, my coaches, my friends. . . . I spent a week in bed in darkness . . . just hating everything."*

"Why should I even think about these medals now being tainted?" asks Kornelia Ender, a former member of an East German Olympic team accused of steroid abuse. *"Why should I even give a thought to what might have been given to me . . . years ago, when I was a child?"*

Remarkably enough, each of these three women is still active in sports despite the pain they've been through as competitors. Sports is a great uplifter. On its simplest level it can keep you healthy; at its peak you brush away tears as the national anthem plays and that medal glistens around your neck. That's why so few of the champions in this book have retired and faded away into a life of obscurity—they, more than most people, are aware of the power of sports to make women healthier, more confident, and, yes, happier.

"The triumph can't be had without the struggle," says former Olympic gold medalist Wilma Rudolph. *"I have spent a lifetime trying to share what it has meant to be a woman first in the world of sports so that other young women have a chance to reach their dreams."*

The women in this book have reached their dreams. Their stories are inspiring, one and all.

I have chosen to present the profiles of *Great Women in Sports* in alphabetical order so as not to give prominence to one sport over the others. Who is to say which is the "best" women's sport? Would it be golf, figure skating, tennis—the traditionally "feminine" pursuits? Or how about some of the sports that used to be off-limits to women—basketball, Ironman triathlon, or NASCAR racing? All are represented here, with many other sports besides, and all deserve equal consideration as worthy roads to glory. The athletes are listed alphabetically in the table of contents, and by sport in the "Who Plays What" section.

Each athlete profile contains hard facts about the athlete, as well as anecdotes about her childhood, early training, and later success in her sport. Wherever possible, a photograph showing the athlete in action accompanies the profile. For quick reference, each entry includes an at-a-glance summary of the athlete's personal stats and career highlights. The comprehensive subject index provides a guide to the athletes and coaches, colleges and universities, leagues and associations, awards and trophies, and many other elements that make up the worlds of these sportswomen.

These great women in sports come from diverse backgrounds, represent a vast array of athletic pursuits, and have experienced unique obstacles and accomplishments. But a common thread unites them all: the pattern that emerges is one of singleminded dedication, hard work, high achievement, *and* the determination to help other young women to do their best as well.

Anne Janette Johnson
March 1996

ACKNOWLEDGMENTS

This book would not have been possible without the help of my editor, Judy Galens. Judy has worked side by side with me every step of the way, from the initial idea to the final credits. I couldn't have asked for a better teammate.

Several others have contributed significantly to this endeavor. Many thanks to Roger Matuz for the inspired idea that started it all; to Kevin Hillstrom and Laurie C. Hillstrom of the Northern Lights Writers Group for their attentive and intelligent proofreading and indexing; to Susan Salas for her diligence and patience in acquiring photographs; and to Pam Hayes for speedily preparing those photos for publication. A special thanks goes out to Marty Laufer of Sportswords, Ltd. and Carol Anne Letheren of the Canadian Olympic Association for their gracious and helpful suggestions.

Other much-needed assistance came from two great librarians, Joan Curtis and Stuart Hoffman, and from Debby Edmund, the babysitter who always arrives with a big bag of goodies.

Just as Olympic athletes go nowhere without good coaching, I am deeply indebted to my high school exposition teacher, Robert Hershey. Through four years at a small Appalachian school, Mr. Hershey taught me everything I would need to do this job. I still think of him every time I sit down to write.

Finally, I wish to thank my husband, Mark Kram, for the wealth of help he gave me on this project—and for his moral support when the going got rough.

FOREWORD

For too long, girls and women have been discouraged from playing sports by a succession of almost desperate myths and stereotypes:

- If she plays sports, she will become "mannish" and "unfeminine."
- If she plays sports, she will develop an eating disorder.
- Because of her anatomical structure, she will suffer more knee injuries in competitive athletics.
- If she trains too hard, her ovaries and bladder will drop.
- Women who play sports are lesbians.
- Women aren't interested in playing sports.
- Women with large breasts can't play golf.

In the 1880s, male doctors even predicted that women who rode bicycles, then symbolic of the independent female, would suffer the dreaded disease of "bicycle face," the distortion of facial muscles from the pain and suffering derived from contact of the female anatomy with a bicycle seat. Spare us!

These myths and stereotypes have arisen from lack of knowledge, fear of the unknown, and the desire of many men to keep the "heady" and powerful cultural institution of sports for themselves. This physical activity called "sport" is not merely fun and games. Rather, sport is one of the most important socio-cultural learning environments ever created. It is no accident that 80 percent of the female executives in Fortune 500 companies identify themselves as having been "tomboys" or sportswomen. Girls and women who play sports derive powerful benefits:

- Women who are active in sports and recreational activities as girls feel greater confidence, self-esteem, and pride in their physical and social selves than those who were sedentary as kids.
- Research suggests that girls who participate in sports are less likely to get involved with drugs, less likely to experience an unwanted pregnancy, and more likely to graduate from high school than those who do not play sports.

Donna A. Lopiano, Ph.D.
Executive Director,
Women's Sports
Foundation

- Half of all girls who participate in some kind of sports activity experience higher than average levels of self-esteem, and less depression.
- One to three hours of exercise a week over a woman's reproductive lifetime (from the teens to about age 40) can bring a 20 to 30 percent reduction in the risk of breast cancer, and four or more hours of exercise a week can reduce the risk almost 60 percent.
- The National Institutes of Health reports that one out of every four women over 60 has osteoporosis (loss of bone mass). There is substantial evidence that weight-bearing exercise, including walking, in combination with calcium supplements, increases bone mass.
- High school girls who participate in sports tend to have higher grades.

The combined effect of ignorance of these benefits and widespread public acceptance of derogatory myths and stereotypes has been exacerbated by the fact that the print and electronic media have failed to fairly portray the female athlete or have rendered her invisible. Until the 1990s, the sports pages devoted more column inches to horses and dogs than women's sports. Even now, 90 percent of all television hours devoted to sports focus on men's sports. The joy and achievements of women in sports are only briefly glimpsed on the occasions of the Olympic Games, coverage of ice skating and gymnastics events (the most feminine rendition of women's sports), or when male sports journalists sensationalize the women who challenge men in head-to-head competition, like hockey goalie Manon Rheaume, jockey Julie Krone, the sailors of America[3], or the Colorado Silver Bullets women's professional baseball team.

If all we know of women's sports is women challenging men, Nancy Kerrigan being attacked, Monica Seles being stabbed, Mary Pierce being abused by her father, or the death of an athlete from an eating disorder, it's no wonder parents are hesitant about encouraging their daughters to play. Can it be that there are no inspirational stories? Can it be there are no female athlete heroes? How can parents know that there is a women's model of sport, that women bring the best of their sensitivity and values to these tests of bodies and minds? Why don't we allow our daughters to feel those special moments of camaraderie between teammates and opponents, too infrequently glimpsed as Navratilova and Evert embrace at the net, as Lobo and Rissotti run with arms upraised in joy upon achieving a national basketball championship, or as Joyner-Kersee drapes her arm around an opponent defeated but so obviously respected?

It is for these reasons that *Great Women in Sports* must be shared with moms and dads and our daughters. The beauty and passion and joy of sports are spectacular and singular experiences that last a lifetime—moments that shape an optimistic view of the world because of the experience of extraordinary possibilities that result from the unity of mind and body. The profiles that follow reveal a balanced view of women in sport—our achievements, our failures, our joys, and our fears. The stories of these great women athletes celebrate their spirit, skill, persistence, and courage, and blow away the mists of prejudice and stereotype. This is the *true* story of women in sports.

MICHELLE
AKERS

Whenever American women's soccer teams have done great work, Michelle Akers has been there. Widely regarded as one of the best soccer players in the world, Akers has helped to move women's soccer into the limelight, initially as part of the first women's world champion team, and more recently as a member of the first-ever U.S. Olympic women's soccer team. Having played professional soccer for nearly a decade—and having been on U.S. national teams even longer—Akers is a fearsome competitor who can truthfully say, "I can score a goal when it's needed."

Born in Santa Clara, California, Akers grew up in the Pacific Northwest, attending public schools in Seattle. She was part of the first generation of American women to benefit from the 1972 federal legislation known as Title IX, which mandates gender equity in sports participation. Suddenly, just as Akers entered grade school, more emphasis was being placed on girls' sports, especially soccer. She was a ready and willing pupil.

Akers was a three-time All-American at Shorecrest High in Seattle. In college at the University of Central Florida, she accomplished the amazing feat of being named an All-American each of her four years in school. She made the roster of the U.S. national team in 1985, just prior to her college graduation, and has been a presence on that team ever since. While other national team members earn a living by coaching—mostly on the college level—Akers has achieved phenomenal success as a professional, playing in Europe. She spent three seasons in Sweden and helped her club, Tyreso, win the Swedish national championship in 1992. Other foreign teams have employed her services as well.

It is as an American champion that Akers has made her mark, though. By mid-1995 she had played in 87 games for the United States, scoring 82 goals. Her most memorable victory came in the first-ever FIFA women's world championship, held in China in 1991. In the tournament, Akers scored 10 goals in six games, including five in one match. She also scored the

SOCCER PLAYER

"It's a tremendous honor to be thought of as the best player in the world. You work toward something your whole life and then all of a sudden the title is there for you."

Michelle Akers is the U.S. Women's National Team all-time leading scorer. (AP/Wide World Photo)

game-winning goal in the gold medal match against Norway, earning a roar of approval from the 63,000 spectators in Guangzhou, at China's Tianhe Stadium. For that victory and other accomplishments in 1991 she earned the Golden Boot Award.

The women's soccer world championship tournament is held every four years. In the interim between the 1991 and 1995 tournaments, problems developed for Akers. Although still widely considered the best American player, she has struggled for some time with Epstein-Barr syndrome, a virus that suppresses the immune system and leaves its victims weak and chronically tired. Akers played soccer for more than two years while suffering from the virus, becoming more and more physically and emotionally drained as time wore on. Since having been diagnosed with Epstein-Barr, she has learned to pace herself—the virus has no cure.

The lingering effects of her illness might have contributed to Akers's disappointing performance in the 1995 women's world championships. Seven minutes into the opening game of the tournament's first round, she suffered a concussion and a knee injury in a collision with another player. She missed three games and was viewed as being in less than top form in a losing match to Norway. The American women's soccer team won a bronze medal in the 1995 world championships, but another world stage had already arisen on the horizon: the 1996 Summer Olympics.

The 1996 Summer Games provide women's soccer with a whole new venue. Previously, women's soccer had not been sanctioned by the International Olympic Committee. Now it will be a regular part of the Summer Games, with 1996 its inaugural year. Although she will be over 30 by the time the 1996 Olympics are played, Akers plans to be a pivotal part of the team. "I always craved the opportunity to play in the Olympics," she told a Knight-Ridder reporter on September 29, 1993. "It will do so much for the future of our sport."

Because American women begin playing soccer at such an early age— and then pursue it in clubs, schools, and leagues—American women's soccer has a higher standing internationally than American men's soccer. The American women are not perceived as playing "catch-up" to better teams from

TITLE IX

On June 23, 1972, President Richard Nixon signed Title IX into law, thereby significantly altering the landscape of American sports. The law says: "No person in the United States shall, on the basis of sex, be excluded from participation in, be denied the benefits of, or be subjected to discrimination under any education program or activity receiving federal financial assistance." Twenty-four years later, Title IX's effectiveness is still being debated. While there is still much room for improvement, great strides have been made. A study appearing in USA Today on November 9, 1995, indicates that 39% of high school athletes were female in 1994–95. That's up from 7% in 1971–72, the school year immediately preceding the implementation of Title IX.

MICHELLE AKERS

American soccer player

Born: February 1, 1966 in Santa Clara, California.

Education: Attended University of Central Florida, earning B.S. in liberal studies/health, 1989.

Career Highlights:
- played varsity high school soccer, 1980–84, three-time All-American
- made U.S. Women's National Team, 1985—
- played for University of Central Florida soccer team, 1984–89, four-time All-American
- named leading goal scorer (with 10 goals) during the inaugural Women's World Cup in China and member of championship team, 1991
- competed for Tyreso Football Club in Sweden, 1990, 1992, and 1994
- scored more goals than any other male or female player in country during Swedish soccer season, 1992
- named leading goal scorer during U.S. Olympic Festival, 1993
- named U.S. Women's National Team all-time leading scorer, 1995.

Awards: Named three-time high school All-American, 1982–84; four-time collegiate All-American, 1985–88; won Hermann Trophy; named U.S. Soccer's Female Athlete of the Year, 1990 and 1991; won Golden Boot Award, given to leading scorer at Women's World Cup, 1991.

other nations. "We're half the soccer-playing population in the United States," Akers told New York's *Newsday* on August 21, 1994. "Women's soccer is part of a huge cultural change around the world. We're starting to become a product when we can sell out 5-to-8,000 seat stadiums." For her part, Akers plans to be part of this "soccer revolution" well into the next century. "I still just love to play," she concluded in the *Los Angeles Times* on May 25, 1995. "I'm enjoying the game. . . . I'm still scoring goals, I'm still beating people, I'm still a force out here. . . . I can play in the year 2000." When that time comes, America's leading scorer will still be welcome on any field.

TENLEY
ALBRIGHT

Before Tenley Albright skated onto the ice at the 1956 Olympic Games in Cortina, Italy, no American woman had ever won a gold medal in Olympic figure skating. Albright brought home the gold and ever since has been considered a pioneer for the many talented American skaters who have come along in her wake. Certainly her accomplishments are a shining example of what can be done with hard work, talent, and a competitive spirit.

Albright was born July 18, 1935, the only daughter of a wealthy surgeon, Hollis Albright, and his wife, Elin. The skater's early life was one of affluence and privilege in a posh Boston suburb. She received her first pair of ice skates at the age of eight and showed such interest in the sport that her indulgent father flooded part of the family's back yard so she could have her own private rink. The following year she had outgrown both the initial pair of skates and the back yard ice patch. She moved on to real figure skates and lessons at the prestigious Skating Club of Boston.

Always a perfectionist about her school work, Albright had to be persuaded to put the same amount of concentration into her skating. After a stern lecture by her coach, Maribel Vinson, the youngster decided to buckle down and learn the compulsory figures that seemed so boring and tedious to perform. As she became more involved with the figures, however, she became fascinated with them—and a star was born.

Illness almost ended Albright's career before it began. In September of 1946 she contracted polio, an extremely serious viral disease that often left its victims partly paralyzed. Fortunately for Albright, she had a mild case and, after three weeks in the hospital, was released. The muscles in her lower back were severely weakened, but the doctors encouraged her to skate, feeling that the exercise would improve the condition. They were right. Just four months after her polio attack, Albright won her first important competition—the Eastern Juvenile Skating Championship.

Titles came easily after that. In 1950 she skated away with the National Junior Championship, and in 1951, at age 15, she won the Senior Eastern Championship. The stage was set for competition in the international arena.

FIGURE SKATER

"The one thing I want to be able to do after it's over is say that was my best. It's better to lose that way than to win with something less than that. But it's fun to win, isn't it?"

—Albright on her hopes for the 1956 Olympics

Tenley Albright skates to a gold in the 1956 Olympics. (UPI/Bettmann)

No one expected the teenaged Tenley Albright to win a medal at the 1952 Olympics. She qualified to represent America, however, and when she got to Oslo, Norway, for the Winter Games she skated brilliantly and won a silver medal. Her feat was doubly remarkable in that she had never even won the U.S. National Championship. That title fell into place just a month later, when she won her first of five consecutive national titles. In 1953, at the tender age of 17, she became world champion.

At this point Tenley Albright's history veers far from the norm for world-ranked athletic competitors. In the autumn of 1953, determined to achieve her other goal of becoming a surgeon, she enrolled in pre-med classes at Radcliffe University. From that time until the 1956 Olympics, Albright combined the demands of a rigorous college education with the demands of her skating. She took a semester break in the autumn of 1955, but she had gone to summer school to keep up with her classmates. A typical day for Albright began at four o'clock in the morning and lasted well into the evening, with several hours of skating in addition to classes and studying.

TENLEY ALBRIGHT

American figure skater

Born: July 18, 1935 in Newton Centre, Massachusetts.

Education: Attended Radcliffe University, bachelor's degree; Harvard Medical School, graduated 1961.

Career Highlights:

- took first place, Eastern Juvenile Skating Championship, 1947
- won National Junior Figure Skating Championship, 1950
- placed first, Women's Senior Eastern Championship, 1951
- earned silver medal, 1952 Olympic Games, Oslo, Norway
- won first place, U.S. National Championship, 1952–56
- took first place, World Figure Skating Championship, 1953, 1955
- received gold medal, 1956 Olympic Games, Cortina, Italy.

Two weeks prior to the 1956 Olympics in Cortina, Albright fell on the ice and cut her right ankle to the bone. The painful injury seemed destined to hurt her chances of winning another Olympic medal, but Albright bandaged the wound and persevered. Her principal competitor in the 1956 Winter Games was another American, Carol Heiss, who was some years younger and very talented. Albright and Heiss placed first and second in the competition after the compulsory figures, and their scores were quite close. That meant that Albright would have to skate flawlessly in the free skate if she wanted the gold medal. Dipping into her reservoir of determination, she did just that, and she became the first American woman ever to win a skating gold medal.

Only when the competition was over did Albright admit that her injury had bothered her. "It is all over now, and I can say that my leg has not stopped hurting once since I cut it two weeks ago," she said, as quoted in the book *Great Skates*. Nevertheless, she returned to America an Olympic champion. Heiss got revenge shortly thereafter by winning the 1956 World Championships, but Albright took another national title a few weeks after that. In nine meetings, Albright beat Heiss eight times.

Albright spurned an offer to skate with the Ice Capades and entered Harvard medical school in 1957. She graduated in 1961 with a specialty in surgery and joined her father's practice in Boston. She has lived there ever since with her second husband, Gerald Blakeley, and her three daughters by a previous marriage. The consummate amateur, Albright never received a single paycheck from her skating. She has served on the U.S. Olympic Committee and the International Olympic Committee and has recently retired from her medical practice.

Skating, Albright once said, is something to be done "for fun." Thus she still dons her skates from time to time and hits the rink, relaxing with the memories of her pioneering Olympic glory.

ALL-AMERICAN GIRLS BASEBALL LEAGUE

"We all might have played baseball in our sandlots, but heavenly days, none of us acted like men, I'll tell you that. . . . It's something born in you—to be a natural athlete."

—Phyllis Koehn, All-American Girls Baseball League

They played real baseball wearing skirts, lipstick, and nail polish. Their teams sported such rampantly anti-feminist names as the Daisys, the Lassies, the Peaches, and the Belles. The members of the All-American Girls Baseball League endured charm school lessons, chaperons, and all sorts of rules aimed at keeping them "womanly." Nevertheless, these extraordinary women entertained crowds of fans for a decade between 1943 and 1954, and their exploits have been warmly re-created in the Penny Marshall film, *A League of Their Own.*

The AAGBL was the brainchild of Philip K. Wrigley, whose fortune from the sale of chewing gum had also enabled him to own the Chicago Cubs. As World War II began to claim many of major league baseball's best players, Wrigley speculated that perhaps a women's league could keep fans interested in the game. He had ample reason to believe this could be true: women's softball leagues had achieved immense popularity in the 1930s and were known to sometimes draw crowds of thousands to games.

In December of 1942 Wrigley announced the formation of the All-American Girls Softball League. Cities in the Midwest were invited to organize teams to begin play in the spring of 1943. As Wrigley saw it, however, his league would be different from other women's softball organizations. He firmly insisted that, along with playing talent, his league participants must display "femininity." Prospective players could not have short hair or wear pants on or off the field. They had to wear makeup and display "charm." Beauty counted as much as talent in filling team rosters. Wrigley's successor as league chairman, Arthur Meyerhoff, described the new venture as "baseball, traditionally a men's game, played by feminine type girls with masculine skill."

The paradox of playing a hard-knocks game while at the same time appearing dainty and well manicured was not lost on the young women who joined the All-American Girls Softball League. The strange requirements became even more amusing when the league switched from softball to standard baseball in 1945. Meyerhoff made sure the press knew that his AAGBL play-

Skirts didn't stop them from sliding in the AAGBL; witness this game between the Racine Belles and the South Bend Blue Sox, 1947. (The Bettmann Archive)

ers were required to attend charm classes as part of their spring training, and that their behavior off the field was monitored by chaperons. Even the women's living arrangements were subject to scrutiny, and any hint of homosexual behavior meant immediate expulsion from the team.

What woman could possibly want to perform under such ridiculous restrictions? The answer is simple: they had few other choices. League player Pepper Paire is quoted in the book *Coming on Strong: Gender and Sexuality in Twentieth Century Woman's Sport* on the subject of the rules on appearance and behavior: "You have to understand that we'd rather play ball than eat, and where else could we go and get paid $100 a week to play ball?"

The All-American Girls Baseball League (re-named with the switch to hardball in 1945) attracted players from nearly every American state and several Canadian provinces. It fielded teams in a number of mid-sized Midwestern cities such as Fort Wayne, Indiana, Peoria, Illinois, and Kalamazoo, Michigan. Conceived as an attraction to replace men's baseball during the years of World War II, the league proved popular enough to out-last the war and the return of major league baseball to the urban markets. Players' salaries ranged from $40-$80 a week during the first years of play to as much as $125 per week in later years. And for a time the league was so successful that it spawned a rival, the National Girls Baseball League, that sparked a bidding war for the best players and brought better salaries to the top stars.

Two forces combined to bring an end to the AAGBL. The first was television, which dealt a devastating blow to many smaller professional and semi-professional sporting events. The other force that undermined women's pro baseball was the onset of male-only Little Leagues. Baseball, once a sand-lot game where both sexes could participate on equal footing, became the province of boys alone—and girls lost the opportunity to hone their skills at an early age. At any rate, the AAGBL ended its existence at the end of the 1954 season, at which time the league had shrunk to a mere five teams.

The history of this unique sporting venture might have become little more than a footnote, but the AAGBL was rescued from obscurity by the film *A League of Their Own,* which recreated the pleasures and pains of perform-ing a "masculine" game while exerting "feminine" charm. The film's director, Penny Marshall, performed a service on behalf of the AAGBL, because in its time it was an extremely viable and profitable sporting venture. Sources esti-mate that in its best years in the late 1940s, the league attracted almost a mil-lion paying customers for a 120-game yearly schedule. Former Rockford, Illinois, player Mary Pratt recalled the league's popularity in *Coming on Strong.* "The fans thought we were the best thing that ever came down the pike," she said. "They really looked up to us."

AMERICA³

The America's Cup yacht race is the oldest competitive event in existence today. For the first 143 years of its history, it was a proving ground for men only, and wealthy men at that. The gender barrier was breached in 1994, when defending Cup champion Bill Koch announced that he was giving his America's Cup boats, a gold mine of research and development data, and several million dollars in seed money, to an all-woman crew—the first in the event's long history. While Koch talked about the chance to "empower" women and the novelty of an all-woman America's Cup team, the women who signed on to race the boat had one clear goal. They wanted to win, not only because they were women, but because they were great sailors.

Koch, an amateur sailor from Kansas, had earned a fortune from oil drilling in his home state. He entered the America's Cup race in 1992 with a radically redesigned boat and an all-new (and all-male) crew. The team, dubbed America³ (America Cubed), won the five-month event even though the crew had less experience than almost any other participating team. Koch—who has described himself as a maverick who likes to shake up the status quo—decided in 1994 to raise the visibility of his project just a bit higher. In an unprecedented move, he declared that America³ would race in the 1995 America's Cup as an all-woman team.

When word got out that Koch was looking for 24 female sailors, he was deluged with some 650 applications. A core crew was chosen in March 1994, and the rest of the team was rounded out a few months later. In terms of personnel, the America³ roster held a number of intriguing members. Experienced sailors such as helmsman Dawn Riley, 1992 Olympic bronze medalist J. J. Isler, 1988 gold medalists Allison Jolly and Lynne Jewell-Shore, and four-time Rolex Yachtswoman of the Year Betsy Alison provided the nucleus of the team. The surprise members included Olympic rowers Stephanie Maxwell-Pierson and Anna Seaton, as well as Alison Townley, holder of 22 U.S. rowing titles. Another surprise teammate was Shelley Beattie, a professional bodybuilder who performed under the stage name "Siren" on television's *American Gladiators* series.

SAILING TEAM

"To those people who say we can't compete with men in the America's Cup—and I don't think there are too many of them—I say we can do it as well or better."

—Katie Pettibone, sail trimmer, America³ team

11

The all-female crew of America³, pictured here on the Mighty Mary, took aboard a male crew member in this race against Stars & Stripes.

(Reuters/Blake Sell/Archive Photos)

A yachting team staffed by rowers and a bodybuilder? At first glance it seems curious, but in fact many members of America³ were chosen not for their sailing experience but for their strength, stamina, and ability to work as a team. Women's team coach Stu Argo explained the philosophy in the San Jose Mercury News: "The major criteria was 'thou shalt be a team player.' We had to figure out who would be able to go the distance and work with the team for the entire year. We had to look at positive attitude first. Then we looked at ability, fitness and coachability."

The 24-member America³ team of 1994–95 embarked on a strenuous training schedule that often lasted up to 14 hours a day. Every woman began each morning with fitness and strength-building exercises. They would then spend hours on board the ship—which, though getting old, was the one that won the 1992 Cup. Late afternoons were spent discussing strategy and determining what mistakes had been made during the day's routine. All of the

AMERICA³ 1995 ROSTER

Position	Name	Age	Hometown
Bow	Susie Leech Nairn	27	Greenwich, CT
Sewer	Merritt Carey	25	Tenants Harbor, ME
Sewer	Sarah Cavanagh	35	Newburyport, MA
Mast	Joan Touchette	24	Newport, RI
Mast	Diana Klybert	36	Chicago, IL
Pit	Lisa Charles	24	Providence, RI
Pit	Christy Evans	31	Marblehead, MA
Pit	Jane Oetking	27	New Zealand
Pit	Linda Lindquist	32	Chicago, IL
Grinder	Stephanie Maxwell-Pierson	30	Somerville, NJ
Grinder	Stephanie Armitage-Johnson	33	Payallup, WA
Grinder	Marci Porter	27	San Ramon, CA
Grinder	Amy Baltzell	28	Wellesley, MA
Grinder	Sarah Bergeron	21	Middletown, NJ
Trimmer	Hannah Swett	25	Jamestown, RI
Trimmer	Merritt Palm	26	Fort Lauderdale, FL
Trimmer	Katie Pettibone	22	Miami, FL
Trimmer	Debbie Pettibone	25	Miami, FL
Main	Melissa Purdy	24	Tiburon, CA
Main Caddie	Shelley Beattie	26	Monmouth, OR
Helm	Leslie Egnot	31	New Zealand
Helm	Dawn Riley	30	Detroit, MI
Tactician	J. J. Isler	30	San Diego, CA
Navigator	Courtenay Becker-Dey	29	Rye, NY
Navigator	Annie Gardner Nelson	35	Miami, FL

America³ coaches were men, simply because women had rarely participated meaningfully in the America's Cup race before.

One of the important on-shore activities for the team was fund raising. Koch had given the boats and about a third of the money needed to participate in the race. The rest had to be raised by donations from corporations and private donors. The task of coordinating this effort fell to veteran sailor Linda Lindquist, a Chicago native who had big boat experience with both male and female crews. "It's all about breaking barriers and setting new goals," Lindquist said as she received endorsements from corporations such as Yoplait Yogurt, Chevrolet, and L'Oreal. All told, a dozen corporate sponsors pledged millions toward a new boat and modest salary stipends for the crew. Other significant money was raised by the sale of t-shirts, hats, and waterproof wallets—all with the women's team logo displayed.

As the America's Cup preliminary races got underway early in 1995, the women's team showed early flashes of brilliance and then slipped into third place behind the other two (all-male) America's Cup contenders from the U.S. Racing with the 1992 boat, the women's team found itself suffering from its hasty assembly of personnel and lack of lengthy training time. Hopes were high when the team's new boat, Mighty Mary, made its debut in March of 1995, but the women continued to struggle and failed to make the two-boat cut for the America's Cup final in the summer of 1995.

The experiment was hardly a failure, however. It provided some of America's best women sailors with a chance to prove their mettle against their male counterparts. And, with the vast publicity the women received—including television commercials and a documentary film—America[3] proved that a viable America's Cup team could certainly include, or even be composed completely of, women. Sail trimmer Merritt Palm of Fort Lauderdale, Florida, said it best: "Maybe we're not as strong as the men, but there's so much more that goes into racing—tactics, driving a boat, trimming sails—all of it. I can't tell you we're going to win, but I know we're going to show what we have. And what we have is tremendous."

EVELYN ASHFORD

Sprinters are not known for their sports longevity. Evelyn Ashford is the exception to that rule.

Ashford's four gold medals in five Olympic appearances rank her among the most successful American Olympians of all time. She first made the Olympic team in 1976 as a 19-year-old college student. She most recently returned to the Summer Games in 1992 as a 35-year-old wife and mother of a seven-year-old child. In between she won two golds in 1984, and a gold and silver in 1988. She won another gold in 1992. Ashford has forged a career that any athlete would be proud to claim.

A California native, Ashford grew up enjoying athletics. She began taking her running seriously in high school after the football coach at her Sacramento-area school challenged her to race some of his male players. "The football coach saw me running in physical education class," she recalled in a June 1986 *Ebony* profile. "I was just running down the field or something and he approached me and said, 'You know, you are really fast. How would you like to run against my best guy on the football team? I think you can beat him. I want to see if you can.' I was game. We ran 50 yards and I beat him. . . . I got a little reputation like that. I started getting free lunches and stuff like that because I beat all the guys. I got very popular that way. There was no envy. It was always very positive."

Ashford was equally successful against competitors of her own gender, and by her senior year in high school she had won numerous state and regional track meets. She accepted a full scholarship to the University of California, Los Angeles in 1975, and it was there that she began to prepare for Olympic greatness. She qualified for the Olympic team in 1976 as a 100-meter sprinter, but she failed to advance into the final rounds of the competition. With great anticipation she awaited the 1980 Summer Games.

Like so many other American athletes, her anticipation soon turned to despair. In 1980, President Jimmy Carter decided that the United States would boycott the Olympics because the Soviet Union had invaded Afghan-

"I don't know about you guys, but I'm EXCITED. I'm 35. I'm not supposed to be running like this."

—Ashford, speaking to the press upon qualifying for the 1992 U.S. Olympic team

Evelyn Ashford wins the 100-meter race and a spot on the U.S. Olympic Team for the 1984 Games. (AP/Wide World Photos)

istan. At the time, Ashford was in the very prime of her career—and sprinters generally do not last long. "I was devastated," she admitted in *Ebony*. "That was my big chance."

Or so she thought at the time. Her persistence in the competitive world of sprinting paid huge dividends when the Olympics rolled around again in 1984. Performing as almost a home town hero in Los Angeles, Ashford won a gold medal in the 100 meter sprint and another as part of the 4 × 100 meter relay. Her time of 10.76 seconds in the 100-meter race set an Olympic record.

Ashford gave birth to a daughter in 1986 and returned to running almost immediately afterwards, regaining her old form and a new measure of emotional equilibrium to boot. Competing against women much younger than herself, she earned a berth on the 1988 Olympic team and won a silver medal in the 100-meter sprint with a second-place finish behind American Florence

EVELYN ASHFORD

American track and field athlete

Born: April 15, 1957 in Shreveport, Louisiana.

Education: Won full scholarship to University of California, Los Angeles, in 1975.

Career Highlights:
• qualified for the U.S. Olympic team, 1976

• won gold medal, 100-meter sprint, and gold medal, 4 × 100-meter relay, 1984 Olympic Games, Los Angeles, California

• took home silver medal, 100-meter sprint, and gold medal, 4 × 100-meter relay, 1988 Olympic Games, Seoul, South Korea

• earned gold medal, 4 × 100-meter relay, 1992 Olympic Games, Barcelona, Spain.

Griffith-Joyner. As a consolation prize, Ashford pinned down a third gold medal as part of a 4 × 100 meter relay team that included Griffith-Joyner, Alice Brown, and Sheila Echols.

Ready to retire? Not Evelyn Ashford. She qualified for the 1992 Olympics as a sprinter *and* member of the relay team. It was at the 1992 Summer Games that she earned her fourth gold, as leader of the 4 × 100 relay. Upon qualifying for what she realized was her last Olympic appearance, Ashford simply gushed to the American press. "I don't know about you guys, but I'm EXCITED," she exclaimed. "I'm 35. I'm not supposed to be running like this."

As pleasant and personable off the track as she was competitive on it, Ashford has parlayed her Olympic success into a solid career. She was a spokesperson for and member of the first-ever Mazda-sponsored track club, and in the mid-1980s she served as a reporter for the cable television program *World Class Woman*.

In a January 1, 1995, *New York Times Magazine* essay, Ashford named Olympic star Wilma Rudolph as the inspiration for her running career. "We definitely had different styles," Ashford wrote. "She was over 6 feet tall; . . . I'm 5 foot 5, though a lot of people don't believe me. But she inspired me to pursue my dream of being a runner, to stick with it."

Few have "stuck with it" more brilliantly than Evelyn Ashford.

TRACY
AUSTIN

TENNIS PLAYER

"At 8, I decided that I wanted to be the best tennis player in the world. Sure, I liked playing with Barbie dolls, but I preferred practicing my backhand."

Tracy Austin has been called the "ultimate tennis prodigy." The youngest member ever elected to the Tennis Hall of Fame, Austin appeared in her first Wimbledon singles tournament at the age of 14, was ranked number one in the world at 17, and won the U.S. Open twice before turning 21. As a freckle-faced youngster in the late 1970s, Austin won a worldwide following of fans who admired the courageous way she faced and beat older, more experienced opponents. Her reign as a top tennis challenger was short-lived, however—injuries and a near-fatal automobile accident effectively ended her dominance of tennis and forced her to re-evaluate her future. Having battled back from serious knee surgery, Austin competes today in the serene knowledge that her biggest and most satisfying victories have taken place off the court.

Born December 12, 1962, in Redondo Beach, California, Austin was the youngest of five children in a tennis-loving family. At the tender age of two she began to imitate her older siblings by swinging a cut-down tennis racket. At four she hit volleys against a wall so fiercely that the coach at the local tennis club took her under his wing and predicted she would be a star. She entered her first tournament at seven and began beating teenagers in competition at eight. "My passion grew as I did," Austin wrote in an April 6, 1993, *Family Circle* profile. "At 8, I decided that I wanted to be the best tennis player in the world. Sure, I liked playing with Barbie dolls, but I preferred practicing my backhand. I loved the challenge, the exertion, the strategy of tennis—and I still do."

Austin was practically unbeatable as an amateur. She won the national title for 12-year-olds in 1974 and the indoor singles championship for girls 16 and under in 1976. The following year she announced her presence to a wider world. With ten national junior titles under her belt, she decided to enter the women's singles competition at Wimbledon. No one expected her to win, but she did manage to advance past a tough first-round match before being retired by Chris Evert in straight sets. Her strong showing at Wimbledon was followed by a U.S. Open appearance that ended in the quarterfinals, earning her *Tennis* magazine's Rookie of the Year award. She was 14 at the time.

Eighteen-year-old Tracy Austin gives it her all in this match against Martina Navratilova in Tokyo, Japan, 1980. (UPI/Bettmann)

All pretenses at a normal life ended in 1978, when Austin turned pro and joined the international tennis circuit. While her fellow classmates at Rolling Hills High School continued their studies, she traveled all over the world for tournaments, playing in both singles and doubles competitions. She won her first major international title, the Italian Open, in May of 1979 and was fourth-seeded for the 1979 Wimbledon tournament. While unsuccessful at Wimbledon that year, she did win the 1979 U.S. Open singles championship, beating Chris Evert Lloyd in straight sets.

Austin was the youngest player ever to win a U.S. Open title and the youngest ever to earn a million dollars as a pro. She was only 17, barely old enough to hold a driver's license, when she was officially ranked number one in the world. Austin's most satisfying tennis victory occurred in 1981 when, after overcoming a painful bout of sciatica, she defeated Martina Navratilova for a second U.S. Open title. "I was ecstatic," she recalled in *Family Circle*. " 'What's next?' I asked myself. 'How can I top what I've already accomplished?' "

Little did she know that her finest work was behind her. The body she had pushed so hard—and so joyously—now began to rebel. From 1982 until 1989 she made only sporadic appearances while enduring injuries to her hamstrings, hip-flexor muscles, sciatic nerve, and shoulders. Then, just as she was set to mount a serious comeback, her plans were altered by fate. On August 3, 1989, a car she was driving was hit by a van that had run a red light. In the first terrible moments after the crash, Austin thought she was paralyzed. Later, at the hospital, she discovered that her right knee had been shattered. The surgery to rebuild her kneecap took five hours to complete. Afterwards, one of her doctors told her she would never play professional tennis again.

Determined to regain at least her ability to walk without a limp, Austin underwent as many as 14 hours of physical therapy a day for months. By the late spring of 1990 she was back on the court hitting volleys, and in 1994 she returned to the pro tour for another year of competition. Her philosophy was significantly altered by the accident and its aftermath, however. "No longer am I driven by the desire to win tournaments," she explained in *Family Circle*. "Instead I have found a new appreciation for life. I had escaped death by a split second—and for that I will always be grateful."

Austin was inducted into the Tennis Hall of Fame in 1992, the youngest person ever to receive that honor. Now married and still as passionate about tennis as ever, she serves as a television commentator at important tennis tournaments (including the Olympic Games), and also as a motivational speaker. Her annual charity event, the Tracy Austin Pro-Celebrity Tennis Tournament, benefits a children's health center in southern California

TRACY AUSTIN

American tennis player

Born: December 12, 1962 in Redondo Beach, California.

Career Highlights:
- earned 10 national junior titles, 1974–76
- competed in Wimbledon and U.S. Open at age 14
- won Avon Futures tournament in Portland, Oregon, 1977—became youngest player ever to win a pro singles title

- won first major international title, Italian Open, 1979
- won U.S. Open singles championship, 1979—youngest player ever to do so
- won Wimbledon mixed doubles title (with her brother John—first brother-sister duo to capture that title), 1980
- took U.S. Open singles championship, 1981.

Awards: Inducted into the Tennis Hall of Fame, 1992.

near her home base of Los Angeles. Although she still competes as her injuries allow, Austin told *People* magazine on May 10, 1993, that she has lost interest in her place in the rankings. "I'm already happy," she said, "and I'm already in the Hall of Fame. They can't take that away from me."

ISABELLE AUTISSIER

SAILOR

"I think the bigger the boat, the longer the race, the easier it is for a woman, because you need more of your brain than muscles."

For Isabelle Autissier, around-the-world solo sailing is a dream come true. A two-time entrant in the grueling, eight month-long BOC around-the-world yacht race, Autissier has shown remarkable endurance and ability as skipper of several state-of-the-art, 60-foot yachts. She is a national heroine in her native France and is known worldwide for her amazing record-setting sail from New York to San Francisco via Cape Horn. When Autissier enters a race, it is not just to prove that a woman can finish. She wants to win. "I think, in France, and in America, that maybe women aren't used to being out in front," she told the *Charlotte Observer* on October 17, 1994. Being "out in front" is what Isabelle Autissier is all about.

Autissier was born October 18, 1956, in the French coastal province of Brittany. She began sailing at age six with the help of her family, exploring the region around La Rochelle in small dinghies. She has said that she began planning her first solo circumnavigation of the globe when she was 12. "As a child, I was never told that something was impossible," she declared in the *Charlotte Observer*. "I was only taught that everything had a price."

Part of that price, in long-distance sailing, is preparation. Autissier took her love of sailing with her to college, where she took an advanced degree in marine sciences. She is an expert on such subjects as weather patterns, currents, and navigation and—when not sailing—teaches college courses in France. The enormous expenses of her sport are partly underwritten by personal appearances and by wealthy French backers who admire her resolve.

Autissier first made headlines in 1991 as the first woman to make a solo sail around the world. She was the sole female entrant in the 1990–91 BOC yacht race, which began and ended along the East Coast of the United States. A four-stage endurance test—making stops in South Africa, Australia, Uruguay, and America—the race is certainly not for sissies. One *Los Angeles Times* reporter joked, "To say the race is grueling is to say it's kind of tough to win a Super Bowl." Experts estimate that the cost of competing in a 40- or 60-foot boat can exceed $2.5 million, but all the technology in the world cannot prepare the racers for the violent storms and other hazards awaiting them at sea.

Isabelle Autissier (center) celebrates with her crew after breaking the New York to San Francisco record. (AP/Wide World Photos)

In Autissier's case, her 60-foot ship, Ecureuil Poitou-Charentes, performed admirably in the 1990–91 BOC challenge. She finished seventh in her class and returned to France for a hero's welcome. Calling the experience a "dream come true," she vowed to enter the race again—and to win it.

First she had another record to smash. In the spring of 1994, Autissier and a crew of three men piloted her new boat, the Ecureuil Poitou-Charentes 2, around Cape Horn from New York harbor to San Francisco's Golden Gate Bridge. Autissier completed this hazardous sail in just 62 days, five hours, and 55 minutes, besting the old record by 14 days. She is only the fourth person in history to set a new record, and the first woman to do so. At her docking in San Francisco Harbor on April 24, 1994, Autissier and her crew members were showered with champagne and cheered by a crowd several hundred strong. "I would like to thank the sea and the waves and the winds because they let us go through," she told the crowd.

ISABELLE AUTISSIER

French sailer

Born: October 18, 1956 in Brittany, France.

Career Highlights:

- distinguished as first and only woman to enter BOC around-the-world solo yacht race
- finished seventh overall in her class in 1990–91 BOC race
- sailed from New York to San Francisco via Cape Horn in record-breaking time

- entered 1994–95 BOC around-the-world race, winning first of four legs, but was unable to complete race due to weather-related boat destruction.

Awards: Holds the record for sailing from New York to San Francisco around Cape Horn. Autissier and three crew members completed the trip in 62 days, five hours, and 55 minutes, besting the old record by 14 days. She is only the fourth person in history to set a new record, and the first woman to do so.

That sail was a shakedown for the more rigorous 27,000-mile BOC race, set to begin in the autumn of 1994. Autissier entered the competition with the Ecureuil Poitou Charentes 2 in Charleston, South Carolina, on September 17, 1994, despite having been swamped by a Gulf Stream wave on her way south for the event. With quickly refurbished electronics and a strong hunch about Atlantic weather patterns, Autissier set off by herself from Charleston, sailing a bit north and east while most of her rivals chose to move in a southerly direction. Her instincts proved true. While her 19 male rivals battled doldrums and other tricky weather systems, Autissier made great time, arriving in Cape Town, South Africa, a full five days before her nearest competitor.

Had the race ended there, Autissier would have won it hands down. Unfortunately, it continued around the Cape of Good Hope, into the Indian Ocean, and on toward Australia. In the midst of the pitiless Indian Ocean, Autissier lost her 83-foot mast during a gale. She never thought of giving up, though. She jury-rigged a new mast and limped into the Kerguelen Islands, where a crew met her and fitted two smaller masts onto the ship. Her plans were to outfit the ship with another 83-foot mast in Sydney, Australia, but misfortune struck once again before she could get there. A huge storm surge hit her boat, rolling it completely over and inflicting massive damage.

Had Autissier been on deck when the wave hit, she would have been washed away. As matters stood, she had no choice but to activate her distress beacons, which sent a radio signal to race officials in Charleston. She spent four frigid days waiting for rescue and was finally airlifted from her listing ship by an Australian helicopter on New Year's Day, 1995. She was 750 nautical miles from Adelaide, Australia, and was brought ashore by the Australian ship HMAS Darwin. A subsequent search for her yacht proved fruitless—the ship was never found.

Such an ordeal might end the careers of some athletes, but Autissier has bigger dreams. After dodging the media for some weeks in the wake of her Indian Ocean adventure, she returned to view in time to see her rival sailors off on the third leg of the BOC challenge. She will probably be back in action when the next BOC race begins in 1998. As a *USA Today* reporter put it on April 22, 1994: "Isabelle Autissier is making a monumental record run."

JENNIFER
AZZI

*"I wish one day there
will be an NBA
system for
professional women
in the states because
I'm sure people will
come over to watch
the matches. People
do like women's
basketball, so it's sad
to be forced to go
overseas after
college."*

Jennifer Azzi is a woman on a mission. She wants to play professional basketball in America.

The former Stanford All-American and member of the 1996 U.S. women's Olympic team has spent the better part of the 1990s playing professionally in Europe. She hopes that the Olympics will spark new interest in women's basketball and lead to the development of a professional league in America. Should such a league become reality, Azzi is sure to become one of its stars. Described as a "classic all-around player," the five-foot-seven-inch point guard has shown great potential since her college days.

Azzi says she is still improving, and no one disputes this claim. Born in 1969 in Oak Ridge, Tennessee, she was not an athletic wonder child. Granted, her junior high team went 50-0 while she played for it, and her Oak Ridge High varsity team compiled an 85-11 record and advanced to the state championship when she was a senior. College recruiters still thought she was a second-tier prospect, though, and even her high school coach described her in a November 20, 1989, *Sports Illustrated* piece as "good at a lot of things, not great at anything."

As a high school senior, Azzi was offered scholarships to Vanderbilt, Ohio State, and Stanford. She chose Stanford, more than 2,000 miles from home, because she thought it offered the best academic package. When she arrived there, the Cardinal women's team was struggling, to say the least. Azzi too struggled as a freshman, once committing nine turnovers in a single game. She was willing to work hard and provide team leadership, however, and by her junior year the Cardinal had improved to a 28-3 record and had won all of its conference games. In recognition of her contribution, Azzi was the only non-senior named to the 1989 Kodak All-American team. She led the Pacific Coast Conference in six statistical categories.

The following season, 1989–90, brought Azzi and the Cardinal to the top. The team only lost once in the regular season and advanced confidently into the NCAA final. There Azzi had the opportunity to lead the Cardinal to

MVP Jennifer Azzi cuts down the net after Stanford beat Auburn in the NCAA championship game, 1990. (AP/Wide World Photos)

a championship victory over rival Auburn, 88-81. The game was played in Knoxville, Tennessee, just 20 miles from Azzi's hometown.

Numerous awards were heaped on Azzi that season, as she was regarded as the best college player in the nation. She won the Naismith and Wade Awards, was a consensus All-American, and received a trophy as the outstanding player in the NCAA Final Four. The hard-working Azzi described her team's NCAA championship as feeling "like I've just eaten the best chocolate-chip cookie I've ever had."

Perhaps a letdown was inevitable. After graduating from Stanford in the spring of 1990, Azzi signed on with International Management Group, a powerful sports agency based in New York City. She had hoped to find a berth in the European professional women's basketball league—but no one seemed interested. Short by basketball standards, and more of a team player than a personal show-boater, she had difficulty finding a place in Europe. When she finally did get called by a team, the experience abroad was anything but ideal. She told the *San Francisco Chronicle* on June 15, 1993: "In Italy, the manager would drive by my house and make sure my lights were out at a certain time. In France . . . they had an idea that you should score 20 points a game. You score 15, and you're gone. And some people have had trouble getting paid—it's cutthroat in a lot of places."

Not surprisingly, Azzi wanted desperately to qualify for the 1992 U.S. women's Olympic team. She was devastated when the squad was announced and she had only made alternate. She did attend the Olympics in Barcelona, but she was never called to play, and the U.S. women's team was defeated by their Soviet Union rivals and had to settle for a bronze medal. Azzi returned to Europe and continued playing there.

History helped Azzi in the wake of the 1992 Olympics. The U.S. Olympic Committee decided to choose and fund a national women's team that would compete in such events as the world championships and the Goodwill Games. Since the players would be compensated, they could be expected to stay with the team for a year or more, practicing and taking on rival women's—and men's—teams. Azzi was one of 17 players who contended for a place on this team in the spring of 1994. This time the coach was not a skeptic, but rather Tara VanDerveer, who had coached Azzi at Stanford. Azzi made the team.

The national team officially became USA Basketball in 1995 with Azzi as one of its stars. The team has had an opportunity to work together and develop an on-court chemistry that was lacking in those Olympic squads that were chosen just prior to the Games. Azzi, who has shown significant improvement as a professional, thinks her best years are ahead of her—and at

JENNIFER AZZI

American basketball player

Born: 1969 in Oak Ridge, Tennessee.

Education: Stanford University, graduated 1990.

Career Highlights:

- named to Kodak All-American team, 1989
- named outstanding member of NCAA championship team, 1990
- played professionally for teams in Italy and France, 1990–93
- earned a berth on the women's U.S. National Team, 1993–95
- chosen as member of Olympic-bound National Team, 1995.

Awards: Winner of Naismith and Wade Awards, voted consensus All-American, and recipient of a trophy as the outstanding player in the NCAA Final Four, 1989; named to Stanford Athletic Hall of Fame, 1995.

least one of them is an Olympic year. "It makes me mad when people say to me, 'Oh, you are still playing?' " she declared in a May 10, 1994, *San Francisco Chronicle* article. "If I was a guy, no one would dare say that. I'm only 25 years old. I feel like I'm still getting better."

Azzi is only one of the Olympic team members who hope that the 1996 Summer Games spark a new interest in the possibility of a professional women's league in America. If that league forms, Jennifer Azzi is likely to establish herself there as she has elsewhere: to quote *Sports Illustrated,* as "an elegant point guard in the mold of Magic Johnson, willing to give it all up in a heartbeat for the good of the team."

OKSANA BAIUL

*"She is that rare
athlete who is also
an artist, without a
doubt the most
musical skater to
appear in a long
time."*

—Martha Duffy on Baiul, Time
magazine, March 7, 1994

A virtually unknown teenaged skater from the Ukraine in 1992, Oksana Baiul made her presence known as the 1993 world figure skating champion and the 1994 Olympic gold medalist. Baiul's long program at the 1994 Olympics—skated nearly flawlessly despite injuries she had sustained earlier that day—placed her squarely on the figure skating map as the new reigning queen of the rink. Her youth and determination assure that she will be a force in figure skating for quite some time. A June 1994 *Life* magazine profile describes the petite Baiul as "the swan of Odessa," a performer who "won our hearts with her natural sweetness and soulful artistry."

Baiul has overcome a series of tragedies so overwhelming they almost seem to have come from the pages of a novel. Deserted by her father when she was an infant and completely orphaned at 13 when her mother died of cancer, she pressed on with her skating, not only because she was winning but because the very process brought her inner peace. "I skate how I feel," she told *Newsweek* on March 7, 1994. "I think it must be a gift from God."

Oksana Baiul was born November 16, 1977, in Dnepropetrovsk, Ukraine. At the time, the Texas-sized province was a part of the Soviet Union, but it has since declared itself an independent country. As a youngster, Baiul's first love was the ballet, but her grandfather bought her a pair of ice skates in the hope that skating would help her to slim down her chubby legs. She began skating at the age of four. In a November 1994 *Seventeen* magazine profile, she recalled that from her first visit to the ice, skating "felt very natural to me. I liked the feeling of spinning on the ice, just gliding along." The local coaches liked what they saw, and before long Baiul's mother—who worked as a French teacher—was spending significant sums for lessons and costumes.

At the age of five Baiul began studying with Stanislav Korytek, one of the finest Ukrainian coaches. Within two years she was winning local competitions. Her progress was steady until tragedy struck in 1991, when her mother died rather suddenly of ovarian cancer. Baiul had never known her father, and her maternal grandparents had died while she was still small. Now

The dramatic and daring Oksana Baiul celebrates her gold-medal perfor-mance at the World Figure Skating Championships in 1993. (AP/Wide World Photos)

she had no adult to care for her. For a few weeks she slept on a cot at the skating rink and cooked her own meals on a hot plate. Then, to make matters worse, her coach departed suddenly for a better job in Canada. "He just bought a ticket and left," the skater remembered in a *Sports Illustrated* piece. "He called me afterward to tell me, and I understood his position. Everyone wants to eat."

At such a life-shattering juncture, many athletes might have quit. Instead, on Korytek's advice, Baiul moved 250 miles away to Odessa to become the protege of Galina Zmievskaya. Zmievskaya—who had coached 1992 Olympic gold medalist Victor Petrenko—not only agreed to coach Baiul, she also provided the young orphan a home. Soon Baiul was sharing a bedroom in a cramped, three-room apartment and spending her days working out with Petrenko and the other elite skaters of the Ukraine. A special bond still exists between Baiul, Petrenko, and their singular coach, Zmievskaya.

Baiul began showing promise at the 1991 Soviet championships, where she placed 12th in singles competition. After two years of working with Zmievskaya, the skater took a silver medal at the 1993 European championship, finishing second to France's Surya Bonaly. Only a few months later, Baiul shocked the international skating community by winning the world championships at Prague. She was 15 at the time—only the legendary Sonja Henie had won a world championship at a younger age.

Baiul's early success was viewed by some observers—particularly the fans of Bonaly and American Nancy Kerrigan—as an aberration, especially when Baiul finished second to Bonaly in the 1993 European championships. Nevertheless, the slender Ukrainian was a favorite to win a medal at the 1994 Olympics in Lillehammer, Norway. Baiul might in fact have been helped by the publicity over the assault on Nancy Kerrigan that nearly forced Kerrigan from competition. So much attention was paid to the American skater that Baiul was all but overlooked—until the Olympic competition began.

Everyone expected Kerrigan to skate as if she had a point to prove, but almost no one was prepared for the artistry and crowd-pleasing performance that Baiul would provide.

As the Olympic skating competition got under way, Kerrigan held a slender lead after the technical program. Baiul finished her technical program strongly for a second place standing. Then, the day of the long program finals, Baiul collided with a German skater during a practice session. Baiul sustained bruises to her back and a gash on her leg just above her skate. The gash required three stitches, and just prior to her long program, Baiul was given a painkiller. Not only would she be skating with a new injury, but Baiul watched as Kerrigan turned in a dazzling performance in her long program.

OKSANA BAIUL

Ukrainian figure skater

Born: November 16, 1977 in Denpropetrovsk, Ukraine.

Career Highlights:
• took 12th place, Soviet Championship, 1991

• finished in second place, European Championship, 1993
• won gold medal, World Championship, 1993
• earned gold medal, 1994 Olympic Games, Lillehammer, Norway.

Baiul, with a lifetime of practice, simply dismissed the monumental obstacles in her path and skated brilliantly that night in Norway. One slight stumble on a triple flip was overlooked by judges who were as beguiled by Baiul's artistic impression as by her daring decision to add extra jumps to her routine. In the end, Baiul won the gold medal by one of the narrowest margins in Olympic history.

If she was just another good skater from a foreign country before the Olympics, Baiul has since been a media darling all over the world. She is a regular performer in the United States and has discussed her life history on television with the likes of Barbara Walters. More liberal rules about accepting fees for performances have allowed Baiul the luxury of training in the United States, but she still calls Odessa home and visits frequently. Oksana Baiul is not the most athletic of the modern skaters, but she is intensely dramatic and daring in her routines. She plays to the audience and to the judges and clearly enjoys pleasing a crowd. A *Time* magazine correspondent reported on March 7, 1994, that Baiul "is that rare athlete who is also an artist. . . . Like the very best dancers . . . she gives the impression that the melody flows from her body rather than that she is reacting to the music."

MYRIAM
BEDARD

BIATHLETE

"In the past, before the Olympic medal, one out of 100 people maybe knew about the biathlon. Now, only one out of one hundred don't know."

Myriam Bedard abandoned the sequins and frills of figure skating as a youth because of the expense. Instead she picked up a rifle and a pair of skis. The rest is Canadian Olympics history.

In 1992, Bedard became the first North American to win a medal in the Olympic biathlon when she took the bronze in the 15-kilometer ski-and-shoot competition. Improving steadily between Olympic appearances, she strode into the 1994 Winter Games in Lillehammer, Norway, and brought home two gold medals for first-place finishes in both the 15- and the 7.5-kilometer races. Bedard's chosen event is one of the most demanding in the Olympics, requiring its entrants to cross-country ski with rifles slung across their backs and then shoot at a series of distance targets. The women's biathlon was only sanctioned by the International Olympic Committee in 1992, so Bedard has been one of the sport's pioneers at the Winter Games.

She has come a long way from her days as a youngster in Canada's Quebec province. Initially interested in figure skating, Bedard switched to the more solitary and grueling biathlon as a young teenager. Her parents, Francine and Pierre Bedard, were baffled by their daughter's choice but supported her when they saw how much the sport meant to her. Growing up in a suburb of Quebec City, Bedard soon learned that it was illegal for her to carry her target rifle on the public buses. Her solution was to dismantle the gun and stash the pieces in a violin case.

Bedard won her first race at the age of 15 in ski boots that were so large she had to stuff tissue in the toes. At 17 she was the Canadian junior champion, and in 1992—the first year women's biathlon was offered at the Olympics—she took home the bronze medal in the 15-kilometer race. She was 23 at the time, considered young for a successful biathlete.

Success did not make Bedard a model Canadian athlete. Four months after her bronze medal victory she refused to sign a contract with Biathlon Canada that would have funneled some of her earnings back into the organization's coffers. The contract also included a "gag order" for media appear-

Myriam Bedard takes aim during her gold medal–winning 15-kilometer biathlon competition at the 1994 Winter Olympics. (AP/Wide World Photos)

ances. When she would not sign, she was suspended from the national team. A compromise was reached shortly thereafter, however, and she rejoined the team in time to win a dramatic 1993 world championship victory in Borovets, Bulgaria. At Borovets, Bedard finished a whopping 16.6 seconds ahead of silver medalist Nadezhda Talanova of Russia, establishing herself as the skier to beat in Lillehammer.

Doubts began to arise about Bedard just prior to the 1994 Olympics. A dedicated loner who practiced in private with a "mystery coach" whose name she has never revealed, Bedard seemed to be slipping out of contention. A series of low placings in the winter of 1993-94 had observers predicting disaster for the Winter Games. They just didn't understand Bedard's strategy: she was saving her strength and her best work for the race that really counted, in Lillehammer.

Distracted by the cheers of the crowd and tired from a sleepless night, Bedard began the Olympic 15-kilometer race in 67th position, third from last.

MYRIAM BEDARD

Canadian biathlete

Born: Loretteville, Quebec, Canada.

Career Highlights:
- finished in first place, Canadian Junior Championship, 1986

- won bronze medal, 15 km, 1992 Olympic Games, Albertville, France
- took home gold medal, World Championship, 1993
- won gold medal, 15 km, and gold medal, 7.5 km, 1994 Olympic Games, Lillehammer, Norway.

She almost hypnotically tuned out the crowd and surged to a lead even though she missed two of twenty shots and earned a two-minute penalty. As it turned out, the penalty didn't matter. Bedard won the 15-kilometer race by nearly a half-minute margin for a gold medal blowout. Just a few days later she entered and won the 7.5-kilometer race by a tight one second. Only some time after that race ended did she discover she had completed it on a mismatched set of skis. "I had one ski that was gliding more. All through the race, the right one was going good and the left one was going bad," she recalled in a March 7, 1994, *Maclean's* piece. "It's funny now because I won. But if I had not won, you'd think about that all your life—one second."

BIATHLON

Although not a winter Olympic sport until 1960 (for men) and 1992 (for women), the biathlon has its origins in ancient Scandinavian society. Early Scandinavians, after inventing skis for transportation across the snowy terrain, soon discovered that stalking prey was easier on skis than afoot. Later, when survival became less of a day-to-day struggle, the combination of skiing and shooting became part of the training of infantry soldiers. This led to the military ski patrol race, which began early this century among European armies. That, in turn, led to the modern biathlon.

Bedard finished her stellar 1994 season by marrying her longtime friend, fellow Canadian biathlete Jean Paquet. The couple have since had their first child. As one of Canada's most successful Olympic medalists, Bedard has become a sought-after motivational speaker and a bona fide hero to Canadian youngsters. She still prefers a quiet and solitary life, though, and she has certainly earned the right to live exactly as she pleases. "I've wanted to share my success . . . with many people," Bedard explained in the *Montreal Gazette.* "[But] I understand now why many artists try to have a home somewhere away from everything, without a telephone. I'm the kind of person who has always been alone, trained alone, with no attention."

Still, there is the upside. And Bedard acknowledges that, too. "I like it when I can strike sparks in people," she concluded in *Maclean's.* "After all, it's why I'm here."

JOAN
BENOIT
SAMUELSON

The diminutive Joan Benoit Samuelson—she stands five feet, three inches and weighs 105 pounds—set new standards for both speed and courage as the first Olympic gold medalist in the women's marathon. Benoit Samuelson, who was the women's marathon world record-holder at the time of the 1984 Summer Games, won the gold easily despite having had knee surgery just months prior to the event. To this day her accomplishments in the 1984 Olympic trials and the Olympics themselves rank among the most thrilling victories ever recorded by a woman runner.

Runner's World reporter Amby Burfoot wrote: "For a three-year stretch during the mid-1980s (1983–85), Joan Samuelson was arguably the greatest marathoner ever. She stormed the '83 Boston Marathon in a startling world record 2:22:43. The next year she ran two marathons, the U.S. Olympic trials and the first Olympic Marathon for women, that have become legendary. In '85, she defeated Ingrid Kristiansen and Rosa Mota in the Chicago Marathon, . . . the most competitive women's marathon of all time." Remarkably, despite numerous injuries and the pressures of parenthood, the popular Benoit Samuelson has not ruled out further marathons, including future Olympic appearances.

The daughter of Andre and Nancy Benoit, Joan Benoit Samuelson was born on May 16, 1957. In an era when women were not encouraged to run or to be athletic, she bucked the trend—even though it could be embarrassing at times. In a December 1991 *Runner's World* piece, Benoit Samuelson recalled that she was so self-conscious about her chosen hobby as a youngster that she tried to hide her interests from everyone. "I'd walk when cars passed me," she said. "I'd pretend I was looking at the flowers."

Living in Portland, Maine, Benoit Samuelson was attracted to winter sports as a youngster and actually preferred skiing until she broke her leg in a slalom race. The running she did as rehabilitation for the skiing injury gradually became more fulfilling than the skiing itself, and she became a high school phenomenon as a middle and longer distance runner. She continued

MARATHONER

"I like having a goal that's way out there. Maybe I won't ever achieve it, but as long as I think I have a chance, then I will keep going."

Marathoner Joan Benoit Samuelson took home Olympic gold in 1984, the first time the women's marathon was offered as an Olympic event. (UPI/Bettmann)

running through her years at Maine's Bowdoin College, where she earned a bachelor's degree in 1979, and through graduate school at North Carolina State University.

Caught in a traffic jam on her way to compete in the 1979 Boston Marathon, Joan Benoit jumped out of her friend's car and ran two miles through the woods to get to the race's starting point on time. Twenty-six miles later she had won the race with a record-setting time of 2:35:15. It was her first Boston Marathon, and it made her an instant star. Suddenly the shy Maine schoolgirl was inundated with requests for appearances and offers for product endorsement contracts. "I hated the publicity," she once told *Sports Illustrated.* "I hated it so much that I seriously considered giving up running so I would be left alone."

Injuries almost accomplished what the publicity hounds couldn't. Faced with chronic heel pain in 1981, Benoit Samuelson once again contemplated retiring from marathon events. Instead she underwent successful surgery on both Achilles tendons and returned to distance running in top form. In her first post-surgery marathon in 1982 she broke the American record for women with a time of 2:26:11. She won her second Boston Marathon in 1983, shattering the world record by almost three minutes with a time of 2:22:42.

Benoit Samuelson's finishing time in the 1983 Boston Marathon easily qualified her for the U.S. Olympic trials to be held in the spring of 1984. The 1984 Summer Games brought a first-ever opportunity for women marathoners, as previously the women's marathon had not been a sanctioned event. Benoit Samuelson trained ardently for the trials, but in March of 1984 she sustained another serious injury, this time to her knee. Her second round of surgery was completed April 25, 1984—just 17 days before the trials.

 **ROAD TO THE OLYMPICS**

Joan Benoit's training for the May 12, 1984, Olympic trials was progressing smoothly until March 16, when her right knee "shut down" completely during a training run. Various non-surgical treatments failed to correct the problem, and finally, on April 25, just 17 days before the trials, Benoit underwent arthroscopic surgery. In an impressive display of tenacity and courage, she decided to run the Olympic trial marathon. Against tremendous odds, Benoit not only ran 26 miles a mere 17 days after knee surgery; she finished in first place, in what writer Amby Burfoot called "the greatest individual marathon effort of all time."

Benoit Samuelson vowed to run anyway. And run she did, not only qualifying for the Olympics but winning the trials with a respectable time of 2:31:04. "I just can't believe I'm going to L.A.," she marveled through post-trial tears. To this day, many observers consider Benoit Samuelson's gritty per-

JOAN BENOIT SAMUELSON

American marathoner

Born: May 16, 1957 in Cape Elizabeth, Maine.

Education: Bowdoin College, bachelor's degree, 1979; graduate work at North Carolina State University.

Career Highlights:

- finished in first place, Boston Marathon, 1979

- took first place, Boston Marathon, 1983

- came in first place, Olympic trials marathon, 1984

- won gold medal, 1984 Olympic Games, Los Angeles, California

- achieved record-breaking finish in America's Marathon, Chicago, Illinois, 1985.

Awards: Named one of *Ms.* magazine's women of the year, 1984; co-recipient of Amateur Sportswoman of the Year award from the Women's Sports Foundation, 1984; Vitalis Award for sports excellence, 1985; Sullivan Award from the Amateur Athletic Union for best amateur athlete in the U.S., 1986.

formance in the 1984 Olympic trials one of the best marathon achievements of all time.

The winning continued in Los Angeles on August 5, 1984. The Olympic marathon started slowly—too slowly for Joan Benoit. She took the lead at the three-mile mark and wondered why she was so outpacing her competitors. Some of them—most notably Norway's Grete Waitz—figured Benoit would falter on her healing knee and fall off the pace. It never happened. By midpoint in the race she led by a 90-second margin. Later she pushed her lead over two minutes. Toward the end she was able to relax, never using the energy she had retained to fight off a last-minute challenge. She won the first-ever Olympic women's marathon with a time of 2:24:52.

Thereafter Benoit Samuelson chose her marathons carefully, rarely appearing in more than one or two a year. Having married Scott Samuelson shortly after the Los Angeles Olympics, she decided to have children, and she actually ran the 1987 Boston Marathon while three months pregnant with her first child. The demands of parenthood kept her from the 1988 Olympics and injuries to her back sidelined her for the 1992 Summer Games. She has said she would like to qualify for the 1996 Olympics because they are being held in America, but in the face of all the American competition her chances are slim. "I'll be 38 or 39 at that time," she told *Runner's World.* "I look at the races some people have been able to run at that age, and I think maybe 1996 isn't too late to think about making the [Olympic] team again."

However her future races pan out, Benoit Samuelson will remain a highly regarded runner with an impressive list of accomplishments—not the least of them the marathon Olympic gold medal. "To say Joanie's life is hectic is a huge understatement," Burfoot noted in *Runner's World,* "but I think maybe that's a good sign. She seems to enjoy the challenge of doing many things well."

BONNIE
BLAIR

Affectionately known as "Bonnie the Blur," Bonnie Blair is the first woman in U.S. history to win gold medals at three consecutive Olympic Games. In 1994 Blair became the first American woman to win five gold medals overall in the Olympics, winter or summer. Add a bronze medal to her gold and she has won more medals in the Winter Olympics than any other American. Blair is a speed skater who has been competing since she was four years old. Shorter and less powerful than some of her Olympic rivals, Blair's near-perfect technique helped her set the world record for the 500-meter speed skating race. Her many victories aside, she is a humble, cheerful, all-American sort of heroine who is happy to be able to participate in a sport that she loves.

Blair was born March 18, 1964, in Cornwall, New York, and quickly took her place among a speed skating clan. The youngest of six children, she was born while her older siblings were competing in a local speed skating event. Her earliest memories revolved around watching her brothers and sisters skate—and skating herself. "I can't even remember learning how to skate," she told *Maclean's* magazine. "It comes almost as naturally to me as walking." By the age of two she was comfortable on the ice, and by four she was entering speed skating races. Shortly after her family relocated to Champaign, Illinois, she won the Illinois state championship for her age class. It was her first major victory. She was seven.

As a pre-teen Blair began training with former Olympic silver medalist Cathy Priestner. Priestner encouraged Blair to concentrate on Olympic-style speed skating, rather than the pack racing that had been Blair's forte in the past. At 16 Blair skated her first Olympic-style race at a qualifying meet for the 1980 Olympic trials. She was an immediate sensation. The last competitor at the meet, she was forced to race alone when her opponent did not appear. She knew she would have to skate 500 meters in under 47 seconds to advance. "I went as hard as I could," she told *Maclean's,* "and when I came across the line it was 46.7." Blair was eliminated later in the Olympic trials, but her brush with the big time encouraged her to work harder in anticipation of the 1984 Winter Games.

SPEED SKATER

"Skating is joy. It's a solitary sport, one in which you can claim all the rewards as your own. Nobody makes you do it. It's just you."

"Bonnie the Blur" heads for her fifth Olympic gold medal, competing here in the 1000-meter event at the 1994 Olympics. (AP/Wide World Photos)

Financial difficulties almost ended Blair's career before it began. She was unable to meet the enormous expenses of coaching and travel that await amateur athletes. Help came from a ten-year fundraising campaign organized by the Champaign police force, who sold bumper stickers and t-shirts promoting the skater. The fundraising gave Blair the backing she needed to train in Butte, Montana, with the U.S. men's speed skating team.

Blair made her first Olympic appearance at the 1984 Winter Games in Sarajevo, Yugoslavia, where she finished eighth in the 500-meter race. Although her times were quite respectable for a first-time Olympian, Blair was disappointed with her performance. She returned home to a more rigorous training program that included skating, weight training, running, biking, and roller skating. The hard work paid off. Blair was the U.S. sprint champion every year from 1985 through 1990, and she broke her first world record in the 500-meter speed skate in 1986.

At five-feet-five-inches tall and just 125 pounds, Blair was much smaller and lighter than her chief rivals, Christa Rothenburger of East Germany and Ye Qiaobo of China. Confident that she could win on technique rather than sheer power, Blair entered the 1988 Olympics in Calgary, Canada, a favorite to win a medal in one of the sprint races. She was so nervous prior to her first heat that she had to eat a peanut butter and jelly sandwich to calm herself. It worked. Minutes after she watched Rothenburger break the 500-meter world record with a time of 39.12 seconds, Blair took the ice and skated the race at 39.10 seconds for the gold medal. The difference between her and Rothenburger was less than the length of a skate blade. A few days later, she won the bronze medal in the 1,000-meter sprint. Blair's American teammates were so impressed by her victory that they honored her by letting her carry the national flag at the closing ceremonies of the Olympics.

After that, Blair was the woman to beat in any international speed skating race. She won her first world sprint championship in 1989, and she was heavily favored as a repeat gold medalist for the 1992 Winter Games in Albertville, France. "Bonnie the Blur" did not disappoint. On a melting track in foggy conditions, she took her second consecutive gold medal in the 500-meter sprint. Then she added a gold medal in the 1,000-meter race—beating Ye Qiaobo by .02 seconds—for good measure.

Few athletes in any sport can hope to win medals at three consecutive Olympics. Blair did just that in 1994 at the Winter Olympics in Lillehammer, Norway, taking the gold in both the 500-meter and the 1,000-meter sprint events. By that time Bonnie Blair was an American hero, loved as much for her open and engaging personality as for her athletic achievements. When she cried as the national anthem was being played after her 1,000-meter victory, fans all over America cried with her. Everyone, including Blair, realized that 1994 would be her last Olympics.

Bonnie Blair stands alone as the only American woman ever to win five gold medals in the Olympics. She capped this fabulous feat by winning both the 1994-95 World Cup and world sprint titles at 500 and 1,000 meters, breaking her own world record in the 500 one last time. Then she retired to help coach other would-be skaters. Honored by the Women's Sports

SPEEDING BULLETS

With racers flying around the track at nearly 40 miles per hour, speed skating is the fastest an individual can move under her own power. Racing skates have extra-long blades to allow for a longer glide without loss of speed, and the blades are often just one thirty-second of an inch thick. The skintight speedskating uniforms, which cover the skater from head to toe in one piece, are designed to minimize wind resistance. The skater must be in a streamlined position, with her upper body virtually parallel to the ground and her head low. The slightest imprecision in body position—elbows not streamlined against the body, head lifted a shade too high—can generate enough drag-time to separate medalists from also-rans.

BONNIE BLAIR

American speed skater

Born: March 18, 1964 in Cornwall, New York.

Career Highlights:

- won Illinois State Championship for her age class at age seven

- named U.S. sprint champion, 1985–1990

- earned gold medal, 500-meter race, and bronze medal, 1,000-meter race, 1988 Olympic Games, Calgary, Canada

- finished in first place, world sprint championship, 1989

- won gold medal, 500-meter race, and gold medal, 1,000-meter race, 1992 Olympic Games, Albertville, France

- took gold medal, 500-meter race, and gold medal, 1,000-meter race, 1994 Olympic Games, Lillehammer, Norway

- won first place, 500- and 1,000-meter races, 1994–95 World Cup and world sprint championship.

Awards: Honored as Sportswoman of the Year by the Women's Sports Foundation, 1994 and 1995.

Foundation as Sportswoman of the Year in both 1994 and 1995, Blair said she was ready for a change of pace. Reflecting on being a coach rather than a performer, Blair told *USA Today:* "I don't miss [competitive skating] so much that I think, 'God, I wish I was doing this.' I know that if I was, I would get my butt kicked."

Gone are the days when helpful policemen had to raise money for Bonnie Blair. With product endorsement contracts and personal appearance fees, she has earned a comfortable living for herself. "Things have gone o.k. for me," she told *Sports Illustrated* recently. "I'm not Michael Jordan, by any means, but I'm in this because I love what I'm doing."

ARLENE
BLUM

"A Woman's Place Is On Top . . . Annapurna." So read the t-shirts that Arlene Blum sold by the thousands to finance the first-ever all-women's expedition to Mount Annapurna, the tenth highest peak in the world. A veteran mountain climber, Himalayan trekker, and expedition organizer, Blum became one of the best-known high altitude climbers when she dared to challenge the idea that women couldn't handle the toughest ascents. Her leadership and stubborn determination helped to pave the way for a whole new generation of climbers—women who go in mixed-sex teams or in all-female teams to the very top of the world.

Arlene Blum was born at the very end of World War II and was the only daughter of a physician and a violinist. Her parents divorced when she was still a baby, and she grew up in Chicago under the care of her maternal grandparents. Her earliest dream was to be a kindergarten teacher, but as she entered high school she found herself in an accelerated science and math program where she had to hold her own academically with boys. Overcoming her initial reluctance to study science and math, Blum prospered in the demanding program and earned top grades. By the time she entered Reed College in Portland, Oregon, she had decided to become a chemist.

"I knew that 'girls weren't supposed to be chemists.' And it's always sort of nice to do things you're not supposed to do," Blum told *Ms.* magazine in 1987. That attitude would propel Blum not only as a research chemist but also as a mountain climber.

While still a college student Blum finished a basic course in high altitude climbing and began attempting ascents of Oregon's volcanic peaks. She became so fascinated by the hobby that she found a way to combine it with her chosen profession—she analyzed volcanic gases on Oregon's Mount Hood for her undergraduate thesis. As a graduate student she widened her horizons, going on expeditions into Mexico and the Andes mountains. She also applied to be part of an expedition to Afghanistan, but she was rebuffed because she was a woman. Prevailing notions at the time held that women couldn't han-

MOUNTAIN
CLIMBER

"People say I've organized all-women's expeditions to show what we can do; but it wasn't like that. It was more a rebellion against being told I couldn't do something, or . . . that women couldn't do something."

Arlene Blum, pictured here on a Himalayan peak in 1982, has walked the entire length of the Great Himalaya range. (UPI/Bettmann)

dle the highest elevations, and that their presence on an otherwise all-male team would hurt morale.

Blum wasn't about to let such sexist considerations ruin her chances at important climbs. When she was turned away from a team that was attempting Alaska's Mount Denali (also known as Mount McKinley), she simply decided to organize her own expedition. Her six-member, all-female team made history on July 6, 1970, when they stood together atop Denali's 20,320-foot summit.

Blum's best-known expedition occurred in 1978, when she led an all-women's team to Annapurna, the tenth-highest mountain in the world. At the time only four teams had succeeded in reaching the summit of Annapurna, a Himalayan peak that is regularly visited by avalanches and extreme weather conditions. Blum financed her team's assault on Annapurna by selling t-shirts and attracting corporate sponsors. A film crew came along to document the climb, and on October 15, 1978, two of Blum's teammates, Vera Komarkova and Irene Miller—along with two Sherpas—reached the summit.

ARLENE BLUM

American mountain climber

Born: c. 1945; grew up in Chicago, Illinois.

Education: Reed College, Portland, Oregon; University of California, Berkeley, doctorate in chemistry.

Career Highlights:
- Organized and participated in first all-female expedition to summit of Alaska's Mount Denali (also known as Mount McKinley), July 6, 1970

- led an all-women's team to Annapurna, tenth-highest mountain in the world, 1978

- walked the entire length of the Great Himalaya Range

- part of scientific team that discovered carcinogenic qualities of a flame-retardant chemical used on children's sleepwear (her analysis of the chemical called Tris led to its being removed from use on American clothing).

The expedition's joy was short-lived, however. Just two days after the first successful summit attempt, another duo, Vera Watson and Alison Chadwick-Onyszkiewicz both disappeared, presumably in an avalanche. Blum was devastated by the loss of her companions, but she refused to concede that they had been killed because they were women. In fact, high altitude mountain climbing is the most perilous sport around, claiming the lives of climbers of both sexes and sometimes their Sherpa helpers as well. For Blum, the ascent of Annapurna was not a tragedy but a triumph, proof that women could achieve—and even suffer—just as men did in the harsh environment of the Himalayan peaks.

In the wake of the Annapurna expedition, Blum capitalized on her fame as a mountain climber, leading challenges on other peaks and teaching trekking courses. She has personally walked the entire length of the Great Himalaya Range. What's more amazing is that her achievements as a climber and expedition organizer are only a part of her contribution to society. Blum was also part of a scientific team that discovered the carcinogenic qualities of a flame-retardant chemical used on children's sleepwear. Her analysis of the chemical called Tris led to its being removed from use on American clothing.

Now in her fifties, Blum has participated in dozens of high-altitude expeditions and has led more than ten herself. As early as 1976 she was a participant in America's bicentennial Mount Everest ascent, and in recent years she has been joined on treks by her daughter, Annalise. In Blum's wake have come a veritable army of women climbers who have attempted all of the world's most challenging climbs. Like Arlene Blum, they too believe that a woman's place is . . . on top.

NICOLE
BOBEK

FIGURE SKATER

"When I was a little girl, all I knew was that I wanted to skate. I wanted to be alone out there, to feel the freedom of it. When I get onto the ice and the music goes on, I come alive."

Nicole Bobek is a world-ranked figure skater, but she might well be any kind of entertainer—a dancer, or a pop singer, or even a movie star. Bobek, the 1995 U.S. champion, is a born performer who can capture an audience with her dazzling smile and her "innocent yet sexy" programs. The center of much attention in tabloids and the mainstream press, Bobek viewed her 1995 national amateur championship as a chance to silence critics who have portrayed her as slipshod in practice and temperamental on tour. Her bronze medal in the 1995 world championships further assured that the blonde teenager was ready to take her place in skating's highest echelon. *Time* magazine, in a February 27, 1995, profile, called Bobek "a true show skater who makes a big, jazzy impression. . . . Bobek has sexy good looks, a smile that reaches the rafters and a playful way with music."

The road to the top has not been smooth for Bobek. In fact, prior to 1995 most of the publicity she received was of the negative sort. She was hardly the victim of an antagonistic media, however. Most of the criticism leveled at her was earned by behavior patterns she has since discarded. Bobek trained with nine different coaches in as many years, trying to outlive her reputation as a "slacker" and a "party animal" who did not care to work hard. In 1995 she mended her reputation by basing herself in Detroit with coach Richard Callaghan, whom she has credited as an inspiration both on and off the ice. But, by December 1995, Bobek had once again switched coaches, this time opting to work with Barbara Roles Williams.

Nicole Bobek was born in Chicago in 1977, the daughter of an unwed Czechoslovakian refugee named Jana Bobek. Nicole's career as a figure skater began at the tender age of three when she discovered a passion for acting out her fantasies on the ice. Even as a youngster she would put music on at the rink and interpret it herself—today she helps to choreograph her routines.

When Nicole's mother lost her job in Chicago, the family moved west to Los Angeles. Nicole was ten at the time, gifted yet prone to bad training

Nicole Bobek smiles for the crowd after a near-perfect routine in the 1995 World Figure Skating Championships. (AP/Wide World Photos)

NICOLE BOBEK

American figure skater

Born: 1977 in Chicago, Illinois.

Career Highlights:
• earned gold medal, Olympic Festival, 1991

• won gold medal, Vienna Cup, 1991

• won U.S. Women's Figure Skating Championship, 1995

• claimed bronze medal, World Figure Skating Championship, 1995.

habits. On the West Coast she worked with two different coaches in three years. As a young teen she relocated to Colorado Springs, where, according to a March 6, 1995, *People* magazine profile, she was regarded as a "discipline problem." From Colorado Springs she moved on to Cape Cod, hoping to train with Evy and Mary Scotvold, Nancy Kerrigan's coaches. This relationship too soured, and in 1994 Bobek moved on to Callaghan in Detroit. At the time she had won only two titles—a gold medal at the 1991 Olympic Festival and a gold at the 1991 Vienna Cup in Austria. Coach Callaghan told *Sports Illustrated* on February 20, 1995, "When I thought about training her, I figured, What have I got to lose?"

He had next to nothing to lose and quite a lot to gain. Under his eye Bobek buckled down, lost some weight, and practiced diligently. Her progress showed at the 1995 U.S. championship, where she beat the favored Michelle Kwan with a "charismatic if technically unambitious performance," to quote *Sports Illustrated*. She went on to win a bronze medal at the world championships, her best showing ever in a major international competition.

Bobek is one of the first athletes who will benefit from changed rules for amateur figure skaters. In previous decades, amateur skaters could not accept any compensation for their performances—they had to pay for all of their coaching, costumes, and much of their travel out of pocket. Those days are gone. In order to keep top amateurs from turning professional prematurely, the International Skating Union, skating's governing body, has inaugurated a $1.95-million, five-event international tournament in which top amateurs compete against one another for points. Some other shows that pay substantial prize money have also been sanctioned by the ISU. In Bobek's case, this means that her training—already underwritten by the U.S. Olympic team— will be further enhanced by her ability to earn real money skating in competitive events.

That very freedom to perform for pay may have cost Bobek the 1996 national title. Multiple commitments in the weeks prior to the January 1996 nationals—including an appearance with *The Nutcracker on Ice*—aggravated an ankle injury and curtailed her practice time. Bobek showed up at the 1996 nationals but was unable to perform her free skate program. The sore ankle flared up and forced her to drop out of the competition. Deeply disappointed, she fought back tears as she told reporters, "I hope everyone doesn't give up on me."

Few skating fans are likely to give up on Bobek as long as she keeps faith in herself. This may prove to be her greatest battle of all. Bobek, who calls herself "just another teenager," will have to shed the image problems that have clouded her career and find a new reservoir of discipline and continuity in order to regain her national title. She certainly knows what needs to be done. "There was never a time when I was confused at what I was doing," she told *People*. "I always knew I wanted to skate, and that's it."

SURYA
BONALY

FIGURE SKATER

"In other sports they don't care how you run. You're faster, and that's it. It's not about your dress."

Controversy has always swirled around Surya Bonaly and her skating career. No one disputes the fact that Bonaly is a powerful, all-out skater with a fabulous command of the most difficult jumps. In a game where artistry and personality count almost as much as athletic ability, however, Bonaly has often been found lacking. Having won five straight European championships between 1991 and 1995, she has yet to bring home an Olympic medal or a world championship. Critics cite everything from her temperamental behavior to her mother's interference for Bonaly's tarnished image. Whatever the case, Bonaly skates into the 1996 Olympics with her amateur status intact and her pure technical ability second to none.

Much of what has been written about Surya Bonaly in the press is sheer fiction. Her first coach, Didier Gailhaguet, and her mother concocted a fabulous story to match the young skater's vibrant black skin and extra-long hair. Bonaly, so the story went, was born on the tropical island of Reunion and abandoned there as an infant. She was adopted by French civil servant Georges Bonaly and his wife Suzanne, who then raised her on a macrobiotic diet that shunned all meat and dairy products but included bird seed. It was also said that Bonaly had never cut her hair going into the 1992 Olympics in Albertville, France.

The truth is simpler. Surya Bonaly was born in Nice, France, and was given up for adoption. She was eight months old when she joined the Bonaly household as an only child. Her parents were indeed careful with their diet, but they allowed Surya treats like chocolate and ice cream. An adventurous family, they liked to travel and take risks. As for her much-publicized pony tail, some fellow skaters have contended that it was a weave.

Bonaly began skating on a rink in Nice when she was about eight years old. Gailhaguet discovered her there when she was 10 and encouraged her parents to invest in serious training. The youngster was immensely talented and apparently fearless, and Gailhaguet found in her a pupil that would make his fame. After a year or so of training in Nice, the coach persuaded Surya's family to move to Paris so she could train at an indoor rink all year around.

Surya Bonaly's characteristic power and athleticism earned her a silver medal in the 1995 World Figure Skating Championships. (AP/Wide World Photos)

SURYA BONALY

French figure skater

Born: Nice, France.

Career Highlights:
- took first place, European Championship, 1991–95
- finished in fifth place, 1992 Olympic Games, Albertville, France
- came in fourth place, 1994 Olympic Games, Lillehammer, Norway
- won second place, World Championship, 1994.

At 16 Bonaly became a French national champion, and the following year, 1991, brought her first European championship. The French were so fond of their star skater that they chose her to administer the athlete's oath at the 1992 Winter Olympics in Albertville. Favored to win a medal at those Winter Games, she finished a disappointing fifth. Her skating was widely perceived to lack the deepest elements of artistic interpretation that determine true champions.

Stung by the bad press she received after the 1992 Olympics, Bonaly moved with her mother to a remote training facility in the French Alps. Coaches came and went, many of them quarreling with Bonaly's mother. While Surya continued to excel at the European championships every year, she made little headway on the international front, being edged out in world class competition by the likes of Oksana Baiul and China's Chen Lu.

"Everyone prefaces their remarks about Bonaly by saying she's a sweet, hardworking kid," wrote Johnette Howard in a March 6, 1995, *Sports Illustrated* profile of the skater. "Then the haymakers start whistling in: She lacks artistic refinement. She's a sore loser. History will forget her unless she wins the worlds or Olympics. She and her mother flub the big things. . . . Plus, they don't play the game by kowtowing to judges and skating officials."

Perhaps the best known of Bonaly's "sore loser" moments occurred in the 1994 world championships. Bonaly was coming off a respectable fourth-place showing at the 1994 Olympics just a few weeks prior to the worlds. At the world championships that year, she skated brilliantly and seemed to have more emotion packed into her routines. Nevertheless, she finished second to Japan's Yuka Sato. The competition was held in Japan, and Bonaly felt that the judges had unfairly scored the event in Sato's favor. Bonaly refused to take the podium for the awards ceremony, and—when she finally did mount the silver medalist's block—she ripped her medal off in protest. The very polite and proper international skating community expressed shock at the skater's behavior.

Since that time Bonaly has struggled to mend her reputation and to maintain her status in the world rankings. She has had variable success, winning another European championship in 1995 and qualifying for the Skate International amateur tour, but her hopes are squarely pinned on the 1996 Olympics. As Johnette Howard put it, "Depending upon the beholder, Surya Bonaly is the most gifted and athletic figure skater in the world today, or she is a unique but squandered talent whose career seems destined to stall at also-ran status." A few more years in the arena will tell.

VALERIE
BRISCO

"I like the competition—when you're out there on the line and all your adrenaline is flowing. I like winning and being recognized as No. 1 in the world. That's what makes it fun."

No runner of either sex had ever won gold medals in both the 200- and 400-meter sprints in one Olympics until Valerie Brisco did it in 1984. A virtual unknown when she entered the Summer Games in Los Angeles, Brisco won three track and field gold medals—for the 200, the 400, and the 4 × 400-meter relay. Brisco was the first woman to take triple gold since the legendary Wilma Rudolph did it in 1960, and no runner since has been able to duplicate the feat. Never as popular with the public as Florence Griffith Joyner, the animated Brisco nonetheless enjoys the regard of the sporting community as one of the best track and field athletes of modern times.

Valerie Brisco's early running career was dedicated to her brother, Robert. Brisco, the sixth of 10 children of Arguster and Guitherea Brisco, was born in 1960 in Greenwood, Mississippi, and raised in Los Angeles. Her family lived in the South Central district of the city, and Brisco and her siblings attended public high school there. Her brother Robert—who had urged her to pursue track—was killed by a stray bullet while training on a field at Locke High School.

The whole Brisco family was devastated by Robert's death, no one more so than Valerie. She determined that she would become a winner in his memory.

At first everything came easy for her. "In high school, workouts weren't the thing for me. I'd just jog and go home—that was it," she told *Women's Sports + Fitness*. Her notorious laziness, and her constant battles with punctuality, did not adversely influence her talent. She was a top-ranked high school sprinter who easily qualified for an athletic scholarship to California State University at Northridge. She entered the college in 1979 and there met the man who would transform her into a world class star.

Bob Kersee was the coach at the California State University when Brisco arrived there. Enthusiastic and demanding, he foresaw Brisco's possibilities immediately and put her on an intense training regimen aimed at making her stronger, faster, and more durable. Kersee "showed me things to per-

Valerie Brisco sets a new world record in this 220-yard dash in 1985.

(UPI/Bettmann Newsphotos)

VALERIE BRISCO

American track and field athlete

Born: 1960 in Greenwood, Mississippi.

Education: Full athletic scholarship to California State University at Northridge, 1979–81.

Career Highlights:

- won gold medal, 200-meter race, gold medal, 400-meter race, and gold medal, 4 × 400-meter relay, 1984 Olympic Games, Los Angeles, California

- set indoor records in the 220-, 440-, and 500-yard races, 1985

- became world champion, 200-meter race, 1986

- won silver medal, 4 × 400-meter relay, 1988 Olympic Games, Seoul, South Korea.

Awards: Inducted into the Track and Field Hall of Fame, 1995.

fect my natural ability, and the first year I trained constantly, I finally believed him," Brisco recalled in *Women's Sports + Fitness*. Her college track career was interrupted in 1981 by marriage to professional football player Alvin Hooks. Brisco left the university to move to Philadelphia with Hooks, who had won a job with the Philadelphia Eagles. A son, Alvin, Jr., was born the next year.

In 1983 Valerie Brisco found herself needing to shed 40 pounds of post-pregnancy weight. She decided to go back into running, and she put herself on a strict diet and a serious workout routine. With her husband sidelined from football by injuries, she decided to go back to California and train with Kersee again. The family moved west, settling in Brisco's parents' small house, which they shared with eight other adults and several children.

Kersee still believed in Brisco, and before long the young sprinter had achieved the best conditioning and discipline of her career. Brisco spent seven hours a day at the track, five days a week. Three times a week she worked out with weights for up to three hours at a stretch. She also did 250 pushups and a staggering 1,000 situps a day. She was more than ready to compete in the 1984 Summer Olympics in her home town.

Because she had been out of track and field for several years, Brisco was not well known when she entered the Olympic Trials and made the U.S. Olympic team. She entered the Games in Los Angeles as a dark horse, but— with a boycott by the Soviet Union and its satellite states—she streaked to victory in both the 200-meter and the 400-meter sprints. When she later participated in the 4 × 400-meter relay for another gold medal, she became the first woman in nearly 25 years to win three track gold medals in one Olympics— and the first athlete ever to win golds in the 200 and the 400 at the same Games.

Brisco had hoped that her success in Los Angeles would bring her an avalanche of endorsement contracts and other offers, but she never achieved the popularity that her fellow 1984 Olympian, Mary Lou Retton, enjoyed. Pestered by suggestions that she might not have done so well had the Soviet Union's runners been present, she set out to prove that she was indeed the fastest woman in the world. In the winter of 1985 she set indoor records in the 220-, 440-, and 500-yard races. The following year she became world champion at the 200-meter distance, beating eight-time champion Evelyn Ashford by a hundredth of a second.

The last Olympic medal Brisco won was at the 1988 Summer Games. There she shared a silver medal with Florence Griffith Joyner, Denean Howard-Hill, and Diane Dixon in the 4 × 400-meter relay. Brisco retired shortly thereafter and, having divorced her husband, set herself to the task of raising a child as a single parent. She was inducted into the Track and Field Hall of Fame in 1995.

ZOLA
BUDD PIETERSE

Zola Budd Pieterse's career illustrates many of the pitfalls that can assail high-level athletes. As the shy South African teenager Zola Budd, the runner faced harrassment by political protesters, pointed questions from the press, and exploitation as a quick meal ticket from some of the people who should have cared about her the most. Even those who had no opinion about South African politics cast her as a villain for tripping Mary Decker in the 3,000-meter finals at the 1984 Olympic Games. A champion-caliber middle distance runner at 17, Zola Budd Pieterse suffered a complete nervous collapse at 21 and declared that she could no longer compete in races. Her enormous potential seemed to have been lost in a morass of politics, family quarrels, and pure bad luck.

Time has brought healing for Pieterse, just as it has for her native land. Today she is married, highly respected in South Africa, and has resumed her running career. The "designated whipping girl of the 1980s," to quote a June 24, 1991, *Sports Illustrated* profile, has endured long enough to put her demons to rest. "I can really say I'm happy now," she told *Sports Illustrated*. ". . . Running is only one part of my life now, not all of it as it used to be, not everything."

The youngest of six children of a white South African couple, Zola Budd was born in Bloemfontein, a small city some 260 miles from the South African capital of Johannesburg. Tragedy played a big part in her decision to become a runner. When she was 14, her beloved older sister died suddenly. Budd took to running—barefoot—to escape the pain of her sister's loss. What Zola and her family discovered was that she had a distinct talent for the longer distance run.

In 1982, at the age of 15, Budd won the South African National Women's Championships at both the 1,500-meter and the 3,000-meter distances. Two years later, at a race in Cape Town, she shattered Mary Decker's world record in the 5,000 meters by more than six seconds. Overnight Zola Budd became an international celebrity, and just that quickly the troubled politics of her homeland began to squelch her career.

Barefoot runner Zola Budd became an international celebrity when she was just seventeen years old. (Archive Photos)

Because Budd broke the world record in South Africa, her mark was never considered official. At that time the nation was barred from official international competitions—including the Olympics—because of its government's discriminatory policies against black South Africans. Soon after breaking the 5,000-meter world record, Budd and her family decided to accept an offer from the London *Daily Mail* that offered the family air fare, British passports, and British citizenship for Budd in return for her exclusive story. Budd and her parents arrived in London in March of 1984, and less than two weeks later she was awarded British citizenship. (Her paternal grandfather had been an English citizen.)

In her autobiography, *Zola*, the runner expressed nothing but bitterness about the quick move to England. "They turned me into some kind of circus animal," she wrote of her father and the staff at the *Daily Mail*. ". . . I was plucked away from everything I loved and put in an environment where I as a person no longer counted." Worse, the fact that Zola Budd was a white South African made her a target for the political protesters in England and elsewhere who opposed apartheid. As 1984 progressed and she entered races in England and abroad, she was jeered from the spectator stands and pressed for her views on her country's politics by reporters. She refused to answer the personal questions, telling *Sports Illustrated* on June 18, 1984: "I just wish the politicians would let me get on with my running."

Her running was spectacular. Racing in tears as the crowds booed her performance, she won Britain's Olympic trials at both the 1,500-meter and 3,000-meter distances. At 17, the runner who *Time* magazine dubbed "an amateur princess, a professional pawn" was on her way to the Olympics and was considered a favorite to beat the popular world champion Mary Decker.

The 3,000-meter race at the 1984 Los Angeles Olympics still stands as one of the most dramatic moments in Olympic history. Midway through the race, Decker tripped over Budd's heel and sprawled onto the track. Budd finished the race seventh and has since claimed that she deliberately held herself back so that she would not be booed on the medal stand. Attempting to apologize to Decker after the race, Budd met with nothing but scorn from her opponent.

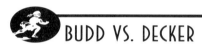

BUDD VS. DECKER

Many people know Zola Budd only in the context of the 3,000-meter race at the 1984 Olympics. Midway through the race, Budd cut into Mary Decker's lane, colliding with her and causing her to fall to the ground, tearing a muscle and losing her Olympic hopes. At the time, Budd was booed by the crowds in the Los Angeles Memorial Coliseum, and she later claimed that she purposely held back for the rest of the race so she wouldn't have to face an angry crowd from the winner's stand; she finished in seventh place. After the race, Budd (who has since been exonerated) attempted to apologize to Decker, who curtly responded, "Don't bother."

ZOLA BUDD PIETERSE

South African distance runner

Born: c. 1967 in Bloemfontein, South Africa.

Career Highlights:

- took first place, South African National Women's Championships, 1,500-meter and 3,000-meter distances, 1982
- finished in first place, Britain's Olympic Trials, 1,500-meter and 3,000-meter distances, 1984
- won first place, World Cross Country Championships, 1985 and 1986.

Returning to England, Budd faced yet more troubles. Her parents divorced, the anti-apartheid demonstrations continued everywhere she appeared, and Decker beat her in several highly publicized rematch races. Nevertheless, Budd managed to win the 1985 and 1986 World Cross Country Championships and set a world record of 14:48.07 in the 5,000 meter and an indoor world record of 8:39.79 in the 3,000.

By 1988, a severely depressed Zola Budd was ready to turn her back on organized sports forever. She had been accused—wrongly—of taking part in a race in Johannesburg, and because of her appearance as a spectator at that South African event, the British team was threatened with suspension from the 1988 World Cross Country Championships. Unable to sleep and nearly suicidal, Budd flew home to Bloemfontein, telling the press: "I have been made to feel like a criminal. I have been continuously hounded, and I can't take it anymore."

The story might have ended there, but back in South Africa Budd began to recover. She married Bloemfontein businessman Michael Pieterse and—very slowly—began to entertain thoughts of running again. In the meantime, her country's political landscape changed dramatically with the end of apartheid and the introduction of majority rule. With South Africa's right to compete in internationally sanctioned events restored, Zola Pieterse returned to the track. She also, at long last, made known her personal views on apartheid. In her 1991 *Sports Illustrated* profile, Pieterse stated: "The Bible says men are born equal before God. I can't reconcile segregation along racial lines with the words of the Bible. As a Christian I find apartheid intolerable."

Zola Pieterse competed in the 1992 Olympics as a South African and was eliminated from the 3,000-meter heat in an early rosund. Soon thereafter she was diagnosed with a liver disorder. Medication and vitamins have since improved her health, and she ran to a fourth-place finish in the 1993 World Cross Country Championships, after which she declared her intention to switch to the 10,000-meter distance. Still in her prime—and now competing with less political and emotional baggage—she may be a contender for many seasons to come.

SUSAN BUTCHER

Over one million t-shirts bearing the logo "Alaska—Where Men Are Men and Women Win the Iditarod" have been sold since Butcher first won what Alaskans refer to as "The Last Great Race."

Susan Butcher is a four-time winner of the annual 1,159-mile Iditarod Trail Sled Dog Race from Anchorage to Nome, Alaska, which had been a male-dominated event until she began participating. Butcher has entered the race each year since 1978, placing first in 1986, 1987, 1988, and 1990. One of only two people to win four Iditarods and the first to win three consecutive races, she held the Iditarod speed record until 1994. In one of the most punishing sports imaginable, Butcher ranks among the very best of all time—male or female. She has helped to smash the notion that men are superior to women in performing feats of endurance and courage.

Butcher was born on December 26, 1954, in Cambridge, Massachusetts. She was the youngest of two daughters of Charles Butcher, chairman of a family-owned chemical company, and Agnes Butcher, a psychiatric social worker. Butcher's parents did not believe in making distinctions between boys and girls, so she and her sister Kate learned such skills as carpentry before they were teenagers. Having helped her father try to restore an old sailboat, Butcher enjoyed the experience so much that she applied to a boat-building school when she was 16. Her application was rejected, she later said, because of her gender. She did not become a boat builder, but she would show greater determination to succeed against odds as a dogsled racer.

From an early age Butcher loved the outdoors and disliked cities. She also preferred solitude. As an eight-year-old she wrote a school essay titled "I Hate the City," in which she described plans to tear down her family home and build a small log cabin that would provide more room for grass. During vacations to the Maine seacoast Butcher played in the surf and spent most of her time with her dog, Cabee. Her parents expected her to become a veterinarian because, as her father commented, she was "more comfortable with animals than she was with people."

Instead of going to college, at age 17 Butcher moved to Boulder, Colorado, and became interested in dogsled racing, or mushing. After two years in Boulder she went to the University of Alaska in Fairbanks to work

After winning her second Iditarod in 1987, Susan Butcher posed with her lead dogs, Mattie (left) and Granite (right). (AP/Wide World Photos)

on a project to save the endangered musk ox. She also wanted to learn mushing, so she bought three dogs. Living in an isolated log cabin in the Wrangell Mountains outside Fairbanks, Butcher hunted for food and practiced mushing. In 1977 she moved with the musk-ox project to Unalakleet, Alaska, where she met Joe Reddington, Sr., who ten years earlier had originated the Last Great Race on Earth, better known as the Iditarod Trail Sled Dog Race. After hiring Butcher to train dogs at his kennel and observing her dedication to mushing, Reddington predicted she would become an Iditarod champion. In her first step toward that goal she entered the 1978 race and finished in nineteenth place.

After participating in the 1979 Iditarod, Butcher made plans to move to Eureka, Alaska. Shortly before she left, in 1980, she met David Monson, a lawyer and sled racer who represented a dog food company. Their courtship began slowly as Butcher tried valiantly to discharge a debt for dog food; by 1985 they were married, and Monson was the full-time manager of Butcher's career. The couple made their home at Eureka, located 100 miles south of the Arctic Circle, where they built four one-room cabins and the 120 dog houses that comprise the Trail Breaker Kennels. After her marriage Butcher won four out of five Iditarods, and in one of her victories, she set a speed record of 11 days, one hour, 53 minutes, 23 seconds.

Since Butcher began racing in 1978 her life has been completely focused on breeding, raising, and training dogs. She has bonded with every dog born at her kennel—as many as 150 Alaskan Husky sled dogs live there at a time—first by assisting at their births, then by giving them names and nurturing them as they grow from puppies into adult dogs. Describing the dogs as her "best friends," Butcher interacts with them as one would with human beings, congratulating a mother dog on the birth of a litter of puppies or commending a young dog for learning a new skill. She even recognizes each dog's individual voice or howl. Butcher's friends and associates say this close bonding accounts for the willingness of the dogs to work hard for her during the grueling Iditarod, and cite it as the reason she wins so many races.

IDITAROD TRAINING

When Butcher's dogs are old enough, she begins a training schedule with an overhead wheel-like device called a dog walker, to which she hooks the dog for a 30-minute walk so she can check how the animal moves. In the fall, before winter weather arrives, she harnesses the dogs to a vehicle with wheels so she and her husband can take them for trips that become increasingly longer as they gain confidence. She pairs a young dog with a more experienced dog for runs through forests on a variety of trails to prevent them from getting bored. The dogs look forward to these outings and enthusiastically submit to the harness. By December, when they are running 25 to 75 miles a day, Butcher begins selecting the 20 dogs for the Iditarod team.

The Iditarod easily ranks as one of the toughest endurance tests in modern sports. Needless to say, Butcher and her dogs have encountered many adventures on the race trail. At the beginning of the 1982 Iditarod, when Butcher's sled careened into a tree, she was bruised and 15 dogs were injured. Shortly after they returned to the race a severe snowstorm completely erased the trail, driving Butcher ten miles off course. She and the dogs were stranded for 52 hours in 80-mile-per-hour winds and 30-foot snowdrifts. They still managed to finish second. During the 1985 Iditarod, Butcher and her team were attacked by a pregnant moose that killed two dogs, injured 13, and hurt Butcher's shoulder. Although they were rescued by a fellow racer who shot the moose, Butcher had to drop out on that occasion.

Butcher has set records in other sled races such as the Norton Sound 250, the Kobuk 220, the Kusko 300, and the John Beargrease race. She has twice been named Women's Sports Foundation Professional Sportswoman of the Year, and in 1990 she and Monson were guests of President George Bush at the White House. The 1994 Iditarod was Butcher's fourteenth, but she did

SUSAN BUTCHER

American dogsled racer

Born: December 26, 1954 in Cambridge, Massachusetts.

Career Highlights:
- won second place, Iditarod race, 1982 and 1984
- took first place, Iditarod race, 1986, 1987, 1988, and 1990

- became one of only two people to win four Iditarods and the first to win three consecutive races
- held the Iditarod speed record until 1994.

Awards: Twice named Women's Sports Foundation Professional Sportswoman of the Year.

not place and her speed record was broken by Martin Buser at 10 days, 13 hours, and 2 minutes. While she was preparing for the race she said it would probably be her last because she wants to take time to have a family and start an animal research center in Eureka.

If Butcher does enter retirement, she will certainly do so with bragging rights.

JENNIFER
CAPRIATI

"I don't regret anything that happened in my career, except that maybe 14 is too young to handle everything emotionally. But I know I don't want to leave tennis the way I did, crying and crawling away."

Jennifer Capriati's tennis career stands as a cautionary tale for any would-be professional athlete: sometimes the highest aspirations are best deferred until adulthood. The youngest player ever to turn pro, Capriati appeared in her first professional tennis match just a month shy of her 14th birthday. She was an instant sensation. The concept of a young, pretty teenager who could sigh over Twizzlers licorice while also blasting her way to the top of the tennis circuit appealed to tennis buffs everywhere. Unfortunately, as time would tell, the pressure to perform at that level proved too great for the sensitive teen. Today, at 20, Capriati is trying to battle back from a case of burnout that led to alienation from family and friends, drug abuse, and more than a year's hiatus from the pro tennis tour.

Jennifer Capriati was born March 29, 1976, on Long Island, New York, to Stefano and Denise Capriati. Her Bronx-born mother, who was a Pan Am flight attendant, met her father in Spain in 1972. Stefano Capriati, a native of Milan, Italy, was a resident of Spain, where he was a movie stuntman and a self-taught tennis pro. They married and settled in Spain.

Stefano Capriati had high hopes for his daughter—even before she was born he told people she would be a tennis star. The family moved to New York so that Jennifer could be born in America, but they spent most of Jennifer's early years living in Spain. When she was a baby, her father did cribside calisthenics with her, propping her backside with a pillow and helping her do sit-ups. At four she could hold her own with a ball machine. Encouraged by her prowess, the family moved to Fort Lauderdale, Florida, where Jennifer began lessons with Chris Evert's father before she was old enough to attend kindergarten.

From age 10 to 13, Jennifer was coached by Rick Macci in Haines City, Florida. Then she went to the Hopman Tennis Academy at Saddlebrook resort in Wesley Chapel, where she got a third coach, Tom Gullickson. But the true driving force in her budding career was her father, whom she called her main coach and whom the other members of her entourage called "the main boss."

*Jennifer Capriati returns a shot off Conchita Martinez during the 1991
Federation Cup; Capriati won the match, 6-4, 7-5, 6-1.* (AP/Wide World Photos)

In retrospect, many observers have suggested that Stefano Capriati was the quintessential "tennis father," pushing his daughter to play against older and more experienced opponents and to make tennis her whole world. A May 30, 1994, *People* profile of Jennifer Capriati quotes her father as having said, "Where I come from we have a proverb: 'When the apple is ripe, eat it.'"

The apple most certainly seemed ripe. In 1988 at age 12, Capriati won the U.S. 18-and-under championships on both hard and clay courts. In 1989 she won the 18-and-under French Open, made the quarterfinals at Wimbledon, and won the junior title at the U.S. Open. Eager for Jennifer to turn pro, her father petitioned the Women's Tennis Council to exempt his daughter from the rule barring girls under 14 from professional tournaments. He was successful—less than a month before her 14th birthday, Jennifer made her pro debut at the Virginia Slims tournament in Boca Raton, Florida, where she advanced to the finals before being beaten by Gabriela Sabatini. By the time she appeared at the August 1990 U.S. Open, she was ranked 16th in the nation.

A SUPERLATIVE PLAYER

In discussing Jennifer Capriati's career as a tennis player, inevitably her many superlative accomplishments are mentioned. She was the youngest female player ever to turn pro (debuting one month before her 14th birthday), the youngest player to play and win a match in the Wightman Cup (1989), the youngest player to participate and win a match in the Federation Cup (1990), and the youngest Wimbledon semi-finalist (1991). Capriati was also the youngest woman to be ranked in the U.S. Top Three.

Even before she took the court as a professional, Capriati had earned a number of lucrative product endorsement deals. These—and her open, pure-teen personality—brought her a level of fame usually reserved for only the very top players. Capriati seemed bound to live up to her legend, however. She reached the semifinals at the 1991 U.S. Open *and* Wimbledon and became the youngest woman in history ever to be ranked in the top ten internationally. She further enhanced her fame by taking the gold medal at the Barcelona Olympics in 1992.

Life on tour began to take its toll as early as 1993. Hounded by the press, Capriati became sullen and uncooperative. She began to feel that her friends liked her only because she was a big tennis star, and as for the tennis, injuries began to erode her ability.

The bottom dropped out when she suffered a first-round loss at the 1993 U.S. Open. "I started out O.K., but at the end of the match I couldn't wait to get off the court," she recalled in a September 26, 1994, *New York Times* profile. "Totally, mentally, I just lost it, and obviously it goes deeper than that one match. I really was not happy with myself, my tennis, my life, my parents, my coaches, my friends. . . . I spent a week in bed in darkness after that, just hating everything. When I looked in my mirror, I actually

JENNIFER CAPRIATI

American tennis player

Born: March 29, 1976 in Long Island, New York.

Career Highlights:
- won U.S. 18-and-under championships on hard and clay courts, 1988
- won 18-and-under French Open, 1989
- made quarterfinals at Wimbledon, 1989
- won junior title at the U.S. Open, 1989
- took home gold medal, women's singles, 1992 Olympic Games, Barcelona, Spain.

saw this distorted image: I was so ugly and so fat, I just wanted to kill myself, really."

The self-destructive urges led to antisocial behavior and eventually to treatment for substance abuse. Capriati has since returned to professional tennis—on her own terms—and is forthright about what happened to her. "I burned out—I'll say it," she admitted in the *New York Times*. Still she thinks she has a brilliant future on the tennis circuit. "It's just a game to me now; I'm playing because it's inside me, I have this desire to play and a talent to play, and I don't want to waste my talent," she said. "I don't care about being No. 1, but I'm ready and willing to give a battle, and that's what sports is all about. Who cares about endorsements and all that stuff? Just give me a racket. There's no ending to my story yet."

ROSEMARY CASALS

"Along the way [in the world of tennis], there have been lots of breakthroughs— lots of 'firsts.' Rosemary Casals has been in on all of them."

—Biographer Linda Jacobs, in Rosemary Casals: The Rebel Rosebud

In a time when tennis was a sport for the rich country club set, Rosemary Casals came along to shake things up. A winner of well over 100 tennis tournaments—including five Wimbledon doubles titles with partner Billie Jean King—Casals earned a reputation as a rebel and an outspoken advocate of gender equity in tournament play. Casals was a fierce competitor who overcame not only the obstacle of being five-feet-two but also covert discrimination against Hispanic players. During her years of peak performance the world tennis circuit saw a number of changes—more than a few sparked by players like Casals herself.

Born September 16, 1948, in San Francisco, California, Casals was given up as a baby by her immigrant parents because they could not earn a living. She was raised by a great-uncle and great-aunt, Manuel and Maria Casals, who took her and her sister into their family. Manuel was a former member of the El Salvador national soccer team, so he infused his adopted daughters with a love of sports. He taught Rosemary to play tennis on San Francisco's public courts and was the only coach she ever had.

Casals earned her reputation as a tennis rebel early in her career. She simply hated the established tennis tradition of having younger players compete against each other on the junior circuit. Whenever she could, Casals would enter tournaments against older and more experienced players, seeking the challenge she could not find with her own age group.

Then there were the problems of race and poverty to overcome. Tennis was traditionally a sport practiced in posh country clubs by the white upper class. Rosie had none of those economic advantages, and her Hispanic heritage further alienated her from most of her opponents. She forged ahead anyway, and in the process became one of the first players to take a tennis court in anything other than traditional all-white clothing. Today most tennis players have followed Casals's example of sporting colorful outfits in competition.

By the age of 17, Casals ranked eleventh in America as a singles player. She advanced to the semifinals of the U.S. tennis championships at Forest

*Rosemary Casals returns a serve to Chris Evert during a match at the
1976 Virginia Slims Tennis Tournament. Casals lost the match.*

(UPI/Bettmann)

Hills, New York, losing an aggressively played match against the top-ranked
player in the world, Brazil's Maria Bueno. In 1966 Casals teamed with Billie
Jean King to win the doubles portion of the U.S. hard-court and indoor tournaments. The well-matched duo also reached the quarter-finals at the 1966
Wimbledon tournament. Casals also teamed with Ian Crookenden in 1966 to
win the U.S. hard-court mixed doubles. Her ranking as a singles player that
same year was third in the country.

Once again teamed with King in the 1967 Wimbledon tournament,
Casals won the doubles crown. She and King also picked up the U.S. and
South African championships that same year. Having earned a great deal of
success on the court, the outspoken Casals decided to try to earn something
else—money. She was not wealthy enough to support herself while engaging
in amateur tennis tournaments, but still she wanted to compete. She was therefore one of the athletes who demanded a change of rules that would allow

ROSEMARY CASALS

American tennis player

Born: September 16, 1948 in San Francisco, California.

Career Highlights:

- teamed with Billie Jean King to win doubles portion of U.S. hard-court and indoor tournaments, 1966
- teamed with Ian Crookenden to win the U.S. hard-court mixed doubles, 1966
- won five Wimbledon doubles titles with partner Billie Jean King, 1967, 1968, 1970, 1971, and 1973
- won inaugural Virginia Slims tournament, 1970
- won the U.S. Open seniors' women's doubles championship (with King), 1990.

professional players to compete in major tournaments. The rules were indeed changed late in 1967, and thereafter Casals was able to make quite a nice living as a touring professional.

Other hurdles remained, however. In the late 1960s and early 1970s, women's tennis tournament winners earned only a fraction of the amount of their male counterparts. Casals, who earned $25,000 in 1970, was the sixth-highest paid women's tennis player in America. She was well aware that such meager earnings were keeping other low income athletes from competing at her level. She was therefore one of a group of women's tennis professionals who threatened to boycott future tournaments unless more prize money could be offered to women and more attention could be focused on their matches.

Tennis's governing body ignored the threats, so an enterprising journalist—Gladys Heldman, editor of *World Tennis* magazine—organized a rival tournament, the Virginia Slims Invitational, to be held on the same day as the prestigious Pacific Southwest Open. Casals was one of seven women who agreed to participate in the Virginia Slims tournament, and she won the $1,600 top prize. In 1972 she was a pioneering participant in the eight-tournament Virginia Slims women's professional tennis circuit. She also continued to tour successfully as a doubles player with Billie Jean King. Thanks to her determination to see more money flow toward women's tennis, Casals saw her earnings nearly triple between 1970 and 1973.

In the mid-1970s, Casals became one of the first members of America's World Team Tennis (WTT) league, which included mixed tennis teams from major U.S. cities. Each meeting between teams included men's and women's singles and doubles games as well as a mixed doubles match. During her years with the WTT Casals played with the Detroit Loves and the Oakland Breakers. She later coached the Los Angeles Strings.

This introduction to the business side of tennis gave Casals new ideas of her own. When her playing career was effectively ended by knee problems in 1978, she sought other challenges within the game. In 1981 she founded Sportswomen, Inc., a California-based sports agency for tennis players of both sexes. The company also inaugurated the Lincoln-Mercury Tennis Classics circuit, a tour that features "classics" matches between former tennis superstars. From its fledgling season in 1984 until the present, the Tennis Classics tour has proven a hit with spectators and has had no trouble attracting sponsors.

As for Casals, she has been a regular participant on the Tennis Classics circuit as well as in seniors' tournaments worldwide. In 1990, she teamed with longtime doubles partner Billie Jean King to win the U.S. Open Seniors' women's doubles championship. It was yet another welcome victory in a long and successful career.

TRACY
CAULKINS

SWIMMER

*"I thought, 'Why
are my records not
falling?' It shows
a lot of progress
when they do. The
women . . . are
not satisfied with
just winning."*

—*Caulkins, upon
retirement in 1984*

Few people "retire" at the age of 21, but that is exactly what Tracy Caulkins did. The University of Florida swimming great who won three gold medals at the 1984 Summer Olympics is an athlete who is content these days to watch her own records fall as a new generation prepares for future Olympic games.

Caulkins was born on January 11, 1963, in Winona, Minnesota. She grew up in Nashville, Tennessee, and attended Harpeth Hall Academy, a private school. She began swimming competitively as a youngster and earned a berth on the Olympic team in 1980, before she even entered college. That year the United States boycotted the Olympic Games, depriving Caulkins of a great chance to enhance her fame. All of the Olympic athletes were disappointed, but none more so than the high school champion from Nashville. She has since said that she trained even harder during college so that she would qualify for the Olympics again in 1984.

That hard training brought fantastic dividends. In 1981 Caulkins enrolled at the University of Florida, where, over a period of four years, she turned in a stunning record as an amateur athlete. Her achievements include 48 national long and short course titles—the most won by any swimmer in U.S. history—62 American records, 15 individual American records, and participation in 11 American record-setting relay teams. From 1980 until 1984 she was widely considered the best and fastest woman swimmer in America.

While at Florida, Caulkins won the Broderick Cup as outstanding collegiate woman athlete of the year in both 1983 and 1984. Although she was a consistent winner throughout her college years—and a winner in the 200-meter and 400-meter individual medleys at the 1982 Pan American Games—her best year as an NCAA swimmer came in 1984. That year she set NCAA records in all four of her individual events (the 200-meter individual medley, or IM, the 400-meter IM, the 100-meter breaststroke, and the 200-meter fly). She also helped the Florida team to win the 800-meter freestyle relay and the 400-meter freestyle relay, both in NCAA record-setting times.

Tracy Caulkins plows through the water to qualify for the finals in the 200-meter IM at the World Swimming competition, 1982. (UPI/Bettmann Archive)

In preparation for the 1984 Olympic trials, Caulkins swam five hours a day, six days per week. Her determination paid off handsomely during the Summer Games in Los Angeles, where she won the 400-meter IM, setting an American record, and the 200-meter IM, establishing an Olympic record. Her third gold medal came as part of a victorious 400-meter relay team. After the Games ended, the United States Olympic Committee recognized Caulkins as "female athlete of the year," a fitting tribute.

Caulkins expresses no regrets as her successors in competitive swimming gradually beat her in the numbers game. After her retirement from competition in 1984, she told the Associated Press: "I thought, 'Why are my records not falling?' It shows a lot of progress when they do. The women . . . are not satisfied with just winning."

Caulkins was inducted into the International Swimming Hall of Fame in 1990. The University of Florida has also honored her accomplishments by

TRACY CAULKINS

American swimmer

Born: January 11, 1963 in Winona, Minnesota.

Education: University of Florida, 1981–85.

Career Highlights:

- won 48 national long and short course titles—the most won by any swimmer in U.S. history
- won 200-meter and 400-meter individual medleys, 1982 Pan American Games
- took home three gold medals at the 1984 Summer Olympics, Los Angeles, California
- set NCAA records in four individual events (200-meter IM, 400-meter IM, 100-meter breaststroke, and 200-meter fly) and two relay events (800-meter freestyle and 400-meter freestyle), 1984.

Awards: Earned Broderick Cup as outstanding collegiate woman athlete of the year, 1983 and 1984; recognized by U.S. Olympic Committee as "female athlete of the year," 1984; inducted into the International Swimming Hall of Fame, 1990.

naming a double swimming scholarship after her and by awarding a Tracy Caulkins Award to Florida's best female swimmer each year.

AMY
CHOW

One of the highest-ranking national gymnasts going into an Olympic year, Amy Chow has a resume that defies every expectation. Some people are great, but this San Jose, California, native is just downright *superior*. Not only has she worked her way onto the U.S. women's gymnastics team, she has also completed high school with a 4.0 grade point average, shown a talent for playing classical piano, and even done some diving on the side. Discipline and determination have paid off handsomely for Chow, who, barring injuries, may contend for Olympic gold in 1996.

Chow is a perfect example of parental aspirations gone awry. She was born on May 15, 1978, the daughter of Susan and Nelson Chow. Both of her parents had emigrated to America from Hong Kong, and her mother had always dreamed of becoming a ballerina. Those unfulfilled dreams were transferred to young Amy, who was taken to her first dancing lesson at the age of three. Unfortunately for her hopeful mother, Amy proved too small for even the pre-school classes at the ballet academies. As a stop-gap measure, her mother put her in gymnastics classes instead. Amy loved gymnastics from the start. By the time she had grown enough to qualify for ballet school, she refused to go.

If her parents were disappointed, their unhappiness did not last long. By the age of eight Amy became the first elite-level gymnast produced by San Jose's West Valley Gymnastics Club. Her coach, Mark Young, described her as "the fastest kid I've ever worked with." As her skills improved, she spent more and more time in practice, while not neglecting her studies—such challenging classes as pre-calculus, chemistry, and psychology—nor her piano practicing. Ranked 23rd all-around at the 1993 Coca-Cola National Championships, she came back from an ankle injury the following year to place fifth at the same competition.

Chow's routines are marked by high-difficulty moves. When working on the bars, she dismounts with a signature double-twisting double back. On the balance beam she can do a standing pike full twist. Her beam dismount

GYMNAST

"When I compete, I tell myself to be calm. It's not something that's the rest of your life. You're in gymnastics for the fun."

Amy Chow (right, with Shannon Miller) took home a gold medal for vault at the 1995 Pan American Games. (AP/Wide World Photos)

AMY CHOW

American gymnast

Born: May 15, 1978 in San Jose, California.

Education: Completed high school with a 4.0 grade point average.

Career Highlights:
- took fifth place, 1993 Coca-Cola National Championships
- earned a spot on the U.S. women's gymnastics team
- won gold medal in vault competition at Pan American Games, 1995.

is said to be "more difficult to perform than to describe." The only obstacle left in her challenge for a national title is her demeanor. Observers say that if she develops a personality to match her skill and perseverance, Chow will truly blossom.

With this in mind, Chow has been working with noted gymnastics coach Geza Pozsar, a colleague of Bela Karolyi who has choreographed routines for Nadia Comaneci and Mary Lou Retton. Chow makes no secret of her admiration for Retton, who has been a lifelong inspirational figure. Chow says of Retton's influence: "It was her spirit. Some gymnasts look so concerned. They look nervous. She looked calm and ready to go. She looked like she was having fun." This sense of playfulness is something Chow has to work to achieve, she admits. She just happens to be a stoic person. Even her high school classmates, she says, are "always trying to pry what I'm doing out of me."

This reticence can even extend to her coaches. In 1993, Amy injured her ankle doing the difficult beam dismount that she had been trying to perfect. The injury ruined a crucial season and led to a 22nd place all-around finish at her first senior national championships. Once healed, Chow worked with her coach, Diane Amos, to simplify the dismount—but not without frustration. Amos spent days trying to get Chow to verbalize what she was feeling inside. Finally, in an unusual burst of honesty, Chow said simply: "I want to do *my* dismount."

"Amy couldn't tell me what was bothering her because I was her teacher," Amos said. "The way she saw it, I'm supposed to tell her *what* to do, not ask her what she *wants* to do. But it was her dismount, and there was no way she was going to do anything else."

With a growing sense of confidence and the help of world-class coaches, Chow is looking forward to a possible Olympic-caliber season in 1996. Not surprisingly, though, the young woman who has spent almost 40 hours a week practicing gymnastics for the last five years has other aspirations as well—a future as a pediatrician, more music studies, and—when she has time—getting a driver's license and a car. "It's an honor to compete for your country, but I don't think I feel any more pressure because of that," she said. "When I compete, I tell myself to be calm. It's not something that's the rest of your life. You're in gymnastics for the fun."

MARY ELLEN
CLARK

Diver Mary Ellen Clark—who won a bronze medal in the 10-meter platform competition at the 1992 Olympic Games in Barcelona—is an eight-time national diving champion and, in her early 30s, a veritable senior citizen in the ranks of world class diving. Facing extremely disabling bouts of vertigo and the general round of injuries that come with age, she nonetheless tried to return to the 1996 Olympics, regarding those Games as her last chance to win further recognition in her sport. Asked about her long years of devotion to diving in a July 8, 1995 *Philadelphia Inquirer* profile, the former national champion stated: "My parents always told me that I should get out of diving when it wasn't fun anymore. But I've always had fun. It's always been a challenge."

Vertigo, which is marked by dizziness and disorientation, occurs when crystals embedded in the inner ear get knocked loose. Doctors have speculated that Clark may have injured herself sometime during her long years of practice, causing episodes of vertigo that begin and end without warning. She suffered her first episode in 1988—and did not qualify for the Olympics that year. The condition reappeared in 1990 and again in 1995. Clark described her condition in the *Philadelphia Inquirer* profile. She explained that when she dives with vertigo she needs her own personal lifeguard. "I need someone to make sure I swim to the top and not down to the bottom," she said. "It can happen."

Diving was not always so difficult for the lively Clark. The youngest of seven children, she began her sport at the age of seven, following her older sisters and brothers into the pool. Her father, Gene, had been a diving team captain at the University of Pennsylvania, and he taught all of his children what he had learned as a collegian. Mary Ellen was a particularly apt pupil, especially on the springboard dive. After graduating from Radnor High School near Philadelphia in 1981, she earned a scholarship to Penn State, and there she began working on the 10-meter platform. In her first year of competition on the 10-meter platform, she finished fifth in the national championships.

In 1987 Clark won her first national championship in an upset victory over Michelle Mitchell. Needless to say, the championship encouraged

"My parents always told me that I should get out of diving when it wasn't fun anymore. But I've always had fun. It's always been a challenge."

Mary Ellen Clark dives off the 10-meter platform during a qualifying heat at the 1992 Olympics in Barcelona, Spain. (AP/Wide World Photos)

Clark to believe she would be one of the two American divers to represent the U.S. in the event at the 1988 Olympics. Instead she finished a disappointing seventh in the 1988 Olympic Trials and—worse—injured her left shoulder at the meet. After that she began to question her future in the sport. "I wondered whether I had it in me to keep going," she told the *Philadelphia Inquirer* on June 20, 1991. "I had some time off. I had to go through rehabilitation, which was painful and tedious. But I decided to give it four more years after 1988."

Clark earned her master's degree in physical education from Ohio State University in 1989 and then moved to Fort Lauderdale, Florida, to train with Ron O'Brien, the coach behind Olympic champion Greg Louganis. Having supported herself by selling Cutco Cutlery door-to-door, Clark was delighted when she received a grant from the Women's Sports Foundation and a public relations job with the McDonalds Olympic Job Opportunities Program. Freed from financial worries, she trained five hours a day, six days a week and quickly regained her national championship form.

At the 1992 Olympic Trials, Clark finished second to Ellen Owen, thereby earning a trip to Barcelona. Her chance at an Olympic medal came at a time when her father had just undergone by-pass surgery, so she was doubly determined to win. Clark finished second in the platform diving preliminaries and trailed only Chinese sensation Fu Mingxia in the finals after six dives. Then she made a crucial mistake: looking ahead to a possible medal, she over-rotated her seventh dive and dropped into fifth place with only one dive to go. "It felt like hours before my last dive," she recalled in a March, 1993 *Women's Sports + Fitness* profile. When the "hours" finally passed, Clark went out and nailed her final dive for a third-place finish and a bronze medal.

VERTIGO, SHMERTIGO

Considering the fact that platform divers hit the water at speeds as high as 30 mph, it's not all that surprising that Mary Ellen Clark would suffer from some dizziness. But her persistent and disabling vertigo that began in January 1995 called for serious treatment and some time off from diving. She tried dozens of approaches to curing vertigo, everything from acupuncture to anti-seizure medication to a potpourri of vitamins and herbs. Finally, after nine months of searching for a cure, Clark found the Upledger Institute and their CranioSacral Therapy, described as a mix between massage and chiropractic techniques. Just weeks after this new therapy began, Clark was back in the pool practicing her dives. And by December 17 she had conquered this dizzying setback sufficiently to win the 10-meter platform event at the Ted Keller Invitational in Fort Lauderdale.

After the 1992 Olympics, most observers expected Clark to retire. For years she had told the press that the 1992 Summer Games were her goal and that she would retire afterwards. She changed her mind after her bronze-medal performance. "I felt I still had better diving in me, that I was still learning about the sport and about myself," she explained in the *Philadelphia Inquirer*. "There was no reason to quit." Since 1993 she has continued to train, facing

MARY ELLEN CLARK

American diver

Born: December 25, 1962.

Education: Graduated from Radnor High School near Philadelphia, 1981; earned an undergraduate scholarship to Penn State; earned master's degree in physical education from Ohio State University, 1989.

Career Highlights:
- won national diving championship, 1987
- took home bronze medal, 10-meter platform competition, 1992 Olympic Games, Barcelona, Spain.

Awards: Named U.S. Diving's athlete of the year, 1993 and 1994; earned a grant from Women's Sports Foundation.

ever younger competitors who also want to savor an Olympic moment. In 1994, for instance, she lost her national championship to 17-year-old Becky Ruehl, but she still competed in the Goodwill Games and the World Championships.

Clark's vertigo re-surfaced in 1995 and literally kept her out of the pool for months. Before she had trained right through the vertigo, but this time she decided to take a rest, try some alternative treatments, and hope that the condition would improve in time for the 1996 Olympic Trials. "I have to look at this as a real grounding experience, to maybe slow down, refocus, then charge into next year and finish my career in Atlanta," she told the *Philadelphia Inquirer*. The 33-year-old diver added: "I don't have to prove anything, but it's a personal challenge for me. I set my own goals and this is a goal. I want to overcome this."

By mid-October of 1995, Clark was back in the pool preparing for her return to competition. And on December 17, she proved that her return was a successful one: she won the 10-meter platform event at the Ted Keller Invitational in Fort Lauderdale, Florida.

ALICE
COACHMAN

Alice Coachman will go down in the history books as the first black woman to win an Olympic gold medal in track and field. The 1948 Olympic running high jump gold medal was only one of Coachman's trailblazing accomplishments. She also won 25 Amateur Athletic Union national titles and was national high jump champion for 12 straight years—many of them during World War II when the Olympics were not held. A dedicated athlete and fierce competitor in an era when American women were supposed to be meek and "ladylike," Coachman helped to break down barriers for blacks and women alike.

"I trained hard," Coachman told the *Albany Herald* on August 16, 1984. "I was sincere about my work. As I look back I wonder why I worked so hard, put so much time into it—but I guess it's just I wanted to win. And competition was very tough. You had to be in shape to win."

Born November 29, 1923, in Albany, Georgia, Alice Coachman was an unrepentant tomboy as a child. She often snuck away to the neighborhood playground to challenge boys in running and jumping contests. "It was a time when it wasn't fashionable for women to become athletes, and my life was wrapped up in sports," she remembered in a July 1984 *Essence* profile. "I was good at three things: running, jumping, and fighting."

Formal sports training for Coachman began in the fifth grade when her teacher, Cora Bailey, recognized her immense talent. Just a few years later Coachman was recruited by the prestigious Tuskegee Institute High School. She represented Tuskegee Institute at the 1939 track and field national championships, even before she had attended her first class at the school. By the time she earned her high school diploma in 1943 she had won the AAU nationals in running high jump and 50-yard dash. Coachman decided to stay on at Tuskegee and work toward a trade degree in dressmaking, which she received in 1946. By that time, she held four national track and field championships: the 50- and 100-meter dashes, the 400-meter relay, and the running high jump.

TRACK & FIELD ATHLETE

"I've always believed that I could do whatever I set my mind to do. I've had that strong will, that oneness of purpose, all my life. . . . I just called upon myself and the Lord to let the best come through."

Alice Coachman soars over the competition to take first place in the high jump at the 1939 National Women's Track and Field Meet. (UPI/Corbis-Bettmann)

ALICE COACHMAN

American track & field athlete

Born: November 29, 1923 in Albany, Georgia.

Education: Attended Tuskegee Institute High School, 1939–43; earned bachelor's degree in home economics from Albany State, 1949.

Career Highlights:
• earned 25 Amateur Athletic Union national titles

• named national high jump champion for 12 straight years

• won gold medal, running high jump, 1948 Olympic Games, London, England; became first black woman to win an Olympic gold medal and first American woman to take a gold medal in a track and field event.

Awards: Inducted into the National Track and Field Hall of Fame, 1975.

In that wartime era, competitions were restricted to a national level. Coachman was recognized as the best in the nation, and as World War II ended she looked forward to trying her skills against international competitors. She got her chance in the 1948 Olympics, held in London, England. One of several black women to qualify for the Olympic team that year, Coachman traveled to England with a sore back and a case of homesickness. She recalled in *Essence* that she was shocked when she arrived in London to discover "my picture was everywhere and everyone seemed to know all about me. All those people were waiting to see the American girl run, and I gave them something to remember me by."

That is an understatement. Holding off a challenge by Britain's D. J. Tyler, the five-foot-eight-inch, 130-pound Coachman completed an Olympic record five-foot, six-and-one-eighth-inch jump for the gold medal. Her feat vaulted her into history as not only the first black woman to win an Olympic gold medal but also as the first American woman to take a gold medal in a track and field event. She was 24 at the time.

Coachman returned home to find herself invited to the Harry S. Truman White House and to a motorcade ride through Georgia, where she was welcomed by throngs of jubilant African Americans. The kind of publicity that surrounds modern athletes never materialized for her, partly due to her race and partly due to her gender. She was a huge hero in the black community, however, and that alone satisfied her immensely.

The Olympics over, Coachman left athletics at the pinnacle of her career and took up teaching high school physical education in her home town of Albany. She earned a bachelor's degree in home economics from Albany State in 1949 and lived quietly in Georgia with her husband (whom she later divorced), their son Richmond and daughter Diane.

Ever since then, Coachman has never sought the limelight, but periodically it finds her anyway. She was named a member of the National Track and Field Hall of Fame in 1975 and has been the subject of numerous historical profiles in the pages of *Ebony* and *Essence* magazines.

By her examples of hard work, long devotion to a sports specialty, and sheer talent, Coachman did more than simply win a nice trophy for her mantelpiece. She literally opened the athletics door to a whole new segment of American society—black women—and served as a standard-bearer for a veritable flood of modern African American women's sports superstars.

COLORADO SILVER BULLETS

There's good news for all the girls out there who are playing Little League baseball alongside their male classmates. Now they, too, can dream of becoming professional baseball players.

The dream was launched in the spring of 1994 when Whittle Sports Properties and the Coors Brewing Company introduced the Colorado Silver Bullets, the first all-female professional baseball team organized to play against men. The Silver Bullets' mission is simple: they want to prove that women can play great baseball, and they want to change the way people think about male superiority in sports.

The idea for an all-women's minor league baseball team was proposed as early as 1984 by former Atlanta Braves executive Bob Hope. At the time Hope tried—with no luck—to interest various franchises in a women's team. After he joined Whittle Communications, Inc. as president of the Sports Properties division, he continued to pursue the possibility. He found a perfect partner in the Coors Brewing Company, one of the nation's biggest brewers of beer. Coors wanted a mainstream but slightly offbeat team to sponsor— something that would garner wide publicity for the company's trademark "Silver Bullet" beer. Hope suggested a women's team, and Coors invested $2.6 million in the idea. In December of 1993 the team, to be known as the Colorado Silver Bullets, won official recognition from professional baseball.

More than 1,300 women showed up at 11 sites around the country to try out for the team in the spring of 1994. Choosing 24 players from this pool of talent proved extremely difficult, since most of the women had not played baseball long enough to amass records on such essentials as batting average or earned run average. "At first, all we had was mechanics: Did the throw look good? Is that a pretty swing?" Hope recalled in a *People* magazine feature. Gradually, however, the most talented players revealed themselves, and after a five-week spring training the final roster was formed.

The first Silver Bullets team faced incredible odds against success. Even though they played against men's semi-pro, minor league, and college

BASEBALL TEAM

"They're not scared. There's no fear factor there. They've gotten hit as hard as anybody, knocked down at home plate, hit in the helmets, cut by ground balls and bad hops. We don't cry. The only time they cry is when I release them."

—Manager Phil Niekro on the Colorado Silver Bullets

Michele McAnany, playing second base for the Colorado Silver Bullets, misses a throw from home while Northern California All-Stars player Cory Bohannon steals the base during an exhibition game, 1994. (AP/Wide World Photos)

teams, they had only prepared for competition during the brief spring training season. Some of the women who made the team were softball stars who had to adjust to hitting and fielding a hard ball. Others were just plain rusty or needed help with their mechanics. Training and moral support were offered by the Silver Bullets' manager, former Atlanta Braves All-Star Phil Niekro. "I think we were a success when we stepped out on the field that first day of spring training," Niekro told *People*.

"Success" as measured by wins came very slowly. The inaugural Silver Bullets team, led by Gina Satriano, Stacey Sunny, Julie Croteau, and Melissa Coombes, managed to win only six of 42 games in their first season of play. No one seemed discouraged, however. Crowds flocked to see the Silver Bullets and clamored for autographs. Each woman received $20,000 for the season—far more than their male counterparts in similar leagues—and received first-

COLORADO SILVER BULLETS 1995 ROSTER

Pos.	Name	Yr.	Age	Ht	Wt	B/T	Occupation	Other Info
P	Billie Jo Charpia	R	23	5'3"	143	R/R	Maintenance Mechanic	Led Baptist College with .392 BA in 1992
P	Melissa Coombes	2	26	5'6"	145	L/L	P.E. Teacher	Led Bullets with .222 BA
P	Pamela Davis	R	20	5'6"	135	R/R	Student	First girl to pitch in Jr. League World Series, '88
P	Alyson Habetz	R	23	5'5"	130	R/R	Student	First girl to play high school baseball in Louisiana
P	Lee Anne Ketcham	2	25	5'4"	150	R/T	Student	Pitched 5 of 6 Bullets wins in 1994
P	Christine Monge	R	21	5'8"	155	R/R	Student	Also played volleyball, soccer, and basketball
P	Gina Satriano	2	28	5'7"	165	R/R	District Attorney	0-3, 6.06 ERA for Bullets in 1994
P	Shae Sloan	2	23	5'10"	150	R/R	Student	0-8, 9.09 ERA for Bullets in 1994
C	Elizabeth Burnham	2	24	5'7"	160	R/R	Student	Starter in 1994; threw out 5 runners
C	Missy Cress	2	24	5'6"	145	R/R	Production Mgr.	Appeared in 3 games in 1994 season
C	Shannon Kimberling	R	25	5'8"	165	R/R	Sporting goods	Hitting star at Oklahoma State University
I	Cara Coughenour	R	27	5'11"	155	R/R	Secretary	Scored 69 points in high school basketball game
I	Laurie Gouthro	2	26	5'6"	126	R/R	Coach	Appeared in one game for Bullets last year
I	Toni Heisler	2	25	5'9"	143	R/R	Coach	Shortstop in on 19 double plays in 1994
I	Tamara Ivie	R	22	5'10"	160	R/R	Student	All-American at Cal State, Northridge
I	Michele McAnany	2	31	5'0"	110	R/R	Teacher	Leadoff hitter; .418 on-base pct.; .212 BA
I	Shannan Mitchem	2	25	5'8"	140	R/R	Marketing	Played 3B, RF, and DH in 1994; .194 BA
I	Pam Schaffrath	2	24	5'8"	150	R/R	Coach	Tied for team lead in doubles (4); hit .164
I	Stacey Sunny	2	29	5'6"	135	R/R	Film Producer	Led team in 7 categories, hit .200
O	Jeanette Amado	2	29	5'2"	130	R/R	Student	Hit .189 in 1994
O	Kim Braatz	2	25	5'7"	140	R/R	Marketing	Missed half of 1994 with back injury
O	Amy Cole	R	23	5'4"	138	R/R	Student	Ranked 8th in ACC with .355 BA
O	Keri Kropke	R	23	5'11"	147	R/R	Actress	Only Bullet without an error in '94
O	Angie Marzetta	R	22	5'5"	141	R/R	Student	2 bronze medals at '94 Olympic Festival

class hotel accommodations and air travel between venues. Cable television aired a number of Silver Bullets games, and Niekro discovered to his chagrin that future opponents were scouting his women by watching them on television.

Fifteen veterans and nine newcomers filled out the Silver Bullets' roster for the team's second season in 1995. The schedule included 44 games, played in 31 states, including Hawaii, and in 12 major league stadiums. Interest in the Silver Bullets continued to be high, with author Stephen King once driving two hours from his home in Massachusetts to watch a game in Maine. Florida Marlins owner Wayne Huizenga has also shown an active interest in the women's team.

Improvement was expected in the second season, and it occurred. The Silver Bullets ended 1995 with an 11-33 record, anchored by the pitching of Lee Anne Ketcham and by hitters Michele McAnany, Sunny, and Coombes. Manager Niekro has increased the pressure a bit, recognizing that the novelty of an all-women's team will wear thin after awhile if the team can't win. "I expect us to be much more competitive, that's for sure," he told the *Atlanta Constitution* in the spring of 1995. "We've got better athletes. Last year we just went out to find athletes and tried to make ballplayers out of them. This year the ballplayers came to us in the tryouts we had. We've had stronger, bigger women come out for the club. Last year we were kind of small and had to play the fundamentals."

Ask the members of the Colorado Silver Bullets, and one point is clear: they do not want to play baseball against other women. Their goal is to compete with—and beat—men's teams. They would even like to see a woman make a men's major league franchise some day. Their critics say it will never happen, that women simply are not strong and fast enough to compete with men at that level. The Silver Bullets, to a woman, would disagree. Julie Croteau told *People:* "A lot of people talk about how important this is to the next generation—and it is."

In the meantime, the Silver Bullets might not revolutionize baseball, but their impact may soften some of the cynicism that has arisen around the professional-level teams. Major league scout Jim Moran noted in an April 1994 *Women's Sports + Fitness* piece that the enthusiasm shown by the Silver Bullets could bring new heart to baseball. He said: "You have honesty here, not some guy making $8 million."

NADIA
COMANECI

In her time she was the quintessential athlete: Nadia Comaneci, the poker-faced sprite who became the first Olympic gymnast ever to score a perfect ten in competition. Comaneci's daring gymnastic performances electrified audiences for the 1976 Summer Games in Montreal, Canada, and she waltzed off with three gold medals, a silver, and a bronze. Her skill in the various women's gymnastic events was unparalleled in 1976, and even to this day she is exerting an enormous influence on her sport.

High drama has been Comaneci's forte both in and outside competition. After winning Olympic medals at both the 1976 and 1980 Summer Games, she languished in her Iron Curtain country of Romania until 1989 before making a thrilling defection to America. When her behavior in the United States began to bring her negative publicity, she admitted that she had been held nearly hostage by the man who helped plan and execute her defection. All this provided grist for television movies and paperback books, but Comaneci is glad those years are behind her now. Recalling those years of turmoil in a March 27, 1995, *People* profile, the former champion gymnast stated: "I do not feel good about all that. That was not me."

Comaneci was born November 12, 1961, in Onesti, Romania. Her native country was a satellite state of the former Soviet Union, rigidly socialist and hostile to Western countries such as the United States. Politics was the last thing on young Nadia's mind, however. As a youngster she loved to run and leap, and she dreamed of becoming a gymnast. When she was only six years old, she was spotted on the playground by a coach named Bela Karolyi. With the permission of Nadia's parents, Karolyi took her into his gymnastics classes, impressed by her fearlessness and maturity beyond her years. As a prospective national gymnast for Romania, Nadia was given everything she needed to excel. She never paid any coaching, travel, costume, choreography, room and board, or entry fees—all of those expenses were paid by the Romanian government.

In her first national competition in 1969, Comaneci placed 13th in the Romanian National Junior Championships. The following year she won

"I know how to smile, I know how to laugh, I know how to play. But I know how to do these things only after I have finished my mission."

—Comaneci, 1976

*Nadia Comaneci performs on the balance beam during the 1979 World
Gymnastics Championships.* (UPI/Bettmann)

the event, her first of five consecutive junior championships. By the time she became eligible for senior international competition in 1975 she was well known beyond Romania for having the audacity—and the ability—to try moves that no woman had ever attempted before in competition. If there were any doubters, they were silenced at the 1975 European championships, when Comaneci won a gold medal in the all-around competition, gold medals in vaulting, the uneven parallel bars, and the balance beam, and a silver medal in the floor exercise. Her spectacular performance beat a host of more experienced gymnasts, including Ludmilla Turishcheva of the Soviet Union.

Americans got their first look at Comaneci when she competed in the 1976 American Cup in New York's Madison Square Garden. As usual, the 14-year-old triumphed, earning several perfect ten scores and easily winning the Cup. On the podium to receive her trophy, Comaneci was urged to kiss the men's gymnastics winner, Bart Conner, for publicity photos. Little did the two teens know that their paths would cross again and eventually lead to marriage.

Nadia Comaneci's most memorable victories occurred at the 1976 Olympics in Montreal, where she earned numerous perfect ten scores on the uneven bars and the balance beam and won gold medals in the all-around competition, the uneven bars, and the balance beam. She also took home a bronze medal in floor exercises and a silver medal in team competition. Her performance in Montreal remains among the most impressive ever staged by a gymnast of either sex.

The world press clamored to learn more about Comaneci, and fans were delighted to hear that she was a happy young girl who played with dolls and restricted her seriousness to her training and performing. By the time she returned to Olympic competition in 1980, Comaneci was arguably the best known entrant in the Summer Games. Nor did she disappoint, earning another gold medal in balance beam, a silver in floor exercises, and a bronze in overall competition. Her Romanian team once again won the silver medal.

Returning to Romania as a national heroine, Comaneci announced her retirement from competition. She was 19 at the time, and her government was fearful that she might try to defect in order to take advantage of her international stardom. Restricted to travel behind the Iron Curtain, Comaneci worked as a state-subsidized coach in Romania, growing ever more disenchanted with life in a socialist country. Rumors that she had an affair with Nicu Ceausescu, son of the Romanian dictator, have never been substantiated, and Comaneci denies any involvement with the Ceausescu family.

At any rate, in 1989 Comaneci left her home on foot one night and walked six hours to the Hungarian border, where she was met by a man named

NADIA COMANECI

Romanian American gymnast

Born: November 12, 1961 in Onesti, Romania.

Career Highlights:

- won five consecutive junior championships beginning in 1969
- won gold medals in all-around competition, vaulting, uneven parallel bars, and balance beam, and a silver medal in floor exercise, European championships, 1975
- earned several perfect ten scores, easily winning the American Cup, 1976
- earned perfect ten scores on uneven bars and balance beam; won gold medals in all-around competition, uneven bars, and balance beam; won bronze medal in floor exercises; and earned silver medal in team competition, 1976 Olympic Games, Montreal, Quebec, Canada
- won gold medal in balance beam, silver medal in floor exercises, bronze medal in overall competition, and silver medal in team competition, 1980 Olympic Games, Moscow, U.S.S.R.
- notable as first Olympic gymnast ever to score a perfect ten in competition.

Constantin Panait. With Panait's help she fled to America by way of Vienna, Austria. For some time after that, Comaneci traveled around America with Panait, staging gymnastic performances and conducting interviews with the press. She appeared uncertain and troubled, and finally her former coach, Karolyi, urged one of his associates, Montreal-based rugby coach Alexandru Stefu, to intervene. Comaneci told Stefu that she was practically being kept as Panait's prisoner, and—as if to prove her point—Panait fled with all of her money and her car.

Comaneci spent the next 18 months living with Stefu and his family. She worked herself back into shape and soon appeared in public again, visibly more at ease. When Stefu died in an accident, Comaneci moved to Norman, Oklahoma, where she began working with coach Paul Ziert. Ziert was also Bart Conner's coach, and Comaneci renewed her acquaintance with Conner while training. The two gymnasts had performed exhibitions together for years, and their close friendship deepened into romance. They became engaged in 1994.

Today Nadia Comaneci enjoys the occasional performance and the more serious duties of coaching and encouraging other would-be gymnastic superstars. One of her proteges is fellow Romanian Dominique Moceanu, who calls Comaneci "alternate mother." Now based at the Bart Conner Gymnastics Academy in Norman, Oklahoma, Comaneci is helping to bring a top ranking to that facility. She and Conner plan to have children in the near future.

The strange saga of Nadia Comaneci has a happy ending. Recent political changes in Romania have opened the country's borders, and she is now able to visit her former home and her family there. Reflecting on his future bride in *People* magazine, Bart Conner said: "She will always be mysterious because she doesn't reveal much of herself." What she has chosen to reveal is nothing less than perfection.

JODY
CONRADT

BASKETBALL
COACH

Jody Conradt has done more to chart the course of women's basketball in America than any other single person. The winningest women's college coach in the game, Conradt has a wealth of impressive credentials: she is the first women's basketball coach to win 600 games, the first women's coach to take an undefeated team to a national championship, and—most important to her—she was the architect of a 12-year undefeated run in the Southwest Conference where her University of Texas Lady Longhorns play. Once thought of as nearly invincible, Conradt is still accorded great respect in an era when many women's basketball programs show the signs of her enormous influence.

Conradt is a true Texan. She has never lived or worked in any other state. She was born circa 1941 in tiny Goldthwaite, Texas—population 1,700. There, even as a child, she showed the characteristics that would follow her into her professional career. Described by those who know her as a classic obsessive-compulsive, Conradt was extremely neat even as a little girl. All of her stuffed animals were kept in exactly the same place, and her closets and drawers were arranged with almost military precision. She was a "tomboy," the daughter of a semipro baseball player, who enjoyed all sports and dreamed of becoming a famous basketball player.

Fortunately for Conradt, women's basketball was quite popular in Goldthwaite. The high school girls' team was successful, often drawing as many or more spectators than the boys' team drew. "Even in the first grade, little girls in my town dreamed about playing for the high school girls' team," Conradt recalled in a *Women's Sports + Fitness* profile. "This was the old, six-girl basketball. It was very slow-paced. I was the kind of player that even I would hate to coach: I shot every time I got the ball."

Conradt attended Baylor University, graduating in 1963 with a degree in physical education. She immediately took a job in a Texas high school, where she coached the same traditional, slow-moving girls' game she had learned in her own basketball days. In 1969 she took her first college coaching job at a small school in central Texas. She moved on to the University of

"You're high if you win and you feel like a failure if you lose. After every loss I contemplate doing something else with my life. Fortunately that feeling passes."

JODY CONRADT

American basketball coach

Born: c. 1941 in Goldthwaite, Texas.

Education: Graduated from Baylor University in 1963 with a degree in physical education.

Career Highlights:

- named winningest women's college coach in the game
- became first women's basketball coach to win 600 games
- her Lady Longhorns qualified for the NCAA championship tournament every year from 1983 to 1994, winning the championship in the 1985–86 season
- became first women's coach to take an undefeated team to a national championship
- led her team on a 12-year undefeated run in the Southwest Conference (1978–1990), totaling 183 consecutive victories against Southwest Conference opponents.

Awards: Inducted into Women's Sports Foundation Hall of Fame, 1995.

Texas at Arlington in 1973, where she served as coordinator of women's athletics. At the time, the University of Texas at Arlington had no women's basketball program. Conradt quickly changed that. "I took the volleyball players and tried to turn them into basketball players," she remembered in *Women's Sports + Fitness.* "It was ridiculous. I had to coach every sport there for women on a $1,200 budget." Somehow she managed: her teams won state championships in basketball, volleyball, and softball.

Conradt's success in Arlington caught the attention of Donna Lopiano, who was then the athletic director at the University of Texas at Austin. Lopiano hired Conradt in 1976 as basketball coach for the Lady Longhorns. The sailing was hardly smooth for Conradt when she arrived in Austin. First, the entire women's basketball team, save one player, had quit to protest the firing of Conradt's predecessor. Second, Conradt was criticized for her salary—a mere $19,000—because she was only the women's basketball coach. "For people at the University of Texas, it was inconceivable to hire someone full-time to coach a silly girls' team," she explained in *Women's Sports + Fitness.*

That "silly girls' team" literally put the University of Texas at Austin on the map. As the quality of high school players improved, and women's basketball became as quick-paced and aggressive as men's, Conradt was ideally situated to influence the direction of the game on a national level. Her Lady Longhorns qualified for the NCAA championship tournament every year from 1983, when the tournament was inaugurated, through 1994. They were ranked in the nation's Top 20 for 16 straight seasons beginning in 1978, and they were top ranked every year between 1984 and 1987. Conradt's 1985–86 University of Texas team was undefeated through regular and post-season play, winning the NCAA national championship.

The achievement that Conradt points to with the most pride is her team's performance in conference play. Between 1978 and 1990, the Lady Longhorns compiled a stunning 183 consecutive victories against Southwest Conference opponents—that's 12 straight years of success. "To think we took care of business for 12 years," Conradt mused in a *Chicago Tribune* piece in 1992. "If I had to name one thing, I think that is a record that is going to be there for a while—at least 12 years."

Revolutionary. That is the best way to describe Conradt's effect on both the game *and* the business of women's college basketball. Not only did her Longhorns win, they served as tireless boosters for women's basketball. Fans and alumni responded. From 1986 until 1991, the Lady Longhorns led the nation in home attendance, averaging 8,481 spectators per game in 1988–89. Before Conradt's arrival in Austin in 1974, the budget for the university's women's athletic programs stood at $72,760. By 1986 it was a whopping $2.4 million, and it has grown considerably since then. "To me, [fan support] is more significant than winning," Conradt told the *Chicago Tribune.* "We proved to a skeptical audience that women's basketball was appealing. That's a part of history no one will attain because it was a first. And you can only have one first."

LYNNE COX

ENDURANCE
SWIMMER

"Everyone always asks, 'What are you going to do next?' There are a lot of swims out there, but I don't feel the pressure of always having to go one goal beyond."

Endurance swimmer Lynne Cox has become more than a decorated athlete—she is a symbol of what can be accomplished when warring nations compromise, when separated peoples are united, and when a simple distance swim proves how close two countries stand to one another. Cox is perhaps the best known American distance swimmer in recent decades, and she has parlayed her fame into quiet but impressive political statements. A swim across the frigid Bering Strait helped dramatize how the Soviet Union and the United States could be better neighbors. A 14-mile swim across the Gulf of Aqaba—against the current—served as a "peace swim" to unite Jordan, Israel, and Egypt. A swim across the Spree River in Berlin, Germany, celebrated the end of that city's Cold War woes.

Cox has been a leading open-water swimmer for 23 of her 38 years. In that time, she has navigated some of the coldest, roughest, most polluted, and most unfamiliar waters in the world. Her conquests include the 40-degree Bering Strait, the 12,000-foot-high Lake Titicaca in Peru, the Nile, Africa's Cape of Good Hope, and Siberia's Lake Baikal. When she isn't swimming for a political cause, Cox says she performs out of simple curiosity. "I want to see what is over there," she told the *San Francisco Chronicle* on March 3, 1994. "I want to see what is under that rock. I want to ask the question that I'm not supposed to ask. They say curiosity killed the cat, but they were wrong."

Cox was born in Manchester, New Hampshire, on January 2, 1957. Her father, Albert, was a radiologist, and her mother, Estelle, was an artist. Lynne and her four siblings all loved to swim, and even at a young age they gravitated to serious competition. When it became evident that the Cox children were becoming better swimmers than their coaches could handle, Albert Cox picked up his family and moved to Los Alamitos, California. "We started competing [in New Hampshire], but all of the good coaches were in California, so they moved us out there," Lynne recalled in the *Los Angeles Times* on October 16, 1994.

Lynne Cox tests the waters of the Bering Sea before her 2.7-mile swim across the frigid waters of the Bering Strait, 1987. (UPI/Corbis-Bettmann)

In 1972, the 15-year-old Lynne Cox set a new English Channel crossing record for both men *and* women. Even then the young swimmer was politically attuned, but gradually as her teen years passed she became less interested in winning trophies and more interested in using her talents and hard work to make a political point. "I don't even remember exactly why I threw [my trophies] out," she explained in the *Los Angeles Times*. "We used to have them displayed all over the place, but I was done with that. They went into a box, and then in the trash. I don't swim for that anymore."

Cox enrolled at the University of California, Santa Barbara, where she majored in history. In the meantime she continued her daring endurance swims, using money donated by sponsors and earned by teaching swimming lessons and giving speeches on the corporate circuit.

Without a doubt her most important distance swim was her 1987 crossing of the Bering Strait, a 2.7-mile swim between Little Diomede Island in the United States and Big Diomede Island in the former Soviet Union. Cox

LYNNE COX

American endurance swimmer

Born: January 2, 1957 in Manchester, New Hampshire.

Education: University of California, Santa Barbara; majored in history.

Career Highlights:

- set a new English Channel crossing record for both men *and* women, 1972
- crossed the 40-degree Bering Strait, a 2.7-mile swim between Little Diomede Island in the United States and Big Diomede Island in the former Soviet Union, 1987
- swam 10 miles across Peru's Lake Titicaca (at 12,000 feet, the world's highest navigable lake), 1992
- completed 14-mile "peace swim" across the Gulf of Aqaba—against the current—to symbolically unite Jordan, Israel, and Egypt, 1994.

made the swim, in waters that were just above freezing, wearing nothing but a bathing suit. "In 2 hours and 6 minutes, I swam across the international dateline . . . from the present into the future," Cox told the *San Francisco Chronicle*. "I made the swim to show that our countries are neighbors." The symbolism was not lost on then–Soviet president Mikhail Gorbachev. In a treaty negotiation with the United States soon after Cox's feat, Gorbachev mentioned her by name in his opening remarks.

Cox has followed that swim with others bearing political messages, including her "peace swim" in the Gulf of Aqaba. Such demonstrations require an enormous amount of planning and logistics, and Cox has been helped through the years by a group of close friends who offer such support. Some of her adventures have literally taken years to plan. "After all of the work, it's always great to finally get into the water," she told the *Los Angeles Times*. "It's like being an artist. You've put out all the paint, and you've gotten everything ready, and you can finally pick up the brush."

The kind of "art" Cox has chosen to pursue can have serious health challenges. Endurance swimmers are prone to heart failure, hypothermia, and all manner of infectious diseases picked up from polluted water. In her swim across Lake Titicaca between Bolivia and Peru, Cox was bitten by some strange aquatic organisms that left huge welts all over her body. In her case, however, her own unusual physiology helps to protect her from damage. Like a seal she has an evenly distributed layer of body fat that insulates her five-foot-six frame from the ravages of cold water. Most women average 20 to 25 percent body fat; Cox has 30 to 35 percent. She also has a normal body temperature of 97.6, a whole degree lower than average. This too helps her avoid hypothermia and its attendant danger—cardiac arrest.

Nearing 40 with an impressive list of achievements to her credit, Cox shows no signs of slowing down. "I don't think that anyone's ever said that

I'm too old to be doing this," she concluded in the *Los Angeles Times*. "You're old when you're old. Why should you be limited by someone else's expectations?" With an evident spark of curiosity in her eyes, she added: "There are a lot of swims out there."

BETH
DANIEL

"Golf is such a streaky, mental game. You take it when you get it, and right now I'm gettin' it."

Her career has had its share of peaks and valleys, but golfer Beth Daniel has learned how to maintain her equilibrium. Daniel joined the LPGA tour in 1979 and almost immediately began winning tournaments and plenty of money. The media hyped her as the "next Nancy Lopez" and predicted that she would break all sorts of records. Instead she struggled in the mid-1980s, earning more press for her infamous temper than for her prowess on the links.

Since then Daniel has confounded almost every prediction made about her during her early years. She is not the "next Nancy Lopez," but she is a solid performer with a Vare Trophy and several million dollars in winnings to her credit. More important, she is not a whining prima donna trying to coast on the tour—she is a hard-working, bona fide talent who has fought her way through adversity.

Daniel, born on October 14, 1956, in Charleston, South Carolina, first drew notice as a collegian at Furman University in her home state. A physical education major, she was a star of a golf team that—incredibly enough—also included Betsy King and Sherri Turner. While all three future LPGA stars were at Furman, the tiny Baptist college won the 1976 NCAA championship in golf. Daniel also won the women's amateur national titles in 1975 and 1977.

Turning pro in 1979, Daniel won a tournament in her first year on the tour and was named Rookie of the Year. She was the tour's leading money winner in both 1980 and 1981—hence the comparisons to Lopez. In 1980 Daniel won LPGA Player of the Year, a significant accomplishment for someone so new to the tour. People compared her to that greatest of all golf stylists, Mickey Wright.

The pressure proved nearly too much for Daniel to handle. She sometimes lost her temper during tournaments, throwing her equipment and screaming at her caddies. Reporters who dared compare her to other golfers got an icy stare. Recalling those days in a 1990 *Sports Illustrated* profile, Daniel declared: "I had the attitude that I'm Beth Daniel and I belong out here, and I'm going to prove it. Golf was a matter of life and death then."

Beth Daniel chips onto the 18th green before winning the JAL Big Apple Classic in 1994. (AP/Wide World Photos)

BETH DANIEL

American golfer

Born: October 14, 1956 in Charleston, South Carolina.

Education: Attended Furman University in South Carolina.

Career Highlights:
- won the women's amateur golf national titles in 1975 and 1977
- won 13 tournaments by 1983
- won four tournaments during the second half of 1989
- won seven tournaments and set a single-season record for prize winnings with $863,578 in 1990.

Awards: Named Rookie of the Year, 1979; designated LPGA Player of the Year, 1980 and 1990; winner of the Vare Trophy for the year's lowest scoring average, 1990.

In fact, Daniel was insecure about her status in the LPGA and was laboring under her own impossibly high expectations. She had won 13 tournaments by 1983, but then her back began to bother her. She would win only one more outing before 1989.

Daniel finished second at the Kemper Open on March 1, 1988, but she did not feel well at the time. Her doctor diagnosed mononucleosis, an ailment that robs its victims of strength. It was while Daniel was recuperating from the illness that she began to take stock of her performance as a golf pro. "I lay on the couch all the time and thought about how much I love golf and how much I missed the competition," she remembered in *The Illustrated History of Women's Golf.* "I came back on tour with new determination."

Her game rebounded dramatically. After being 29th on the money list in 1987, she moved to 17th in 1989. She turned in nine Top 10 finishes early in 1989 and then won four tournaments during the second half of the year, including the Greater Washington Open. By the end of 1989 she was second on the money list—and in Player of the Year voting—to Betsy King.

Finally, in her 12th year on tour in 1990, Daniel achieved the level of serenity and achievement she had always wanted. She won seven tournaments, set a single-season record for prize winnings with $863,578, and walked off with the Vare Trophy for the year's lowest scoring average. Again she was named LPGA Player of the Year.

Daniel told *Sports Illustrated* that she has come to terms with her celebrity and the attention it brings her, as well as with the day-to-day pressures of the LPGA. "I've realized that winning a major requires a lot of patience," she said. Smiling, she added: "Golf is such a streaky, mental game. You take it when you get it, and right now I'm gettin' it."

DOMINIQUE
DAWES

GYMNAST

"Don't set your goals to be a star; set your goals to be the best that you can be and go from there."

She's known as "Awesome Dawesome," a top-ranked gymnast who is still on a scoring roll at a time when most of her peers in the field have bandaged their wounds and retired. Dawes, one of the first two black American women ever to make the United States Olympic gymnastics team, also holds the honor of being the first black woman to win a national gymnastics championship. She is muscular and fearless, yet graceful and multi-talented, and she plans to be a force to be reckoned with at the 1996 Summer Games and beyond.

As the 1994 American national champion in gymnastics, Dawes became the first woman in 25 years to earn first place in every category of competition at the championship event. Her petite stature and slender figure disguise the truth about this performer: she is perhaps the strongest, most agile and daring participant in gymnastics today. The legendary Mary Lou Retton extolled Dawes in an April 7, 1995, *USA Weekend* magazine piece as a "real '90s gymnast, explosive and athletic. Nobody does it like her."

Dawes was born in 1976 in Silver Spring, Maryland, a suburb of Washington, D.C. Far from being pushed into sports by overzealous parents, she had to do some pushing of her own. As an active six-year-old, she jumped on the family furniture and tumbled down the stairs until her mother—fearful for the child's safety—enrolled her in gymnastics classes at a nearby club in Wheaton, Maryland. The club was run by a former University of Maryland gymnast named Kelli Hill, herself just out of college. Despite her own youth, Hill recognized Dawes's natural talent immediately and encouraged Dominique's parents to give her all the lessons they could afford.

Dawes proved quickly that she had the stamina and determination to reach the top in her sport. In the late 1980s coach Hill moved her operation to the Hill's Gymnastic Training Center in Gaithersburg, Maryland. Gaithersburg is a good 40-minute drive from Silver Spring on one of the busiest arteries leading into the nation's capital. Nevertheless, Dawes rose each morning at five o'clock to make the trip to Gaithersburg in time for a two-hour

Dominique Dawes performs in a qualifying round at the 1993 world championships. (Reuters/Kevin Lamarque/Archive Photos)

GREAT WOMEN IN SPORTS

morning workout before school. After school ended, she would spend an additional five hours in the gym practicing, almost always under the watchful eye of Kelli Hill. Dawes showed promise in each area of gymnastic specialty, especially the floor exercise. By 1991 she was ranked 13th nationally in compulsories, third in optionals, and ninth overall. Her achievement was particularly impressive in that she was not working with a well-known Olympic coach or at one of the more prestigious Olympic training centers.

Asked her goals by the *Washington Post* on June 30, 1991, the 14-year-old Dawes said she wanted to make the 1992 Olympic Team. And if she failed? "I'll try for 1996," she declared. "If I don't make it then, I'll switch sports." Coach Hill could not ask for a protege with more focus.

As it turned out, Dawes did not have to wait until 1996 to make an Olympic team. She first announced her superiority at a dual 1992 U.S.-Japan meet by scoring a perfect 10 in floor exercise. At the U.S. National Championship that same year she placed first in the uneven bars and fourth in the all-around, easily qualifying to travel to Barcelona. Her number four ranking in the all-around was doubly impressive in that she finished within one-tenth of a point of winner Kim Zmeskal, the 1991 world champion and a favorite to win a medal at the 1992 Summer Games. As for Dawes, her performance at the Barcelona Olympics was a slight disappointment. She won a team bronze medal but finished 26th overall. Her inability to win any individual events did not faze the young athlete, however. She looked at Barcelona as a learning experience, a rare opportunity for a high school student to travel, receive worldwide attention, and come home with honors.

Dawes's difficult schedule-balancing act became easier when she moved in with her Gaithersburg-based coach so that she would have more time to train. The decision paid off when she won two silver medals at the World Championships and finished second in the individual all-around competition at the 1993 National Championships. Her accomplishments at the Nationals also included a first place finish in the vault and the balance beam—longtime nemesis Shannon Miller won the uneven bars and the floor exercise. In an August 31, 1993, interview with the *Washington Post,* Dawes admitted that she felt somewhat inferior to Miller, who had beaten her in the 1993 World Championships in Birmingham, England. "I think Shannon works harder than I do," Dawes said. "When I see her work out, it seems like she's trying harder than anyone else. If I want to beat her, I have to train harder and longer."

Sometimes having a tough opponent can be inspiring. Dawes returned to her Gaithersburg gym and set herself to the task of surpassing Miller—and any other up-and-coming competitor who might be waiting in the wings. Her

DOMINIQUE DAWES

American gymnast

Born: 1976 in Silver Spring, Maryland.

Education: Graduated from Gaithersburg High School, 1994; accepted athletic scholarship to Stanford University but deferred enrollment until after summer of 1996.

Career Highlights:

- placed first in uneven bars, fourth in the all-around at U.S. National Championship, 1992
- won team bronze medal, 1992 Olympic Games, Barcelona, Spain
- won two silver medals, World Championship, 1993
- finished second in individual all-around competition with first place finish in vault and balance beam, U.S. National Championship, 1993
- won U.S. National Championship, 1994 (became first woman in 25 years to earn first place in every category of competition)
- won two events—floor exercise and uneven bars—at 1995 U.S. Nationals.

hard work paid off in August of 1994 at the National Championships held in Nashville, Tennessee. There, in a brilliant showing, she took the national all-around championship and *first place in all four women's events:* the vault, uneven bars, balance beam, and floor exercises. No one had accomplished such a feat in 25 years, and the last gymnast to do it had been competing at a time when the field of opponents was much weaker. Dawes became an instant celebrity, sought after for television interviews, magazine profiles, and—of course—autographs. "It's kind of overwhelming," she said of her sudden success in an August 30, 1994, *Washington Post* profile. "It seems kind of neat for me, that it's only been done one time before. It's neat for my own self-esteem. It means I've accomplished something very unusual. I just went out there to hit my sets. I never imagined I'd win all the events."

When talk turned to the 1996 Olympics, however, Dawes demurred. "I don't want to say anything about the next few years because I want to make sure that if I stay around for Atlanta, my body will be able to hold up—both physically and mentally," she explained. "You're concentrating all the time in this sport. I'm really excited right now, but I don't like to get overexcited about competitions. You know there will be good days and bad days. And I know I still will have some bad days." Fourth-ranked in the world as late as 1995, Dawes was expected to make the Olympic team not only on her own merits but also for her leadership qualities, so necessary in a sport dominated by youngsters.

Having graduated from Gaithersburg High School in 1994, Dawes accepted an athletic scholarship to Stanford University but deferred enrollment until after the summer of 1996. In the meantime she began taking courses at the University of Maryland—medicine is one possible field of study she says she would like to pursue.

Dawes credits her parents for their patience and generosity in allowing her to pursue her gymnastics goals. "They just let me do it, and if I didn't want to, I didn't have to," she told *USA Weekend*. "But whenever I wanted to go to the gym, they would take me." As for her own advice to other Olympic hopefuls, Dawes told *Ebony* in February of 1995: "Don't set your goals to be a star; set your goals to be the best that you can be and go from there."

MARY
DECKER SLANEY

TRACK & FIELD
ATHLETE

*"I dream about being
healthy. That's all I
need to be."*

Mary Decker Slaney is nothing less than an American running legend. In her prime years in the early 1980s she competed against no one but the clock, compiling 36 American and 17 world records. In 1982 alone she was the fastest woman at *every* distance between 800 and 10,000 meters. She was also the first woman to run 880 yards in less than two minutes, and her American record in the 1,500-meter race (3:57.12) still stands. As the popular and ebullient Mary Decker she won the 1982 Sullivan Award as best amateur athlete of the year and took home the prestigious Jesse Owens award as well. In the first-ever World Track and Field Championships in 1983, she cruised to gold medal finishes in both the 1,500-meter and the 3,000-meter races.

Olympic victories have been another matter. Few world champions have ever had worse luck than Slaney whenever the Summer Games roll around. Stress fractures sidelined her in 1976 when she was a high school senior. An American boycott in 1980 kept her home at a time when she was dominating the world running scene. Then, in 1984 when she finally made it to the Games, she was tripped in one of the most dramatic 3,000-meter races ever run. It is quite unfortunate that, to this day, Mary Decker Slaney is remembered by some fans more for what she didn't win—an Olympic medal—than for her numerous American and world victories.

The determined runner, born Mary Decker on August 4, 1958, in Bunnvale, New Jersey, was a record-setter as a teen in the 800-meter and 1,000-yard distances. She began running at the age of 11, when she entered and easily won a local cross-country race for grade school students. "The run was fun," Slaney recalled in the *Christian Science Monitor*. "Even if I hadn't won, I would still have been captivated by the competition. But I knew I liked it, and right then it didn't seem like it was going to be that hard. After that, all I wanted to do was run."

Run she did. At 13 she clocked a 4:55 mile and set an age-group world record in the 800-meter race. Although her coaches recognized her as natu-

Mary Decker Slaney pulls ahead of the pack in this 2,000-meter race at the 1988 Michelob Invitational Track Meet. (UPI/Corbis-Bettmann)

MARY DECKER SLANEY

American track & field athlete

Born: August 4, 1958 in Bunnvale, New Jersey.

Education: Attended University of Colorado at Boulder on a track scholarship, 1977–78.

Career Highlights:

- compiled 36 American and 17 world records in the early 1980s

- established herself as the fastest woman at *every* distance between 800 and 10,000 meters, 1982

- became the first woman to run 880 yards in less than two minutes

- cruised to gold medal finishes in the 1,500-meter and the 3,000-meter races, World Track and Field Championships, 1983.

Awards: Won the Sullivan Award as best amateur athlete, and the Jesse Owens award, 1982.

rally gifted they also noted that she was willing to work hard. Perhaps, in retrospect, she worked just a little bit *too* hard.

Her wholehearted devotion to running eventually caught up with her in the form of painful and long-lasting injuries. X-rays taken in 1974—the year after she joined the women's track circuit—revealed numerous improperly healed stress fractures in her lower legs. The stress fractures caused her to miss the 1976 Olympics and necessitated surgery for compartment syndrome, a muscle condition, while she was still a teen.

Having recovered from the surgery by 1980, Mary Decker returned to championship form. Beginning that year, she broke records—both indoor and out—in such events as the mile, the 1,500 meter, the 2,000 meter, and the 3,000 meter. It is safe to say that she would have brought home some Olympic medals had America competed in the 1980 Summer Games, but at that time President Jimmy Carter decided that the Americans should boycott because of the Soviet Union's invasion of Afghanistan. Mary Decker buried her disappointment by competing in other international track and field events—and she began to prepare for 1984.

Even casual Olympics observers will remember the fateful 3,000-meter race Mary Decker ran at the 1984 Olympics in Los Angeles. As the race neared its midpoint, she was tripped by South African Zola Budd and fell flat onto the track in obvious pain. Unable to finish, she limped off to the showers, spurning Budd's attempts to apologize. A decade later, the runner recalled her disappointment in a *People* magazine profile. "Even though I had people telling me [Budd] did it intentionally, I never thought she did," Slaney said. "I don't hate her. I hated the fact that it was an opportunity for me that got messed up."

Slaney—who married in 1985—kept running, grimly determined to outlast her injuries and outrace her opponents. She set a new world mile record in 1985 and qualified for the Olympics in 1988 with Olympics Trials victories in the 1,500 meter and the 3,000 meter. The injuries kept coming, however, and she was not a featured performer in the 1988 Summer Games.

With a new round of Achilles tendon and heel surgery behind her, Slaney tried one last time to make the 1992 Olympic team. "I think women reach their peak in their mid-30's," she told *Sports Illustrated* on July 29, 1991. Unfortunately for Slaney, a whole new generation of runners had come of age, including American Lynn Jennings and a host of competitors from the Unified Team, Africa, and Cuba. Undaunted, the feisty Slaney set her sights on the 1996 Summer Games, even though she is nearing 40 and has a teenaged daughter. In what is perhaps the most ironic comment on her career, she told *People:* "I dream about being healthy. That's all I need to be."

If health and luck would fall into place, the talent is certainly there. Inside at least, Mary Decker Slaney is still a little girl who runs for fun.

DONNA
DE VARONA

*"My philosophy as a
commentator is to
never upstage an
event. You're there to
lend what the
pictures don't tell, to
bring out the moment
of truth."*

Olympic gold medalist, television sportscaster, pioneering activist for gender equity in sports—all of these roles have been filled by Donna de Varona in the course of her extraordinary career. De Varona was the youngest American on the 1960 Olympic team. She was the first woman hired as a sports reporter on a major television network. She helped to establish the Women's Sports Foundation, and she has testified before Congress on issues pertaining to women's sports. Her life has been dedicated to expanding opportunities for women athletes, herself included.

Donna de Varona was born in San Diego, California, in April of 1947. She grew up in a conventional home with warm and supportive parents. "My parents were there for us. I don't remember a dinner when they weren't there for us," she recalled in a *Women's Sports + Fitness* interview. De Varona's father was a Hall of Fame rower and an All-American football player at the University of California. He encouraged young Donna to develop her swimming talents, serving as her first coach and making sure she attended meets.

De Varona told *Women's Sports + Fitness* that even as a youngster she realized what she was missing in athletics. "I got in trouble until I started to swim," she said. "I was always on the boys' playground trying to play baseball, and they wouldn't let us play. I spent all my money on bubble gum so I could bribe my way into the little league, and I wound up with a uniform with number 0 on it. I picked up the bats."

Swimming provided de Varona the challenge she needed as an athlete. A strong swimmer from the age of three, she entered her first race at nine and was soon training under California's best coaches. Her specialty was the 400-meter medley, the sport's toughest race, in which competitors must swim four laps, each in a different stroke: freestyle, butterfly, breast stroke, and backstroke. At the tender age of 13 de Varona qualified for the Olympic team in the 400-meter medley. She was the youngest member of the American team and was thrilled to be in Rome, even though her event was cancelled.

Donna de Varona displays her trophy awarded for scoring the most points in the National Amateur Athletic Union Women's Swimming Championships, 1964. (AP/Wide World Photos)

Throughout her high school years de Varona managed to maintain a B average while training as much as six hours a day. After amassing a veritable treasure trove of trophies and medals, she once again qualified for the Olympic team in 1964. This time the 400-meter medley was run, and she won the gold medal in the event. She also picked up a gold medal as a member of the 400-meter freestyle relay team. By the time she retired from competitive swimming in 1965 she had set 18 world swimming records.

"Retirement" was more or less forced upon de Varona because she had to find a way to support herself while attending college at the University of California, Los Angeles. "When I quit swimming I was the All-American girl, the swimmer, the blonde, the UCLA coed, the relatively good student," she recalled in *Women's Sports + Fitness*. ". . . I'm happy I grew up in the sixties because it forced me to question everything. I think it makes me better and more thorough in my work." One of the things de Varona questioned was

DONNA DE VARONA

American swimmer and broadcaster

Born: April, 1947 in San Diego, California.

Education: Undergraduate degree from University of California, Los Angeles.

Career Highlights:
- qualified for the Olympic team in the 400-meter medley at age 13; she was the youngest member of the American team

- won gold medals, 400-meter medley and 400-meter freestyle relay, 1964 Olympic Games, Tokyo, Japan

- set 18 world swimming records by the time she retired from competitive swimming in 1965.

the tradition that television sportscasting was all male. While still a college student she became the first female broadcaster on ABC's *Wide World of Sports,* and after graduating from UCLA she decided she liked sportscasting enough to make it a career.

Finding regular work as a female sportscaster was almost as difficult as winning the 400-meter medley. In her early years de Varona traveled all over America, accepting temporary assignments when regular anchor men got sick or went on vacation. "It took me years to get off the pool deck," she admitted in a *Sports Illustrated* piece. She was a well-known and widely recognized sports hero, however, and eventually she settled on network television—NBC and ABC—as a reporter at the Olympic Games. De Varona served as an interviewer and nightly recap anchor at the 1972 Olympics, the 1976 Olympics, and the 1984 Summer and Winter Games. "My trial was Sarajevo [in 1984]," de Varona recalled in *Women's Sports + Fitness.* "I was there by myself, no producer, no assignments. I hustled everything myself. I just went out, grabbed a crew, did spots and wrote stories. That was my test because I was just back at ABC and we were in a crisis situation with the problems of scheduling and snow." Life was easier at the 1984 Summer Games in Los Angeles, but when the Olympics ended de Varona was still dissatisfied with the progression of her career.

Reflecting on her service at the 1984 Olympics, de Varona told *Sports Illustrated:* "I don't feel the rewards came after that. You do good work, and then wait and wait for another good assignment." Waiting for opportunities is not Donna de Varona's style. She was a founding member of the Women's Sports Foundation in the mid-1970s and, as early as 1975, she served on President Ford's Commission on Olympic Sports. She has testified on behalf of Title IX legislation in front of both houses of Congress, and she has helped to create support groups for women athletes similar to those that exist for men. "I will always be an activist," de Varona declared in *Women's Sports + Fitness*. "That is a lifetime commitment."

Other commitments have entered the picture for de Varona as well. She is the mother of two young children and in fact brought her infant son to the 1988 Winter Olympics in Calgary, which she was covering for ABC. She has also benefitted from the popularity of cable television, adding Turner Network Television to her list of stations for which she does reporting. De Varona has had a spectacular career, but she would like to see women do even more as television sportscasters. "It's too easy to play the victim," she told *Sports Illustrated*. "We're making progress. It's coming. It's just taking longer than I ever thought it would."

GAIL
DEVERS

"Every hurdler in the world has got to be intimidated by Gail because they all know rule No. 1: remove the hurdles and there's no way they can outsprint her."

—Bob Kersee, Devers's coach

Miraculous—that's the only way to describe Gail Devers's career. Devers has won gold medals in the 100-meter sprint at both the Olympics and the World Championships. She also has gone gold over the 100-meter hurdles as recently as 1995. That's not a bad resume for someone who once thought her feet would have to be amputated.

A promising athlete in college, Devers became stricken with Graves' disease—a serious thyroid disorder—in 1988. She literally went from an appearance at the Seoul Olympics to being so ill that she could only crawl or be carried. Devers has estimated that she came within 48 hours of having her feet surgically removed due to the rigors of the radiation treatment she underwent for her condition. Saved by a change in therapy, she has mounted possibly the greatest comeback in track history. A former Olympic and world gold medalist in the 100-meter sprint, she has been concentrating on the 100-meter hurdles in more recent years. She won a gold medal in that event at the 1993 World Championships in Stuttgart, Germany.

Devers was born and raised in San Diego, the daughter of a Baptist minister. "We were a *Leave It to Beaver* family," she recalled in a May 10, 1993, *Sports Illustrated* profile. Her strict parents imposed all sorts of rules on Devers and her brother, and Devers never seemed to mind. She dreamed of becoming a school teacher, using her girlfriends as model "pupils." She began running track in high school, first as a distance runner and only later as a sprinter. By her senior year of high school she had won the 100-meter sprint and the 100-meter hurdles at the California high school track championships. She was offered a scholarship to the University of California, Los Angeles.

The naive and sheltered Devers arrived at UCLA with great curiosity about her new college track coach, Bob Kersee. In the *Sports Illustrated* profile, she remembered that she expected him to be "an old white man." Instead she met a dynamic young individual who sized up her potential in an instant. After only a few practices, Kersee informed Devers that she would some day break the U.S. record in the 100-meter hurdles and that she would make the

Gail Devers flies over the hurdles to win the 100-meter hurdles final and qualify for the 1992 Olympic Games. (AP/Wide World Photos)

1988 Olympic team. As if he were reading a crystal ball, Kersee predicted gold medals in Devers's future. "Regardless of whether his predictions were going to turn out to be true or whether he was just trying to motivate me, I liked them," Devers admitted in *Sports Illustrated.* "I hadn't run track until high school. I started as a distance runner. I hadn't had much coaching. So I thought that if he had all this faith in me, he'd coach me well. For quite a while Bobby believed in me more than I believed in myself."

As a senior at UCLA Devers set a new American record for the 100-meter hurdles. She easily qualified for the 1988 Olympics in that event, but when she got to Seoul her performance was inexplicably stale. Returning from the Summer Games, she began to experience strange weight fluctuations, fits of shaking, memory loss, migraine headaches, and temporary loss of vision in one eye. At times she menstruated without stopping, and the slightest scratch could cause her skin to bleed profusely. Doctors found a cyst on her thyroid gland, and the radiation treatments prescribed to correct the problem completely destroyed her thyroid. Worse, the treatments caused her feet to swell and ooze. She had to be carried around her apartment and could do virtually nothing on her own.

The condition of Devers's feet became so severe that her doctors thought they would have to amputate. As a last measure they changed her medication, and she began a dramatic recovery. In a month she was able to walk, and a year later, at the 1991 world championships in Tokyo, she won a silver medal in the 100-meter hurdles.

The 1992 Olympics brought both triumph and disappointment. Devers won the 100-meter sprint in the closest finish ever recorded in an Olympic race—a mere one-hundredth of a second. In the hurdles, she jumped out to a commanding lead, only to trip over the final barrier and slide on her knees to a fifth-place finish. When fellow American Gwen Torrence suggested—without naming names—that some of the 100-meter competitors were using performance-enhancing drugs, Devers did not involve herself in the controversy even though Torrence seemed to be pointing a finger at her. "All I take is Cynthroit," she explained in the *New York Times* on August 2, 1992. ". . . It fools my body into thinking I have a thyroid." Coach Kersee was a bit more emphatic in his defense of his star sprinter. "I'm tired of all these sour grapes," he complained to the *New York Times.* "Anybody who believes Gail has ever taken performance-enhancing drugs can kiss my butt."

Indeed, Gail Devers has never failed a drug test, and she emphatically denies using anything but the medicines she needs to combat her thyroid condition.

GAIL DEVERS

American track and field athlete

Born: San Diego, California.

Education: University of California, Los Angeles.

Career Highlights:
- won silver medal, 100-meter hurdles, World Championships, 1991

- won gold medal, 100-meter sprint, in the closest finish ever recorded in an Olympic race, 1992 Olympic Games, Barcelona, Spain
- earned gold medal, 100-meter sprint, World Championships, 1993
- won 100-meter hurdles, U.S. Track Championship, 1995 (and holds the American record in the event).

A different kind of controversy awaited Devers at the 1993 World Championships. There, once again, she raced to a photo finish in the 100-meter sprint, this time beating Jamaican Merlene Ottey by only several one-hundredths of a second. The finish was so close that Devers and Ottey were both given the same time on the scoreboard—only later did the judges announce that Devers had won. The decision was not popular with the crowd at the event in Stuttgart, and in the ensuing media crush Devers was almost reduced to tears. She finally rallied, however, and stood up for herself. "I'm leaving this meet happy," she concluded, as reported by *Track & Field News* in November of 1993. "I believe everything happens for a reason, and this was just my time."

Since 1994, when her world ranking in the 100-meter sprint dropped to ninth, Devers has been concentrating on the hurdles. She won the 100-meter hurdles at the 1995 U.S. Track Championship and holds the American record in the event. The athlete has admitted that she once considered herself "too small" to run hurdles, but her years of training with Kersee have given her confidence. It's no wonder. Asked about Devers's chances as a hurdler, Kersee told *Track & Field News* in May of 1993: "It's obvious there is no hurdler in the world as fast as Gail. The matter of control between hurdles, and how much time she spends in the air from takeoff to touchdown, will be the difference in how fast she runs the hurdles. But every hurdler in the world has got to be intimidated by Gail because they all know rule No. 1: remove the hurdles and there's no way they can outsprint her."

Devers credits at least a part of her success to the lessons she learned from her long illness. "I'm stronger as a person; it's not hard for me to concentrate on the job at hand," she told *Track & Field News*. "I've said before that there's nothing that can come up in my life that I can't get over after going through what I did." She added of her experience: "I wouldn't wish it on anyone, but I'm happy I went through it. I think back . . . to March of 1991, when I was wondering if I would ever walk again, let alone run."

BABE DIDRIKSON ZAHARIAS

"Before I was even out of grade school, I knew what I wanted to be when I grew up. My goal was to be the greatest athlete that ever lived."

In her heyday she was known simply as "Babe," perhaps the most multi-talented sportswoman ever to take to a field. Today, Mildred Ella Didrikson Zaharias is widely considered the best female athlete of the first half of the twentieth century. Babe could run. She could throw the javelin. She could high-jump. She could figure skate, play golf better than most men, and she could blow a mean harmonica. She even designed her own line of sportswear and made a fortune selling it to wealthy patrons.

Babe Didrikson Zaharias was an American original and one of the most beloved sports superstars of all time.

Born June 26, 1913, in a gritty Texas oil town, Babe was the daughter of Hannah Marie Olson, a former figure skater, and Ole Didriksen, a carpenter and furniture refinisher (Babe later changed the spelling of her surname to Didrikson). The nickname Babe grew out of "Baby," which is what her parents called her when she was young. The Didriksen family always struggled financially, and all of the seven children were expected to find jobs as soon as they were old enough. As a seventh grader, Babe spent her after-school hours working in a fig-packing plant. Later she sewed potato sacks.

Athletic activities were a welcome diversion for the active Babe Didrikson. She wanted to be the best at everything she tried, and she almost succeeded. As a youngster she played baseball and basketball with the boys in her neighborhood, and she could outrun her peers of both sexes. She also enjoyed swimming and diving. Self-conscious about her looks, she decided that excelling in sports would help her to make a name for herself and to earn the affection and attention she craved.

She first went out for organized sports in high school, including basketball, baseball, golf, swimming, tennis, and volleyball. Unfortunately, her level of success in any sport she tried tended to alienate the other students, so she had few friends. Before she graduated from high school she was offered a place on a basketball team sponsored by the Dallas-based Employers Casualty Company. The only way she could persuade her parents to allow her to leave

Babe Didrikson (right) clears the hurdles to set a record and win this 80-meter hurdle race, 1932. (Archive Photos/Popperfoto)

school early was to promise that she would finish her course work—*and* hold a steady job with the insurance firm. Babe played her first game with the Employers Casualty team the very night she arrived in Dallas and thrilled spectators by singlehandedly outscoring the entire opposing team.

In the off-season, Babe was a member of Employers Casualty teams in swimming, diving, and track. The latter sport in particular fascinated her, although she had never even seen a track meet before moving to Dallas. Becoming acquainted with the various skills, she practiced to the point of exhaustion, and within just a few months she had set national records in the javelin and baseball throws and regional records in the shot put, high jump, and long jump.

At the Amateur Athletic Union (AAU) women's track and field championship in 1932, Babe competed as a one-woman team representing Texas and won six of the eight events she entered, accumulating *by herself* nearly twice as many points as all 22 members of the second-place team. The Olympics beckoned, and Babe Didrikson could hardly wait to get there.

Babe's performance at the 1932 Olympic Games in Los Angeles was nothing short of sensational. Restricted to entering just three events due to a recent rule change, she chose the javelin throw, the 80-meter hurdles and the high jump. Amazingly, she set world records in both the javelin throw and the 80-meter hurdles, winning gold medals in both, and she tied for first in the high jump. She was later awarded the silver medal in the high jump because the judges objected to the fact that her head crossed the bar before her feet. In recognition of her performance in the AAU championships and at the Olympics, the Associated Press named Babe 1932's Woman Athlete of the Year.

Gold medals were fine, but Babe needed to eat. Soon after the Olympics, she announced that she would turn pro and become—of all things—a golfer. Although not a "natural" at the sport, she practiced until her hands were raw, then bandaged them and practiced some more. While she was learning the game, she supported herself and her extended family by making personal appearances and playing in exhibition games, including brief stints with several major league baseball teams. She even worked up a vaudeville routine that included a tumbling exhibition and some harmonica music.

HEADING TOWARD SILVER

In the 1932 Olympics Babe Didrikson became the first woman to hold triple medals in running, jumping, and throwing events. Her jumping medal—a silver in the high jump—was cause for disappointment and controversy, however. While Babe's record-breaking jump of 5 feet, 5.25 inches tied that of American Jean Shiley, Olympic officials objected to Babe's unorthodox jumping style: Didrikson dove head and shoulders first over the bar. Because of this unusual method, and because the judges needed to break the tie, they ruled that Babe would get the silver medal and Shiley would get the gold. In 1937, the rule that penalized Didrikson's "diving" technique in the high jump was rescinded.

By 1934 Babe felt confident enough about her golf game to enter some serious amateur tournaments. In 1935 she won the Texas Women's Amateur Championship, exciting such jealousy among some of the other competitors that they petitioned the United States Golf Association to disqualify her from amateur play. Since there was only one professional ladies' golf tournament in existence at the time, Babe returned to promotional work—this time strictly as a golfer—and ended up sharpening her game by playing in exhibition matches with some of the best male golfers in the world. At one such match early in 1938, she was teamed with wrestler George Zaharias, nicknamed the "Crying Greek from Cripple Creek." The two established an immediate rapport and were married on December 23 of that year. Zaharias subsequently quit wrestling and managed his wife's career.

In 1940 the USGA agreed to allow Babe to re-apply for amateur status if she did not make any paid appearances for three years. She fulfilled the requirement and re-entered golf as an amateur in 1943. Babe dominated the sport throughout the rest of the decade, winning 17 straight tournaments, in-

BABE DIDRIKSON ZAHARIAS

American track and field athlete, golfer

Born: June 26, 1913 in Port Arthur, Texas.

Died: September 27, 1956 in Galveston, Texas.

Career Highlights:

- competed as one-woman team representing Texas in Amateur Athletic Union (AAU) women's track and field championship, winning six of eight events she entered, 1932

- set world records and won gold medals in both javelin throw and 80-meter hurdles; won silver medal in high jump, 1932 Olympic Games, Los Angeles, California

- won the Texas Women's Amateur Championship in golf, 1935

- won 17 straight golf tournaments, including the Western Women's Open, the National Women's Amateur, and the British Women's Amateur, 1943–49

- co-founded the Ladies Professional Golf Association (LPGA), 1949.

Awards: Named Associated Press Woman Athlete of the Year, 1932, 1945, 1946, 1947, and 1954; named AP Outstanding Woman Athlete of the Half Century, 1950.

cluding the Western Women's Open, the National Women's Amateur, and the British Women's Amateur. In an echo of her Olympic days, she was named AP Woman Athlete of the Year in 1945, 1946, and 1947.

Feeling that women golfers should have access to all the advantages enjoyed by their male counterparts, Babe Didrikson Zaharias was a co-founder of the Ladies Professional Golf Association (LPGA) in 1949. By lining up corporate sponsors, the LPGA was able to initiate more professional tournaments and provide larger cash prizes to women entrants. Babe herself became the star of the fledgling tour, winning more tournaments and taking home more prize money than anyone else. Her involvement lent credibility to the young organization and to women's professional athletics in general. In 1950, the Associated Press named her the Outstanding Woman Athlete of the Half Century.

By 1952 Babe had lost some of her legendary energy and spirit. She was diagnosed with rectal cancer and underwent surgery for the condition, vowing to return to the LPGA tour as soon as she was better. Just a few months after her operation she made good on the vow, and by 1954 she had won top honors at five more competitions, once again winning AP's Woman Athlete of the Year award. She continued golfing—and serving as a spokesperson for the American Cancer Society—into early 1955 but grew steadily weaker and eventually ruptured a disk in her back. Another operation revealed that the cancer had invaded her spine. She retired from the tour in mid-1955 and died a little more than a year later, on September 27, 1956, at the age of 43.

In a *Sports Illustrated* article published shortly after her death, longtime friend and admirer Paul Gallico paid tribute to the woman he called a "champion of champions." Gallico wrote: "It may be another 50 or 75 years before such a performer as Mildred Didrikson Zaharias again enters the lists.

For even if some yet unborn games queen matches her talent, versatility, skill, patience and will to practice, along with her flaming competitive spirit, . . . there still remains the little matter of courage and character, and in these departments the Babe must be listed with the champions of all times."

CAMILLE
DUVALL

The inclusion of waterskiing as an Olympic event in 1996 has come too late for Camille Duvall, the beautiful slalom champion who dominated waterskiing in the mid-1980s. Duvall was women's slalom champion in 1984 and 1985 and a top winner of prize money through much of the decade, further capitalizing on her fame by working as a model and endorsing lines of equipment and apparel. Known in her time as the "Golden Goddess of Waterskiing," Duvall earned further kudos by working with her brother, Sammy, as a popular brother-sister combination at various slalom events.

Raised by parents who were themselves amateur enthusiasts of the sport, Duvall began waterskiing at the age of four, perched on one ski alongside her father. Later she advanced to solo efforts and was initially pulled by a rope from the bow (rather than the rear) of the Duvall family boat, with the boat running in reverse. This maneuver, her father determined, lessened the alarming noise of the engine and the fear it imposed on the young Camille.

Encouraged by both of her parents, Duvall persisted and by the age of six had won her first tournament, one of many she entered throughout the United States. She also underwent rigorous training at a private lake her father leased near the family's home in Greenville, South Carolina. There Duvall benefitted from the tutelage of live-in coaches and the expertise of former world-class water-skiers such as Linda Giddens and Ricky McCormick. But it was probably the intense personal drive generated by her dynamic father, coupled with the daily competition between Duvall and her younger brother, that most influenced the budding skier.

From a "little bitty ten-year-old," Duvall matured into a disciplined and skilled athlete. Measuring five feet eleven inches tall, she utilized her height, strength, and superior arm length to excel in slalom skiing, an event that requires zig-zag skiing between buoys in the water. The "Golden Goddess" nickname was coined to reflect not only her athletic ability but her tanned, statuesque physical appearance as well. An attractive and shapely sun-bleached blonde, Duvall always attracted an impressive number of spectators for her

Blonde and statuesque, Camille Duvall was known as the "Golden Goddess of Waterskiing."

Camille Duvall shoots up a wall of water while competing in the women's slalom event of the U.S. vs. the World All-Stars Water Ski tournament, 1987. (UPI/Corbis-Bettmann)

appearances—a fact that made a mockery of the difference between men's and women's monetary compensation in waterskiing events.

In fact, throughout her career Duvall earned minimal financial rewards from skiing itself. In 1984, for example, she claimed less than $18,000 in purses—and she was one of the best-paid skiers on tour. Her annual income was supplemented by equipment endorsements, teaching contracts, personal appearances, and her work at a school for skiers that she and her brother operated together in Florida. Nevertheless, Duvall deserves recognition as one of the first successful professional women's water-skiers, a competitor who helped advance the popularity and visibility of her sport.

A part-time actress and model who was once featured in commercials for Fuji film, Duvall once told *Sports Illustrated* that professional waterskiing was finally beginning to afford "the very best skiers . . . a house,

CAMILLE DUVALL

American water-skier

Born: Greenville, South Carolina.

Career Highlights:
- won her first tournament at the age of six
- became U.S. women's slalom champion in 1984 and 1985.

a BMW and a Rolex." As one of the first women to qualify for those perks, she helped to popularize yet another athletic endeavor in which women have long excelled.

BECKY
DYROEN-
LANCER

"All I can do is compete against myself, within myself, and hope for the best."

A rules change for the 1996 Olympic synchronized swimming event means less limelight for Becky Dyroen-Lancer, but the winner of the 1994 World Aquatics Championship doesn't mind too much. Dyroen-Lancer, arguably the greatest performer in the history of individual, duet, and figures swimming, will perform in the Olympics as part of an eight-member team. One observer likened that to "putting Mary Lou Retton in a gymnastics chorus line."

Just how dominating has Dyroen-Lancer been? Like Babe Ruth, she specializes in grand slams. At least eight times in her career, she has swept the individual, duet, and figures events at major aquatics competitions, while also sharing in team gold medals. Fellow synchronized swimmer Kristen Babb-Sprague, who won the 1992 Olympic gold medal in Barcelona, noted that her rival "will go down as one of the most incredible athletes in the sport ever." Regardless of her achievements in the 1996 Olympics, Dyroen-Lancer has made her name as the new champion of synchronized swimming.

Born February 19, 1971, in San Jose, California, Becky Dyroen-Lancer seemed an unlikely candidate for athletic greatness. Her early years were fraught with anxiety, as she faced a congenital defect that had produced a hole in her heart. At the tender age of five she underwent open heart surgery to repair the birth defect. No one expected that the operation would endow her with a heart that could withstand the rigors of synchronized swimming.

Ironically, Dyroen-Lancer's heart is perhaps her greatest asset today. "What Becky does in the water is a combination of what a gymnast or figure skater does," U.S. National Team coach Charlotte Davis told *USA Today*. "But for a skater, the ice is always firm. Becky has to do the same moves, but in a constantly changing medium." Says Chris Carver, Dyroen-Lancer's personal coach: "You need the aerobic base of a swimmer, and you have to tread water as well or better than a water polo player—and you'd better be able to make it look easy." As for intangibles such as heart, expression, and competitiveness, Dyroen-Lancer has these bases covered too. "Becky is a sweet per-

Becky Dyroen-Lancer performs the routine that won her a gold medal in the 1995 Pan American Games. (AP/Wide World Photos)

son out of the water," Davis said. "But if I were an opponent watching her, I'd be very intimidated."

Dyroen-Lancer got involved in synchronized swimming at the age of ten. "It looked like loads of fun. It was so entertaining," she recalled. "Everyone was together in costumes doing the same routine. When you're that age, you don't see any of the hard work that goes into it." That realization came when she buckled down and got serious about the sport. "About age 13, I started to realize the demand synchronized swimming had on my time," Dyroen-Lancer said. "It was always work, but I never took it serious at that age, because it was so natural for me. I was pretty self-motivated. I remember in the beginning I was getting some pretty low scores. I didn't place very well. But I just kept setting high goals and kept going after them. It's hard for me to believe what I've accomplished. Sometimes it seems like a dream."

Aided by her husband, a former ballet dancer, Dyroen-Lancer practices six to eight hours a day, six days a week. She is no happier about her

BECKY DYROEN-LANCER

American synchronized swimmer

Born: February 19, 1971 in San Jose, California.

Career Highlights:
• swept the individual, duet, and figures events at major aquatics competitions more than eight times in her career

• won 1994 World Aquatics Championship.

schedule now than she was at 13. "That's the toughest thing," she said. "We [swimmers] probably spend more hours training than I think a lot of sports do physically. You can't spend eight hours shooting arrows in archery. There are so many different aspects to this sport. It's like gymnastics training in different disciplines, day after day after day." She added: "It does seem that the better you get, the more of a sacrifice it becomes. I guess that's true in sports and life in general. A lot of it is keeping up the motivation and the drive. All I can do is compete against myself, within myself, and hope for the best."

The biggest disappointment in Dyroen-Lancer's career occurred in 1992, when she was edged out of the Barcelona Olympics by Kristen Babb-Sprague. "It wasn't my time," Dyroen-Lancer admitted. "Kristen had put in the work and time, and 1992 was her time." Little did Dyroen-Lancer know that, by failing to make a solo appearance in Barcelona, she would *never* get to swim a solo routine in the Olympics. A rules change has eliminated solo and duet competitions. "In a way I feel bad," said the world champion solo swimmer. "But it will be a lot less work for me. And I really like the feeling of working with a group. I think that's more exciting."

As for sharing the spotlight, Dyroen-Lancer says she prefers an element of anonymity. "I don't look at myself as some big historical figure," she said. Still, her teammates are certain to welcome the leadership of a proven competitor in a sport that comes from the heart.

TERESA
EDWARDS

Teresa Edwards stands as living proof that women can be as long-lasting and successful in professional basketball as men. Edwards made her first Olympic appearance as a basketball player in 1984 as part of a gold medal-winning U.S. team in Los Angeles. She won another Olympic gold medal for basketball at Seoul in 1988, and she added a bronze medal at the Barcelona Olympics in 1992. The Georgia native will make a record-breaking fourth Olympic appearance in the 1996 Summer Games, performing in her home state in front of a family that has supported her dreams for years. Regarded as one of the best female basketball players in the world—"the Michael Jordan of women's basketball"—Edwards brings vast experience and quality leadership to the U.S. women's basketball team.

Born in 1964 in Cairo, Georgia, Teresa Edwards grew up in a single-parent family, with four brothers. Her mother, Mildred Edwards, gave up her own dreams of becoming a nurse to support her large family, and she had some decided views on women playing sports. Try as she might, however, Mildred could not drag Teresa away from the sandlot baseball, football, and basketball games she enjoyed playing with the local boys. When her brothers shot hoops through an old bicycle rim nailed to a pine tree, Teresa joined in as well. No one in Cairo ever expected that Teresa would become one of the nation's most famous women's basketball players, however—the sport was just a favorite hobby for an active girl.

Edwards made her debut in a structured basketball program as a seventh grader at her local public school. She kept her participation on the team a secret from her mother as long as she could. "She kept coming home late from school and laying it off on some teacher," Mildred Edwards recalled in *Sports Illustrated*. "Then one day she said, 'I need a new pair of sneakers because I made the team.' I said, 'Girl, you can't play basketball.' And Teresa said, 'Mama, I made the team.'"

It was only the first of many teams Teresa Edwards would make in her spectacular basketball career. After being a high school All-American, she

Teresa Edwards (left, with Mary Ethridge) wipes a tear after winning an Olympic gold medal in 1988. (UPI/Corbis-Bettmann)

GREAT WOMEN IN SPORTS

TERESA EDWARDS

American basketball player

Born: 1964 in Cairo, Georgia.

Education: attended the University of Georgia on an athletic scholarship.

Career Highlights:
- won gold medal as part of U.S. team, 1984 Olympic Games, Los Angeles, California
- named a consensus All-American in 1985 and 1986
- won gold medal as part of U.S. team, 1988 Olympic Games, Seoul, South Korea
- won bronze medal as part of U.S. team, 1992 Olympic Games, Barcelona, Spain
- played professional basketball in Italy and Japan.

attended the University of Georgia on an athletic scholarship, where she was named a consensus All-American in 1985 and 1986 as a junior and a senior. Leaving college before she finished her degree requirements, Edwards found work playing professional basketball in Italy and Japan. By the early 1990s she was earning better than $200,000 a year as a starter for the Nagoya, Japan, team sponsored by Mitsubishi. The long seasons overseas proved difficult, though. Edwards did not have the time to master the foreign languages of her host countries, and she was lonely and homesick.

The opportunity to play basketball for an American team was always welcome. Edwards first made the U.S. Olympic team while still a college student in 1984. She qualified again in 1988 and again in 1992. Her long history with the U.S. national team has included victories and setbacks, which she as the senior member of the squad has been uniquely positioned to understand. Edwards was part of Olympic basketball teams that won gold medals in 1984 and 1988. She was a member of a hastily assembled U.S. team that performed disappointingly in Barcelona, with a sound defeat by the former Soviet Union team. Now she is a member of a fully subsidized U.S. women's team that has been playing together for more than a year in anticipation of the 1996 Summer Games.

Her close friends describe Edwards as a genuine and easygoing person who has never let her six-figure salary dictate her lifestyle. She is not a fancy dresser, and when she does spend money, she tends to lavish it upon family members. Her mother is living in a house bought by Edwards, and her younger brothers receive help with their college tuition. Theresa Grentz, the coach of the 1992 U.S. Olympic women's basketball team, told *Sports Illustrated* of Edwards: "She can't be bought. Values are important to her. Her humility and her simplicity of life make her very special to be around."

In 1989 Edwards finished the requirements she needed to earn her bachelor's degree in recreation. When she is not traveling, she still makes her home near Cairo, Georgia. The citizens there honored her not too long ago by renaming the street on which she lived as a child. Now, when she visits the old family home, she drives down Teresa Edwards Street.

The future looks bright for Edwards as well. When she is finished working with the U.S. women's team in 1996, she expects to be one of the first women players chosen for a planned American women's professional basketball league. Edwards's longevity in basketball rivals any of her male counterparts—she is enjoying the game as much as ever and shows few signs of slowing down. The five-foot-eleven guard is set to make history as the first American to play basketball in four consecutive Olympics. Then she may turn around and make history again, as one of the first American women pros.

KORNELIA ENDER

SWIMMER

Was Kornelia Ender an Olympic medal-winning sprint phenomenon, or was she a steroid-fueled product of a corrupt East German swimming program? Today the answer is still shrouded in mystery. Ender won four gold medals at the 1976 Summer Games and set a fantastic 23 world records in her career. Her performance at the Olympics made a mockery of her American rivals and included the unprecedented feat of two gold medal sprint victories in the space of 28 minutes. Although her achievements are clouded by the possibility that she was given steroids—without her knowledge or assent—Ender still stands as one of the most successful Olympic swimmers of all time.

"I didn't lift weights much. I was agile, naturally strong. I did drills. I had a naturally perfect freestyle stroke. I was used as an example to others."

Kornelia Ender was born in 1958 in the German Democratic Republic, known in the West as East Germany. Her father was an army officer, and her mother a nurse. "I was a robust child, I was nice, but I was tough," Ender told *Sports Illustrated* in 1992. "When I didn't get what I wanted, I'd stamp and scream." What she wanted most was to swim. She was outstanding by the time she turned six, and at 11 she was enrolled at the Chemie Club training center in Halle. There, living away from home, she swam six to seven miles a day. Her workouts were supervised by a coach and a team doctor.

"After every workout I got a 'cocktail' with vitamins," she recalled. "I drank it because I wanted to recover as fast as I could." Quickly she added: "You must understand that no one, not swimmers or coaches or doctors, ever spoke about drugs. Sports officials never talked to us about anything. We never questioned what we were being given. I wish I could ask Coach Langhein, but he died of cancer in 1982."

At the age of 13 in 1972, Ender anchored two East German Olympic silver medal-winning relay teams and won an individual silver in the 200-meter medley. For four years after that, she was virtually untouchable in butterfly and freestyle sprints. A *Sports Illustrated* reporter once wrote that she "propelled herself into the water with such authority as to give the impression that she was pulling the pool toward her." She certainly was a physically imposing specimen, standing five-feet-eleven and weighing 167 pounds, all of it muscle.

Kornelia Ender trains in Montreal before turning in four gold medal per-formances in the 1976 Olympics. (Archive Photos)

Before the 1976 Olympics in Montreal, East German women swim-mers had never won a gold medal in Olympic competition. Suddenly in Montreal, the GDR team burst into prominence, winning gold medals in 11 of 13 events and setting eight world records. Ender was a big part of that suc-cess story. She won the 100-meter and 200-meter freestyle sprints, the 100-meter butterfly, and she anchored a 400-meter medley relay team that won gold. Every one of her races broke the world record. Even more amazing, Ender swam two of the individual events in less than half an hour—the 100 butterfly and the 200 freestyle, in which she was substituting for Barbara Krause. "I went as hard as I could in the 100 butterfly," she told *Sports Illustrated.* "In the 200 I imagine I might have gone two-tenths of a second faster if I'd been fresh."

Some of her American opponents—most notably Shirley Babashoff—suggested that the East German swimmers had cheated by using performance-enhancing drugs. At the time Babashoff was accused of being a sore loser, but

KORNELIA ENDER

German swimmer

Born: 1958 in what was then the German Democratic Republic, or East Germany.

Career Highlights:

- won two silver medals as part of East German relay teams, and won individual silver in 200-meter medley, 1972 Olympic Games, Munich, Germany

- set 23 world records between 1972 and 1976

- won four gold medals—100-meter and 200-meter freestyle sprints, 100-meter butterfly, and (as anchor) 4 × 100-meter medley relay team—1976 Olympic Games, Montreal, Canada.

with the fall of the Berlin Wall in 1991, 20 former East German coaches admitted they had given anabolic steroids to selected athletes in those years. Ender's name was not mentioned in connection with steroid use, and she denies having ever used performance-enhancing drugs. "I don't think I was the type who needed something," she told *Sports Illustrated*. "I didn't lift weights much. I was agile, naturally strong. I did drills. I had a naturally perfect freestyle stroke. I was used as an example to others."

Ordinarily, a swimmer like Ender would be given a hero's life in East Germany. But she was ostracized when she chose to retire after the 1976 Olympics. She married a fellow swimmer but divorced him in 1982 after having one child. A stint in medical school ended when one of her professors simply wouldn't pass her. Instead of achieving her dream of being a doctor, Ender became a physiotherapist. She remarried in 1984 and had a second daughter shortly thereafter.

Ender's troubles with the repressive East German government continued into the late 1980s, and she and her husband tried to leave the country after her husband was dropped from the state bobsled team. In 1989 Ender applied for an emigration visa, only to find her every move observed by the secret police. She and her family finally found refuge in West Germany late in 1989.

Today Kornelia Ender practices physiotherapy in a private physician's office in Germany. She swims an occasional seniors race, but does not pursue swimming seriously anymore. It pains her to think that her Olympic achievements are clouded by the possibility of cheating. "Why should I even think about these golds now being tainted?" she complained in *Sports Illustrated*. "Why, when I didn't know anything then or now? Why should I even give a thought to what *might* have been given to me . . . years ago, when I was that child you see in the pictures?"

JANET EVANS

"I never saw myself as being small. Size doesn't matter as long as you can get to the end of the pool faster than anybody else."

Janet Evans took to the water when she was a year old, and by the time she was 17 she had set three world records. Often considered too small for competition, Evans made up for her lack of size with hard work and determination. She is the only American woman ever to win four Olympic gold medals in swimming and the rare competitor who has won gold at two consecutive Olympics. She was the darling of the 1988 Games in Seoul, and now she is swimming's *grande dame,* racing against rivals who were just little girls when she won her first Olympic gold. Despite her record-breaking success, she has remained humble and tries to be "Just Janet," a young woman who loves to swim.

Fame has been particularly kind to Evans. William A. Henry III noted in a *Time* magazine profile on July 27, 1992, that, as "the world's most famous woman swimmer," Evans has "cashed in." Product endorsements, motivational speeches, and a perennial berth on the U.S. swimming national team have provided the athlete with a comfortable income and the freedom to train vigorously for the longer-distance events in which she excels. If she is no longer quite as fast as she was in 1988, neither is anyone else—all three of her world records were set in the 1980s and have yet to be surpassed.

Evans was born on August 28, 1971, in Placentia, California. She grew up there, learning to swim soon after she learned to walk. At five she competed in her first race. By the age of 15 she had earned a national ranking, winning the Phillips Performance Award at the U.S. Open Swim Meet for breaking Tracy Caulkins's 400-meter individual medley meet record. She was a junior in high school when she set national high school records for the 200-yard individual medley and the 500-yard freestyle. Even then Evans was something of a celebrity, though she tried to keep her life away from the pool as normal as possible. She signed her first autograph at 15. "It was really weird when that started," she recalled in a March 26, 1990, *Sports Illustrated* profile, "because I thought *I* was one of those little kids."

Janet Evans celebrates her gold-medal victory in the women's 400-meter medley during the 1988 Olympic Games. (AFP/Bettmann)

"Little" might be one way of describing Evans as she easily qualified for her first Olympics in 1988. At the time she was just over 5 feet tall and weighed 102 pounds. A *Sports Illustrated* reporter who watched her climb the block for her gold medal 800-meter freestyle race—surrounded on both sides by enormous, muscled East German rivals—described her as looking like "an age-group swimmer who had somehow stumbled into the wrong race." In fact, Evans's lithe figure proved a significant asset. She won the Olympic gold in the 400-meter individual medley, set a world record in the 400-meter freestyle in a gold medal performance three days later, and capped the Summer Games by taking the gold medal in the 800-meter freestyle. Evans was the only American woman who won individual gold medals in swimming that year, and her perky personality and obvious youth charmed the viewers at home. "Evans was the bright spot for the U.S. women swimmers," wrote Bruce Anderson in *Sports Illustrated* on October 3, 1988. ". . . And she beamed and bubbled and giggled with delight at winning." She was 17 at the time.

The reality of celebrity began to affect Evans's life when she returned home after Seoul. She enrolled in Stanford University in 1989 but stayed only two years, relinquishing her eligibility when the National Collegiate Athletic Association set new rules reducing the amount of practice time for collegiate swimmers. Freed from her academic duties—she had been an "A" student—Evans accepted product endorsements and moved to Austin, Texas, to train with coach Mark Schubert. By 1990 she was ranked in the top three in the world in an astonishing five events.

ATLANTA IN '96

In '88, Janet Evans was 17 and thrilled to be taking home three gold medals from her first Olympics. By '92, at the age of 21, she was already a bit weary of her competitive life, feeling the pressure of being a reigning champion. As for '96, Evans asserts that she is looking forward to these Summer Games; they will give her an opportunity to enjoy the "fun" of the Olympics again as she really has nothing left to prove. "My body has changed, and if I never swim an 8:16 (her 800-meter world record) in my life again, I'm not going to consider it the end of the world. I was able to swim more than 10 seconds off that and still win a world championship. The way I look at that now, that just tells me it was a pretty amazing thing when I did it."

Try as she might, Evans could never duplicate her world record-setting times in the 400-meter, 800-meter, and 1,500-meter freestyle. The 400-meter and 1,500-meter records were set in 1988 and the 800-meter in 1989, when Evans was at her "little" and lithesome best. She found, as she entered her twenties, that she had to compensate for changes in her figure and weight. She was able to do this, and she returned to the 1992 Summer Games in Barcelona favored to win gold again in her two best races, the 800-meter freestyle and the 400-meter freestyle. She did win the gold in the 800-meter, but she had to settle for a silver in the 400-meter freestyle— and she did not qualify for the relay team.

JANET EVANS

American swimmer

Born: August 28, 1971 in Placentia, California.

Education: enrolled in Stanford University in 1989; stayed two years.

Career Highlights:

- won gold medal in 400-meter individual medley, won gold medal and set a world record in the 400-meter freestyle, won gold medal in the 800-meter freestyle, 1988 Olympic Games, Seoul, South Korea

- won gold medal in 800-meter freestyle and silver medal in400-meter freestyle, 1992 Olympic Games, Barcelona, Spain

- distinguished as only American woman ever to win four Olympic gold medals in swimming

- owns World Championship medals in 800-meter freestyle, 1993 and 1994.

The Janet Evans of the 1992 Summer Games was no longer a giggling teenager. In retrospect, she told *USA Today* on July 7, 1995, she was not even happy. "Swimming was the be-all and end-all of my life," she recalled. "I listened to all the stuff about why I wasn't as fast as before. I felt the pressure, and it made me a little bitter. And that kept me from going as fast as I might have." Still her achievements were nothing to take lightly. Evans is the first American woman to win four Olympic gold medals in swimming, and she has five medals overall.

As if to prove her naysayers wrong, Evans has been particularly dominating in the 800-meter freestyle since 1993. She owns back-to-back world championship medals in the event, for 1993 and 1994, and her strongest competition may come not from abroad but from American Brooke Bennett, who, a young teenager herself, is being described as "the next Janet Evans." In fact, while Evans qualified for the 1996 Olympics in the 800-meter freestyle, she finished behind Bennett in the trials. Asked about facing competitors who were in grade school when she won her first Olympic gold, Evans told *USA Today:* "I'm looking forward to it. . . . I like the competition."

Evans is one athlete who has never let her success go to her head. "There are so many people out there in the world, and I have a world record. Why me?" she asked, as quoted in *Newsmakers 1989.* "It's kind of weird. I try not to think about it too much, but it still boggles my mind."

CORY
EVERSON

After winning the Ms. Olympia title six times, Cory Everson changed careers, starring in the 1992 film Double Impact with Jean-Claude Van Damme.

Few bodybuilders of either sex can rival the success enjoyed by Cory Everson, a six-time Ms. Olympia and the dominant female bodybuilder of the 1980s. Everson won the first Ms. Olympia bodybuilding competition she entered in 1984 and simply owned the event every year after that until 1990. She was a bodybuilder with a difference, counting on her stunning good looks and winning personality to help nail her titles. A favorite with judges and fans alike, she has continued to be closely associated with the sport even though she no longer competes.

Born the second of three children in Deerfield, Illinois, in 1959, Everson inherited athletic genes from her German-born parents. Her father, Hank Kneuer, had been a successful gymnast, and her mother ran track. As a youngster Corrina Kneuer was encouraged to develop her own athletic talents, and she especially liked track and field events. A straight-A student in public school, she won an athletic scholarship to the University of Wisconsin, where she proceeded to win four Big 10 pentathlon titles in four years. She also earned a bachelor's degree in interior design.

While a student at Wisconsin, Cory met strength coach Jeff Everson, who encouraged her to try bodybuilding. Their working association at the school soon deepened into a romance, and they married in 1982. That same year, Cory's budding career in strength training nearly ground to a halt. A strange swelling in her left leg sent her to the hospital, where doctors puzzled over the condition for several weeks. Finally, as the swelling began to ease by itself, a blood test revealed that she suffered from a rare genetic enzyme deficiency that can cause dangerous blood clots and unpredictable swelling. Medication improved the condition, and Everson resumed bodybuilding in 1983.

Everson and her husband felt that her combination of superb conditioning and natural beauty might prove a winning formula in the Ms. Olympia competition. They moved to Los Angeles, California, in 1984, and sure enough, Everson won her first Ms. Olympia title that year, the first time she entered

Cory Everson flexes her muscles in competition for the 1987 Ms. Olympia title; she won her bid for the title, her fourth straight victory. (UPI/Bettmann)

CORY EVERSON

American bodybuilder

Born: 1959 in Deerfield, Illinois.

Education: attended University of Wisconsin on an athletic scholarship; earned a bachelor's degree in interior design.

Career Highlights:

- garnered four Big 10 pentathlon titles in four years
- won Ms. Olympia bodybuilding competition six years in a row, from 1984 through 1989.

the contest. A Ms. Olympia title confers enormous prestige upon its recipient—as well as an annual earnings potential of almost a million dollars. Everson proved to be a durable champion, winning six straight Ms. Olympia crowns and cashing in with product endorsements and personal appearances all over the world. During the height of her fame she marketed her own line of athletic clothing and cosmetics, based on her own aversion to flashy outfits and heavy makeup.

Everson retired from competitive bodybuilding in 1989 while she was still at the top. She has never really left the sport behind, however. In 1992 she appeared in the Jean-Claude Van Damme movie *Double Impact,* playing—what else?—a tough fighting woman. Everson has also enjoyed a successful career writing about bodybuilding and other women's fitness issues in a special column, "Cory's Corner," in *Muscle & Fitness* magazine. Although she continues light weight training and aerobic exercises, she says she has no nostalgia for her days as a serious bodybuilder. "It's an unnatural state," she explained in *People* magazine. On the other hand, she has no qualms about her muscular physique and how it enables her to win roles in action films. "Julia Roberts isn't believable as being able to hurdle a truck and not hurt herself and go and kick two guys in the face," she said. ". . . You have to look believable."

CHRIS
EVERT

TENNIS PLAYER

Chris Evert was such a good tennis player, and such a consistent winner, that her style was sometimes described as *boring*. From the early years of the 1970s until 1989 Evert dominated her sport, turning a long rivalry with Martina Navratilova into high drama and pulling down Grand Slam event victories as regularly as the seasons change. Evert was ranked number one in the world almost every year between 1975 and 1981, and she spent 17 consecutive years in the World Top Ten. She entered 56 Grand Slam tournaments in her career and won 18 of them, making the semifinals a phenomenal 52 times. Her career, to quote *Tennis* magazine correspondent Mike Lupica, "is not just one of the great accomplishments in all of tennis history, it is one of the great individual accomplishments in sports history."

She began her career as "Chrissie" Evert, a teenaged ingenue with a two-handed backhand and a powerful slow-court baseline drive. Born December 20, 1954, in Fort Lauderdale, Florida, she was ideally situated to become a tennis star. Her father, Jimmy Evert, was a teaching professional who lavished attention on his children and saw to it that they learned the game at very early ages. "I really admired my dad and put him on a pedestal, and I wanted his attention," Evert remembered in a May 25, 1992, *Sports Illustrated* interview. "Whether it's ego or insecurity or whatever, when you start winning and getting attention, you like it, and that feeling snowballs. You start to feel good about yourself. You feel complete and proud of yourself."

Both of Evert's parents encouraged her to pursue tennis to the exclusion of all else except her studies, and she grew up with few friends and hardly any social life to speak of. On the court, however, she displayed flashes of brilliance that augured well for a professional career. At the age of 16 she advanced to the semifinals at the U.S. Open, losing to Billie Jean King. Reporters dubbed her the "Little Ice Maiden" for her grim and unemotional style, but off court they enjoyed calling her "Chrissie" and emphasized her youth and obvious skills.

"I was very insecure when I was young. I was shy and introverted. When I went out on the tennis court, I could express myself. It was a way of getting reactions from people."

151

Chris Evert was the first player ever to win 1,000 matches. (*Archive Photos*)

Evert retained her amateur status until 1973 and then joined the professional tour. By that time she had already advanced to the semis at both the U.S. Open and Wimbledon, and she had won the first of four Virginia Slims tournaments in 1972. Evert established herself firmly in the World Top Ten and by 1974 was ranked number one in the United States. She earned the top world ranking the next year and kept it in 1976, 1977, 1980, and 1981. With none of the apparent attitude problems that plague younger players, in 1976 the "Ice Maiden" became the first woman to reach a million dollars in career prize money.

Between 1973 and 1979 Evert won 125 consecutive matches on clay, garnering 24 tournament titles. She won at least one major singles title every year for 13 consecutive years, and her record of 52 semifinal appearances in 56 Grand Slam events makes her one of the all-time most successful Grand Slam players. She was also dominant in Wightman Cup singles competition, going undefeated through 26 matches and helping the U.S. team win 11 Cups in 13 years. Evert achieved all of this without ever losing her low-key demeanor, even when she faced more emotional opponents such as Navratilova.

"When I look back and see myself with that little grim, fixed expression, I wonder, because that's not me," Evert admitted in *Sports Illustrated.* "I think my father instilled it in me at a young age. I remember his telling me, 'Don't show any emotion: it will be to your advantage because your opponent will be frustrated.' And you know, it worked. So I stayed with it. But it wasn't me the person. It was just me the tennis player."

As a tennis player, Evert was one of the best. As Lupica put it, "It was not just tennis on display, it was character." He added: "Evert was the first tennis girl, and she was forced to grow into a woman with a camera always parked right in front of her, and she handled it all with a sort of grace that you had to see year in and year out to fully appreciate. She made a seamless transition from ingenue to leading lady to grande dame. When it was time for her to go, she left with dignity."

The first player ever to win 1,000 matches and 157 tournaments, Evert held onto her number one ranking until 1981. By that time her rivalry with Navratilova was in full swing, and it became an exciting staple of women's tennis through much of the 1980s. Although Navratilova got the best of Evert more than vice versa, Evert did score some late-career victories over her nemesis, most notably in the 1985 and 1986 French Open events. Evert appeared in one Olympics, in 1988, and did not win a medal. She retired from the tour in 1989 having won almost $9 million in prize money and having earned easily that much again with product endorsements and personal appearance fees.

Reflecting on her decision to retire in a *Women's Sports + Fitness* interview, Evert said: "I wanted in essence to stop when I was on top, and I was

CHRIS EVERT

American tennis player

Born: December 20, 1954 in Fort Lauderdale, Florida.

Career Highlights:

- won 125 consecutive matches on clay, including 24 tournaments, between 1973 and 1979

- ranked number one in the world almost every year between 1975 and 1981, and remained in the World Top Ten 17 consecutive years

- entered 56 Grand Slam tournaments, winning 18 of them

- became the first woman to reach a million dollars in career prize money, 1976

- won at least one major singles title every year for 13 consecutive years

- set record of 52 semifinal appearances in 56 Grand Slam events, making her one of the all-time most successful Grand Slam players

- remained undefeated through 26 matches in Wightman Cup singles competition, helping the U.S. team win 11 Cups in 13 years

- first player ever to win 1,000 matches and 157 tournaments.

Awards: Inducted into the International Tennis Hall of Fame in 1995.

ranked number four and I felt like I was on top in certain ways, and I just didn't want to have to go through the week-in and week-out grind any more. I've done my time." Having married her second husband, skier Andy Mill, she decided to start a family. They now have a son, Alexander.

"Being a mother . . . having Andy as my husband, living in Aspen and Boca Raton, doing broadcasting and fulfilling my endorsements is definitely enough for me," Evert explained in *Sports Illustrated*. "You know, it's funny, I'm not an overly ambitious person; I don't feel like I have to excel, I don't think I will ever be as intense in anything I do as I was in tennis."

Chris Evert was inducted into the International Tennis Hall of Fame in 1995.

MAE
FAGGS

Mae Faggs was the first American woman to participate in three Olympic Games. In spite of her short stature—just five feet tall—she became a legendary sprinter and was the first of many award-winning Tennessee State University Tigerbelle track athletes. It was not until a runner of Faggs's skill and competitive drive joined the Tennessee State track team that the university began to support the development of track as a viable sport. Track coach Ed Temple, who called her the "mother of the team," credited her with getting the Tigerbelles started and initiating the development of the track program. She was highly regarded by other athletes for her team spirit and her willingness to help others. Track star and Olympic gold medalist Wilma Rudolph, who also attended Tennessee State, credited Faggs with giving her invaluable assistance during her career.

Aeriwentha Mae Faggs was born on April 10, 1932, in Mays Landing, New Jersey. She was the only girl and the second of five children born to Hepsi Faggs, a domestic worker and a needle maker in a musical instrument plant, and to William Faggs, a factory worker. Mae began running track when she was in elementary school and as a teen became a member of the Police Athletic League (PAL) in Bayside, Long Island. She ran for the PAL from 1947 until 1952.

In 1947, Sergeant John Brennan decided to form an Amateur Athletic Union (AAU) team using runners from all over the Long Island region. Brennan became Faggs's coach, mentor, and trusted friend. After watching her win consistently at local track events, he told Faggs he felt she was ready to enter the trials for the 1948 U.S. Olympic team that were to take place in Providence, Rhode Island. Faggs traveled to Providence and won a berth on the Olympic squad, becoming the youngest American member to compete that year.

Her first Olympic appearance at the Summer Games in London was a bit of a disappointment. She competed in the 200-meter dash and the 400-meter relay but lost both events. Youth was on her side, however, and she returned home vowing to improve her skills. In 1949 at the AAU national in-

TRACK & FIELD
ATHLETE

Three-time Olympian Mae Faggs was one of the earliest members of Tennessee State University's legendary Tigerbelle track team

Mae Faggs is on the verge of breaking the finish line and the American record in the 100-yard dash during the Women's Amateur Athletic Union Track and Field Meet in 1955. (AP/Wide World Photos)

door meet she won the 220-yard dash, setting an American record of 25.8 seconds. For the following three years she held the 220-yard dash title consistently, with no challenge to her record.

In 1952, Faggs set an American indoor record in the 100-yard dash at Buffalo, New York, and was a member of the winning 880-yard relay U.S. National Team at the British Empire Games in London. As she had predicted, she returned to the Olympics a second time and earned her first medal as a member of the winning 400-meter relay team at the 1952 Summer Games in Helsinki, Finland.

Mae Faggs entered Tennessee State University in 1952 having participated in two Olympics. With the opportunity to earn a college degree on an athletic scholarship, she brought her competitive spirit, her experience, and her leadership skills to her new Tigerbelle team. At the time she entered the university, the track program there was in its embryonic stages. Through her

MAE FAGGS

American track & field athlete

Born: April 10, 1932, in Mays Landing, New Jersey.

Education: entered Tennessee State University on athletic scholarship, 1952.

Career Highlights:

- won the 220-yard dash, setting an American record of 25.8 seconds, at the AAU national indoor meet, 1949; for the following three years she held the 220-yard dash title, with no challenge to her record

- set an American indoor record in the 100-yard dash at Buffalo, New York, 1952

- won (as part of team) 880-yard relay for U.S. National Team at the British Empire Games in London, 1952

- earned gold medal as member of 400-meter relay team, 1952 Olympic Games, Helsinki, Finland

- won bronze medal as member of 400-meter relay team, 1956 Olympic Games, Melbourne, Australia

- won (as part of all-Tennessee State University team) 440-yard relay; won gold medals in 100-yard dash and 220-yard dash, at National AAU women's championships, 1956.

Awards: Won 26 trophies, three plaques, and nearly 100 medals during four-year track career at Tennessee State University; named AAU All-American, 1954, 1955, and 1956; inducted into the Helms Hall of Fame and the National Track and Field Hall of Fame at Charleston, West Virginia, 1956.

---

efforts on behalf of the program, the selection of Ed Temple as coach, and an intensive development plan, a world-class track team was born—thanks in no small part to Faggs's performance as the team's anchor. By the end of her four-year track career at Tennessee State, she had won 26 trophies, three plaques, and nearly 100 medals; she set records in the 100-meter and 200-yard dashes, and she led the Tigerbelle relay team to an American record in the 440-meter relay with a time of 49.1 seconds.

In 1956, Faggs and an all-Tennessee State University team won the 440-yard relay at the National AAU women's championships. At that same competition Faggs won gold medals in the 100-yard dash and the 220-yard dash. Named AAU All-American for a third consecutive year, she easily qualified for her third Olympic appearance. At the 1956 Olympic Games in Melbourne, Australia, Faggs and her all-Tennessee State team won the bronze medal in the 400-meter relay. Later that same year, in recognition of her achievements, she was inducted into the Helms Hall of Fame and the National Track and Field Hall of Fame at Charleston, West Virginia.

Throughout Faggs's years in track, she demonstrated leadership skills and an ability to encourage and inspire. These talents, coupled with her desire to increase the opportunities available to young people, led her to embark on a teaching career in Cincinnati, Ohio, that lasted 32 years. She retired in 1989 but remains active in community affairs. Since her retirement she has also worked part time in a program that aids freshman athletes at Cincinnati's Xavier University. Thus, even in her life outside track, Faggs has assumed the nurturing role that her coach, Ed Temple, attributed to her early in her career.

AMY
FENG

TABLE TENNIS
PLAYER

"Table tennis was not easy for me. But I worked very hard. I hoped one day to be in the Olympics."

American athletes have long felt the sting of playing against opponents from other countries who have been trained in state-supported sports schools. Amy Feng, the top-ranked female table tennis player in the U.S., has a different take on the topic. Born near Beijing and selected for a special sports school at the age of 11, Feng became disgruntled with the sport-as-a-life approach of her native country and emigrated to America in 1992. No longer a slave to her sport, she feels that the move away from China can only improve her game.

"Table tennis in China takes so much time," said Feng, who currently resides in Wheaton, Maryland, and trains in Augusta, Georgia. "When you are 18 or 19, maybe you want to try some other things. I didn't want to stop playing table tennis, but I wanted a little more time to try other things. I didn't have enough time. Table tennis in China—it's your life."

Feng, who was born April 9, 1969, began playing the game with her father, a high school teacher, just for fun. As her skills improved, however, she and her parents began to see table tennis as an opportunity to win notice in the highly structured Chinese society. After being selected for one of China's elite sports schools in 1980, the ambitious girl found herself in a tightly controlled environment with few options beyond pursuing her sport. A typical sports school day would begin at six in the morning with an hour of running and calisthenics, followed by nearly six hours of table tennis and two hours of schooling. The routine hardly ever varied.

"Table tennis was not easy for me," Feng admitted. "But I worked very hard. I hoped one day to be in the Olympics."

When she arrived at the school, Feng was ranked third out of 12 girls. After two years, she was number one. "But five hours of table tennis a day is too much," she said. "You cannot think for that long. After awhile, you are just playing, not thinking *how* you are playing. I loved to play, at first. After a while, I had no choice. They make you play."

From 1985 to 1990, Feng was women's champion of the Chinese state of Tianjin, placing fifth or higher each time in the Chinese national champi-

AMY FENG

Chinese-born American table tennis player

Born: April 9, 1969 in Beijing, China.

Career Highlights:
- named women's champion of the Chinese state of Tianjin, 1985–1990
- placed second in the Chinese national championships, 1986
- won U.S. table tennis championship, 1995.

onships. In 1986 she was ranked 26th in the world and placed second in the Chinese national championships. Feng was succeeding, but she ran afoul of the baffling bureaucracy in her native land. "When I finished second in China, I felt I should go to the worlds," she said. "But the coach did not like me, so he did not choose me to go. In China, if the coach likes you, you can do anything. You can play on the world team—*anything*. Because there are so many good players in China, anyone from No. 1 to No. 20 can go to the worlds and win."

Feng's career—and life—took a major turn in 1991 when she met Andrew Tan, a U.S. citizen and amateur table tennis buff, who'd taken a vacation to China to train. Tan's excursion was rather like one of those baseball fantasy camps for the ping-pong set, and not surprisingly, he found himself completely overmatched when he scrimmaged with Feng. Nevertheless, the two players struck up a friendship by correspondence when Tan left China. They married in 1992.

Feng has found the U.S. system of athletics much more to her liking. "Here, it is better," she explained. "Here, any person can go to world competition or the Olympics. They don't give everyone an even chance in China. This is a very fair country. Here, there's more freedom." Even freedom has a price, however. Deprived of the top-notch competition she faced in China— and relieved from the demands of practicing five or more hours a day—Feng has seen her game suffer. She was ranked 40th in the world in 1995, down from 26th in the late 1980s. Where once her training regime was subsidized by the state, she now has to pay most of her own coaching and travel fees.

Still, things have managed to work. Feng, who won the 1995 U.S. table tennis championship, is taking classes to improve her English. To support her career she coaches and takes other part-time jobs as her schedule allows. Her favorite dream? To play against some of her former countrywomen at the Olympic Games.

"I know everybody who plays in China," she said. "I could end up playing someone from my old country. Before, they didn't give me the chance to go to the worlds. Right now, I would just like to beat them."

America would like it, too.

GIGI
FERNANDEZ

"I'm very proud for Puerto Rico. I'm very proud for the U.S. I'm very proud."

—Fernandez on winning the 1992 Olympic gold medal

A stellar career in tennis has made Gigi Fernandez famous and beloved in her native island of Puerto Rico as well as in the wider world. Gigi's accomplishments include a 1992 Olympic gold medal, a world doubles championship, a doubles crown at Wimbledon, and a championship at the French Open—all "firsts" for a Puerto Rican player. Often teamed with Mary Joe Fernandez (no relation), Gigi has proven herself to be one of the toughest and most consistent doubles players in recent history, a competitor who could *and did* beat a Spanish doubles team in Barcelona for Olympic gold.

Born in 1964 in San Juan, Gigi was first introduced to tennis on her eighth birthday, when she received lessons as a gift from her parents. Almost as soon as she picked up a racket, she found that the game came naturally to her. She was ranked number one in Puerto Rico as a junior player, enabling her to win an athletic scholarship to Clemson University in South Carolina.

Gigi had not been known to practice diligently until she arrived at Clemson. As she grew serious about her game, her ability improved dramatically. While still a college freshman she advanced to the finals in the NCAA singles championship, a feat that fueled her decision to turn professional in 1985. That same year she was recognized by *Tennis* magazine as a "player to watch" for achieving a singles ranking of 23rd in the world.

The real turning point in Gigi's career came after an encounter with tennis great Martina Navratilova. At the time Gigi was a relative unknown on the tour, struggling to find the will and the discipline to win. Navratilova approached Gigi at a Wimbledon players' party, complimented her performance in a match against Pam Shriver, and suggested that she had a brilliant career ahead of her. Gigi was astonished.

"It was thrilling to me," she later recalled in the *New York Times*. "I was ranked about 150 in the world and I weighed about 170 pounds. I had lost about 14 matches in a row in the first round and I was eating in frustration, porking out on ice cream and chocolate chip cookies—anything I could get my hands on." After talking to Navratilova, Gigi said, "I decided to change

Gigi Fernandez exults after her first round upset victory over Sebine Hack at the 1994 U.S. Open. (Reuters/Corbis-Bettmann)

my diet and habits. I went home for a week and thought about what kind of tennis player I wanted to be."

Gigi Fernandez was skilled as a singles player, but she found her real niche and greatest success in doubles. She has garnered six Grand Slam women's doubles titles to date, including the U.S. Open in 1988, 1990, and 1992, the French Open in 1991 and 1992, and the Wimbledon championship in 1992. Her highest ranking as a doubles performer came in 1991, when she hit number one.

The Olympic gold medal easily ranks amongst Gigi's most satisfying accomplishments, even though it caused her some controversy in Puerto Rico. Gigi knew she would have no chance to advance into medal rounds in the Olympic competition unless she competed for the United States. Still it was one of the most difficult decisions of her life, since she knew she would be criticized on her home island. Any criticism was short-lived, as Gigi and her partner Mary Joe Fernandez beat the Spanish team of Arantxa Sanchez Vicario

GIGI FERNANDEZ

Puerto Rican tennis player

Born: 1964 in San Juan, Puerto Rico.

Education: Won athletic scholarship to Clemson University in South Carolina.

Career Highlights:
- attained U.S. Open doubles title, 1988, 1990, and 1992
- ranked number one as a doubles performer, 1991
- garnered French Open doubles title, 1991 and 1992
- won Wimbledon doubles championship, 1992
- partnered with Mary Joe Fernandez to win gold medal, 1992 Olympic Games, Barcelona, Spain.

and Conchita Martinez in Barcelona at the 1992 Summer Games for an Olympic gold medal. Interviewed after the thrilling gold medal match, Gigi expressed her happiness for both of the countries she was representing at the Games. "I'm very proud for Puerto Rico. I'm very proud for the U.S. I'm very proud," she said.

Pride works both ways. While tennis is not considered a major sport in Puerto Rico, Gigi has nevertheless captured her countrymen's admiration. As the first Puerto Rican to win an Olympic gold medal—and the first female Puerto Rican athlete to turn professional—she has paved the way for a new generation of female athletes on her island home. "In a way, it's kind of neat," she remarked in *Hispanic* magazine, "because it's opening a door for female athletes in Puerto Rico. Before, it was taboo for a female to make a living out of a sport. Girls are supposed to get married and have kids, so now maybe this opens the door."

LISA
FERNANDEZ

Unbeatable. That's what softball pitcher Lisa Fernandez is. Considered by many to be the best all-around player in fast-pitch softball today, Fernandez compiled a four-year college record of 93-7 with the University of California, Los Angeles Bruins and led the Bruins to two national championships. Her winning percentage—in college alone—is .930, and that does not include all the shutouts she has pitched for elite amateur teams and the U.S. women's softball team. Oh, yes, and this might be the place to add that she bats around .400 and plays a mean third base.

"Once in a while, you run across a young ballplayer who is too unreal to be true," writes Mike Downey in the *Los Angeles Times.* "A natural. A 'phenom,' as they used to say. Someone with the sizzle of Sandy Koufax, the dazzle of Fernando Valenzuela and the ability to inspire complete and utter disbelief, like someone out of fiction, a Roy Hobbs, a Joe Hardy, a Sidd Finch. Here is such a person. . . . A pitcher worth a thousand words." Lisa Fernandez is, in short, a living, working legend.

Excellence in softball beckoned her from the start. She was born in Long Beach, California, and raised in Lakewood, California, by a father who emigrated from Cuba and a mother who hailed from Puerto Rico. Her father, Antonio, had played semi-pro baseball in Cuba and moved to softball when he arrived in America. Her mother also enjoyed softball. Not surprisingly, both parents encouraged Lisa to get an early start in the sport. As a toddler she chased a rolled-up sock that her mother tossed around the house. As soon as she could throw, she began practicing batting in her back yard.

"All I knew was softball," Fernandez told *USA Today.* "We were always playing. I was the batgirl for my mom's slow-pitch team. When I was old enough, I started playing."

Fernandez gauged her progress by the type of mitt her mother used to catch her pitches. At first a regular baseball glove was sufficient, but as Lisa progressed, her mother had to switch to an extra-padded mitt. Next came shin guards and a catcher's mask. Once Lisa was ready to play, her mother chose

"I've always thought of myself as an all-around player, but I definitely love pitching the most. I love having that control. I love having the game in my hands."

163

Softball phenom Lisa Fernandez is distinguished by her exceptional versatility. (AP/Wide World Photos)

the opposition carefully. "My mom didn't allow me on a team I could dominate," Fernandez recalled in *USA Today*. "She didn't want me to be a big fish in a little pond. So I always played on teams where there were better players, where I had to work hard to get better."

In her very first outing as a softball pitcher, Fernandez lost 28-0, walked "about 20 batters" and "must have hit another 20." She got better quickly. At 11 she won her first Amateur Softball Association championship. During her career at St. Joseph High School in Lakewood she pitched 69 shutouts, 37 no-hitters, and 12 perfect games. She established an earned run average that would amaze even James Bond—0.07—and was a four-time All-American who spent her summers touring with amateur teams.

This success was extremely satisfying for a girl who had been told she would never pitch softball at the top level. When Fernandez was a young teen, she sought the advice of a nationally recognized pitching coach. He took one look at her stature (a mere five-foot-six) and declared that she was not tall enough and was not built right for softball success. She was so stung that she cried—and then she set out to prove him wrong.

"I didn't have a lot of the natural abilities other people had," Fernandez confessed in the *Long Beach Press-Telegram* in 1992. "I didn't have exceptional speed. I wasn't very tall and I wasn't blessed with tons of power. But the one thing that God gave me was the determination to want to be the best and the desire to want to go out there and compete. I know a lot of times kids get tired of the game after playing it for so long. I just never seem to reach that point. I always see that there's more that I can do. That keeps me going."

Fernandez arrived at UCLA in 1989 and as a freshman in 1990 pitched the Bruins to an NCAA championship. She was named a first-team All-American and All-PAC 10 each of her four years while the team won two championships. As a senior for the Bruins, she had a 0.25 ERA, struck out 348 batters in 249 and 2/3 innings, and batted .510. When she wasn't pitching, she played third base. In addition to her service to the Bruins, she also played for Team USA, winning six games en route to a gold medal at the 1991 Pan American Games. She has appeared on two gold medal-winning Olympic Festival teams as well.

Fernandez earned a degree in psychology at UCLA, but she has pursued softball as a career since leaving college. In addition to playing for the perennial champion Raybestos Brakettes, she has conducted clinics and received modest athletic footwear endorsement contracts ("It's nothing like Shaquille O'Neal," she says). After helping her team to win yet another Olympic Festival gold medal in 1995, she began looking forward to a whole new goal—playing for the first-ever U.S. Olympic women's softball team.

LISA FERNANDEZ

American softball player

Born: Long Beach, California.

Education: Attended University of California, Los Angeles, earning degree in psychology.

Career Highlights:
- won first Amateur Softball Association championship at age 11
- pitched 69 shutouts, 37 no-hitters, and 12 perfect games throughout college career (four-time All-American)

- played for Team USA, winning six games en route to a gold medal, 1991 Pan American Games
- appeared on three gold medal–winning Olympic Festival teams
- played for two U.S. World Championship teams.

Awards: Named the American Softball Association's woman of the year, 1991 and 1992; named Olympic Athlete of the Year in softball, 1992 and 1993.

"I remember watching the '84 Olympics, thinking that someday I wanted to run around with the flag in front of everyone," Fernandez told the *Washington Post* in 1995. She may well be America's pitching ace—and one of its slugging leaders—in the 1996 Summer Games. Fernandez possesses a whole arsenal of pitches, from off-speed curve balls to the lethal "riseball" that whizzes to the plate and rises in the strike zone. Even though she is at the top of her game, she practices constantly and is never satisfied with her performance. "Repetition is everything," she declared in the *Los Angeles Times*. "If you can throw a ball over the plate nine times out of 10, you've got to keep trying for 10 out of 10."

This attitude has led to new challenges for Fernandez. Late in 1995 she was the top draft pick of a new women's professional softball league that will commence play in California after the Olympics. All of her success notwithstanding, Fernandez does not see herself as some sort of Wonder Woman endowed with heaps of natural ability. "God didn't give me that many physical talents," she concluded in *USA Today*. "But one thing He did give me was a lot of heart and a lot of tenacity. I always tell myself never to be satisfied."

MARY JOE
FERNANDEZ

A well-known name on the women's professional tennis circuit, Mary Joe Fernandez has been playing professionally since the age of 14. It has only been since 1990, when she started playing the women's circuit full-time, that she has begun to make a serious bid to become a top-ranked player. Probably her brightest moment in tennis was when she and doubles partner Gigi Fernandez of Puerto Rico captured the gold medal for the United States at the 1992 Olympics in Barcelona, defeating Spain's own Arantxa Sanchez Vicario and Conchita Martinez as King Juan Carlos looked on. Mary Joe also won a bronze medal in Olympic singles competition, and she has reached three Grand Slam finals.

Born in 1971 in the Dominican Republic to José and Silvia Fernandez, Mary Joe moved with her family to Miami when she was six months old. At age three she began to play tennis. Her sister Silvia recounted in the *New York Times* that Mary Joe often tagged along to her elder sister's tennis lessons. To keep her occupied, José bought her a racket and a bucket of balls that she could bounce off a wall. Just two years later she was good enough at volleying to qualify for lessons with a pro.

Mary Joe showed talent for tennis very early on. At age ten she won the United States Tennis Association Nationals for players 12 and under. At 11, she won the Orange Bowl singles title for players 12 and under. She proceeded to win the title again at age 14 for 16-and-under, and at age 16 for 18-and-under. She also won the United States Tennis Association championship for 16-and-under players and the U.S. Clay Court Championship for her age in 1984. Mary Joe played in her first professional tournament when she was 13, competing as an amateur. She beat her first-round opponent, 33-year-old Pam Teeguarden, but then lost the following match. That same year, she defeated the world's tenth-ranked player, Bonnie Gadusek, reaching the quarterfinals of the Lipton tournament. Mary Joe is also the youngest player ever to win a match at the U.S. Open.

As a 14-year-old freshman at Carrollton School of the Sacred Heart, Mary Joe began to feel pressure to turn pro and play the professional circuit

Mary Joe Fernandez celebrates a victorious match against Gabriela Sabatini in 1992. (UPI/Bettmann)

full time. She resisted the temptation and became a straight-A student at Carrollton. "I just decided that if I was going to go to school, I was going to do it right," she told *Sports Illustrated* in 1991. "And I wasn't ready to sacrifice being with my friends."

Instead Mary Joe entered four Grand Slam tournaments and various other selected events over the next three-and-a-half years, working them around her high school classes. Many credit her balanced approach with preventing her from burning out on the game as so often happens with precocious tennis teens. Nevertheless, she was able to gain valuable experience from the few events in which she competed. In her very first Wimbledon match as a 14-year-old, she faced her idol, Chris Evert Lloyd, losing in straight sets. She also missed her high school graduation because she was competing in the semifinals of the French Open.

In her first year as a full-time participant on the pro tour, Mary Joe won 40 of 50 singles matches and two tournaments, including her first ever

MARY JOE FERNANDEZ

American tennis player

Born: 1971 in Dominican Republic.

Career Highlights:

- won U.S. Tennis Association Nationals for players 12 and under at age ten, and for 16-and-under players at age 13

- captured Orange Bowl singles title for players 12 and under at age 11, for 16-and-under at age 14, and for 18-and-under at age 16

- won U.S. Clay Court Championship for her age in 1984

- won gold medal (with Gigi Fernandez) in doubles competition and bronze medal in singles competition, 1992 Olympic Games, Barcelona, Spain.

professional tournament championship in the Tokyo Indoors. With endorsements, her earnings topped $1 million in 1990 alone. Unfortunately, she also sustained several injuries that year, including a hamstring tear, a knee sprain, and tendinitis in her shoulder. These setbacks convinced Mary Joe that she needed a sound conditioning program to build upper body strength and overall fitness. Ever since, she has employed a strength coach.

Mary Joe's highest ranking as a pro came early in 1991, when she reached number four in the world. Recent years have seen her move more into doubles play, where she has been particularly effective with a variety of partners, including her Olympic co-medalist, Gigi Fernandez (no relation). Mary Joe was a millionaire before she was old enough to buy liquor, having earned more than a million dollars by age 19. Since then, her career earnings have topped $2.5 million—not including the value of the gold in that Olympic medal.

PEGGY FLEMING

FIGURE SKATER

"She remains the sport's artistic bellwether."

—E. M. Swift on Fleming in Sports Illustrated, *September 19, 1994*

On February 10, 1968, in Grenoble, France, Peggy Fleming launched the modern era in figure skating. Graceful, beautiful, and balletic, Fleming won the Olympic gold medal in Grenoble and then came home to a heroine's welcome in America. The only U.S. competitor to win a gold medal in the 1968 Olympics, she became the first in a long line of American skating superstars. As E. M. Swift noted in a September 19, 1994, *Sports Illustrated* profile, "Her skating appeared effortless, and therein lay its magic. She seemed to flow from one element to the next, seamlessly, weightlessly, like something blown about by the wind. No skater in any era could surpass Fleming's lyrical elegance on the ice. . . . She remains the sport's artistic bellwether."

Compared with many figure skating champions, Fleming came to the sport relatively late. She was born July 27, 1948, in San Jose, California, and lived there until she was nine. Then her family moved to Cleveland, and it was in that colder climate that she first strapped on skates. She took to the sport immediately and within two years had entered her first competition. In 1960, at the age of 11, she won the Pacific Coast Juvenile Figure Skating Championship.

In those days skating was considered a sport for the wealthy, who could well afford the expensive coaching fees and reserved rink time. Fleming's father was a press operator for newspapers, and he worked part-time jobs in order to help defray his daughter's expenses. The Fleming family returned to California in 1960, and most of Peggy's training over the next few years was conducted there. She rose quickly through the amateur skating ranks, winning the Pacific Coast Women's Championships in 1963 and her first of five straight U.S. championships in 1964. At 15, Fleming was the youngest skater ever to win a U.S. championship.

Fleming's quick success was actually aided by a tragedy. In 1961, a plane carrying the U.S. skating team crashed in Czechoslovakia, killing everyone on board. The untimely accident eliminated many of Fleming's more experienced American competitors. It also brought greater publicity

After winning the gold medal at the 1968 Olympics, Peggy Fleming turned pro, appearing here in the 1972 production of "Holiday on Ice." (Archive Photos)

for the young skater from California, who was touted as the "new hope" for American figure skating. Fleming accepted the pressure with grace and good humor. She attended the 1964 Olympic Games in Innsbruck, Austria, and finished a respectable sixth in the competition. Shortly thereafter she won her second national title and placed second in the 1965 North American Championships.

Fleming was ready to win medals in international competition, but one hurdle remained. After placing third at the 1965 World Championships, she realized that the high altitude of the venue—Colorado Springs, Colorado—caused her to become fatigued during her routine. In what was perhaps the ultimate family sacrifice, Fleming's father took a job with a newspaper in Colorado Springs so that Peggy could move there to train. In June of 1965 Fleming began preparing for the Olympics at the Broadmoor World Arena, while simultaneously attending classes at nearby Cheyenne Mountain High School. Her daily schedule included workouts from seven until eleven in the morning, and again from five until eight p.m.

The high altitude training made a difference. In Davos, Switzerland, Fleming won the 1966 World Championship, skating for a perfect score in the compulsory figures and earning high marks for her classically choreographed free skate. She won a fourth national championship and a second world title in 1967, and she was favored to win the gold medal at the 1968 Olympics in Grenoble.

As those Olympic games got under way, the world became aware of Peggy Fleming and her family's long years of financial sacrifice on her behalf. She took the ice in Grenoble wearing one of the many costumes her mother had made for her on the home sewing machine—a chartreuse skirted leotard trimmed with rhinestones. In fact the Olympic competition was nearly over before it began. Fleming entered the free skate portion with a commanding lead, having once again excelled in the compulsory figures. Despite simplifying two of her more difficult jumps—completing a single Axel instead of a double and failing to complete two rotations in her double Lutz—Fleming easily won the Olympic gold medal. She was the only American gold medal–winner at the 1968 Winter Games.

Years later, recalling her moment of Olympic glory, Fleming admitted that she had been extremely nervous during competition. "When everyone began saying I was sure to win, I felt an enormous burden of responsibility not to let myself or my country down," she told *Good Housekeeping* in February of 1992. The pressure of national expectations—and her family's shaky finances—convinced Fleming to turn professional soon after the 1968 Olympics ended.

PEGGY FLEMING

American figure skater

Born: July 27, 1948 in San Jose, California.

Career Highlights:

• won the Pacific Coast Juvenile Figure Skating Championship at age 11, 1960

• earned Pacific Coast Women's Championship, 1963

• won five straight U.S. Championships, 1964–68

• garnered World Championship, 1966 and 1967

• won gold medal, 1968 Olympic Games, Grenoble, France.

Few skaters before or since have enjoyed the popularity of Peggy Fleming in her heyday. In an era when White House invitations to athletes were uncommon, she traveled to Washington to meet the president. In 1980, she was the first skater ever to perform live at the White House. Her talents were showcased on television specials and in ice shows, especially the Ice Follies and Holiday on Ice. More recent generations recognize her as the ABC television commentator for skating events. Her influence on the sport itself is no less significant. At a time when the trend in skating was moving more toward athletic bravado, Fleming won championships with routines that accented balletic grace and fluidity of motion. Fellow skater Dick Button once said of Fleming: "She is a delicate lady on ice. With some skaters, there is a lot of fuss and feathers, but nothing is happening. With Peggy, there's no fuss and feathers, and a great deal is happening."

The mother of two grown sons, Fleming undertook a 30-city skating tour as recently as 1991. She is, according to E. M. Swift, "a lingering star who seems never to wear out her welcome."

DAWN FRASER

"I'm usually pretty relaxed, but there have been other times when I've been nervous. Once in a meet in Australia I started to peel off my warm-up suit and an official stopped me. I'd forgotten my bathing suit."

Swimming is a sport that loves youth, but Australian Dawn Fraser proved the exception to the rule. Fraser was a seasoned 19 when she won her first Olympic gold medal in 1956 and a veritable senior citizen when she won her third Olympic gold in 1964. The first woman to freestyle 100 meters in less than a minute, Fraser overcame a late start in the swimming world to endure as a world champion and Olympic medalist through almost a decade of competition.

Fraser was born in 1937, the youngest of eight children of a Sydney shipwright. Her father had been a professional soccer player, but he knew nothing about swimming and did not encourage his children to try the sport. They found the local municipal pool anyway, and Dawn spent all of her spare time there. Unfortunately, she did not have very much spare time—her mother was ill, and Dawn had to pitch in and help with the housework.

As she grew older, Fraser was tempted into local meets by her brothers, who felt she could be a champion. Without proper coaching she was all heart and no finesse, but she managed to make a name for herself anyway. She was 14 when she swam for the first time under the watchful eye of Harry Gallagher, one of Australia's noted swimming coaches. Gallagher convinced her family to invest in swimming lessons, promising them that Dawn had the talent to be an international star.

Fraser had some catching up to do, and she worked extremely hard in preparation for the 1956 Olympics. The Summer Games were held in Melbourne that year—a convenient location for the Aussie swimmer. A relative unknown at the time, she blitzed the 100-meter freestyle in 1:02, easily taking the gold medal. When a reporter sympathized with her for "not getting started sooner," Fraser stared him down and predicted that she would be at the 1960 Olympics in Rome as well. "I'd sort of like another of these," she said, fingering her medal.

True to her predictions, Fraser did indeed return to the 1960 Olympics, this time as a defending champion in the 100-meter freestyle. She again won the gold in the 100-meter race and narrowly missed taking a medal

Dawn Fraser relaxes in the pool after taking a practice swim in preparation for the Empire Games in 1958. (UPI/Bettmann)

in the 400-meter freestyle. Fraser earned some bad press at the 1960 Summer Games as well. Told that she wouldn't be needed for her country's 400-meter relay team, she went shopping on the day of that race. When she returned, she was informed that she would be swimming after all, and that the race was only 45 minutes away. She refused to participate on such short notice, and as a result was banned from the Australian team. Pleading her case at home after the Games, she was quickly re-instated.

Two medals might have been enough for many swimmers, but Fraser pressed on. She would be 27 at the 1964 Olympics in Tokyo, but she was also still in top form and a regular winner both on the national and international level. Just seven months before the 1964 Summer Games, she was involved in a serious automobile accident that killed her mother and injured herself and her sister. Her injury was a broken neck, and the doctors predicted that she would not swim again. They were wrong. "I had to fight back," Fraser explained. "That's what life is all about."

DAWN FRASER

Australian swimmer

Born: 1937 in Sydney, Australia.

Career Highlights:
- won gold medal in 100-meter freestyle, 1956 Olympic Games, Melbourne, Australia
- captured gold medal in 100-meter freestyle, 1960 Olympic Games, Rome, Italy
- acquired third consecutive gold medal in 100-meter freestyle, 1964 Olympic Games, Tokyo, Japan.

Fraser entered the 1964 Olympics with the nickname "Granny," based on her age. She proceeded to prove that she had not slowed down a bit, winning her third consecutive gold in the 100-meter freestyle. Finally, having proven that swimming is not necessarily the exclusive pursuit of the very young, she retired. She is a hero Down Under to this day.

JULI
FURTADO

Mountain bike champion Juli Furtado has her sights set on a new prize: the first-ever Olympic gold medal to be awarded in her sport. Mountain biking will be introduced as an Olympic event at the Summer Games in Atlanta, and Furtado—former world champion and national champion mountain biker—seems poised to take the Olympic crown just as she has so many others. A true Renaissance athlete, Furtado came to cycling after a career as a ski racer. Her excellence has rarely been challenged in the 1990s.

A native of New Jersey, Juliana Furtado launched her athletic career as a promising youngster on the U.S. ski team. Five operations later, however, she was forced off the slopes and into physical therapy, which eventually included, among other things, riding a bike. This she did with gusto: in her first year of competitive riding, she reigned as the National Road Champion, having dispatched the field with a masochistic 60-mile solo breakaway. "Skiing had come easy to me," she later told *Bicycling* magazine, "so I almost expected to excel in cycling. I never had to struggle."

Furtado's coach, David Farmer, has called her "a natural—someone who would excel even on the tennis court. And she's extremely focused." Convinced that road racing in the U.S. would not suit her in the long run because of her "horrible sprint," Furtado chose mountain biking instead and took to the dirt trails near her Colorado homestead. There she revealed herself to be a talented climber, an even more talented downhiller, and a consummate bike handler. In short, she was a natural. Her ski experience was helpful—mountain bikers can sometimes reach speeds in excess of 50 miles per hour on downhill routes. Control and clear thinking are essential.

The first year of mountain biking's world cup—and Furtado's first full year off-road—the Colorado phenom reigned as the world cross-country champion. That 1991 inaugural championship title augured things to come. The same year, Furtado added a litany of National Off-Road Bike Association (NORBA) first-place finishes to her resume, including the National Series overall title. She defended her championship the next year, and what's more, she

MOUNTAIN
BIKER

"I almost expected to excel in cycling. I never had to struggle."

JULI FURTADO

American mountain biker

Born: New Jersey

Career Highlights:

- reigned as the National Road Champion in first year of competitive riding
- became world cross-country champion, 1991

- won National Off-Road Bike Association (NORBA) overall title, 1991, 1992, 1993, 1994
- garnered world championship victory in downhill event, 1992.

Awards: First woman to be named Cyclist of the Year by *Velo News*, 1993.

---

notched a world championship victory in the downhill event, making her the first pro ever to win the rainbow jersey in both the downhill *and* cross-country events.

In 1993 Furtado was unstoppable. "I felt sorry for the other girls," she admitted to *Bicycling* magazine. Reeling in one win after another, Furtado owned a tremendous psychological edge on the competition. She nailed every one of the six NORBA nationals *and* all but one of the ten sanctioned Grundig World Cup skirmishes. In seven months' time, she collected 17 first-place finishes—out of 18 races entered. And when Furtado won, she won big: in every World Cup victory but one, she scorched the field, winning by no less than 60 seconds. *Velo News* was impressed enough to name her 1993's Cyclist of the Year, making her the first woman to join an exclusive club that includes such luminaries as Miguel Indurain, Greg LeMond, and Ned Overend.

The following year was less spectacular. Reigning for her fourth consecutive year as the NORBA women's national champion, Furtado placed second to Alison Sydor in the Grundig World Cup final. And—having announced in a pre-race press conference that she was off-form—she failed to place in the world championships. The year ended with the tragedy of her mother's suicide.

By 1995 Furtado was "weathering the storm," though she confessed to *Velo News*: "My training has been lackadaisical. I've lacked motivation for it. But when the racing begins, I'll try my hardest—I always do." Her motivation should certainly return as the 1996 Summer Games approach and she vies for a place on the first-ever U.S. Olympic mountain biking team. More history could be in the making for this intrepid cyclist and her daring cross-country rides. The world will be watching.

CARIN
JENNINGS
GABARRA

Sacrifice has been the name of the game for Carin Jennings Gabarra. A forward with the U.S. national women's soccer team, Gabarra has been a star and a featured member since 1991, when she won the Most Valuable Player award at the World Championships. Gabarra has played through long separations from her husband. She has lost jobs, or held three at a time in the off-season to help pay the bills. She has even endured injury-related setbacks in her quest to be on the first Olympic U.S. women's soccer team. All the same, she still loves the game.

The Rancho Palos Verdes, California, native attended the University of California, Santa Barbara, where—as Carin Jennings—she was a four-time All-American forward. She joined Team USA in preparation for the 1991 women's World Championships. At the world championship tournament, she scored six goals in as many games to help the Americans win the gold medal. Afterwards she was given the Golden Ball, the tournament's trophy for Most Valuable Player.

Trophies do not pay the bills, however. After the world championships, Jennings married soccer coach Jim Gabarra and took a "forced year" off from her sport. "The national team didn't have any games, and I didn't want to play for a club," she told *USA Today*. Unlike some of her Team USA mates, she did not want to relocate to Europe to play in a women's professional league. Instead, in 1993, she took a job as head women's soccer coach at the U.S. Naval Academy in Annapolis. She also headed a series of soccer clinics nationwide, sponsored by an athletic shoe manufacturer.

Those jobs meshed well with her renewed work with the national soccer team in 1993. A talented forward who is one of the best dribblers in the world and who can score or engineer the perfect assist, Gabarra leads the U.S. team in assists and has 48 international goals. So high is her reputation that she was named U.S. Soccer Federation Female Athlete of the Year in 1992— the year she did not play in an organized game.

SOCCER PLAYER

"She freezes players with her moves. It looks like she walks around them."

—U.S. Soccer coach Tony DiCicco

Carin Gabarra has amassed 48 international goals during her career.
(© D. Pensinger/Allsport Photography USA Inc.)

In a *USA Today* profile, Gabarra said that she enjoys coaching, even when she is tempted to jump in and show her less-talented players how to execute the perfect pass. "Sometimes it might be beneficial to step in and demonstrate, show the difference between what they're doing and how I want them to do it," she noted. "But generally, I think you have to step aside from the playing while you coach."

A nagging back injury has caused Gabarra to reduce her playing time in recent years, but she is still a featured performer with Team USA. When she retires from playing, she expects to coach for a very long time. Speaking of herself and her fellow national team members, she told *USA Today:* "We're the first generation of players who could play at a competitive level our whole life. Coaching is something most of us want to get into."

CARIN JENNINGS GABARRA

American soccer player

Born: 1965 in Rancho Palos Verdes, California.

Education: University of California, Santa Barbara.

Career Highlights:
- attained All-American status four years in a row during collegiate career
- played for gold medal at World Championship, 1991
- leads the U.S. team in assists and has 48 international goals.

Awards: Given Golden Ball (awarded to most valuable player) at the World Championships, 1991; named U.S. Soccer Federation Female Athlete of the Year, 1992.

ZINA GARRISON

"Things are changing a little bit in tennis, but not a lot. Tennis is still not visible in many homes. If you don't have cable, you don't see it much. I really think if the black community took interest, we'd see lots of new talent."

One of the top rated and highest paid tennis professionals in the world and the first black woman to reach the Wimbledon finals since Althea Gibson did so in the late 1950s, Zina Garrison can truly be classified as a trailblazer. Among the few black women to achieve success in a game dominated by whites, she appears not to be disturbed by her singular status. She believes it is her personal attributes—the talent and dedication she brings to the game—that are most important.

Garrison had none of the childhood advantages that produce budding tennis stars. She was born in 1963 in Houston, Texas, the last of seven children born to Mary and Ulysses Garrison. Zina's 42-year-old mother was so sure that she would have no more children that she gave her youngest daughter a name beginning with "Z." With many years between Zina and her older siblings, she grew up almost as isolated as an only child.

Tragedy struck the Garrison family when Zina was still a baby. Her father died unexpectedly of a stroke, and her brother Willie developed a fatal brain tumor after being struck in the eye by a baseball. The sudden losses bound Zina tightly to her mother and to her brother Rodney, who took her with him to nearby MacGregor Park, a municipal playground with tennis courts.

At MacGregor Park, Garrison enjoyed watching local tennis coach John Wilkerson give private lessons. Eventually Wilkerson gave her a wooden racket and showed her the fundamentals of the game. She was an enthusiastic student who showed natural talent, and before long Wilkerson was coaching her with an eye toward the major national tournaments. Garrison told the *Chicago Tribune* that her coach constantly reminded her that she faced a distinct disadvantage when she met opponents who had been nurtured by well-paid, country club professionals. Garrison remembered Wilkerson telling her, "You have to be two and three times better than the others."

No problem. Garrison challenged the stereotypes and put them to rest. In 1981, at the age of 17, she won the junior singles titles at both

Zina Garrison sends the ball flying over the net in this U.S. Open match in 1994. (AP/Wide World Photos)

Wimbledon and the U.S. Open. The following year she turned professional soon after graduating from Ross S. Sterling High School. By the end of 1982 she had achieved a respectable 16th in the world tennis rankings.

With Wilkerson as her full-time coach, Garrison embarked on a hectic round of tennis tournaments in the United States, Europe, and the Far East. She was rarely able to return to Houston, and she worried about her mother constantly. Her fears were well-founded: Mary Garrison died of an illness related to diabetes in 1983. For years afterward, Zina Garrison struggled to accept her mother's death and to come to terms with her grief. She turned to the tennis courts for release, rising in 1985 from ninth in the rankings to fifth. That same year she reached the semifinals at Wimbledon and the quarterfinals at the Australian and U.S. Opens, earning $274,470 in prize money.

The emotional turmoil that Garrison felt eventually led her into an eating disorder that robbed her of her health and strength. By 1986 her problems had become acute, and she changed coaches and sought therapy. She re-

ZINA GARRISON

American tennis player

Born: 1963 in Houston, Texas.

Career Highlights:

• won, at the age of 17, junior singles titles at Wimbledon and U.S. Open, 1981

• reached semifinals at Wimbledon and quarterfinals at Australian and U.S. Opens, earning $274,470 in prize money, 1985

• earned a gold medal in doubles play (with Pam Shriver) and a bronze medal in singles competition, 1988 Olympic Games, Seoul, South Korea

• ranked fourth internationally, 1989

• advanced to the finals at Wimbledon, beating Monica Seles and Steffi Graf along the way, 1990

• won French Open, 1990.

Awards: Voted "Most Impressive Newcomer" by Women's International Tennis Association, 1982; named "Player Who Makes a Difference" by *Family Circle* magazine, 1992.

---

bounded by the 1988 Olympics, where she earned a gold medal in doubles play with Pam Shriver as her partner, and a bronze medal in singles competition. Her winning ways continued into 1989, when she was ranked fourth internationally and became the last person to defeat the legendary Chris Evert in a tournament.

Garrison's best year to date was 1990. She advanced to the finals at Wimbledon—beating Monica Seles and Steffi Graf in the process—only to lose to Martina Navratilova. Still, the near-victory at Wimbledon helped Garrison to earn more product endorsement contracts, including a substantial one with Reebok footwear. Newly married to Houston executive Willard Jackson, Garrison found herself busier than ever, juggling tournaments, endorsements, and personal appearances. She told the *Detroit Free Press* that she actually welcomes the hectic lifestyle. "I enjoy it," she said. "I just have to get used to it and I should learn how to say no."

Zina Garrison is well known for her community service work. Since 1988 she has supported youth organizations, anti-drug programs, and projects designed to improve the lot of the homeless through funding from the Zina Garrison Foundation. In the summer of 1992 she opened the Zina Garrison All-Court Tennis Academy, which provides opportunities for economically disadvantaged children to increase their self-confidence through tennis. Her mission is to encourage young people who may be potential tennis professionals, especially African Americans and other minorities. In honor of all her work on behalf of disadvantaged youngsters, Garrison was named 1992 "Player Who Makes a Difference" by *Family Circle* magazine.

Garrison is one athlete who doesn't mind being a role model. "It's hard for black kids, Mexican kids, white kids to have much self-image when their parents are away on jobs making money," she told the *Chicago Tribune.* "I tell them they don't have to be an athlete to acquire self-image. Be what you are. Writer. Student. Let it happen, and draw off that." As for herself, Garrison claims that her learning years in the Houston public parks imbued her with a strength that has carried her to success. "You have to be meaner . . . to come from the parks," she concluded in the *Chicago Tribune.* "Those 'scars' . . . left me stubborn and tough and determined not to quit. I'm known for that. I never give up."

ALTHEA GIBSON

"I hope that I have accomplished just one thing: that I have been a credit to tennis and my country."

Althea Gibson's accomplishments in tennis rank among the most inspiring in modern professional sports. At a time when the game of tennis was completely dominated by whites, Gibson emerged with enough talent and determination to win multiple championships at Wimbledon and the U.S. Open in the late 1950s. Gibson was not only the first black woman to compete in these prestigious tournaments, she was also the first black person ever to win a tennis title. She became a role model for blacks of both sexes who sought the right to compete in previously segregated sporting events. Gibson forged into the previously all-white field of women's tennis with the conviction that racism could not stop her, and she handled difficult situations with a grace and earthy humor that brought her a firm following among American sports fans.

The oldest of five children, Gibson was born in Silver, South Carolina, on April 25, 1927. At the time of her birth, her father was working as a sharecropper on a cotton farm. The crops failed several years in a row, and the impoverished Gibson family moved to New York City, where they settled in a small Harlem apartment.

Gibson grew up in the ghetto, a restless youngster who longed to "be somebody." School was not the answer for her. She often played hooky to go to the movies and had little rapport with her teachers. As she entered her teen years, she was sent to the Yorkville Trade School where her problems only worsened. She was even threatened with reform school if her truancy and attitude problems continued.

Even before she was of legal age to drop out of school, Gibson applied for working papers and quit attending classes. She held a series of jobs but was not able to keep any of them very long. By the time she was 14, she was a ward of the New York City Welfare Department. The social workers there helped her to find steady work, and they steered her into the local Police Athletic League sports programs.

Gibson's first contact with tennis was through the game of paddleball. The game is similar to conventional tennis but uses wooden paddles

Althea Gibson reaches for victory at Wimbledon in 1957; she won both singles and doubles competition that year. (Archive Photos/Express News)

instead of rackets. Somehow paddleball appealed to Gibson the way nothing had before, and before long she switched to tennis itself, using a second-hand racket given to her by a caring city employee. Soon Gibson's natural talent had brought her to the attention of members of the interracial New York Cosmopolitan Club. They sponsored her for junior membership and paid for private lessons with a tennis professional named Fred Johnson. Given this chance at a different kind of success, Gibson curbed her anti-social behavior, buckled down, and practiced her tennis. Just one year later, in 1941, she won her first important tournament, the New York State Open Championship.

In 1944 and 1945 Gibson captured the national Negro girls' tennis championship. This success drew the backing of two influential patrons, a pair of surgeons who agreed to provide Gibson room and board *and* tennis lessons if she would return to high school. Gibson accepted the offer and moved to Wilmington, North Carolina, where she lived with one of the surgeons and his family and practiced tennis on his private court. Beginning in 1948 she won the first of nine consecutive Negro national championships, a feat that quickly brought her recognition within the white tennis community as well.

Gibson graduated tenth in her class at North Carolina's Williston Industrial High School in 1949. She then accepted a tennis scholarship to Florida Agricultural and Mechanical University in Tallahassee. She wanted to study music, as she could play the saxophone and had a fine singing voice. Counselors at the college persuaded her to stay with tennis, and she majored in physical education instead.

Her biggest battle during those years was the fight to secure the right to compete in major tennis tournaments against white opponents. Many of the clubs that hosted the tournaments did not admit blacks. In 1950 Gibson sought an invitation from the United States Lawn Tennis Association to play in the national grass court championships at Forest Hills, Long Island. The invitation never came. Other tournaments at private clubs barred her as well. Frustrated but undefeated by the rampant racism, Gibson expressed her disappointment in a dignified and professional manner. Before too long she began to find allies in prominent positions. One such ally, the editor of *American Lawn Tennis* magazine, wrote an editorial that lambasted the "color barrier" in tennis, especially where it applied to Gibson. That editorial, as well as her own public demeanor, opened the doors of big-time tennis to Althea Gibson.

In 1952 Gibson was ranked seventh nationally in women's singles competition. The following year she dropped to 70th. She considered leaving the sport entirely, especially after she earned a bachelor's degree in 1953 and

ALTHEA GIBSON

American tennis player

Born: April 25, 1927 in Silver, South Carolina.

Education: Attended Williston Industrial High School in North Carolina; accepted a tennis scholarship to Florida Agricultural and Mechanical University, where she earned a bachelor's degree in 1953.

Career Highlights:
- won New York State Open Championship, 1941
- captured the national Negro girls' tennis championship, 1944 and 1945
- won the first of nine consecutive Negro national championships, 1948
- won singles and doubles championships at Wimbledon, 1957 and 1958
- won U.S. Open at Forest Hills, 1957 and 1958.

took a teaching job at Lincoln University in Missouri. Her former coaches encouraged her to press on, however, and in 1955 she was chosen as one of four American women sent on a "good will" tennis tour of Southeast Asia and Mexico.

Black people seeking equal treatment in all walks of American life pointed proudly to the success of Althea Gibson in 1957 and 1958. Gibson appeared at Wimbledon both years, seeded first on both occasions, and she won the singles *and* doubles championships both years. She also won the U.S. national championship at Forest Hills in 1957 and 1958. Then, still at the top of her game, she shocked the world by announcing her retirement. She admitted that the most pressing reason for her decision was money—she simply did not make enough playing tennis to meet her needs.

The lure of sports was powerful, however. By 1963, after being unsuccessful as a singer and actress, Gibson embarked on another quest just as ground-breaking as the first. She qualified for the Ladies Professional Golf Association (LPGA) and began competing in important golf tournaments—the first black woman to achieve that honor. Gibson never had the success with golf that she had with tennis, however. She took home little prize money, although she participated in the LPGA tour from 1963 until 1967. As late as 1990 she attempted a comeback with the LPGA but failed to qualify.

In the 1970s and 1980s Gibson served as a tennis coach and mentor to athletes, especially young black women. Having married a New Jersey businessman named William A. Darben, Gibson concentrated her efforts in Essex County, New Jersey, where she served for many years on the Parks Commission. She also took posts with the New Jersey State Athletic Control Board and the Governor's Council on Physical Fitness. Gibson retired in 1992, save for personal appearances in connection with golf or tennis events.

Althea Gibson's contribution to American sports is unparalleled. Her determination to play in the top tennis tournaments at a time when blacks had little access to exclusive tennis clubs helped to create a climate of acceptance that persists to this day. Elitism may never be completely eliminated from sports such as golf and tennis, but the contributions of Althea Gibson—and their effect on subsequent generations of black American athletes—are of lasting value to the sporting world.

DIANA
GOLDEN

Diana Golden did not begin as a great athlete. During her early years, she was awkward and not athletically inclined. Always the last to be picked for a team in gym class, Golden even began to hate sports. Then, because it looked like fun, Golden took up skiing. By the time she was 12 years old she had become fairly proficient at skiing and was actually enjoying participating in a sport. But then her right leg mysteriously fell out from under her. Discovering she had cancer, doctors told her that her leg would have to be removed. Golden was devastated, wondering how she could be so young and have a disease like cancer.

Recovering her optimism in the wake of her leg amputation, Golden quickly realized that she was still *alive,* whether she had one leg or not. Within a few weeks, she was once again speeding down the ski slopes. A new type of ski competitor was born—one who could dominate races for disabled participants *and* hold her own amongst two-legged skiers.

Golden remained a weekend skier until her junior year in high school when David Livermore, the ski coach at Massachusetts Lincoln-Sudbury High School, asked her to join the team. By watching Golden ski only once, Livermore realized her potential and began training her. Experiencing the personal satisfaction of intense physical training, Golden left her "klutzy" body behind. By her senior year in high school she was in top shape and competing in the World Games for Disabled Athletes in Geilo, Norway. By the end of that year, as the greatest athlete on the United States Disabled Ski Team, she won the World Handicapped Championships.

While having only one ski to control gave Golden great form and precision on the slopes, it required more skill than regular two-legged skiing. Yet Golden did not believe that simply adapting to her disability and her subsequent accomplishments made her a hero. As her public image and her private reality began to clash in her second year at Dartmouth College, Golden withdrew into herself. After making a commitment to the Christian religion, she felt a conflict between her new-found faith and the pressure to win on the

SKIER

"I was a klutz. If you had ever told me that I would make being an athlete my profession, I would have laughed at you and my family would have laughed at you. They still laugh."

191

slopes that came with her achievement. As her struggle intensified she trained less and less. By the beginning of her senior year at Dartmouth, Golden realized she had skied only three times since her sophomore year.

As graduation loomed closer, Golden began to wonder why she had let the media manipulate her by pressuring her to maintain her status as a hero and role model. Realizing that she had been pushed away from something she loved, Golden questioned the power of the media and the conflict it had caused with her faith. After graduating she took a job as a computer software salesperson, but she quickly became bored with the direction her life was taking. Finally, after repeated urgings by friends, Golden agreed to go on a ski weekend. Surprising all of her friends, Golden jumped onto the most difficult slalom course and sailed flawlessly down the hill.

Golden realized her love for the powder and the exhilaration of speeding down the slope had never completely vanished. Needing to get back into shape, she began a rigorous training routine with both disabled and "normie" (two-legged) skiers. Despite her "disadvantage," Golden watched and learned from the two-legged skiers and was soon even passing them on the slopes. A new and even greater challenge awaited Golden as she reentered the competitive arena: in order to successfully compete in national championships she needed a sponsor. Approaching the Rossignol Ski Company, Golden challenged them to back her not as a disabled skier but as a skier who would win. Seeing her confidence and her amazing ability on the slopes, the company quickly agreed.

Success then followed Golden wherever she set her skies down. With her return in 1985 she won four gold medals and nineteen championships. In 1985 she began racing against two-legged skiers in formal competition. Meeting frustration not only because she lost but also because the organizers of the competition made disabled skiers go last, Golden decided to fight for a rules change. Near the end of 1985 the United States Ski Association did indeed alter the governing rules. After fifteen "natural" competitors had skied, places were to be reserved for disabled skiers, thus providing not only equality but also exposure for disabled skiers. The new procedure became known as the Golden Rule, in honor of Golden.

From 1986–1990 Golden dominated the World Ski Championships, while she also won the Olympic gold medal in 1988 in the giant slalom for disabled skiers. Now that she was not required to ski on slopes that had been virtually destroyed by previous competitors, she began to provide competition for "normal" skiers. In 1987 she placed tenth out of forty in a slalom race as the only disabled skier in the competition. Golden saw this as her greatest victory, even more so than the four consecutive gold medals at the world disabled championships.

DIANA GOLDEN

American skier

Education: Attended Dartmouth College.

Career Highlights:
- won the World Handicapped Championships as a senior in high school
- won four gold medals and nineteen championships
- placed tenth out of forty in a slalom race as the only disabled skier in the competition, 1987

- won gold medal in the giant slalom for disabled skiers, 1988 Olympic Games, Calgary, Canada.

Awards: Won the Beck Award for being the best American skier in international competition, 1986; named Female Skier of the Year by the U.S. Olympic Committee, and U.S. Female Alpine Skier of the Year by *Ski Racing* magazine, 1988.

As a result of her efforts for disabled athletes, Golden was the recipient of many prestigious awards. In 1986 she won the Beck Award for being the best American skier in international competition. In 1988 she was named Female Skier of the Year by the U.S. Olympic Committee, while *Ski Racing* magazine named her U.S. Female Alpine Skier of the Year.

Golden retired from competitive skiing in 1991. She told people she intended to take up rock climbing and teaching both one- and two-legged skiers. But before she did that she went to Utah by herself for four days and walked across the desert on two forearm crutches, determined to find out more about herself and her athletic ability. When Golden returned she was ready to begin her new life. Being a role model may be enough for some people, but for Diana Golden, being *successful* was more to the point.

EVONNE GOOLAGONG

"Tennis is my whole life, and I could not imagine any other."

Evonne Goolagong was the first Aboriginal Australian to achieve prominence in a sporting endeavor, and to this day she is one of the most successful athletes ever to come from Down Under. A five-time Wimbledon finalist, Goolagong faced some of the greatest women's tennis players in history and showed herself their equal in every respect. Having won well over a million dollars in the course of her career, she emerged victorious at two Wimbledon tournaments, one French Open, and four Australian Open championships.

Evonne Fay Goolagong was born on July 31, 1951, in New South Wales, Australia. She was the third of eight children born to Kenneth and Linda Goolagong, both of whom were part Aboriginal. The Goolagongs were very poor and lived in the tiny town of Barellan, where Kenneth worked as a farm laborer, sheep shearer, and occasional mechanic. Young Evonne spent whole days playing with tennis balls, and even at the tender age of five she earned pocket money by retrieving balls at the local tennis club. She received her first tennis racket at the age of six and quickly began devoting every spare hour to the sport.

Goolagong learned tennis basics from members of Barellan's War Memorial Tennis Club. When she was ten years old, she began working with Vic Edwards, perhaps Australia's best-known tennis coach at the time. Edwards lived in a suburb of Sidney and owned his own tennis school. So impressed was he with Evonne's natural talent and desire that he invited her to live with his family and train at his school. Goolagong was not forgotten by the townspeople of Barellan, however. They raised money to help foot her bills and buy her the clothing and equipment she would need to compete on a national level.

Having won many of the important Australian amateur championships, Goolagong embarked on her first international tour in 1970. She won seven of 21 tournaments she entered in such countries as Great Britain, Holland, France, and Germany. She lost in the first round at Wimbledon that

At the start of a great career, Evonne Goolagong heads to victory in this 1971 Wimbledon match. (AP/Wide World Photos)

EVONNE GOOLAGONG

Australian tennis player

Born: July 31, 1951 in New South Wales, Australia.

Career Highlights:

- won the French Open and Wimbledon singles competition, 1971
- won Australian Open singles competition, 1974–77
- won Australian Open doubles crown, 1971, 1974, 1975, and 1976
- helped Australia to win Federation Cups, 1971, 1973, and 1974
- won Wimbledon singles competition, 1980.

Awards: Elected to the International Tennis Hall of Fame, 1988.

year, but the experience of playing in such an important event gave her greater confidence and poise.

In 1971 Goolagong turned professional and lost no time establishing herself on the tennis tour. She beat fellow Australian Helen Gourlay to win the French Open and then stunned the favored Margaret Smith Court with a Wimbledon finals victory. Smith Court, who was also Australian, hailed Goolagong as her logical successor on the international tennis scene—quite an honor, as Smith Court had been a top-ranked champion for many years.

Throughout the 1970s and into the 1980s, Goolagong remained among the top players in professional tennis. She made the Wimbledon finals three more times in the 1970s, losing to Billie Jean King in 1972 and 1975 and to Chris Evert in 1976. No one could touch her at the Australian Open, however. She won that event every year between 1974 and 1977, and she also won the Australian doubles crown in 1971, 1974, 1975, and 1976. Goolagong was a mainstay of Australia's Federation Cup team, which won Cups in 1971, 1973, and 1974 and reached the finals in 1975 and 1976.

By 1980 many observers were writing Goolagong off as a has-been. She surprised them all by winning Wimbledon that year, beating the likes of Hana Mandlikova, Wendy Turnbull, Tracy Austin, and Evert in the only Wimbledon singles finals round ever to end in a tie-breaker. Goolagong's 1980 Wimbledon victory was doubly impressive since she was by that time a mother, having married Roger Cawley and given birth to the first of their children. No woman with children had won a Wimbledon singles final in sixty-six years.

Goolagong retired from tennis in 1983, having won $1,399,431 in prize money. She was elected to the International Tennis Hall of Fame in 1988.

SHANE GOULD

When Shane Gould got home from the 1972 Munich Summer Olympics, she said, "I'm tired. I'm looking forward to school. I wish to be an ordinary teenager." Not an easy order when, at 15, you've won five Olympic medals, including three golds that set world record times. The young Australian phenomenon had American women swimmers so spooked at Munich, they wore t-shirts that read: "All that glitters is not Gould." It didn't help much.

Gould, born September 4, 1956, in Brisbane, Queensland, could swim underwater at the age of three. At six she began professional lessons and at 13 started the serious training that would bring her to international acclaim and the amazingly low heart rate of 40 beats per minute. By 1971 she held every women's freestyle record up to 1500 meters.

Her 1972 Olympic victories came in the 200-meter and 400-meter freestyles and the 200-meter individual medley. She took a silver medal in the 800-meter and a bronze in the 100-meter freestyle races, which were her first freestyle losses in two years. Gould's parents were nearly as big a presence as their daughter at the Summer Games that year. Her mother, Shirley Gould, had already written a book, *Swimming the Shane Gould Way*.

In a classic case of early burnout, Gould announced her retirement just a year after the 1972 Olympics. At 18 she married a 25-year-old Bible student named Neil Innes. After their outdoor wedding, Gould told reporters: "Instead of saying the formal vows, we made up our own. It seemed to be in line with what we believe. We like the open air and surfing."

SWIMMER

"All that glitters is not Gould."

—Slogan on t-shirts worn by U.S. women swimmers at 1972 Olympics

197

SHANE GOULD

Australian swimmer

Born: September 4, 1956 in Brisbane, Queensland, Australia.

Career Highlights:

- took home gold medals for 200-meter and 400-meter freestyles and 200-meter individual medley, 1972 Olympic Games, Munich, Germany

- won silver medal in 800-meter freestyle and bronze in the 100-meter freestyle, 1972 Olympic Games, Munich, Germany.

STEFFI GRAF

They call it the Grand Slam, and it is tennis's biggest challenge: victories in the Australian and French Opens, Wimbledon, and the U.S. Open, all in the same year. So improbable is a Grand Slam that only five players have done it in the history of the professional tennis tour. Steffi Graf is one of them.

During her career, Graf has been the best women's tennis player in the world, twice spending long periods of time as the game's top-ranked player. She burst onto the tennis scene in 1986 as a precocious 16-year-old and has stood at or near the top of the rankings virtually ever since. Her Grand Slam occurred in 1988, the same year she won a gold medal at the Seoul Olympics. Graf stands poised to dominate tennis perhaps through the rest of this century.

Stephanie Maria Graf was born June 14, 1969, in Mannheim, West Germany, and grew up in the small German town of Bruhl. Her father, Peter, and mother, Heidi, were both tennis players. When Graf was three years old, she began to drag out her father's rackets and ask to play. Eventually, Peter Graf sawed off the end of one of his rackets and gave it to Steffi, who was soon bouncing the ball off walls and breaking the family's lamps. A makeshift tennis court was constructed in the family basement, consisting of two chairs connected by a string. Peter and Steffi used this "court" to play mock tournaments, with the victor winning ice cream with strawberries on top.

Peter Graf quickly realized that his daughter had extraordinary talent. He was so sure she could be a champion that he quit his job as an automobile insurance salesman and opened a tennis club in Bruhl. Steffi, with her father as full-time coach, began to beat other players her age. She was six when she won her first junior tournament, and by the age of 13 she had won both the European championships in her age group and the German junior championship in the 18-and-under division. In 1982, at the age of 13, she quit school and joined the women's professional tour, becoming the second-youngest player ever to be given a ranking, number 124. Just two years later she advanced to the quarterfinals at Wimbledon and won a gold medal in a tennis demonstration at the 1984 Olympic Games.

> *"I am never afraid to lose to anybody. All I want to do is play good tennis and have fun. I want so much to hit it hard—and have it go in."*

199

Steffi Graf's powerful forehand has served her well, as in this victorious U.S. Open final in 1988. (UPI/Bettmann)

Graf came into her own in 1986 with a victory over Chris Evert at the Family Circle Cup tournament. She went on to win eight of 14 tournaments she entered in 1986 and came in second in three others. In an effort to improve her game even more, she began a strict training program that included running, weightlifting, jumping rope, and playing tennis. The hard work paid off in 1987 when she finally won the French Open, defeating Martina Navratilova in the finals. At the time Graf was the youngest-ever French Open champion. She also advanced to the finals at Wimbledon and the U.S. Open, falling to Navratilova on each occasion. But Graf did well enough in other tournaments to become the number one-ranked player in the world. She lost only two of 72 matches she played in 1987 and won 11 of the 13 tournaments she entered.

In 1988 Graf made history by becoming only the third woman ever to win all four Grand Slam tournaments in the same year. She triumphed over Chris Evert to win the Australian Open, shut out opponent Natalia Zvereva in the French Open final, staged a dramatic come-from-behind victory over the favored Navratilova at Wimbledon (she also won the doubles title, paired with Gabriela Sabatini), and defeated Sabatini 6-3, 3-6, 6-1 to take the U.S. Open. Just a few days after nailing down the Grand Slam, Graf added an Olympic gold medal, the first awarded for tennis in modern times.

A loss to Arantxa Sanchez Vicario at the French Open was the only thing that kept Graf from winning a second Grand Slam. She was victorious in the 1989 Australian Open and defeated Navratilova in the Wimbledon finals and the U.S. Open. When Graf beat Mary Joe Fernandez in the finals of the 1990 Australian Open, she'd won eight of the last nine Grand Slam tournaments. Between June 1989 and May 1990, Graf won 66 straight matches, the second-longest winning streak in the history of women's tennis.

A new challenger arrived in the 1990s: Monica Seles. Graf suffered her first loss to Seles in the finals at the 1990 French Open, and her game began to suffer just a bit. Graf's biggest victory in the next two years was another Wimbledon title—but Seles did not participate in that tournament. In several dramatic head-to-head confrontations in 1992, Seles got the best of Graf. Seles beat Graf in the French Open. Graf beat Seles at Wimbledon. Seles went on to win the U.S. Open after Graf was eliminated in the quarterfinals. Soon enough, Seles had toppled Graf from the number one ranking.

What appeared to be the decade's most exciting tennis rivalry was interrupted by tragedy. On April 30, 1993, Seles was stabbed at a tournament in Germany by an emotionally disturbed fan. When asked why he did it, the attacker said he was a big fan of Graf and wanted her to be the number one-ranked player again. He got his wish, because Graf did resume her top ranking—but she was mortified that anyone might act so irrationally and use her as an excuse.

STEFFI GRAF

German tennis player

Born: June 14, 1969 in Mannheim, West Germany.

Career Highlights:

- attained number one ranking in the world, losing only two of 72 matches and winning 11 of the 13 tournaments she entered, 1987
- won French Open, 1987, 1988, and 1993
- triumphed as Grand Slam champion, winning Australian, French, and U.S. Opens, and Wimbledon, 1988
- earned gold medal in singles competition, 1988 Olympic Games, Seoul, South Korea
- won Australian Open, 1988, 1989, 1990, and 1994
- won U.S. Open singles competition in 1988, 1989, 1993, 1994, and 1995
- won Wimbledon singles, 1988, 1989, 1991, 1992, 1993, and 1994; won Wimbledon doubles title (with Gabriela Sabatini), 1988
- won 66 straight matches between June 1989 and May 1990, the second-longest winning streak in the history of women's tennis.

Without Seles to challenge her, Graf again dominated women's tennis in 1993, winning the French Open, Wimbledon, and the U.S. Open. For the third time, Graf had won at least three of the four Grand Slam tournaments in a single year. She was happy to be back on top, though troubled by Seles's injury.

Only an upset by American Mary Pierce in the semifinals of the French Open deprived Graf of yet another Grand Slam attempt in 1994. A repeat Grand Slam does not seem out of the question for the sturdy Graf, who is still under 30 and at the top of her game. The return of Seles to competition in 1995 has given new impetus to Graf as well—she defeated Seles in the finals of the 1995 U.S. Open and might see her as an opponent at the 1996 Olympic Games. Graf is fifth on the all-time list in Grand Slam singles titles for women and fourth on the all-time tournament titles list for women.

Needless to say, tennis has made Steffi Graf a very wealthy woman. She had earned $13 million in prize money through 1994 and many millions more through product endorsements and her own line of clothing, the Steffi Graf Collection. Few opponents have emerged with the potential to unseat Graf in recent years. She enjoys all-around ability that has allowed her to remain a strong contender for better than a decade. Her topspin forehand may be the best in the history of women's tennis, and her powerful serve and lightning speed give her tremendous edges against her rivals. As Navratilova once said of Graf: "I think she can do pretty much anything."

MICHELE
GRANGER

Someone once called Michele Granger "college softball's sultana of strikeouts." A world-class pitcher since her high school years, Granger holds the all-time NCAA record for strikeouts (1,640), strikeouts for one season (484), and strikeouts in a game (26). She has pitched more than 25 no-hitters, including five perfect games. Granger burst onto the scene as a star of the 1986 women's softball world championships, where she pitched a one-hitter and a perfect game en route to the gold medal. Since then she has dazzled at the Pan American Games and the Olympic Festival, as well as the University of California at Berkeley. Women's softball will be a sanctioned sport at the 1996 Summer Olympics, and the determined southpaw Granger is sure to be a figure on America's team.

Although only 26 years old, Granger says she is past her prime as a softball pitcher. She claims that she peaked in the eighth grade, when she had more time to practice and fewer demands on her energy. She began playing softball in the third grade as a righthanded shortstop and moved to the pitching mound two years later when her parents became managers of her team. Her father, Mike Granger, encouraged her to use her whole body to pitch, rather than just her arms. Some of his training techniques were almost bizarre—when Michele grew tired or frustrated with the sport, he would goad her to greater perfection by catching her pitches bare-handed and teasing her. He taught her to throw at a small opening in a piece of wood and even tied her to a tree to help correct over-stepping in her delivery. "One time somebody wrote an article and it sounded like [my father] was abusing me," Granger told the *Philadelphia Inquirer*. "It wasn't like that."

Her father's training efforts produced results. Granger's underhanded "riseball" has been clocked at better than 70 miles per hour. Since the pitching rubber is closer to home plate in softball, that speed translates to a 96-m.p.h. fastball in baseball. Small wonder that Granger exploded as a world class pitcher while still in high school, being named 1986 Sportswoman of the Year in the sport by no less than the U.S. Olympic Committee. At 14 Granger

"Not only do all of us on the team that were chosen feel a special obligation being a first-time sport in the Olympics, but we also feel an obligation to a lot of the players that didn't make it, and for the players that helped us get in the Olympic sport."

Michele Granger, the "sultana of strikeouts," pitches a one-hitter to lead the U.S. team to a gold medal at the 1987 Pan American Games. (AP/Wide World Photos)

and her Santa Monica Raiders won the 18-and-under national championship. At 16, as a pitcher for Team USA, she hurled a no-hitter at the world championships. The next year, 1987, she took the U.S. to a gold medal at the Pan Am Games. At a time when most athletes are just getting started, she was inducted into the Amateur Athletics Hall of Fame.

Recruited by numerous colleges, Granger chose the University of California, where she broke the NCAA record for strikeouts and posted a 0.16 earned run average as a senior. She graduated in 1993 with a double major in history and mass communications. While still in college she teamed with fellow pitchers Lisa Fernandez and Debbie Doom to breeze undefeated through nine games as Team USA won yet another Pan American gold, in 1991.

For some time after she graduated from college, Granger considered retiring from fast-pitch softball. She had married an attorney named John Poulos, and she thought she wanted to settle down and have a family. Instead, new challenges arose that changed her mind. One was the inclusion of softball as a medal sport at the 1996 Olympic Games. Although nursing tendinitis in her left rotator cuff, Granger auditioned for, and won a spot on the first woman's Olympic softball team.

Granger has been pitching with the team in preparation for the first-ever Olympic softball tournament in 1996. The three-time winner of the Bertha Tickey Award, given to the outstanding pitcher in the ASA Women's Major Fast Pitch National Championship, she will be a force on the rubber as the Americans try to nail the first Olympic softball gold medal. After that she will become a pioneering member of the Women's Professional Fast-Pitch League, destined for a team in California.

Granger is a modest woman who talks about improving her game rather than bragging about her strikeout record. Softball, she told the *St. Paul Pioneer Press,* is "a game and an individual battle." She added: "When I'm done with one batter I forget about it and move on to the next. . . . Strikeouts are what I do. It's nice to get the records for the type of thing you are known for."

 A NEW LEAGUE

Michele Granger was asked as a teenager if she would want to play professional softball if the opportunity arose. "Only if I'd get paid enough," the seventeen-year-old whiz kid replied. Apparently the Women's Professional Fastpitch league is offering enough, because Granger has signed on to play in the league's inaugural season. President and CEO Mitzi Swentzell is planning to have six teams in the league, playing a 72-game schedule starting in the summer of 1996. In a draft held in November 1995, Granger was drafted along with Lisa Fernandez, Dot Richardson, Sheila Cornell, and Julie Smith.

MICHELE GRANGER

American softball player

Education: Attended University of California at Berkeley, graduating in 1993 with a double major in history and mass communications.

Career Highlights:

- pitched a one-hitter and a perfect game en route to the gold medal at the women's softball world championships, 1986
- took the U.S. to a gold medal at the Pan American Games, 1987
- helped Team USA breeze undefeated through nine games to win a gold medal, Pan American Games, 1991
- broke the NCAA record for strikeouts and posted a 0.16 earned run average as a college senior, 1993.

Awards: Named Sportswoman of the Year in softball by the U.S. Olympic Committee, 1986; inducted into the Amateur Athletics Hall of Fame, 1987; named three-time winner of the Bertha Tickey Award, given to the outstanding pitcher in the ASA Women's Major Fast Pitch National Championship.

FLORENCE
GRIFFITH
JOYNER

She was known as "Flo Jo," the athlete who won Olympic medals while sporting elaborately painted nails and flamboyant track attire. Others dubbed her "the world's fastest woman" when she set world records in the 100- and 200-meter dashes in 1988. Whatever the nickname, Florence Griffith Joyner was a blur on the track at the Summer Olympics in Seoul, and to this day she remains one of the most visible and popular female athletes in America. "Throughout the history of track and field, there have only occasionally been athletes whose personalities and performances transcended their sport," wrote a *Ms.* magazine reporter in 1988. "Florence Griffith Joyner has joined the immortals, rising to their status on the force of her amazing athletic achievement, aided by the singular nature of her personality and approach to life."

Delorez Florence Griffith was born December 21, 1959, in Los Angeles, California. The seventh of 11 children, she was raised in the Jordan housing project in the tough Watts section of Los Angeles by her mother, Florence, a seamstress. Her parents were divorced when she was four, and her mother had a hard time earning enough money to support the family. This was the young runner's first important lesson. "We learned something from how we grew up," Griffith Joyner told the *Sporting News*. "It has never been easy, and we knew it wouldn't be handed to us, unless we went after it."

Griffith Joyner, known as "Dee Dee" to her friends and family, showed early signs of becoming her own person. In kindergarten, she braided her hair with one braid sticking straight up. In high school she wore her pet boa constrictor like a necklace. Her mother tried to discipline the young rebel and steer her along a path of Christian righteousness. The daily Bible readings and hours spent at church on Sundays were not appreciated at the time, but Griffith Joyner now understands what her mother was trying to do. "Everybody in the family survived," she told *Newsweek*. "Nobody does drugs, nobody got shot at. I used to say it was because we were afraid of Mama's voice. We didn't know how poor we were. We were rich as a family."

TRACK & FIELD
ATHLETE

"I work hard to keep things around me positive. At a basic level, my belief in God lets me believe that I can achieve almost anything."

Florence Griffith Joyner jubilantly finishes the 100-meter dash to win one of three gold medals at the 1988 Olympics. (AP/Wide World Photos)

At the age of seven Griffith Joyner began to compete in 50- and 70-meter dashes at the Sugar Ray Robinson Youth Foundation, a program for Los Angeles children. She almost always won, even when competing against boys. Griffith Joyner likes to joke that she learned to run by chasing jack rabbits in the Mojave desert—she often went there to visit her father. However she developed her talent, it showed itself early on. In 1973 she won the annual Jesse Owens National Youth Games, and the following year she won again. When she graduated from Jordan High School in Los Angeles in 1978, she held school records in sprint and long jump events.

After high school Griffith Joyner attended California State University at Northridge, but she ran out of money, quit school, and worked as a bank teller. Her track coach at Northridge, Bob Kersee, persuaded her to return to college and helped her to apply for financial aid. Kersee was an enthusiastic and ambitious coach, and he saw possibilities in "Flo Jo" that she did not even see herself. When he changed jobs in 1980 and went to the University of California at Los Angeles, Griffith Joyner followed him. "UCLA didn't even offer my major . . . but my running was starting up, and I knew that Bobby was the best coach for me," she explained in *Ms.*

In 1980 Griffith Joyner barely missed qualifying for the Olympics in the 200-meter race. In 1982 she ran the 200 meters in 22.39 seconds for the NCAA championship. The following year she was NCAA champion in the 400 meters. Griffith Joyner qualified for the 1984 Olympics in her home town of Los Angeles, but she finished second in the 200-meter sprint there to fellow American Valerie Brisco.

THE PRESIDENT CALLS

In 1993 President Bill Clinton announced that Florence Griffith Joyner, along with former NBA basketball star and U.S. Congressman Tom McMillen, would co-chair the President's Council on Physical Fitness and Sports. The Council advises the President on ways to promote fitness and sports programs for all Americans. Griffith Joyner hopes to use her position to encourage all Americans, but especially children, to exercise and eat right. She does admit that her own lifestyle is less than perfect. "I don't always have the best eating habits," she told a reporter for the New York Times Magazine. *"I like butter and ice cream. There are days I should work out and I don't. But it's never too late to change old habits."*

The silver medal finish undermined Griffith Joyner's verve for her sport. After the 1984 Summer Games, she took a job as a customer service representative for a bank, working in the evenings as a hair dresser and nail stylist. Her training fell off, she began to gain weight, and she broke her engagement to hurdler Greg Foster. Then a new source of inspiration entered her life and enabled her to regain her old form—and then some.

Florence Griffith had known Al Joyner since the 1980 Olympic trials. Joyner—himself an Olympic athlete and brother of track star Jackie Joyner-Kersee—convinced Griffith to return to serious training. The two began dat-

FLORENCE GRIFFITH JOYNER

American track & field athlete

Born: December 21, 1959, in Los Angeles, California.

Education: Attended California State University at Northridge and University of California, Los Angeles.

Career Highlights:
- won Jesse Owens National Youth Games, 1973 and 1974
- won 200-meter race for the NCAA championship, 1982, and the 400-meter race for the NCAA championship in 1983
- earned silver medal, 200-meter sprint, 1984 Olympic Games, Los Angeles, California

- won silver medal, 200-meter sprint, 1987 world championships

- earned gold medals, 200-meter dash, 100-meter dash, and as part of 4 × 100-meter relay team; won silver medal as part of 4 × 400-meter relay team, 1988 Olympic Games, Seoul, South Korea.

Awards: Received Jesse Owens Award and Sullivan Award for amateur athletics, 1988; named by President Bill Clinton as co-chair of the President's Council on Physical Fitness and Sports, 1993; elected to the Track and Field Hall of Fame, 1995.

ing and were married on October 10, 1987, in Las Vegas, Nevada. By that time, Griffith Joyner had quit working with Kersee in favor of her husband, and she had won a silver medal in the 200-meter sprint at the 1987 world championships.

Griffith Joyner always brought her unique sense of style onto the track. Her outfits were different, to say the least—she wore white bikini bottoms over one-legged tights, painted her long nails bright colors with inspirational designs. "Looking good is almost as important as running well," she once said. "It's part of feeling good about myself."

During the U.S. Olympic trials in July of 1988, Griffith Joyner shattered the world 100-meter record with a time of 10.49 seconds—more than a quarter second better than the previous record held by Evelyn Ashford. This strong showing made Griffith Joyner a favorite heading into the 1988 Olympics, and she did not disappoint. With fingernails sporting gold polka dots and Olympic rings, she broke the world record in the 200-meter sprint twice, in the semifinals and the finals. Her 100-meter dash final of 10.54 seconds was not counted as an Olympic record because she was running with a wind, but it brought her the gold medal nevertheless. Adding to her two sprint gold medals, she won a gold as part of the 4 × 100-meter relay team and a silver medal for the 4 × 400-meter relay. Her joyous enthusiasm at the end of each successful race—hugging her husband, her sister-in-law, her former coach—is one of the frequent replay moments from those Summer Games.

Following the Olympics, some of Griffith Joyner's competitors claimed she had used illegal anabolic steroids to build up her strength. Griffith Joyner denied the charges emphatically and passed all of the drug tests she was asked to take. "I am anti-drugs," she proclaimed in New York's *Newsday*. "Chasing all those records and giving the young kids coming up something to chase, that's what the sport is all about." Apparently, few track pundits believed the rumors, because Griffith Joyner won both the 1988 Jesse Owens Award *and* the 1988 Sullivan Award for amateur athletics.

With endorsement contracts of every sort pouring in, Griffith Joyner retired from running early in 1989. She stayed in the limelight, however, designing a line of sportswear for Starter and appearing as an actress on television shows. She also has made several fitness videos that have sold extremely well. In 1993 President Bill Clinton named Griffith Joyner to the President's Council on Physical Fitness and Sports, which advises the president on ways to promote fitness and athletics for all Americans.

Elected to the Track and Field Hall of Fame in 1995, Griffith Joyner has mulled the idea of a return to competition in time for the 1996 Olympics. If she did run, it would be in the 400-meter race. The mother of a young daughter, Griffith Joyner is still a visible sports personality who particularly likes to work with children. "I always encourage kids to reach beyond their dreams," she told the *New York Times Magazine*. "Don't try to be like me. Be better than me."

JOAN GUETSCHOW

BIATHLETE

After winning the North American Championship and the U.S. Nationals in 1992, Joan Guetschow was named the U.S. Biathlon Association's Woman Biathlete of the Year.

Joan Guetschow, of Minnetonka, Minnesota, isn't your typical homecoming queen. Nor, for that matter, your regular National Honor Society member. Guetschow can often be found toting a nine-and-a-half-pound, .22 caliber rifle. She got it as a Christmas present in the late 1980s when, as a champion cross-country skier, she caught the biathlon bug. Once she was considered a long shot—pardon the pun—to succeed. No more. Today, Guetschow, a competitive swimmer and champion triathlete who joined her high school ski team in suburban Minneapolis to keep in shape for track, is among the headliners on the U.S. women's biathlon team.

Guetschow, who was born September 9, 1966, won 12 letters in high school in swimming, track, and cross-country skiing. She was an All-American honorable mention in swimming and was team MVP in all three of her sports. In college at the University of Minnesota and Central Oregon Community College, she was an All-American skier, and in 1988 she was the 10 kilometer college champion.

Her first real claim to fame was winning the Olympic trials in Lake Placid in 1990, finishing first in the 7.5-kilometer event and second in the 15-kilometer competition. She took part in the 1992 Olympic Games in Albertville, France, where the women's biathlon became a medal sport for the first time; unfortunately, no American biathletes took home any medals that year.

Guetschow surprised many people—including herself—by advancing so far in the demanding biathlon. After dedicating herself to the sport, she changed residences 18 times and held 13 different jobs while training.

"I've had some bad luck, too," she told the *Minneapolis Star Tribune,* in something of a whopper of an understatement. Guetschow, who speaks fluent Finnish, broke her left hand in 1990, her right arm in 1991, and suffered a serious leg and shoulder bruise in a roller skiing accident. In 1989 she cut off the tips of two toes while mowing her lawn. She also skis with medication to control an irregular heartbeat. Small wonder that the makers of the pain-

Joan Guetschow prepares to take aim during the 4 × 7.5-kilometer biathlon relay at the 1994 Olympic Games. (AP/Wide World Photos)

JOAN GUETSCHOW

American biathlete

Born: September 9, 1966.

Education: Attended University of Minnesota and Central Oregon Community College.

Career Highlights:

• named All-American skier throughout college career

• named 10 kilometer college champion, 1988

• placed first in 7.5-kilometer event and second in 15-kilometer competition, Olympic Trials, Lake Placid, New York, 1990

• won North American Biathlon Championship and U.S. Biathlon Nationals, 1992.

Awards: Named U.S. Biathlon Association Woman Biathlete of the Year, 1992.

killer Nuprin nominated her for a comeback award in 1992. In that year she won both the North American Biathlon Championship in Alaska and the U.S. Biathlon Nationals.

Guetschow, the 1992 U.S. Biathlon Association Woman Biathlete of the Year, admitted that she almost had to scratch her biathlon career before any of her big victories occurred. "My first thought (after the mowing incident) was I was going to go back to swimming," she said. "I thought the injury would really mess my balance up. But the doctors made a special insole for my foot, and I worked extra hard on balancing that foot, so I don't notice it now."

With the injuries behind her, she can contemplate a long future in the biathlon. "Skiing is a good long-term sport," she explained. "You can train for it in a variety of ways, whereas about all you can do to train for swimming is swim more. Also, women skiers peak later, usually in their 30s, whereas anything much above 20 is getting old for a swimmer."

We haven't heard the last of Joan Guetschow.

DOROTHY HAMILL

Still one of America's favorite ice performers, Dorothy Hamill won the hearts of a nation when she skated for an Olympic gold medal in 1976. Known as much for her signature hairstyle as for her talents, Hamill combined athletic prowess with the grace and musicality of a dancer. In her time she was acknowledged as the best freestyle skater in the world. Hamill's amateur career was marked by three national titles, an Olympic gold medal, and a world championship. Since turning professional in 1976, she has almost single-handedly saved the Ice Capades from extinction, first by performing with the troupe, and later by purchasing the entire show and recasting it according to her own tastes. It is safe to say that Dorothy Hamill has left a significant mark on both amateur and professional figure skating in the United States.

Hamill began skating at the age of eight on a pond near her home in Greenwich, Connecticut. After watching some of her friends skate backwards, she begged her parents for lessons. They enrolled her in a group class at a local rink. Her progress was rapid, and she became immersed in the sport. Few skaters have ever worked harder than the young Dorothy Hamill as she sought to perfect her skills. After age 14 she never again attended public school, using private tutors instead so that she could skate seven hours a day, six days a week. As is often the case, her family made significant financial sacrifices to help her pursue her dream. The demands of international competition and training often meant long periods away from home for Dorothy and her mother, especially after the skater became a teenager.

At the 1971 world championships, Hamill finished seventh overall. She was 14 at the time. Encouraged by that success, she began to work with renowned skating coach Carlo Fassi in Colorado. Fassi had also trained Peggy Fleming, and he noticed immediately that his new protege was stronger and more athletic than Fleming. Together Fassi and Hamill created routines that showcased Hamill's spectacular jumping ability and her well-known "Hamill camel" spin (a camel spin into a sit spin). Fassi also helped Hamill perfect her compulsory figures, one of the weaker aspects of her performance repertoire.

FIGURE SKATER

"I don't think enough people realize that skaters get better as they get older."

215

Dorothy Hamill proudly holds up the gold medal she won in the women's figure skating event at the 1976 Olympics. (UPI/Bettmann)

Hamill won her first of three consecutive national championships in February of 1974. That same year her performance at the world championships helped to make her name a household word. At the world competition in Munich, Hamill was warming up prior to her appearance when suddenly the audience began to boo loudly. Thinking that the spectators were booing her, she burst into tears and fled the ice. When she discovered that the jeers were aimed at the judges for their scoring of the prior skater, Hamill dried her eyes, returned to the ice, and turned in a fabulous performance. She won the silver medal.

In prime condition for the 1976 Olympics, and with three national championships to her credit, Hamill was favored to win a medal at the Winter Games. In a March 7, 1994, profile of the skater, *Sports Illustrated*'s Steve Wulf wrote of her Olympic performance: "In four nearly flawless minutes at the Olympic Ice Hall in Innsbruck, . . . she walleyed, toe-looped, Salchowed, Axeled and Lutzed her way into our hearts, finishing her performance with

DOROTHY HAMILL

American figure skater

Born: 1956.

Career Highlights:
- won three consecutive national championships, 1974, 1975, and 1976

- received silver medal, world championships, 1974
- earned gold medal, 1976 Olympic Games, Innsbruck, Austria
- won gold medal, world championships, 1976.

her signature Hamill camel. The nearsighted girl in the pink dress further endeared herself to millions by squinting to see her scores. . . . The gold medal was hers, and as she stood shyly, demurely on the platform, she seemed to have stepped out of a storybook. And what a storybook name, Dorothy."

The pressure of competition had always been quite difficult for Hamill to handle. She often became sick to her stomach before she performed, and she carried a lucky rag doll to the rink side with her at important events. Having won the Olympic gold and her first world championship in 1976, Hamill announced that she would turn professional. She signed a seven-figure contract with the Ice Capades and embarked on a two-year tour as part of that troupe. Her immense popularity led to television shows and product endorsement deals—and to a whirlwind romance with actor Dean Paul Martin. The two were married in 1982 but separated two years later. Martin was killed in a plane crash in 1987.

Touring with the Ice Capades proved even more stressful than amateur competition, and Hamill quit the show in the early 1980s. In 1983 she appeared in a televised ice version of *Romeo and Juliet*. Its success marked a new direction in Hamill's career. In 1987 she married sports physician Ken Forsythe, and together they produced the well-received show *Nutcracker on Ice*. Soon after that acclaimed show closed, Hamill received the news that the Ice Capades had sought Chapter 11 bankruptcy and planned to fold up operations.

"It was breaking my heart to think there would be no more Ice Capades," Hamill told *Sports Illustrated* on March 7, 1994. "It wasn't just that I once skated for the company, it was also the thought of all those skaters out of work." In short, Dorothy Hamill bought the Ice Capades and breathed new life into the artistically moribund troupe. One of her greatest successes with the rejuvenated Ice Capades was the 1994 show *Cinderella . . . Frozen in Time*, in which she skated the lead. After just one year of ownership, Hamill and her partner were able to sell 80 percent of the Ice Capades to another buyer for the same price they had paid for the entire company.

Having made her mark on both amateur and professional skating, Hamill—the mother of a young daughter—has found new levels of enjoyment on the ice. "I cringe whenever I see tapes of myself [in the Olympics]," she told *Sports Illustrated*. "I wasn't very good, not compared to what they can do today, to what I can do today." She continued: "I don't think enough people realize that skaters get better as they get older." Perhaps the difference lies in the fact that Hamill need no longer prove herself, either to judges or to an audience. Reflecting on her newfound success with the Ice Capades, Hamill concluded: "My first dream came true when I was 19, which is a little early to start asking, What next? So I had to find another dream, and this is it."

MIA
HAMM

A member of the U.S. national women's soccer team, Mia Hamm ranks among the team's most accomplished scorers. That should come as little surprise to anyone who followed Hamm's collegiate career at the University of North Carolina, which won every NCAA soccer championship played while Hamm was a student there. By the time her college days were done in 1993, Hamm was the Atlantic Coast Conference's all-time leading scorer, with 103 goals. Arguably the top college soccer player of recent years, she has brought her talents to the national team in preparation for the 1996 Olympic Games.

Mia Hamm says she grew up on a soccer field. The daughter of a military fighter pilot and a ballet dancer, she followed her older siblings to soccer practice as soon as she could walk. "Basically the soccer field was where I was baby-sat," she told *Seventeen* magazine in June of 1994. By the time she was five, she grew weary of sitting on the sidelines and joined in. She played pee wee soccer on a mixed-sex team and even then enjoyed making goals.

As an "Army brat," Hamm moved frequently with her family, but most of her early years were spent in Texas. It was in Wichita Falls that the 14-year-old Hamm caught the eye of John Cossaboon, coach of an Olympic development team. She spent a year with that team and then, at the tender age of 15, was given a chance to perform at the 1987 U.S. Soccer Federation tournament. There she worked with U.S. team coach Anson Dorrance, who also coached at the University of North Carolina.

Hamm recalled her debut at that tournament in a *Sports Illustrated* profile: "I was a nightmare. I had no idea how to play, and when I first did fitness with the national team, I thought I'd die." Instinctively Hamm knew, however, that she had found her niche in the game. She wanted to work with Dorrance—and she wanted to play for the national team.

First things first. Hamm entered the University of North Carolina in 1989 and, as a freshman, was a force on an undefeated, NCAA champion Tar Heel squad. In 1990 she led the nation in scoring on the college level, with 24 goals and 19 assists. Named women's college soccer player of 1992, she

SOCCER PLAYER

"Mia has this amazing ability to go right through defenders—as if by molecular displacement."

—Anson Dorrance, Hamm's coach at the University of North Carolina

The U.S. Soccer Federation has named Mia Hamm the Female Athlete of the Year in both 1994 and 1995. (© *Tony Quinn/Allsport Photography USA Inc.*)

turned in a spectacular season that year and the next, leading the NCAA as a senior with 32 goals and 33 assists.

Hamm achieved her other goal as well. In 1990 she became a factor in Team USA play and was a member of the first-ever women's world champion soccer team in 1991. At the first world championships, Hamm started five of the team's six games and contributed two goals. Two years later, she led all players with six goals at the World University Games, where the U.S. won the silver medal. And in 1994, during the qualifying tournament to determine World Cup finalists, Hamm scored six more goals. That year she was named Female Athlete of the Year by the U.S. Soccer Federation.

Hamm continued to shine for the U.S. team in 1995, leading the team to a 19-2-2 overall record with 19 goals and 18 assists. For the second year in a row she was named Female Athlete of the Year. Her only disappointment occurred at the world championship tournament, where her team bowed out only after a thrilling 1-0 defeat in the semifinal against Norway.

MIA HAMM

American soccer player

Born: 1972.

Education: Graduated from University of North Carolina, 1993.

Career Highlights:

- helped North Carolina Tar Heels to four NCAA championships, 1989–93

- named Atlantic Coast Conference's all-time leading scorer, with 103 goals, 1989–1993

- led the nation in scoring on the college level, with 24 goals and 19 assists, 1990

- played on first-ever women's world champion soccer team, starting in five of six games and contributing two goals, 1991

- led all players with six goals at the World University Games, where the U.S. won the silver medal, 1993

- led U.S. team to a 19-2-2 overall record with 19 goals and 18 assists, 1995.

Awards: Named women's college soccer player of 1992; named Female Athlete of the Year by the U.S. Soccer Federation, 1994 and 1995.

Remaining challenges include the 1996 Olympics and the tantalizing possibility of professional women's soccer in America. As for Mia Hamm, she is hardly satisfied to rest on her current laurels, no matter how fantastic they may be. "I've had some wonderful years, . . . but I don't want to sit and look at all the trophies," she told *People* magazine. "I don't want to live in the past— I want to live *now!*"

BETH
HEIDEN

*"I'm happiest when I
skate for myself."*

Overshadowed in her Olympic sport by the exploits of her famous brother Eric, Beth Heiden is nevertheless an athlete who deserves recognition. Beth, a former world champion speed skater and bronze medalist in speed skating at the 1980 Winter Olympics, has been equally successful in bicycle racing *and* cross-country skiing—a feat that stands as testament to her superb conditioning and iron determination. Certainly she stands as one-half of one of the most famous brother-sister athletic duos in history—and one of the rare competitors who has won big in three different sports.

Beth Heiden was born and raised in West Allis, Wisconsin, a picture-perfect venue for a would-be skater. As a youngster, because she was a girl, she drifted into figure skating. Her brother Eric chose speed skating and hockey. As they grew up together, however, Beth became more and more interested in speed skating. She was petite and slender, so as she became immersed in the sport she had to overcompensate for her physical limitations by being tough mentally. That she certainly was. "There was many a time when Beth wanted to hit the ice, and I'd say, 'Aw, let's forget it today,'" Eric Heiden recalled in *The Olympic Factbook*. "But her tenacity would get the better of me—and that's what made the difference between success and failure."

In 1972 both Heiden siblings began training with coach Dianne Holum, the 1972 Olympic gold medal winner in the 1500-meter race. Holum detected greatness in both Heidens and put them on a training program that included bicycling, weightlifting, duck-walking, and hours of skating. The intense daily workouts began to take their toll on the less muscular Beth, but she doggedly pursued perfection and didn't complain when she was injured. In 1979, skating against women who were bigger and stronger, she won a world championship by adding an equal dose of guts to her flawlessly executed striding technique.

When Beth Heiden arrived at the 1980 Winter Games, expectations were high that she would skate away with pockets full of gold. Both she and her brother were greeted as conquering heroes, and Eric Heiden proceeded to

Combining guts and determination with a flawless stride, Beth Heiden races to a third-place finish in the World Speed Skating Sprint Championships, 1980. (AP/Wide World Photos)

BETH HEIDEN

American speed skater, cyclist, skier

Born: 1959 in West Allis, Wisconsin.

Education: Attended University of Vermont.

Career Highlights:
• won speed skating world championship, 1979

• earned bronze medal, 3000-meter race, 1980 Olympic Games, Lake Placid, New York

• won bicycle racing world championship, 1980

• won cross-country skiing NCAA championship in the 7.5-kilometer event, early 1980s.

fulfill the expectations by winning a stunning five gold medals. Beth was less successful. Her world championship the year before had been based on *overall* performance in four events. At the Olympics, each event is awarded separately, so while Beth finished seventh, fifth, seventh, and third in four races—the best overall—she won only a bronze medal for the 3000-meter race.

When some members of the press chided her for not keeping pace with Eric, Beth, who was also skating on an injured ankle she told no one about, broke down. "I'm happiest when I skate for myself, but this year I have to skate for the press," she growled. "The hell with you guys."

Stung by her treatment at the Olympics, Beth moved on to new challenges. Having trained extensively on a bicycle to complement her skating, she won a world championship in the sport of bicycle racing in 1980. While working on her degree in physics at the University of Vermont in the early 1980s, she took up cross-country skiing on a whim and soon found herself winning the NCAA championship in the 7.5-kilometer event. After college she helped to create and develop extensive cross-country facilities in Michigan's Upper Peninsula.

Throughout their stellar athletic and academic careers, both Eric and Beth Heiden remained happy because they never sought to capitalize on their laurels. Not for them the endorsements and public appearances so common among Olympic medalists. Instead, they concentrated on excellence in sporting endeavors and in the classroom. For Beth Heiden, a world championship and an Olympic appearance were only two milestones on a long road of victories.

CAROL
HEISS JENKINS

The old saying goes, "Always a bridesmaid, never a bride." Figure skater Carol Heiss must have felt like that sometimes as she competed in national and world championships against her friendly rival, Tenley Albright. For several years Heiss finished second—consistently—to Albright, including at the 1956 Olympics. Then Albright retired, and Heiss stepped into the spotlight. She won every U.S. championship from 1957 to 1960, and every world championship from 1956 to 1960. And then, in 1960, she won the Olympic gold medal, fulfilling a promise she'd made to her dying mother years before.

Heiss literally grew up on the ice. She began her skating career with a pair of roller skates at age three, and she was so exuberant about skating that her mother, Marie, decided to give her ice skating lessons. Carol, her sister Nancy, and her brother Bruce were all enrolled at a local rink, and all showed early promise. When Carol was six, her mother took her to Manhattan and signed her up for lessons at the New York Figure Skating Club. The coach there, Pierre Brunet, told Mrs. Heiss that Carol could become a champion— if she practiced as much as eight hours a day, every day.

The whole Heiss family showed a singular devotion to skating. Both parents worked long hours in order to meet the staggering expenses of lessons for three children. Mrs. Heiss took her work with her to the rink, chaperoning her children on a long bus ride from their home in Queens to downtown Manhattan. Carol got up every morning at 5:30, skated from 7:00 until noon, attended classes at the Professional Children's School, and skated again after school. She had hardly any life to speak of beyond the rink and her studies.

Her time was not wasted, however. In 1953, at the age of 13, Heiss finished second to Albright at the U.S. senior national championships. Albright was almost five years older than Heiss. Urged on by her mother, Heiss continued to practice with an eye toward the 1954 world championships and the 1956 Olympics. Then misfortune struck. Two weeks before the 1954 worlds, Heiss collided with her sister during a practice session. Her sister's skate slashed Heiss's Achilles tendon, forcing her out of the worlds and into a long

"When I saw the sun shining while I was skating, I felt it was a lovely day to win a gold medal."

—Heiss, before winning the gold medal at the 1960 Olympics

Carol Heiss performs compulsory figures for the judges at the 1960 Winter Olympics; she was awarded the gold medal for her performance there. (AP/Wide World Photos)

and painful recovery. Heiss did improve in time to compete in the 1954 U.S. nationals, where she finished second to Albright again. The Albright-Heiss battle continued in 1955, when once again Heiss earned silver medals in both the national championships and the worlds.

By the time the 1956 Olympics rolled around, Carol Heiss's mother was gravely ill with cancer. Mrs. Heiss's treatments required long, hot baths every day, so when she and Carol traveled to the Olympics in Cortina, Italy, they stayed in a hotel rather than with the rest of the American team. Reporters jumped on them, calling them "snobby" and suggesting that the duo thought they were too good for the official accommodations. Heiss never let on that her mother was so sick. Instead she concentrated on beating Albright while her mother was still alive to witness a gold medal.

At the 1956 Olympics Heiss skated her very best but still finished second to Albright by a narrow two-point margin. Just two weeks later the pair met

CAROL HEISS JENKINS

American figure skater

Born: January 30, 1940 in Queens, New York.

Education: Attended New York University.

Career Highlights:
- took first place, U.S. figure skating championships, 1957–1960

- won world championships, 1956–1960
- earned silver medal, 1956 Olympic Games, Cortina, Italy
- won gold medal, 1960 Olympic Games, Squaw Valley, California.

again in competition at the world championships. For the first time, Heiss took a lead into the free skating portion of the program and then skated perfectly in the short and long programs. After years of performing in the shadow of Tenley Albright, Heiss was finally a world champion. Tragically, her mother died only a few months later—and Heiss vowed to win an Olympic gold medal in her honor.

Time was on Carol Heiss's side during all those years of second-place finishes. Albright was older, and she retired from skating in 1957. With her chief rival out of the way, Heiss blossomed and became one of the most durable world champions of all time, winning the worlds every year between 1956 and 1960. She also won four national titles beginning in 1957. Remarkably, she accomplished all of this while attending college at New York University and taking care of her younger siblings and the family home. Even more remarkably, her principal rival in the late 1950s was her own sister, Nancy.

Heiss was favored to win a gold medal at the 1960 Olympics in Squaw Valley, California, and she did not disappoint. Over the four days of competition, she built a tremendous lead over her opponents, finally emerging after the free skate with a gold medal and a 65-point lead over the silver medalist. After the medal ceremony, Heiss told reporters that she'd stayed in competition to fulfill the vow she'd made to her mother. "I gave her my promise," she said. "I only wish she could be here now."

With a fifth world championship to her credit in 1960, Heiss retired from amateur skating. She married fellow gold medal figure skater Hayes Alan Jenkins and embarked on a career that included appearances in ice shows, films, and television. "It cost my family a great deal to help make me a champion," she said. "It's time for me to pay back."

After leaving the ice shows, Heiss settled in Akron, Ohio with her husband and three children. She began a second career as a skating coach, and she has had the thrill of seeing her pupils succeed. One of them, Jill Trenary, became the 1990 U.S. figure skating champion, and another, Tonya Kwiatkowski, is the 1996 U.S. silver medalist.

SONJA
HENIE

FIGURE SKATER

"I want to go into
pictures, and I want
to skate in them. I
want to do with
skates what Fred
Astaire is doing with
dancing."

—Henie, upon turning pro, 1936

Modern figure skating is deeply indebted to Sonja Henie, one of the greatest athletes of this century. Before Henie wrought a revolution in the sport, "figure skating" was just that—a boring, staid tracing of figures on ice with little flair and less action. Henie changed all that. A born entertainer, she was the first skater to incorporate the principles of ballet into her routines. She was also the first woman to perform spins and jumps that had long been used by male skaters. More important, through her live ice shows and a series of Hollywood movies, Henie enlarged the audience for figure skating and made it what it is today—a thrilling entertainment.

Born April 8, 1912, in Oslo, Norway, Henie was blessed from the beginning with every attribute a skater might need. Her father was a wealthy fur salesman and a former amateur cycling champion who encouraged his children to compete. Her mother was willing to travel all across Europe with her to find coaches and outdoor ice rinks—in those days indoor ice rinks were rare. Private tutors were hired to educate her while she concentrated on her skating. Her talent was evident from a very early age.

Henie entered her first Olympics in 1924, when she was 11 years old. Because she was still a child, she competed in a knee-length skirt, rather than the calf-length outfits the older women wore. Her fur-trimmed costume afforded her greater ease of movement, and she performed some moves that were downright shocking for the time, including a jump into a sit spin. A surprised panel of judges awarded her third place in the free style portion of the competition, but her poor showing on the compulsory figures lowered her score dramatically. She finished in last place.

Far from being discouraged, the youngster poured all her energies into skating. In 1927, at the tender age of 14, she won her first of *ten consecutive world championships*. No other skater before or since has dominated the sport as thoroughly as Henie did between 1927 and 1936.

Soon after winning her first world championship, Henie saw a ballet performance by Russian great Anna Pavlova. The young Norwegian was pro-

Sonja Henie revolutionized the sport of figure skating. (UPI/Bettmann)

SONJA HENIE

Norwegian figure skater

Born: April 8, 1912 in Oslo, Norway.

Died: October 12, 1969.

Career Highlights:

- won an unprecedented ten consecutive world championships, 1927–1936

- earned gold medal, 1928 Olympic Games, Saint-Moritz, Switzerland
- earned gold medal, 1932 Olympic Games, Lake Placid, New York
- earned gold medal, 1936 Olympic Games, Garmisch-Partenkirchen, West Germany

foundly influenced by Pavlova's artistry, and she tried to incorporate ballet-style choreography into her skating routines. At the time this was a brave departure from convention, and audiences loved it. Henie's sense of drama, athletic perfection, and graceful, balletic performances wrought a permanent change in figure skating and paved the way for today's skating superstars.

Henie won Olympic gold medals in 1928, 1932, and 1936 before retiring from amateur skating. At the height of the Great Depression she had become an international star with enough clout that she could announce that she planned to be in motion pictures. The idea of an ice skating movie might seem quaint today, but Henie starred in a number of them, most notably *One in a Million,* the story of a skater's rise to Olympic glory, and *Thin Ice.* Typically, Sonja Henie films were short on plot and long on her trademark skating routines, but in an era before television these films were an introduction to skating for millions of American viewers.

Within a year of turning pro, Henie had earned in excess of a quarter of a million dollars. She became a millionaire by 1940, an accomplishment that outstrips even the male athletes of her generation. With her sunny personality and obvious love of skating, Henie popularized the sport and served as a role model for American skating hopefuls of both sexes, including Dick Button, Tenley Albright (the first American woman to win an Olympic gold medal), and Carol Heiss.

When live television began to cut into the film industry, Henie stopped making movies and returned to traveling ice shows. For a time she had her own company, Sonja Henie's Hollywood Ice Revue, but an unfortunate bleacher collapse at one of her shows caused the venture to fold. After that Henie could be seen in other ice shows and on television specials. Gradually her appearances dwindled, and in 1956 she retired.

Dividing her remaining years between homes in Norway and the United States, Henie lived happily with her third husband, Niels Onstad. In the mid-1960s she developed leukemia and spent the rest of her life fighting the disease. Her death on October 12, 1969, at the age of 57 robbed the skating world of one of its brightest stars. By today's standards, Henie's routines were almost ridiculously simple, her jumps far from spectacular. Her contribution to skating is secure, however, because she combined all of the elements so important to the sport today: high drama, athletic prowess, and—perhaps most important—"star power." A champion in her own day, she is a legend in ours.

LYNN HILL

Lynn Hill has loved climbing from a young age and has distinguished herself as one of the best female climbers in the world. But her mission also includes establishing equality between female and male climbers. In the World Cup competition in France in 1989 she showed her ability to climb a course as well as any man and thus struck a blow for women's rights in the sports arena. Fueled by a love for her sport and a determination to eliminate sexist attitudes toward women competitors, Hill has played a large role in the advancement of professional rock climbing worldwide. As Paul McHugh put it in the *San Francisco Chronicle,* Hill is singlehandedly "blazing a trail to the top for other women, in what's been a male-dominated sport for a century. Yet Hill's sense of style has meant that athletic success, even on gritty, gut-wrenching ascents . . . requires zero sacrifice of femininity."

Not only is Hill one of the top five rock climbers in the world, she is the world's foremost *female* rock climber. In a sport that requires intense muscular strength, low body fat, and unbreakable concentration—skills that have been typically regarded as "male" attributes—Hill has proven herself through her accomplishments. Capitalizing on her skill, natural talent, and experience, she has quickly risen to the top of the sport.

Hill became a crowd favorite at climbing competitions in the 1980s, where she dominated the women's category over the years and made great strides toward defeating her top male rivals. At a World Cup competition in Lyon, France, in 1989, she delivered a performance that brought down the house. A longtime advocate of women being allowed to compete on the same courses as men, Hill got her wish in the final round, where she scaled the same course as her top male competitors.

Courses on the competition's synthetic cliff can be manipulated to increase the difficulty of the climb, and the course is made increasingly more difficult until only one climber can finish the route. On that particular day only two men were able to finish the course. The second-place woman competitor fell after the first move up from the stage. Then Hill, in a dramatic

Lynn Hill displays her world-class climbing skills on a synthetic course.
(UPI/Corbis-Bettmann)

climb, made it to the very last move of the route before falling (sustained by a safety rope, of course), thus demonstrating in front of thousands of people that she was indeed among the top rock climbers in the world.

Hill has been naturally inclined toward climbing since a young age—she started participating in the sport at age 14. A self-described tomboy, she enjoyed running, jumping, and climbing anything she could. When her older sister invited her on trips to climbing areas in Joshua Tree National Monument and Yosemite National Park, both in California, Hill quickly fell in love with the sport. Soon she was taking part in difficult three- and four-day climbs up cliff faces like the legendary 3,600-foot El Capitan peak. While her pure love of climbing played a large part in her determination to master climbs of greater and greater difficulty, her compact, powerful build and intense training habits made her physically up to each new challenge. "People may have described me as a tomboy when I was a kid," she told the *San Francisco Chronicle,* "as if I wasn't what a girl's supposed to be. Yet if extreme athletics improves you as a person, why can't that be feminine?"

As Hill began to become more serious about her sport and more competitions cropped up, she settled into a strict training regimen. Aside from numerous practice climbs, she also runs and lifts weights. Standing five feet two inches tall and weighing 100 pounds, Hill nearly set a new world record for her body weight by bench pressing 150 pounds.

Hill first realized her ultimate potential as a climber when she scaled a wall named Ophir Broke in Telluride, Colorado, at the age of 19. The hill was rated one of the more difficult in the world and Hill became the first woman to execute the climb. She then began to devote herself to full-time climbing while making ends meet any way that she could. In 1980 she even appeared on the televised sports program *Survival of the Fittest,* which ran competitors through various obstacle courses. She won the grand prize four years in a row, earning $30,000 as a result. In 1993 Hill moved permanently to New Paltz, New York, to attend the College at New Paltz, where she eventually earned a degree in biology. Conveniently, the college is located just a few minutes' drive from the Shawangunk cliffs, the best rock climbing region east of the Rocky Mountains. While training at the "Gunks," as they are called, Hill met Russ Raffa, a sales representative for the Patagonia clothing firm. Raffa became her climbing partner and eventually her husband.

With more economic security, Hill was able to lead the itinerant lifestyle necessary to stay competitive internationally, traveling to Europe on a regular basis to compete in weekly contests for purses of up to $5,000 an event. If she needed more proof that rock climbing was a career without a great deal of security, she found out the hard way in May 1989. After finishing a routine climb on a limestone cliff in Buoux, France, she mistakenly neglected to tie a safety knot in her rope and fell 85 feet to the ground. Miraculously, Hill emerged from the fall with only a broken foot and a dislocated elbow, and her desire to compete completely intact. She began rehabilitation and within four months returned to win the women's division in a contest at Arco, Italy.

Hill's comeback could not have been more complete. The accident gave her a firsthand look at the possible dangers of the sport and seemed to double her concentration. By the end of the same year, she had more major

NANCY FEAGIN

Lynn Hill is not alone on the face of the world's tallest cliffs. World-class climber Nancy Feagin has both benefitted from and continued Hill's trailblazing efforts. Feagin is the only woman who has climbed the longest wall of Yosemite's El Capitan—3,400 feet of granite—in a single day. In Utah's Zion National Park, she climbed Moonlight Buttress solo, a trek which involved spending the night alone, tied to the rock wall. Her ability to conquer fear helps mightily in these quests. "I just try to ask," she told the Christian Science Monitor in 1993, "'Is this a realistic fear or not a realistic fear.'" Unrealistic fears are dismissed, and realistic fears are dealt with by trying to calmly change the situation. "It's very logical," she claims.

LYNN HILL

American rock climber

Born: C. 1961, grew up in Los Angeles, California.

Education: Received B.S. in biology at College at New Paltz, New York, c. 1983.

Career Highlights:
• became the first woman to scale Ophir Broke in Telluride, Colorado, 1980

• garnered more major wins than any other female climber by the end of 1989

• made rock climbing history by becoming the first woman to complete a grade 5.14 climb, in Cimai, France, 1990

• free-climbed the "Nose" route on Yosemite's El Capitan, a feat once thought impossible for any climber, 1994.

wins than any other female climber. Then, in 1990 in Cimai, France, Hill made rock climbing history by becoming the first woman to complete a grade 5.14 climb.

Although Hill achieved a fair amount of economic success as a competitive climber, she has retired in order to devote her climbing skills to personal goals. In 1994 she free-climbed the "Nose" route on Yosemite's El Capitan, a feat once thought impossible for any climber. Still one of the best known practitioners of her sport, Hill earns a good income from teaching and from endorsements of climbing and athletic gear. She told the *San Francisco Chronicle:* "Athletics means you can commit and be disciplined and endure. Those are good qualities in any human being. If we say such things make a man more of a man, we should also say they make a woman more of a woman. Someone who's balanced, active, natural."

NELL
JACKSON

**TRACK & FIELD
ATHLETE AND
COACH**

*"The 220 was the
longest event a
woman could run
then. There were a
lot of so-called
'studies' around then
showing how
'dangerous' it was for
women to run longer
distances. . . . It
didn't make a great
deal of sense to me,
but there was nothing
I could do about it."*

Race and gender were not issues for Nell Jackson. Winning was all that mattered. In a career spanning more than 40 years, she was an Olympic athlete, a coach, a college professor, and a scholar—despite the many stumbling blocks placed before black women in our society. Having herself excelled in a sport once considered "unfeminine," she helped to change the image of women's track and field, paving the way for the many successful athletes of our own time.

Nell Cecelia Jackson was born in Athens, Georgia, on July 1, 1929, one of three children born to Burnette and Wilhemina Jackson. The Jackson family moved to Tuskegee, Alabama, while Nell was still young, and she grew up there in an environment that fostered athletic endeavor. Tuskegee University was home to one of the nation's prominent women's track and field teams, and young Nell grew up dreaming of being part of that organization. Talented in swimming, basketball, and tennis as well as track and field, she switched to running full time as a teenager.

Jackson's specialty was the 220-yard dash. She would have liked to have run longer races, but it simply wasn't possible. "The 220 was the longest event a woman could run then," she explained in the book *After Olympic Glory: The Lives of Ten Outstanding Medalists*. "There were a lot of so-called 'studies' around then showing how 'dangerous' it was for women to run longer distances, that they would upset their chemical and physical make up. It didn't make a great deal of sense to me, but there was nothing I could do about it. So I ran the 220."

After graduating from Tuskegee High School in 1947, Jackson attended Tuskegee University, where she majored in physical education and served as a star member of the women's track team. She had only finished her freshman year when she qualified for the United States Olympic team as a sprinter in 1948. Her showing at the Summer Games in London was disappointing to her, because she failed to place in either of her events—the 200-meter sprint and the 4 × 100-meter relay. The following year, however, she

*Athlete, coach, and scholar Nell Jackson devoted her life to women's ath-
letics.* (AP/Wide World Photos)

NELL JACKSON

American track & field athlete and coach

Born: July 1, 1929 in Athens, Georgia.

Died: April 1, 1988 in Vestal, New York.

Education: Graduated from Tuskegee High School in 1947; attended Tuskegee University, where she majored in physical education, earning her bachelor's degree in 1951; did graduate studies at Springfield College, earning a master's degree there in 1953; finished her doctorate of philosophy degree at the University of Iowa, 1962.

Career Highlights:

- set an American record of 24.2 seconds in the 200-meter dash, a record that stood for six years, 1949
- named national AAU champion in the 200-meter dash in 1949, 1950, and 1951

- won silver medal in the 200-meter dash and gold medal in the 4 × 100-meter relay, Pan American Games, Buenos Aires, Argentina, 1951
- worked at Tuskegee University as head track and field coach, 1954–1962
- coached U.S. women's Olympic track and field team, 1956 and 1972
- managed U.S. national women's track and field team, 1964, 1965, 1966, 1969, 1972, and 1977
- became first black American assistant athletic director, women's track coach, and professor of physical education at Michigan State University, 1973.

Awards: Named to the National Track and Field Hall of Fame, 1989.

set an American record of 24.2 seconds in the 200 meter, a record that stood for six years. She was also national AAU champion in the 200 meter in 1949, 1950, and 1951.

At the first Pan American Games held in 1951 in Buenos Aires, Argentina, Jackson won a silver medal in the 200 meter and a gold medal in the 4 × 100-meter relay. Throughout her running career from 1944 through 1952 she always placed sixth or better in any 200-meter event in which she participated.

In the early 1950s Jackson had to choose between athletics and academics. She earned her bachelor's degree from Tuskegee in 1951 and immediately embarked upon graduate studies at Springfield College. She took a master's degree there in 1953 and continued her education with summer study at the University of Oslo, Norway.

Another dream came true for Jackson in 1954, when she accepted the post of head track and field coach at her alma mater, Tuskegee University. She worked at Tuskegee from 1954 until 1962, with time off in 1956 to coach the U.S. women's Olympic track and field team. Jackson had the distinction of becoming the first black woman head coach of an Olympic team. She repeated as head coach of Team USA in 1969, in preparation for the World University Games, and 1972, for the Olympics once again. Jackson also served as a manager of the U.S. national women's track and field team, beginning in 1964 and serving through 1965, 1966, 1972, and 1977.

All this and scholarship, too. Jackson finished her doctorate of philosophy degree at the University of Iowa in 1962. Immediately she began rising through the academic ranks, beginning as an assistant professor of physical education at Illinois State University in Normal and moving to the University of Illinois in Urbana-Champaign in 1965. In 1973 she became the first black American assistant athletic director, women's track coach, and professor of physical education at Michigan State University. Her legacy of research and scholarly publications includes the 1968 textbook *Track and Field for Girls and Women*. She was also producer of the film *Grace in Motion*.

Jackson's last post, from 1981 through 1988, was as director of physical education and intercollegiate athletics at the State University of New York (SUNY) at Binghamton. She died on April 1, 1988, in Vestal, New York, after a short illness. Just a year after her death she was named to the National Track and Field Hall of Fame, in honor of a lifetime spent in devotion to women's athletics.

LYNN JENNINGS

*"I have the killer
instinct . . . on the
starting line. Would
you want a surgeon
to say, 'Gee, I really
hope I do a good
job on this heart
transplant'? No. You
want him to say, 'I'm
going to open up that
chest, I'm going to
take that heart out,
I'm going to shove a
new one in there, and
it's going to work.'"*

One of the most successful distance racers of all time, Lynn Jennings proved to a generation of cross-country runners that fame and fortune could be found in that sport. Jennings was a three-time world cross-country champion and also a winner at indoor and outdoor track meets and marathons. Any race from 3,000 meters to 15 kilometers would find Jennings leading the field, powered by an iron resolve and a deadly kick. The only American runner, male or female, to medal at a distance of more than 800 meters at the 1992 Summer Olympics, Jennings has forged a career spanning two decades. "I feel like I've been on this steady, relentlessly paced journey," she said in *Runner's World* in 1993. "There hasn't been one defining moment in my career—there have been many defining moments, each one feeding into the next."

Many successful distance runners hail from warm-climate countries such as Kenya. Jennings grew up in snowy New England and still lives there, relishing a training schedule that varies little through the seasons. She was born July 1, 1960, in Harvard, Massachusetts, a small town about 40 miles west of Boston. Growing up so close to a major American city, with a close and supportive family, Jennings was encouraged to set her sights high and work toward her dreams.

"I remember being 16 years old, and saying that I would be the best runner in the world at age 30," she recalled in *Runner's World*. ". . . I just knew I had the mental tools and that I was going to be an exceptional adult runner. And I knew I wouldn't get to college and find out there was something else I wanted to do with my life."

As a teen Jennings had reason for her confidence. Under the coaching of John Babington of the Liberty Athletics Club track team, she won the junior national cross-country championships in 1976 and competed in the 1976 Olympic 1,500-meter trials. Coach and athlete came to a parting of the ways in 1978 when Jennings insisted upon running in the Boston Marathon against Babington's advice. Jennings finished the marathon in 2:46 as an un-

Three-time world cross-country champion Lynn Jennings crossed the finish line in third place for the bronze medal at the 1992 Olympics. (AP/Wide World Photos)

official competitor, but she also sustained a knee injury that required surgery and affected her performance for quite awhile.

Jennings attended Princeton University, graduating in 1983. Just as she had predicted, she failed to find any course of study that attracted her so much as running, and by early 1984 she had re-dedicated herself to her sport. In order to "perfect my craft without anyone looking over my shoulder," in her own words, Jennings moved to Newmarket, New Hampshire, a small mill town on the Great Bay. There she began to fulfill her teenaged dream of being the best runner in the world.

Jennings failed to qualify for the 1984 Olympic team in the 3,000 meters, but she suffered few setbacks after that. In 1985 she won the first of eight TAC national cross-country championships, the last seven of them consecutive. In March of 1986 she finished just behind Zola Budd Pieterse at the world cross-country championships, and in 1988 she won the TAC 3,000 meters. That same year she qualified for the U.S. Olympic team in the 10,000-meter run, finishing sixth in Seoul.

In many sports, hitting age 30 is a death knell. Not so for distance running—women especially often hit their stride after 30. Jennings is certainly a case in point. In March of 1990, just months before her 30th birthday, Jennings became the first American in 15 years to win the world cross-country championship. The world cross is considered perhaps the toughest race to win of any track and field event, because the field of competitors includes champions in various distances from 1,500 meters to the marathon. Jennings happened to like the cross-country race better than road or track competitions, and she performed superbly on the world level throughout the early 1990s. By 1992 she had won three back-to-back world cross-country championships, and in 1993 she finished third.

If asked, Jennings would say that her favorite amongst her numerous titles and championships is the bronze medal she won at the 1992 Summer Olympics. Jennings finished third in the 10,000-meter race behind Derartu Tulu of Ethiopia and Elana Meyer of South Africa, setting an American record of 31:19.89. Remembering that race, Jennings told *Runner's World:* "*Nobody* expected me to do well, and I reveled in it. I *knew* I was going to come home with something in my pocket. Whether it was gold, silver or bronze didn't matter."

Small wonder that *Runner's World* chose Jennings as American Female Runner of the Year—against stiff competition—five times, including three consecutive times in 1991, 1992, and 1993. At one point the editors of the magazine quipped, "Maybe we should retire the Runner of the Year title for American women. Or better yet, rename it the Lynn Jennings American Runner of the Year Award."

LYNN JENNINGS

American distance runner

Born: July 1, 1960 in Harvard, Massachusetts.

Education: Attended Princeton University, graduating in 1983.

Career Highlights:
- won eight national cross-country championships, the last seven of them consecutive, 1985, 1987–1993
- finished in second place, world cross-country championships, 1986
- won world cross-country championship, 1990, 1991, and 1992
- earned bronze medal, 10,000-meter race, 1992 Olympic Games, Barcelona, Spain.

Awards: Named American Female Runner of the Year by *Runner's World* magazine five times, including three consecutive times in 1991, 1992, and 1993.

The year that statement was made, Jennings proved her enormous versatility by winning, among others, the national 3,000-meter and 10,000-meter indoor races, a Bud Lite Couples 5-K, the Tufts Women's 10-K, the Tulsa Run 15-K, and her eighth national cross-country championship.

Nike shoes has sponsored Jennings since 1985 and, oddly enough, helped her to meet her husband. New shoes were always sent to her New Hampshire home via United Parcel Service. The delivery man on her route, Dave Hill, became her husband, training companion, and chief booster. Jennings has also resumed training with John Babington, and she feels that she has some victories left to win. "I never take a day off," she admitted in *Women's Sports + Fitness,* "but I do get regular massages and make sure I sleep and eat well. My body has handled high-mileage training really well, although I wouldn't recommend double workouts and mega-mileage for most runners."

What she *would* recommend is cross-country running, especially for teens. "Cross-country provides the basis of excellence for track success," she explained in *Runner's World.* "And most kids get their start as runners in high school cross-country. I'd like to think that my success with cross-country could serve as a kind of beacon to them."

LYNN
JONCKOWSKI

Anyone for a little ride on the back of a 1,500-pound, *angry* Brahma bull? For Hall of Fame cowgirl Lynn "Jonnie" Jonckowski, rodeo bull riding proved the ticket to athletic fame that she had sought all her life. A two-time winner of the world bull riding championship, Jonckowski has earned her victories at great price: she has been kicked, thrown, run over, and slammed by bulls, both inside and outside the ring. Her sport demands physical and mental toughness, and Jonckowski has never felt at a loss in either department. "I ride the same bulls as men," she told *Women's Sports + Fitness*. "But I'm not out there to compete with the guys. I'm just playing the same game, which is to beat the bull."

A resident of Billings, Montana, Jonckowski grew up pursuing athletics with a vengeance. "I had to be better than everyone," she said. "I don't know where the competition comes from, but it just burns a hole in you." She did not ride bucking bulls as a youngster, however. Her chosen sports were track and field events, triathlon, pentathlon, and body building. On the side, as a hobby, she rode horses.

Jonckowski had dreams of making the Olympics as a pentathlon participant, but during training for the 1975 Olympic trials she tripped on a hurdle and injured her back. Doctors told her she would never be able to compete in track and field events again. Bitterly disappointed, she cast around for another outlet for her competitive spirit, and she found it unexpectedly close to home. In 1976 she saw a poster for an all-women's rodeo. She went to the rodeo and entered the bull riding contest, having never sat atop a bull before.

"It was the biggest rush in the world," Jonckowski recalled. "The bull was so powerful that when I got onto it, I instantly saw how athletic it was. But I didn't know enough to be afraid of it."

Jonckowski learned fast. Just a year later, at a bull riding school, she got kicked right in the face by one of the bulls she had ridden. On that occasion, her nose was literally knocked off her face. It was the first of many serious injuries that would befall Jonckowski over the years as she pursued the

244

LYNN "JONNIE" JONCKOWSKI

American bull rider

Born: July 22, 1954 in Fargo, North Dakota.

Career Highlights:

- took second place to become reserve champion, world women's bull riding championship, 1985

- won world women's bull riding championship, 1986 and 1988

Awards: Named to Cowgirl Hall of Fame in Hereford, Texas, 1991.

violent sport. Nor did she find a pot of gold in the rodeo ring. The costs of training and travel exceeded the amount she could win in events. "I built up thousands of dollars in debt," she said. "I had to drop my health club memberships, so I was using innovative training techniques—sit-ups on the rails of the barn, running through the tall alfalfa pastures with sand buckets."

When she finally did contend for her first world championship, in 1986, Jonckowski had yet another scrape with a bull. On her first of three rides (six seconds each), the bull stepped on her after she had fallen. The nerves behind her knee were crushed, raising the specter of blood clots that could cost her the leg—or cause a heart attack. Jonckowski refused to give up. The next day she had her friends lift her onto another bull for the rides that won her a world women's bull riding championship. She repeated as world champion in 1988.

Jonckowski continues to enter bull riding events, even though she has endured even more injuries in the 1990s. A member of the Cowgirl Hall of Fame in Hereford, Texas, since 1991, she has erased her credit card debts by working as a motivational speaker and a sportswear model. Known affectionately as the "Belle of Billings" in her hometown, Jonckowski is thrilled with the way her odd career has turned out. "Any time you have the freedom to do what you want to do and exercise that freedom, you're a champ," she said. "And, to raise my hands and have 30,000 people cheer—I love it!"

JOAN JOYCE

*"There's too great an
element of luck in
women's team sports.
My success in
softball, no matter to
how slight a degree,
still depends on my
teammates."*

The year was 1962, and two legends were ready to square off against each other. One was Ted Williams, the last baseball player to hit .400 in a season. The other was Joan Joyce, a 22-year-old softball phenomenon with a fastball that simply could not be hit. Williams the batter faced Joyce the pitcher in an exhibition in Waterbury, Connecticut. Whatever the former Boston Red Sox star was expecting, he soon found himself fishing for air. With 10,000 fans cheering her on, Joan Joyce fired more than 30 pitches at Williams, who managed only one weak tapper to the infield and a few foul tips. Mostly Williams just missed. Like everyone else who faced Joan Joyce.

Joyce is one of the most successful athletes the world has ever produced. For better than 20 years she dominated softball with her unhittable fastball and her ability to bat like a major leaguer. Joyce's teams—most notably the Raybestos Brakettes of Connecticut—were perennial championship winners, largely because of their star pitcher's penchant for hurling no-hitters in key games. With Joyce's help, the Raybestos Brakettes won 12 national amateur titles in 18 seasons as she pitched 105 no-hitters and 33 perfect games. A tournament umpire once quipped that Joyce was "one of the three best softball pitchers in the country, and two of them are men."

Like so many other women athletes, Joyce gravitated to softball because she was barred from playing baseball. "I started playing softball at eight because my father played it and because it was the only sport open to me at the time," she told *Sports Illustrated* in 1973. By the time she was a teenager, Joyce had developed the fastball that some sources say reached 116 miles an hour at the height of her career. At the age of 18 in 1958 she joined the Raybestos Brakettes of Stratford, Connecticut, and—with the help of veteran teammate Bertha Tickey—she took the team to the first of three consecutive Amateur Softball Association national championships.

Joyce attended Chapman College in Orange, California, and while there she helped the Orange Lionettes to win a national championship by defeating her former team, the Raybestos Brakettes. In college she also played

Pitching phenom Joan Joyce dominated women's softball for more than two decades. (AP/Wide World Photos)

basketball and volleyball. When she graduated she moved back to Connecticut, opened a travel agency, and returned to the Brakettes.

Major League Baseball could only wish for such a dependable winner as the Raybestos Brakettes. The team is one of the all-time strongest dynasties in all of organized sports, winning national championships almost every year between 1958 and 1992, including sixteen straight between 1971 and 1986. Joyce was the dominating force behind the Brakettes in the early to mid-1970s. She led the team to a 1974 world championship, the first won by Americans. How lethal was Joyce? In 1973, to take an example, she pitched back-to-back shutouts over 16 innings with 34 strikeouts against the Santa Clara Laurels en route to the national championship. That was typical. An opponent once told *Sports Illustrated*: "Beating Joan Joyce would make my life complete!"

In 1975 Joyce retired from amateur softball to become a founding member of the International Women's Professional Softball Association. Although slowing down somewhat, she still led her new team, the Connecticut

JOAN JOYCE

American softball player

Born: c. 1940.

Education: Attended Chapman College in Orange, California.

Career Highlights:
- pitched 105 no-hitters and 33 perfect games to lead the Raybestos Brakettes to 12 national amateur titles in 18 seasons
- helped the Orange Lionettes to win a national championship
- led the Raybestos Brakettes to a 1974 world championship, the first won by Americans
- led the Connecticut Falcons to the first-ever World Series victory in professional softball.

Awards: Inducted into the National Softball Hall of Fame, 1983; named to the Women's Sports Foundation Hall of Fame, 1990.

Falcons, to the first-ever World Series victory in professional softball. Working in the professional softball league was for most of its players a labor of love—salaries for a whole summer season of play ranged from $1,000 to $3,000. Joyce, by contrast, was well compensated in recognition of her status in the sport.

Interestingly enough, Joyce admitted having a love-hate relationship with team sports. "I've always been an athlete, and as long as I play women's team sports my success won't be totally my own," she told *Sports Illustrated*. With that in mind, she retired from softball and sought a berth on the LPGA tour. She earned a place on the tour on her second try, at the age of 37.

Few awards have eluded Joan Joyce. In 1983 she was inducted into the National Softball Hall of Fame, and in 1990 she was named to the Women's Sports Foundation Hall of Fame. During her career she was named to 18 ASA All-American teams and was Team MVP eight times. Her amateur career record was 507-33, her professional record 101-15. Her lifetime batting average was .327.

Joyce was women's softball's Babe Ruth and Ty Cobb rolled into one. Just ask Ted Williams.

JACKIE
JOYNER-KERSEE

If amateur athletics has a queen, that monarch would have to be Jackie Joyner-Kersee. Described everywhere as the greatest multi-event track and field athlete of all time, Joyner-Kersee has won three Olympic gold medals, one silver, and one bronze, and has competed in every Summer Olympics since 1984. Her list of accomplishments is impressive: the first American woman to win a gold medal in the long jump, the first woman in history to earn more than 7,000 points in the seven-event heptathlon, the world record holder in the heptathlon since 1986, and the first athlete in 64 years to win gold medals in both a multi-event and a single event in track and field. Amazingly, she is still a force to be reckoned with, and she shows no signs of slowing down.

America loves Jackie Joyner-Kersee. Not only has she been a stand-out Olympian, she has also dazzled fans and opponents alike with her winning personality, her grace and intelligence, and her commitment to the community. She has never let success go to her head but has instead worked to promote physical fitness among young people, especially in urban environments. In the February 1995 issue of *Women's Sports + Fitness,* she said: "I find it touching, in a sense, that people want my autograph and they're in tears. I think, my God! I'm just happy that I'm in the position I'm in and that people would even take the time to talk to me. . . . I understand the position I'm in, but I also know that tomorrow there's going to be someone else. So I try to keep things in perspective."

Joyner-Kersee was born March 3, 1962, in East St. Louis, Illinois, a poverty-stricken city on the Mississippi River. The younger of two children of teenaged parents, she grew up dreaming of a better life for herself and her brother Al. Together the young Joyner siblings took part in sports activities at the publicly-funded Mayor Brown Community Center in East St. Louis. It was there that Jackie Joyner was introduced to track events. After watching the 1976 Olympics on television, she became determined to try to make the U.S. team herself one day.

Almost immediately the versatile young athlete began laying the foundations for her big dreams. At the age of 14 she won the first of four straight

TRACK & FIELD ATHLETE

"You would think it would be easier to focus now, but because of all the things I've already accomplished, sometimes it's harder. I can't think I'm going to go out there and win just because I'm Jackie Joyner-Kersee."

Jackie Joyner-Kersee takes the lead in the 100-meter hurdle portion of the 1992 Olympic heptathlon. (Reuters/Bettmann)

national junior pentathlon championships. She also played basketball and volleyball and earned honor roll grades. Recruited by many top flight colleges, she accepted a scholarship to the University of California, Los Angeles. She chose well: a coach was waiting there to help her achieve her fullest potential.

Bob Kersee met Jackie Joyner in 1980, when she was still playing basketball as a primary sport. He convinced Jackie—and the athletic brass at UCLA—that she should concentrate on multi-event track. She was already a good long jumper and a winner at the 200-meter sprint. Her brother Al Joyner helped her to learn to run hurdles and throw the javelin and shot put. By 1982 Jackie had chosen the demanding heptathlon as her event, and the following year she qualified for the world championships. Her first international competition ended in disappointment when she pulled a hamstring muscle and had to withdraw.

She has had few disappointments since. At her first Olympic appearance in 1984 she won a silver medal in the heptathlon, missing the gold by only .06 seconds in her final event, the 800-meter run. At the 1986 Goodwill Games in Moscow she set a new world record in the heptathlon with 7,148 points. She broke that record three weeks later in Houston on a day when temperatures reached 100 degrees. Those two performances earned Jackie Joyner the 1986 Sullivan Award and the Jesse Owens Award. That same year she married Bob Kersee, and the two have worked closely together ever since.

Joyner-Kersee's performance at the 1988 Olympics was one of the outstanding accomplishments of those games. She won gold medals in both the heptathlon and the long jump and set yet another world record in the heptathlon, with 7,291 points. Those Summer Games were marked by the enthusiasm and affection displayed by Joyner-Kersee and her sister-in-law Florence Griffith Joyner as they congratulated each other on their medal-winning races.

 THE HEPTATHLON

Before Jackie Joyner-Kersee set her sights on it, the heptathlon was a virtually unknown event in America. It has since become a track and field favorite, especially during the Olympics. For the heptathlon, athletes amass points by running a 200-meter dash, completing both high and long jumps, throwing a javelin and a shot put, running the 100-meter hurdles, and doing an 800-meter run, all in the space of two days. The seven-event series demands skills in a variety of areas that most athletes choose as specialties.

More glory awaited Joyner-Kersee in the 1992 Olympics in Barcelona. There she won the heptathlon gold medal again and added a bronze in the long jump. She further endeared herself to her fans by being a gracious "loser" in the long jump to her friend Heike Drechsler of Germany. Asked if she planned to retire after the Games in Barcelona, the animated Joyner-Kersee declared that she fully intended to stay in competition until 1996, so she could begin and end her Olympic career with appearances in Summer Games on American soil.

JACKIE JOYNER-KERSEE

American track and field athlete

Born: March 3, 1962 in East St. Louis, Illinois.

Education: Attended University of California, Los Angeles, 1980–84.

Career Highlights:

- won four straight national junior pentathlon championships as a teenager
- became first woman in history to earn more than 7,000 points in the seven-event heptathlon
- earned silver medal in heptathlon at the 1984 Olympic Games, Los Angeles, California, missing gold by only .06 seconds in 800-meter run
- set new world record in heptathlon, Goodwill Games, and broke that record three weeks later in Houston on a 100-degree day, 1986

- won gold medals in both heptathlon and long jump, 1988 Olympic Games, Seoul, South Korea, becoming first athlete in 64 years to win gold medals in a multi-event and single event in track and field, and first American woman to win a gold medal in long jump
- garnered gold medal in heptathlon and bronze in long jump, 1992 Olympic Games, Barcelona, Spain.

Awards: Won Sullivan Award for best amateur athlete, athlete of the year citation from *Track & Field News,* and Jesse Owens Award, all 1986; named amateur sportswoman of the year by McDonald's, 1987; received honorary doctorate from the University of Missouri, 1989.

Through a decade of tough competition, Joyner-Kersee's stamina has rarely flagged. She has suffered from injuries in her Achilles tendon, hamstring, and groin, however, and is no longer considered an automatic winner in her preferred event. No one, male or female, has ever won a multi-event medal at 34, the age Joyner-Kersee reached just before the 1996 Olympics. She remains undaunted, though. "That's the ultimate challenge—to do something nobody has been able to do," she told *Women's Sports + Fitness.* "I would love that."

Needless to say, Joyner-Kersee has lately been facing much younger competitors both in the U.S. and abroad. Asked the secret of her longevity in a January 1993 *Women's Sports + Fitness* profile, she replied: "A lot of it has to do with how you take care of your body while you're young, and I've always taken care of myself. One good thing about multievent is that I don't have to compete every weekend, like sprinters do. The most heptathlons I do in a year is two, and then I break the events up and work on them at different meets."

One of the only African American women athletes to win lucrative product endorsement contracts, Joyner-Kersee is conscious of her status as a role model. "I feel that as an African American woman the only thing I can do is continue to better myself, continue to perform well, continue to make sure that I'm a good commodity," she concluded in *Women's Sports + Fitness.* "If doors aren't opened for me, then maybe it will happen for someone else."

CAREN
KEMNER

American women's volleyball—like basketball—often sends its best stars abroad to play professionally in Europe. There, our women athletes hone their skills and build their experience in a high-stakes, competitive arena, against players more seasoned than those in colleges and amateur leagues. Caren Kemner is one of U.S. Volleyball's key performers, and she has benefitted from time in Europe as well as almost a decade of work with Team USA. The 1996 Olympics will mark the third Olympic appearance for the six-foot-one-inch, 175-pound player whose coach has described her as "one of the best in the U.S."

Kemner was born and raised in Quincy, Illinois. She loved sports—all sports—and tagged along after her brothers to their various games. "I remember my older brother putting me in goal and kicking balls at me, and you had to hold your own because you didn't want to hear about it over dinner," she joked in the *Los Angeles Times*. Kemner also spent hours whacking tennis balls against a wall or practicing her softball pitches. "It was like I always knew I was supposed to be in sports," she said.

Always big and strong for her age, Kemner played many sports in high school, including volleyball. "It takes a lot of physical gifts, so everything has come a little easier for me," she admitted in the *Times*. "But it requires a lot of good luck and the ability to never underestimate yourself." As a high school student, Kemner led her Quincy Notre Dame team to three consecutive Illinois state volleyball titles. Moving on to the University of Arizona, she was named a second-team All-American during her sophomore year.

Kemner joined the U.S. national volleyball team in 1985 at the age of 20. She saw her first Olympic action in 1988 in Seoul, South Korea, where she turned in 66 kills, 18 blocks, and passed a team-leading 119 serves in five matches. Unfortunately, Kemner's performance in Seoul was not enough to lift the Americans into medal contention. The Cubans won the gold medal, the Soviet Union the silver.

Considered the best all-around player on the U.S. team—and heavily recruited for professional league play in Europe—Kemner reached a crisis

"I always knew I was supposed to be in sports."

point as the 1980s ended. "I felt I was burned out. I felt a lot of frustration in my own life," she explained in the *Los Angeles Times*. "For the first time, I stepped away and regained my personality, which I had lost in sports. There are only so many hours in a day that your life can revolve around volleyball."

Re-establishing her links with herself and her family, Kemner took a six-month hiatus from her sport. She returned to the U.S. team in July 1990 in time to help the Americans win a bronze medal at the world championships. For her efforts on the team's behalf Kemner was nominated for the prestigious Sullivan Award for amateur athletics. She earned yet another Sullivan Award nomination the following year when she was named Most Valuable Woman Player in the World by the Federation Internationale de Volley-Ball (FIVB). That award stemmed as much from Kemner's professional play on teams in Brazil, Japan, and Italy, as it did from her work for her native land.

Caren Kemner is considered one of the best volleyball players in the United States. (© Otto Gruele, Jr./Allsport Photography USA Inc.)

The U.S. women's volleyball team had its best showing ever in the 1992 Olympics, winning a bronze medal behind Cuba and a Unified Team from the former Soviet Union. Kemner's contribution to the 1992 bronze medal victory included a team-high 127 kills and seven aces, a performance that led her to be named to FIVB's 1992 "Super Four."

Greater subsidies for practice and play with Team USA have given players like Caren Kemner the luxury of staying in the United States and working with a stable roster of fellow teammates. The improvement has been noticeable. After a dismal sixth place showing at the 1994 world championships, the U.S. women's team won a silver medal at the 1995 Pan American games, facing tough competition from Cuban and Brazilian teams. Kemner has contributed experience and leadership to the American team in preparation for the 1996 Summer Games, where she will be one of four returning starters from the 1992 Olympic team.

U.S. national team coach Terry Liskevych has expressed great relief that he can count on the likes of Caren Kemner to build his next Olympic team. "Caren, without question, is one of the best athletes I've ever coached, male or female," Liskevych told the *Los Angeles Times*. The coach added that

CAREN KEMNER

American volleyball player

Born: Quincy, Illinois.

Education: Attended the University of Arizona.

Career Highlights:
- led her Quincy Notre Dame high school team to three consecutive Illinois state volleyball titles
- helped U.S. women's volleyball team win a bronze medal at the world championships, 1990
- led U.S. team to bronze medal with a team-high 127 kills and seven aces, 1992 Olympic Games, Barcelona, Spain
- helped U.S. women's team win a silver medal at the 1995 Pan American games.

Awards: Named Team USA MVP, 1986–88, 1990–91; nominated for Sullivan Award for amateur athletics, 1990 and 1991; named Most Valuable Woman Player in the World by the Federation Internationale de Volley-Ball (FIVB), 1991; named to FIVB's "Super Four," 1992.

she would be "a big factor in our becoming the best team in the world." As for herself, Kemner has equally high ambitions. "I have to win a gold medal for myself," she said. "I'm not worried about making an impression on the sport for myself. If I go down as one of the greater players . . . , that would be a great compliment."

NANCY KERRIGAN

FIGURE SKATER

"With dozens of American flags waving and Kerrigan beaming proudly at center ice, one had the feeling that at least one demon had been exorcised. The attack in Detroit was behind her."

—Steve Rushin for Sports Illustrated coverage of 1994 Olympics

Through no design of her own, Nancy Kerrigan became one of the world's most famous athletes during the winter of 1994. Struck by a club-wielding assailant, she collapsed inside Detroit's Cobo Arena on a snowy January afternoon, sobbing from an injury to her right knee. As the public came to know the particulars of her attack, turning what initially seemed sense-less violence into riveting drama, Kerrigan the Victim became more famous than Kerrigan the Skater. At the close of the 1994 Winter Games weeks later, however, the Skater easily overshadowed the Victim, with a remarkably com-posed performance in the women's free skating competition that earned the 24-year-old far more than a silver medal.

Kerrigan began chasing an Olympic dream while still a child. Raised in a modest home in Stoneham, Massachusetts, she often found herself at the neighborhood ice rink, following in the footsteps of two older brothers who played ice hockey. Father Dan Kerrigan was a welder, and almost from the moment Nancy laced up her first pair of skates, he sacrificed his earnings to support her training. It was a considerable investment from the start, and as Nancy began winning local and regional competitions, her father was forced to work odd jobs and take out loans for thousands of dollars.

The early training years were trying for Kerrigan. She would rise reg-ularly at 4 a.m. to skate before attending classes at Stoneham High School. Sometimes the Kerrigans did not have enough money to purchase a new pair of skates. Nancy would complain about her outsized pair. "Suffer in silence," her mother would respond.

With her combination of talent and toughness, Kerrigan established herself as an elite competitor at the age of 19 when she won the National Collegiate Championships. At the time she was a student in a business pro-gram at Emmanuel College, an institution near her home in Stoneham. In 1989 she took the stage as one of the top three skaters in the country, win-ning a bronze medal at the U.S. Olympic Festival. The next year she won the

*Nancy Kerrigan triumphantly completes her free skating program at the
1994 Olympics; in spite of adversity, she came home with the silver
medal.* (AP/Wide World Photos)

NANCY KERRIGAN

gold at the same competition. It was no surprise when Kerrigan earned the right to represent the United States at the 1992 Winter Games in Albertville, France.

During the 1992 Olympics Kerrigan began her ascent into celebrity. Her performance didn't beat out gold medalist Kristi Yamaguchi, but it was good enough for a bronze and a secure place in the hearts of many Americans. Following the Olympics, Kerrigan won her first national championship, but soon thereafter cracks began to show in her routines. At the world championships in Prague in 1993, Kerrigan led the field going into the free skate but fumbled in her long program and dropped to a dismal tenth. It was a humiliating showing that sent her into a fit of tears. Before national television cameras she said, "I just want to die."

That her family had dedicated their lives and savings to her career only heightened Kerrigan's sense of failure. The bronze medal at the 1992 Olympics won her a pile of press clippings but none of the lucrative endorsements that might have secured her financial future. For that, she knew she needed a gold medal at the 1994 Olympics.

To prepare for the competition of her life, Kerrigan trained with a fierce intensity that left little room for anything but skating. The hard work paid off: she won two major international competitions in 1993—the Piruetten in Hamar, Norway, and the AT&T Pro Am in Philadelphia. Then she set out to defend her national title in Detroit before heading to Lillehammer.

What happened then ranks as one of the most bizarre moments in the history of sports.

"Why me? Why now? Help me! Help me!" Kerrigan's pained call for help seconds after the attack was captured by television cameras and newspapers worldwide. Suddenly she found herself awash in publicity, hounded by reporters who camped in the driveway of her parents' home and followed her everywhere she went. And her ability to compete in the Olympics was seriously in doubt, with injuries to her kneecap and quadriceps tendon.

As the details of the assault became known, America learned that the attack had been engineered by the husband of rival skater Tonya Harding, an athlete who had almost always finished second to Kerrigan in head-to-head competition. This revelation brought an avalanche of sympathy and support for Kerrigan, who was named to the U.S. Olympic team even though she had been unable to compete in the nationals.

Another athlete rocked by the same trauma might never have resurfaced in the competitive arena. Kerrigan simply dug her heels in deeper. Her public sobbing at the world championships in Prague was behind her, and the

NANCY KERRIGAN

American figure skater

Born: October 13, 1969 in Massachusetts.

Education: Attended Emmanuel College in Massachusetts, receiving an associate's degree in business, 1989.

Career Highlights:

- won the National Collegiate Championships, 1988
- earned bronze medal, U.S. Olympic Festival, 1989
- won gold medal, U.S. Olympic Festival, 1990
- received bronze medal, 1992 Olympic Games, Albertville, France
- won national championship, 1993
- won two major international competitions—Piruetten in Hamar, Norway, and AT&T Pro Am in Philadelphia, 1993
- earned silver medal, 1994 Olympic Games, Hamar, Norway.

Boston "working-class blood in her veins," as one reporter noted, brought out her fighting spirit. Doubly angered that the U.S. Olympic Committee had decided to allow Harding to compete in the Games, Kerrigan vowed to beat her nemesis and all other competitors as well.

A nearly flawless performance in the technical program put Kerrigan in first place at the Lillehammer competition. She knew she would have to skate well in her free program in order to win the gold. The 1994 Olympic Winter Games women's free skate was one of the most widely watched athletic competitions in U.S. television history. Harding broke a lace on her skate and fumbled through her program, earning only polite applause. In contrast, Kerrigan skated with passion and verve, executing her difficult jumps perfectly and smiling brightly at the crowd. For all that, she narrowly missed winning the gold medal and had to settle for a silver.

Americans love winners, and in Nancy Kerrigan's case a silver medal was just fine—considering what she endured to earn it. She returned home to a hero's welcome, which she deemed "corny," and she embarked on a professional career that has more than earned back all the money her parents spent on her training. Today Kerrigan is newly married and a featured performer in ice shows. The endorsement contracts have materialized, including a big one with Campbell's soup.

Sports Illustrated correspondent E. M. Swift observed about Nancy Kerrigan: "She is tough and honest. She can be sarcastic and biting and carries a bit of a chip on her shoulder. She is provincial, loyal, determined, ungrateful, graceful and proud, and she comes from a loving family and neighborhood. Deal with it, America. Princesses are for fairy tales. She's one of us."

BETSY KING

GOLFER

"I tell all my students to look at Betsy King, the unemotional and classy way she handles herself. That's the way to be a consistent winner."

—Ed Oldfield, golf pro

Membership in the LPGA Hall of Fame is one of sport's most prestigious prizes. Only 14 women have qualified in more than 40 years, principally because the entry requirements include 30 tournament victories, including at least one major LPGA title. Betsy King is the most recent inductee into this elite group of world champion golfers, and for her the honor took nearly 20 years to achieve.

Oddly enough, King is a Hall-of-Famer in a sport that she didn't particularly like as a youngster. In high school and college she preferred basketball and field hockey, only turning to golf when injuries ended her participation in those other sports. Her early struggles on the LPGA tour were made easier by her Christian faith, which has sustained her through good years and bad.

King was born in 1955 in Reading, Pennsylvania, and grew up in the small town of Limekiln. Both of her parents were dedicated athletes who encouraged her and her brother to participate in sports. King was an excellent student who earned honor roll grades and still found enough time to engage in numerous extracurricular activities. She was a star of her Exeter Township High School basketball team and batted .480 as a shortstop on the softball team.

King's father was a doctor who well knew the benefits of all sorts of sports. He began giving Betsy and her brother golf lessons when they were ten. In the *New York Times,* Dr. King recalled that the lessons led to some childish mischief. "[Betsy] and her brother . . . used to hit golf balls toward the house," he said. "One time, from upstairs, I could hear her brother saying, 'I hit the house with a 4-iron today.' I was on them pretty good after that. I told them to keep it on the course."

After high school King attended Furman University in South Carolina. She majored in physical education and played basketball, field hockey, and golf. A knee injury she sustained in a field hockey game effectively ended her participation in both of the more rigorous sports, so she decided—reluctantly—to concentrate on golf. In 1976 the Furman team, including King and future LPGA pros Beth Daniel and Sherri Turner, won the NCAA champi-

LPGA Hall of Famer Betsy King chips onto the eighth green during the JAL Big Apple Classic in 1990. (AP/Wide World Photos)

onship in golf. That same year King shot the best amateur score at the U.S. Women's Open, finishing in a tie for eighth place. She decided then and there to turn pro.

At first King struggled on the LPGA tour, averaging 74.26 strokes per round through her first four years. Her best finishes were two second places—in 1978 at the Borden Classic and in 1979 at the Wheeling Classic. "For a lot of reasons, it's hard for me to remember my first few years on tour," King admitted in *Golf* magazine. "But I do recall that I reached a point where I thought I might never win a tournament. I think I'd even begun to come to terms with that. I thought, well, I'm going to be the best non-winner who's ever been out there."

Being an also-ran was just not good enough, however. In 1980 King sought the help of teaching pro Ed Oldfield, who told her that her game would have to be "rebuilt from top to bottom." Learning a whole new swing was a difficult and wrenching task, but King worked at it patiently, enduring months when her game was worse than ever. In *Golf* magazine, Oldfield confessed: "Most pros probably couldn't handle changing their swing altogether. It takes an exceptional person. I quickly realized that Betsy King was that person. She was so patient, so trusting, so sincere. I'd never seen anyone who wanted to be the best player in the world more than Betsy King. She was willing to do whatever it took."

A new interest in Christianity also helped King to deal with the pressures of the tour. Her faith helped her to get perspective on her competitiveness. "In the past I tended to compare myself to other people," she explained in *Golf Digest*. "I used to resent people who would beat me. I'd want to win at everything, if it was just playing cards."

King won her first LPGA tournament in 1984, the Kemper Open. Having put her also-ran status to rest, she proceeded to win two more tournaments and to lead the LPGA in earnings for 1984. At season's end she was named Player of the Year. Over the next two seasons she won four more tournaments, and in 1987 she took her first major title with a win in the Dinah Shore Women's Open. King won the Vare Trophy in 1987, given to the player with the lowest scoring average. (The trophy is named after Glenna Collett Vare, an American who won a record six U.S. women's amateur championships in the 1920s and 1930s.)

In 1989 King turned in a phenomenal season, with six tournament victories, including the Women's Open. The next season she successfully defended her Women's Open crown with a stunning come-from-behind victory over Patty Sheehan. At one point in the Open, King was a full 11 strokes behind Sheehan. She just didn't give up. "They're not going to know what hap-

BETSY KING

American golfer

Born: 1955 in Reading, Pennsylvania.

Education: Attended Furman University in South Carolina.

Career Highlights:

- helped Furman University team win the NCAA championship in golf
- won Kemper Open, her first LPGA tournament, in 1984
- took first place in Dinah Shore Women's Open, 1987 and 1990

- won the Women's Open, 1989 and 1990
- earned LPGA championship, 1992
- won ShopRite LPGA Classic, her 30th career victory, which enabled her to be inducted into the LPGA Hall of Fame, 1995.

Awards: Named LPGA Player of the Year, 1984, 1989, 1993; won the Vare Trophy, 1987 and 1993; inducted into LPGA Hall of Fame, November 11, 1995.

---

pened down the road," she told *Sports Illustrated* after the tournament. "They'll see the winner's name and won't know what occurred." King also won the Nabisco Dinah Shore Women's Open for the second time in 1990.

As the 1990s progressed, King struggled with her swing, but she kept winning all the same. As victor in the 1992 LPGA championship, she credited her win over a younger field to her years of experience. She was named LPGA Player of the Year in 1993, led the tour in earnings with $595,992, and took home her second Vare Trophy.

The final goal for King was induction into the LPGA Hall of Fame. She needed 30 tour victories to qualify, and by 1994 she had won 29. Nine times in 1994 King held the lead in the final round of a tournament but could not win. The pressure to get that final victory was hurting her game. "I know people mean well and try to encourage you, but a lot of people were asking about it and mentioning it," she recalled in *Golf* magazine. "There's been a lot of prayer on my part to keep perspective, and I haven't always done well with that. I did feel it was unfair that anytime I was close to the lead, people were saying if I didn't win, I lost it. I used to count the days that went by when someone didn't mention the Hall of Fame. Those were few and far between."

King's slump lasted 20 months. Finally, in 1995, she won at the ShopRite LPGA Classic, her 30th career victory. "The pressure's off," a relieved King exclaimed in the *New York Times*. The LPGA Hall of Fame inducted Betsy King on November 11, 1995. At the time she led the LPGA in career earnings with $5,374,022.

Betsy King is renowned for her seriousness and deep concentration during tournaments. Off the links she is a shy person who shuns contact with fans or the press as much as possible. "I think sometimes people think you're cocky or standoffish because you're shy," she explained in *Golf Digest*. "I have a hard time handling the [fans] coming up. I've never felt my job is to make sure I give 5,000 autographs every week. It's scary in a way, when people put you on a pedestal. I feel like right away it limits any kind of relationship you can have."

King, who lives in Scottsdale, Arizona, might turn to coaching when her golf career comes to an end. In the meantime, she continues to tour, attending Christian fellowship meetings with fellow athletes whenever possible. With her the religious faith is more than a convenient show—she donates an estimated 10 percent of her earnings to charity and has been known to miss tournaments when their scheduling conflicts with her charitable duties.

BILLIE JEAN KING

Few tennis stars have done more to popularize the sport than Billie Jean King. King was not only one of the most successful players of the 1960s and 1970s, she was also an ardent activist for women's rights, both inside and outside the sporting arena. Remembered by many today for her trouncing of Bobby Riggs in a 1973 exhibition tournament, she forged a long string of career victories in singles, doubles, and mixed doubles competition. Her 21 Wimbledon championships are a record for that prestigious tournament. Just as important, King was one of the major forces in a movement to bring women's tennis prize money into parity with men's. And in a broader context, she helped to found the Women's Sports Foundation, an organization dedicated to the aid and support of women athletes.

"I couldn't stand to lose. It used to just kill me! But I felt in the long run that if I really wanted to achieve my goals I would have to lose."

Born Billie Jean Moffitt on November 22, 1943, King grew up in Long Beach, California. Her family enjoyed athletic endeavors—not tennis—and Billie Jean found early success as a softball player. (Her brother, Randy Moffitt, pitched for the San Francisco Giants.) Billie Jean entered tennis later than many pro players do, not receiving her first formal lessons until she was about 11. That same year she had progressed enough to beat a college junior in straight sets.

In 1959 King entered the eastern grass court championships, where she lost to the 1959 Wimbledon champion, Maria Bueno. King's performance there brought her to the attention of coach Frank Brennan, who convinced her to relocate to Saddle River, New Jersey, and work at his tennis school. Just two years later, in 1961, King teamed with fellow Brennan protege Karen Hantze to win the doubles title at Wimbledon. At the time they were the youngest team ever to take the doubles crown.

That championship was the first of 20 Wimbledon titles that would come to King over a period of almost 20 years. All told, King won six singles, 10 doubles, and four mixed doubles championships at Wimbledon between 1961 and 1979. She appeared in a phenomenal 27 final rounds there during her career. King's doubles partners in various Wimbledon tournaments included Hantze, Rosie Casals, and Martina Navratilova.

Billie Jean King swoops down to return the ball in a successful bid for the 1972 French Open crown. (AP/Wide World Photos)

In the late 1960s King was ranked number one in the world in women's tennis. Not the kind of person to waste that sort of clout, she became a vocal and determined crusader for equal prize money for women players. King became the first woman ever to win $100,000 in prize money, and she did so in 1970. However, the top male winner of 1970, Rod Laver, earned three times that much and won only a third of the number of tournaments that King won. Billie Jean King decided enough was enough. She banded with other top-ranked female tennis stars and threatened to boycott the big tournaments unless women were given more prize money. This threat in turn led to the creation of the Virginia Slims Tournament, the first tennis tournament strictly for women.

On the court in the late 1960s and early 1970s, King was queen. She won the Wimbledon singles title in 1966, 1967, 1968, 1972, 1973, and 1975. She also took the U.S. Open at Forest Hills in 1967, 1971, 1972, and 1974. In amongst these consistent victories, she racked up a French Open singles

BILLIE JEAN KING

American tennis player

Born: November 22, 1943 in Long Beach, California.

Education: Attended Los Angeles State College (now California State College at Los Angeles).

Career Highlights:

- won twenty-one Wimbledon titles, including six singles, 1966–68, 1972–73, and 1975; ten doubles, 1961–63, 1965, 1967–68, 1970–73, and 1979; and four mixed doubles, 1967, 1971, 1973–74

- won U.S. Open singles competitions, 1967, 1971–72, and 1974; doubles competitions, 1964, 1967, 1974, 1977, 1980; mixed doubles competitions, 1967, 1971, 1973, 1976

- won Australian Open singles championship, 1968 and 1971; mixed doubles championship, 1968

- took French Open singles and doubles crowns, 1972; mixed doubles, 1967–70

- helped U.S. Federation Cup team to win seven Cups in nine attempts by winning 51 of 55 singles and doubles matches.

Awards: Voted into the International Tennis Hall of Fame, 1987.

---

crown in 1972 and the Australian Open singles championship in 1968 and 1971. She therefore won all four Grand Slam events, just never in the same year.

King was at the very top of her game in 1973 when she was challenged to a singles match against self-proclaimed "male chauvinist" Bobby Riggs. Riggs, a former Wimbledon champion, was a middle-aged tennis hustler with a larger-than-life personality. Even though he was 25 years older than King, the oddsmakers favored him to beat her on the tennis court. Their showdown was performed before a live crowd of 30,472 in the Houston Astrodome and has been estimated to have drawn a television audience in the millions. Riggs arrived for the match surrounded by scantily-clad women, and, not to be outdone, King had herself carried onto the court on a red-draped divan supported by four men dressed as ancient slaves. Once the match started, King became deadly serious. She not only beat Riggs, she beat him soundly. Then she used the victory as a rallying point for equal rights in sports.

King continued to play professionally until 1983 and retired when she was still ranked 13th internationally. Her late-career victories were often in doubles play, including a 1979 Wimbledon doubles championship and a 1980 U.S. Open women's doubles title. She was particularly formidable as part of the U.S. Federation Cup team, helping the U.S. to win seven Cups in nine attempts by winning 51 of 55 singles and doubles matches. King was 40 when she retired, and in one of her last tournament appearances she advanced to the semifinals at Wimbledon, there losing to 18-year-old Andrea Jaeger. King's prize money total of $1,966,487 would have been many times greater had she reached her peak in more recent times.

Since leaving tennis, King has enjoyed a second career as an advocate for equity in women's sports. She remains active with the Women's Sports Foundation and is a frequent speaker at motivational seminars and women's conferences. Divorced from her husband, Larry King, she has admitted to having had some lesbian relationships—an admission that cost her some endorsement contracts but enhanced her reputation as an honest and forthright individual. She was voted into the International Tennis Hall of Fame in 1987.

KAROLYN
KIRBY

Someone once said that Ginger Rogers could do everything Fred Astaire did—except backwards, and on high heels. Beach volleyball is like that, in a way. It's volleyball played almost singlehandedly, on ever-shifting terrain in temperatures that sometimes hit 140 degrees. Even the best team volleyball players often look completely foolish in a beach volleyball game. Karolyn Kirby, widely acknowledged as the best American beach player of all time, had to learn new skills to be competitive on the sand.

"It's a very different game, and you don't have instant success," Kirby noted in the *San Francisco Chronicle*. "The first year or so I spent trying to figure out how to play the game. You go out in the sand and you can't jump or move; you trip and fall when you try to set. And once you get the basics down, you're bothered by the sun and wind. It's a very humbling experience."

It's safe to say that Kirby has the basics down today. She is the first women's beach volleyball player ever to earn $200,000 in prize money. Her gold medal at the 1994 Goodwill Games—at which she was paired with Liz Masakayan—sent a message to the international community that America would be looking for gold when beach volleyball debuts as an Olympic sport in 1996. Kirby has been the top-ranked American beach volleyball player virtually ever year since the 1990s began, and although she has changed partners several times, she always seems to win. Her 1995 totals alone included three tournament titles, an overall record of 71-31, and $46,495 in prize money from appearances in 17 events.

Kirby's life story is something of a joke among beach volleyball players. Blonde and tanned, she looks like a quintessential California girl—and she even lives in San Diego. Looks can be deceiving, though. She was actually born and raised in Brookline, Massachusetts, the same town that produced presidential candidate Michael Dukakis. She was an athletic youngster, but she never played volleyball until high school. She discovered the sport as a freshman and "fell in love" with it. "I was swimming competitively, but I

BEACH
VOLLEYBALL
PLAYER

"The first year or so I spent trying to figure out how to play the game. You go out in the sand and you can't jump or move; you trip and fall when you try to set. And once you get the basics down, you're bothered by the sun and wind. It's a very humbling experience."

burned out on that," she said in the *Los Angeles Times*. "I was looking at what else there was. It was either field hockey, soccer, or volleyball."

With no experience, Kirby made the varsity volleyball team at her high school and spent four years playing there. As a junior she was invited to join the junior Olympic team, an honor that further deepened her commitment to the sport. As a senior she sent a tape of her performance along with an application to Utah State University, site of the NCAA champion volleyball team. To her surprise, she was accepted and offered a full scholarship. Reluctant to try her skills at such a competitive school, Kirby almost turned the scholarship down. Her father helped her to change her mind. "When I was in high school, he and I would sit around and talk about playing volleyball and going to the Olympics," Kirby told the *Boston Globe*. "I was so nervous, I didn't know if I wanted to go to Utah State. But he encouraged me to do it. He had the vision I lacked." Kirby added that her father died just before she left for Utah State.

Kirby was named an All-American at two different schools, Utah State and the University of Kentucky. She transferred to the latter school when her Utah State coaches moved there in 1983. Known primarily for her setting skills, she made the Olympic training team in 1983 and served as an alternate to the 1984 Olympic team. When her association with the national team ended in 1987, she turned professional, playing in Europe and South America.

Kirby's introduction to beach volleyball came in the summer of 1985, when she was captain of the U.S. national volleyball team. She and fellow team member Angela Rock were taking a day off when they noticed an open beach volleyball tournament on Mission Beach. On a whim they entered, figuring with their volleyball skills they could easily win a few rounds. They soon discovered otherwise. The sand shifted when they tried to jump or set. There was so much more court to cover with just two players. And each of them had to use every volleyball skill—set, spike, dig, and block. In short, the two Olympians lost every game. "It was uno, dos, adios," Kirby recalled in the *Los Angeles Times*. "And we didn't even know these people we lost to. It was embarrassing."

Beach volleyball intrigued Kirby, however, and in 1987 she decided to join the Women's Professional Volleyball Association and spend her summers playing beach volleyball. She rejoined Angela Rock on the beach, and after a year of learning the nuances of the game she began to win. In 1991 she and Rock won 12 of 17 events with a 98-14 record. They split $135,000 in prize money. Kirby was named tour Most Valuable Player in 1991 and 1992.

Partnerships in beach volleyball shift almost as often as the sand itself. After winning the 1992 world championship with Nancy Reno, Kirby

KAROLYN KIRBY

American beach volleyball player

Born: C. 1962 in Brookline, Massachusetts.

Education: Attended Utah State University on scholarship; transferred to the University of Kentucky in 1983.

Career Highlights:
- paired with Liz Masakayan to win gold medal at the 1994 Goodwill Games
- attained top-ranking among American beach volleyball players virtually every year since the 1990s began
- won three tournament titles, achieved an overall record of 71-31, and earned $46,495 in prize money, 1995.

Awards: Named All-American at both Utah State and University of Kentucky; named MVP of the Women's Professional Volleyball Association, 1991 and 1992.

found herself without a partner as eight top players left the WPVA for a rival tour. The split proved to be lucky for Kirby, though it certainly did not seem so at the time. Her new partner, Liz Masakayan, was a two-time All-American graduate of UCLA with experience on the national team. Kirby and Masakayan were ranked first and second nationally when they teamed up, and they proved the rankings true over the next two seasons, winning a gold medal at the Goodwill Games in 1994 and earning an estimated half million dollars in prize money between them. The prospects looked bright for this dynamic duo to cruise into the 1996 Olympics together, but Masakayan injured her knee severely late in 1994 and had to quit the tour in mid-1995.

A champion like Kirby has not gone begging for partners since. She re-teamed with Nancy Reno late in 1995 and is looking forward to a future that includes an Olympic medal. Once considered elusive and private, Kirby has emerged to help the struggling WPVA as its chief booster and spokesperson. In addition to her prize money, she has endorsement contracts with athletic wear manufacturers that have helped her to enjoy a comfortable lifestyle.

One thing that rankles Kirby is the trivialization of women's beach volleyball and the suggestion that it is little more than a "babes in bikinis" show. The former All-American and national team captain maintains that beach volleyball is a much tougher contest than team volleyball on a flat surface, requiring a full complement of skills and superb physical conditioning. As for the attire she wears during tournaments, Kirby told *Women's Sports + Fitness:* "This is what you wear at the beach. It's not as if we used to play in pantaloons and then switched to swimsuits to get on TV."

OLGA KORBUT

"After I delivered my son, two or three years later, I would have done brilliantly. I could have stayed in competition for 10 more years. . . . But this is fine. I am a great realist in all aspects of life. Whatever I can do . . . here it is."

She has been called the "first of the pixies" and an "amazing Soviet sylph." She dazzled the world at the 1972 Olympic Games in Munich and ignited a gymnastics revolution among young girls who wanted to be like her. Olga Korbut, with her radiant smile and daring performances, did more to popularize women's gymnastics than any star before her. Her influence on the sport is still strong today.

"Women's gymnastics previously had been more like an athletic ballet, and its champions were adults," wrote Leigh Montville in *Sports Illustrated.* "Larissa Latynina of the Soviet Union had been 29 and a mother when she won six gold medals [in 1964] in Tokyo. Now, here was this waif throwing herself around the uneven bars and backward off the balance beam in a series of moves that seemed almost death-defying. What mature woman could do what she did? Or would even try? Some gymnastics purists called Korbut 'a circus act,' but to the public she was a wonder."

This "wonder" was born in 1956 in Grodno, Belarus, which was then known as Byelorussia, part of the Soviet Union. Korbut, the youngest daughter of an engineer and a cook, grew up in a region where gymnastics were popular, and she followed her older sister into training. At 11 Korbut qualified for one of the Soviet government's sports schools. There she worked with coaches Yelena Volchetskaya and Renald Knysh, who pushed her to try ever more difficult and innovative stunts on the balance beam and the uneven parallel bars.

Korbut climbed quickly through the gymnastic ranks, and in 1969 she placed fifth at the Soviet national championships. The following year she won her first national title, on the vault horse, and was named to the Soviet world championship team. Just as she was beginning to experience success, she suffered an injury and illness that kept her out of training for quite some time. Known as a lackadaisical trainer before the illness, she buckled down afterwards and practiced wholeheartedly. When she returned to competition in 1972, she placed third in overall performance at the Soviet national championships and qualified for the 1972 Olympic team.

Olga Korbut stunned audiences at the 1972 Olympics and changed the face of gymnastics. (Archive Photos/Express Newspapers)

Korbut was 17 years old, four-feet-eleven inches tall, and about 90 pounds when she arrived at the Olympic Games in Munich. Surprisingly enough, she did not even win the all-around event that year. Her achievements were spectacular nonetheless. The Soviets took the team gold medal, then Korbut won individual golds in floor exercise and balance beam. A blunder on the uneven parallel bars cost her the gold in that event, but she won the silver. Audiences were delighted with the young Korbut, her bright smiles and bouts of disappointed tears when her performances did not suit her. What no one knew at the time was that Korbut represented the future of gymnastics—the young, slender, fantastically daring athlete who performed with all the exuberance of a child.

After the Olympics, Korbut took a triumphant tour of America and Europe. She met President Richard Nixon, got her picture taken with Mickey Mouse, spent a day boating with the British prime minister, and met the Shah of Iran. Back home in the Soviet Union, she was just another successful ath-

OLGA KORBUT

Belarusan gymnast

Born: 1956 in Grodno, Belarus (then Byelorussia, part of the Soviet Union).

Career Highlights:

- placed fifth at Soviet national championships, 1969
- took first place at Soviet national championships, vault horse competition, 1970
- helped Soviet team win team gold medal; won individual golds in floor exercise and balance beam, and silver in uneven parallel bars, 1972 Olympic Games, Munich, Germany
- won silver medal, balance beam competition, 1976 Olympic Games, Montreal, Canada.

lete in a long series of champions, but in the rest of the world she was loved for her spontaneous personality and obvious talent.

Korbut recalls those days in wonder. "I look at that little girl now and see that it was a shame she wasn't prepared for any of this," she told *Sports Illustrated.* "She couldn't comprehend what was happening. She was thinking, Why are these people bothering me?"

Korbut appeared in the 1976 Olympics but was overshadowed by Nadia Comaneci. Returning to the Soviet Union after a winter tour of America, she announced her retirement and took a job as a coach in Minsk. She married a Soviet musician named Leonid Bortkevich and had a son, Richard. The stage seemed set for a quiet, productive life, but fate intervened.

Soon after completing a 1989 gymnastics tour of America, Korbut discovered that she had developed thyroid problems and exhaustion related to radiation poisoning. She had been living in Minsk when the Chernobyl nuclear reactor exploded in 1987 and, like many of the other residents of Belarus, she had been exposed to the dangerous fallout that spread in the wake of the accident. Unlike the numerous anonymous citizens, however, Korbut could capitalize on her celebrity to publicize the fate of the sick citizens—especially the children. Since 1990 she has served as the spokesperson for the Emergency Help for Children Foundation, a nonprofit company set up to help the victims of the Chernobyl disaster.

"I would like everyone in the world to be aware of how terrible it is in Byelorussia," Korbut told *People.* "Maybe we can only save one child or two children. I hope there are people in this world who want to help. No matter how little or how large, it will count."

In 1991, when relations between Russia and America grew friendly, Korbut moved to the United States and settled in Atlanta with her teenaged son. She teaches gymnastics there and is still actively involved with fundraising for the sick children she left behind in her native land. She has undertaken several national tours, but the aging process has taken its inevitable toll on her talents. "I always thought there should be a separate classification for older gymnasts," she confided in *Sports Illustrated*. "There should be different expectations for someone in a mature stage of womanhood than for a young girl. The audience should not cheer only out of fear. There should be an appreciation of the beauty of gymnastics. . . . A gymnast should be able to stay in the sport for a long time."

PETRA
KRONBERGER

SKIER

"If I am to believe the newspapers, I am supposed to be a superstar. The trouble is, I don't feel like one, and I am very glad that at least my friends and family still treat me like a normal person."

She tried her best to dodge the limelight while at the top of her sport, but Petra Kronberger became a skiing star anyway. Quite possibly the most dominant female skier ever to snap into a set of bindings, Kronberger became the first woman ever to win a competition in each of ski racing's five events—slalom, giant slalom, Super G, downhill, and combined. Even more remarkably, she accomplished this feat in just 38 days during the winter of 1990–91. A three-time World Cup winner and holder of two Olympic gold medals from the 1992 Winter Games, Kronberger never considered herself anything but a "country girl" who happened to do well on the slopes.

Her life was hard as a child. She was born February 21, 1969, in the tiny town of Pfarrwerfen, Austria, and spent the first few years of her life living on a farm owned by her maternal grandparents. Her father earned a meager living driving a cement truck, and her mother tried to help out by working as a cleaning woman and a dishwasher in a restaurant. Kronberger's younger brother, Robert, died after a flu-like illness at the age of 13 months. Perhaps as a result of the tragedy, young Petra began to behave more like a boy than a girl, choosing vigorous sports and working hard on her skiing.

Kronberger began skiing at the age of two and, with her father's help, was winning trophies by the time she was six. At 10 she left home to live at a *Skihauptschule,* a special school for athletes in Bad Gastein. She stayed there for four years and then transferred to a similar school in Schladming. Plagued with injuries, she was not a strong skier as a young teen, and when she graduated from school she took a job as a bank clerk.

Kronberger's fortunes on the slope began to turn in 1988 when she scored an impressive 15th at the tough Leukerbad, Switzerland, course. She made the 1988 Olympic team representing Austria, finishing 11th in the combined (downhill and slalom) and an impressive sixth in the downhill. She really began to dominate in 1990, when she won her first of three consecutive World Cups and became the first woman to win in every discipline during the course of a single season. In the 1990 season alone, Kronberger out-scored

Petra Kronberger was a three-time World Cup champion in the early 1990s, and won two gold medals at the 1992 Olympics. (AP/Wide World Photos)

10 other nations—singlehandedly. She basically had the overall-points championship wrapped up by the New Year.

It was at that season's end, however, that Kronberger's career began to close. A crash at the world championships in Saalbach, Austria, forced her out for the rest of 1991. And although she came back in 1992 to capture her third consecutive overall title and two gold medals at the Winter Games in Albertville—in slalom and combined—the pain from her knee injury was just too much to bear.

Prior to the 1992–93 World Cup season, Kronberger announced her retirement. "I have reached everything possible in the world of ski racing," her press release stated. "I know that many will say 'Petra is crazy to renounce all that money.' . . . My health is more important."

Money there certainly was—in abundance. Sources estimate that Kronberger earned as much as $300,000 a year during her brief reign as the

PETRA KRONBERGER

Austrian skier

Born: February 21, 1969 in Pfarrwerfen, Austria.

Career Highlights:
• won three consecutive World Cups, 1990, 1991, and 1992

• captured two gold medals, in slalom and combined, 1992 Olympic Games, Albertville, France.

queen of ski racing. Still, she never saw herself as anything but a shy country girl from a tiny Austrian town, a modest bank clerk who happened to ski on the side. Sometimes it doesn't take years to establish greatness, as Kronberger proved—a year or two, a couple of titles, and the odd skiing "first" have made her one of the sport's all time greats.

JULIE KRONE

At four-feet-ten-and-a-half inches tall and 100 pounds, Julie Krone is about the average size for a professional jockey. What is unusual about her is that she is a successful woman in the male-dominated sport of horse racing. In 1993 Krone made history, becoming the first woman jockey to win one of horse racing's Triple Crown races when she rode Colonial Affair to victory in the Belmont Stakes. One of the nation's top jockeys—and the winningest woman jockey in history—Krone has spent her entire career trying to prove that women can win on the race track.

"In a lot of people's minds, a girl jockey is cute and delicate. With me, what you get is reckless and aggressive."

Julieanne Louise Krone was born July 24, 1963, in Benton Harbor, Michigan. She and her older brother grew up on a farm in tiny Eau Claire, Michigan, where they learned to ride horses under the tutelage of their mother, Judi. When she was two, Julie rode a horse for the first time with her mom, and soon she would ride by herself. "I was a wild kid," she told *Ms.* magazine. "I got bit, I got stepped on, I got kicked in the head. I got dumped five miles from home; the pony ran back and I had to walk."

When she was five, Krone began entering and winning horse shows where she competed against riders up to 21 years old. After passing up a chance to join a circus, she decided she wanted to be a jockey. At 16, during her spring vacation from school, she was given a job walking horses at Churchill Downs, the famous race track in Louisville, Kentucky, that is home to the Kentucky Derby. In 1980 Krone became an apprentice jockey at Tampa Bay Downs in Tampa, Florida. She won her first race there, on February 12, 1981, riding a horse named Lord Farkle.

Within a couple of years, Krone was racing at larger, more famous tracks in Maryland, Delaware, and New Jersey. In both 1982 and 1983 she was the leading jockey at the Atlantic City, New Jersey, race track. By the mid-1980s, Krone was one of the top five riders on the East Coast of the United States. She earned praise as an intelligent rider, a jockey who made horses "run for her," and she showed an ability to communicate with the horse she was riding.

Julie Krone works out at New Jersey's Monmouth Park, site of several hundred of her victorious races. (AP/Wide World Photos)

Krone learned early on that she would have to show she was tough enough and strong enough to be a good jockey. Most horse trainers thought that women tired out during races and weren't able to control the 1,000-pound horses through the stretch. Krone scoffed at this attitude and allied herself with trainers who had faith in her. "I guess I don't think it's that big a deal that I'm a woman competing against men," she said in the *Chicago Tribune.* "Who cares about that? Times have changed." On the subject of fans, she stated: "I only hear 'Go home, have babies, and do the dishes,' after I've lost. I know they'll be cheering for me when I come out the next day and win."

As an up-and-coming jockey, Krone experienced her share of problems. At the age of 17 she was caught with marijuana and received a 60-day riding suspension. In 1980, at Maryland's Pimlico Park, she fell off her horse and broke her back, losing four months of riding to the injury. Then, in the summer of 1986, she faced another crisis when an altercation with jockey Miguel Rujano turned ugly off the track. Krone was fined $100 on that occasion for punching Rujano and hitting him with a lawn chair. He was fined the same amount and suspended for five days for hitting Krone with his riding whip and knocking her into a swimming pool.

Krone worked hard to put her problems behind her and mend her image. She continued to be successful on the track, becoming one of only three riders, male or female, in the history of Monmouth Park in New Jersey to win six races in one day. In 1987 she became the first woman to win four races in one day in New York and the first woman to win a riding title (winning the most races in one year) at a major racetrack, for her 130 wins at Monmouth Park. She repeated as champion in 1988 and 1989 and won three straight titles at the Meadowlands, also in New Jersey, between 1988 and 1990. In 1988 she passed Patricia Cooksey's career record of 1,203 victories, earning the rank of all-time winningest female jockey.

In 1992 Krone's horses won $9.2 million in purses, ranking her ninth in the nation. Still Krone was labeled as a jockey who couldn't win the big races. All that changed at the 1993 running of the Belmont Stakes, the last leg of the prestigious Triple Crown. Krone was riding Colonial Affair, a long shot, in the Belmont Stakes that day. Halfway through the race she felt a surge of confidence, and sure enough, she guided Colonial Affair to the first-place finish. "It was like a dream come true," Krone told *Sports Illustrated* of her first Triple Crown victory.

On a fateful day at Saratoga Race Track in August of 1993, Krone was seriously injured when her horse fell and she was kicked by another mount. She suffered a shattered right ankle, a badly cut left elbow, and a bruised heart. Only a two-pound protective vest she was wearing saved her life. An orthopedic surgeon inserted 14 screws and two metal plates into Krone's lower leg and ankle to correct the injuries and predicted that she would not ride for at least a year. Enduring agonizing rehabilitation and bouts of depression, Krone fought her way back and returned to the track in May of 1994. "Once you've almost lost something you really love, like I almost lost racing, it means even more to you," she confessed to the *Detroit Free Press*.

Krone is the best female jockey in the history of racing and one of the better jockeys riding today. She has won purses worth just under $54 million, of which she is given 10 percent, and she is closing in on 3,000 career victories. Even her 1995 marriage to TV sports producer Matthew Muzikar did not keep her off the track—she rode a full card at Saratoga on her wedding day, sped home to don her bridal gown in time for an evening wedding, celebrated until two in the morning, and returned to Saratoga the next morning for another day of racing. When not on the track, she likes to read, ski, lift weights, and do aerobics.

JULIE KRONE

American jockey

Born: July 24, 1963 in Benton Harbor, Michigan.

Career Highlights:
- became one of only three riders, male or female, in the history of New Jersey's Monmouth Park to win six races in one day
- became the first woman to win four races in one day in New York, 1987
- became first woman to win a riding title (winning the most races in one year) at a major racetrack, for 130 wins at Monmouth Park, 1987; repeated as champion in 1988 and 1989
- won three straight titles at New Jersey's Meadowlands, 1988–90
- passed Patricia Cooksey's career record of 1,203 victories, earning the rank of all-time winningest female jockey, 1988
- ranked ninth in the nation for winning $9.2 million in purses, 1992
- took first place, riding Colonial Affair, in the Belmont Stakes, the last leg of the prestigious Triple Crown, 1993.

Describing her love of horses, Krone told New York's *Newsday:* "Shakespeare says, 'There's no secret so close as between a horse and a rider,' and it's true. You just look in their eyes. The horses with a lot of talent always seem like they're looking into the way beyond. They always have the look of eagles in their eyes. It's very romantic."

MICHELLE
KWAN

Experienced and poised beyond her years, Michelle Kwan is the figure skater to watch for the 1998 Olympics. The California teenager is a seasoned veteran of world skating competition and the 1996 World and U.S. national champion. Cheerful and endearing, Kwan has won fans worldwide as much for her winning personality as for her winning skating. She has been known to execute difficult back-to-back triple jumps in a program and then clown in front of television cameras like the teenager she is.

All clowning aside, skating is a serious business for Michelle Kwan. She trains diligently and is known throughout the skating ranks for her character and discipline. Unlike some of her peers who have been dogged by questions about their training practices and dedication to the sport, Kwan carries no negative baggage. Former champion Peggy Fleming—herself a teenaged national champion—called Kwan "a wonderful example for our athletes today."

As for Michelle, she makes makes no secret of her ambitions. "I dream about the Olympics," she told *USA Today*. In fact, she has been dreaming Olympic dreams for a very long time.

She was born in 1980 in Torrance, California, the youngest daughter of immigrants from Hong Kong. Her father, Danny, works for Pacific Bell Telephone. Her mother, Estelle, runs the family restaurant, the Golden Pheasant. Michelle first took to the ice at the age of five, following her older sister onto a rink at the local shopping mall. A few years later, she watched the 1988 Olympics and was completely smitten. She knew immediately that she had found her calling.

Kwan began private lessons in 1986 and won her first junior competition two years later. As a middle school student she was accepted into the prestigious—and expensive—Ice Castle International Training Center in Lake Arrowhead, California. The Ice Castle offers on-site housing and tutoring for its top skaters, and both Michelle and Karen Kwan became top students there. The exuberant Michelle once described her training facility as a "slumber party—except when you have to get up early and practice."

"I always dreamed about going to the Olympics and seeing the Olympic rings."

1996 U.S. figure skating champ Michelle Kwan pauses during a workout at the Los Angeles Sports Arena in 1995. (AP/Wide World Photos)

In 1992 Kwan placed ninth at the junior nationals. She was "bored" with junior competition, however, and behind her coach's back she decided to take the qualifying test for the senior level. She passed, and her furious coach, Frank Carroll, gave her a good scolding. Then he watched in amazement as the young teenager held her own against the older competition.

In 1993 Kwan placed sixth at the U.S. nationals, earning the distinction of being the youngest competitor in 20 years. Even greater laurels waited in the wings. The next year, at the tender age of 13, she finished second to Tonya Harding at the nationals. That silver medal finish in an Olympic year would ordinarily have qualified Kwan immediately for the U.S. Olympic team. Instead, she was politely informed that she would have to serve as an alternate, since Nancy Kerrigan was knocked out of the national championships by an assault. Ever gracious and likeable, Kwan accepted her position with no complaints. "I think it's fair," she said of Kerrigan's inclusion on the Olympic team. "What I've gotten already is incredible."

MICHELLE KWAN

American figure skater

Born: 1980 in Torrance, California.

Career Highlights:
- placed sixth at the U.S. nationals, earning the distinction of being the youngest competitor in 20 years, 1993

- finished second at the U.S. nationals, 1994 and 1995
- finished fourth at the world championships, 1995
- won the U.S. championship, 1996
- won the World championship, 1996.

Michelle Kwan attended the 1994 Olympics as the alternate to the American figure skating team. Ever since then she has been America's darling, the skater whose ability and budding artistry belie her age. She won her second silver medal at the 1995 national championships, this time behind Nicole Bobek, and she finished fourth at the 1995 world championships.

Kwan's years of playing second fiddle came to an end in 1996, when she won the U.S. championship with a dramatic and crowd-pleasing free skate based on music from the opera *Salome*. Kwan's performance demonstrated her newfound maturity as an artist as well as her ability to hit the triple jumps in the heightened atmosphere of competition. Still, at the performance's end, as she easily nailed down the gold medal, Kwan made faces at the camera, pretended to shoot herself in the head, and flashed a huge grin at the cheering audience. At fifteen, she became the youngest national champion in thirty years—the last woman to win at her age was a sprite named Peggy Fleming.

Barring any serious injury, Kwan could easily skate in two upcoming Winter Olympics—1998 and 2002. By the latter date she will be an ancient 21. Few of her competitors on the national scene show the same amount of durability, save perhaps her own sister.

Recent changes in amateur status have helped Kwan and her family to offset the exorbitant costs of training. Her yearly rink, coaching, and travel fees can run in excess of $60,000. She has been able to earn money competing in the Skate America and Skate International events for amateurs, and in 1995–96 she did very well in those competitions, often beating world champion Chen Lu and world silver medalist Surya Bonaly.

Kwan is a disciplined worker who misses few opportunities to perform. Her decision years ago to enter the senior ranks has clearly been vindicated by her success there, and she says she enjoys skating more now than she ever did. "I've really gained by all the experiences I've had," she confided in the *Detroit Free Press*. "It's been good for me to skate in front of big audiences. I've learned a lot from the older skaters." Her only worry? She's still growing. "You really feel it when you gain a pound because you feel off-balance going up for jumps," the high school student said.

With her sights clearly set on the 1998 Winter Games, Kwan says she benefitted enormously from her exposure to the 1994 Olympics, even though she was only an alternate. "I got an idea what the Olympics were like," she said. "Everything is preparation for everything."

Step by step, Michelle Kwan is on her way.

SILKEN
LAUMANN

The sport of rowing has produced few competitors with more courage than Silken Laumann. The former world champion and perennial Olympic hopeful came back from a severe injury just months before the 1992 Olympics and won a bronze medal in the heavyweight single sculls race. No one—not Laumann, not her coaches, and certainly not the doctors who treated her—ever expected her to win an Olympic medal in 1992. She did so on sheer will, her body responding to its splendid conditioning. She has been a Canadian hero ever since.

Laumann was born and raised in Mississauga, Ontario. Her parents, Hans and Seigrid Laumann, owned a small window-cleaning company. She began sculling with her sister Danielle on the Credit River in 1982 when she was 17. Just two years later, the Laumann sisters won a bronze medal in double sculls at the 1984 Summer Games in Los Angeles. For Silken, this victory seemed the beginning of a fabulous sports career. She could hardly foresee the ups and downs her fortunes would take over the next decade.

Problems began to surface as early as 1985. Rowing in almost constant back pain, Laumann discovered that she had a lateral curvature of the spine. The condition had been present since her birth, but the motion of sculling aggravated it. Determined not to let it slow her down, Laumann worked through the defect and kept at her sport. Then, with another partner, she finished a disappointing seventh at the 1988 Summer Olympics in Seoul. This defeat, coupled with her medical condition, led Laumann to consider giving up sculling.

Laumann was dissatisfied with the way Canada's rowing teams were run. She thought she should be working harder, and in 1989 she began training with the men's rowing team and their new coach, Michael Spracklen. "I had worked hard before," she told *Maclean's* magazine, "but with Mike, I knew that I was putting my effort into something that would work."

It worked, all right. In July of 1991 Laumann won the World Cup of rowing as an individual racer in the women's heavyweight division. The World

ROWER

"There is some part of me that wants to achieve excellence in something and, in rowing, I found something that I was really good at."

In defiance of a painful injury, Silken Laumann rowed her way to a bronze medal at the 1992 Olympic Games. (AP/Wide World Photos)

Cup is awarded to the athlete who compiles the most total points in a series of races. Even better, Laumann took the world championship in the 2,000-meter singles, a feat that *Maclean's* calls "rowing's holy grail." The championship race was quite exciting, with Laumann exchanging the lead with challenger Elisabeta Lipa of Romania more than a half dozen times.

The two gold medal victories in 1991 elevated Laumann to the top ranks in her sport and made her the force to beat at the 1992 Summer Games. At those Games, Silken Laumann proved that even the most dire adversity could not rob her of her dreams.

A little more than two months before the 1992 Olympics, Laumann was scheduled to row in a regatta in Essen, Germany. She was required to be in the race just to show Rowing Canada that she was ready for the Olympics. Prior to her race, Laumann was warming up when her boat was struck by a two-man German scull. She never saw the boat until it hit her, and the men never saw her until impact, either. The accident literally drove the side of her boat into her leg, breaking a bone, tearing muscles, and sending splinters deep into her skin.

"The muscles on the outside of my right leg were peeled back and hanging down to the ankle," Laumann explained in *Maclean's*. "I think that's why the doctors thought I would never row again. In a person of average fitness, they would have just cut the muscle off. The blood wouldn't get back up there and the tissue would die. But my muscle has lived. It's basically astounding, and I guess I'm surprising a lot of doctors."

Everyone told Laumann at the time that rowing in the 1992 Olympics would be out of the question. Laumann disagreed. In her hospital bed she began doing exercises to keep her upper body in shape. After several operations and a skin graft, she returned to her scull. She missed only 26 days of training and returned to rowing before she could walk.

Her gutsy performance at the Barcelona Olympics will not soon be forgotten. Leaving a leg brace on the wharf and easing into her scull in obvious pain, Laumann overcame her disability to row to a bronze medal finish behind Elisabeta Lipa and Annelies Bredael of Belgium. Laumann was thrilled that her Olympic dream had not been shattered by the injury. She told *Maclean's*: "I chose to work on the premise that there was a little light at the end of the tunnel, and that I could work towards that light."

Laumann continues to be a world-ranked single sculler and also an important member of the Canadian women's quadruple sculling team. She won gold medals in single and quadruple at the 1995 Pan American Games but then had the ill fortune to see them yanked because she had taken an over-the-counter decongestant during race week.

ROW, ROW, ROW YOUR BOAT

The boats used for competitive rowing, called shells, can attain speeds ranging from about 10 miles per hour for a single scull to more than 13 miles per hour for an eight (the shells that are crewed by eight rowers plus a coxswain). That kind of speed may not seem too impressive to someone living in the age of internal combustion, but for a human-powered watercraft it's truly remarkable. The speed of a racing shell is not constant, however, and spectators will observe that the motion of the hull through the water is jerky. The reason, of course, is that the power being applied through oar strokes is intermittent.

Laumann trains on Elk Lake near Victoria, British Columbia, her work subsidized by contracts with athletic clothing companies and by the Canadian government. A college graduate with a degree in English, Laumann contributes articles to rowing magazines and is contemplating a future career as a journalist. In the meantime, she is satisfied with the course her career has taken in sports. She concluded in *Maclean's*: "There are not that many areas of your life where you can be one of the best in the world."

SILKEN LAUMANN

Canadian rower

Born: C. 1965 in Mississauga, Ontario.

Education: Earned degree in English from University of Victoria.

Career Highlights:

- paired with her sister Danielle to win a bronze medal in double sculls, 1984 Olympic Games, Los Angeles, California

- won the World Cup of rowing as an individual racer in the women's heavyweight division and took the world championship in the 2,000-meter singles, 1991

- earned bronze medal, women's single sculls, 1992 Olympic Games, Barcelona, Spain.

VIRGINIA
LENG

Equestrian sports have long provided women with an equal opportunity for serious competition. Especially since World War II, when women began to demand and receive berths in major equestrian events, women on horseback have pretty much done it all. Few have been more successful than Great Britain's Virginia Leng, a two-time Olympic medalist, five-time European champion, and two-time world champion in the demanding "three day event." Leng—who once rode through an Olympic competition with a broken ankle—has won dozens of three day event titles with a series of dependable and spirited horses.

The three day event combines dressage, cross-country, and show jumping in a competition that lasts three or four days. The dressage comes first, followed by a tough cross-country race through some 20 kilometers of roads and tracks, a steeplechase of up to three and a half kilometers, and a special cross-country course that might have 32 obstacles stretched over eight kilometers. The last day's show jumping test is a mere formality compared to the cross-country, but it serves to show that the horses are sound after their long second day run.

Not surprisingly, the British are enthusiastic three day event participants, with even amateur fox hunters joining in to test their horses' mettle. Since the 1950s a number of women have excelled at England's premier three day event, called Badminton after the course on which it is run. Margaret Hough became the first modern woman Badminton winner in 1954, and close on her heels Sheila Willcox won the race in 1957, 1958, and 1959. Even Princess Ann, daughter of Queen Elizabeth, finished fourth at Badminton in 1974 and brought home team and individual silver medals from the 1975 European championships.

As for Virginia Leng, she could never remember a time when she wasn't fascinated by horses. Her father was an officer in the Royal Marines, and she grew up on the move as a military child, living in Malta, Singapore, the Philippines, Canada, and Cyprus, among other stops. No matter where

EQUESTRIAN

"I suppose I'm considered a bit of a perfectionist, I'm never satisfied with anything but the best. And I think being humble, and not getting conceited about anything [is important], because we can all ride, it's just a question of who rides better on the day."

she went, she rode horses. By her own account, she jumped her first fence at the age of three. As a youngster she belonged to the Pony Club, and as a teen with her first important horse, Dubonnet, she won a team gold medal at the 1973 Junior European championships. "I would never have got where I am without the Juniors," she said.

Leng's competitive riding career was almost ended before it had begun. After winning a Canadian pre-Olympic three day event in 1975 she was considered as a candidate for the 1976 British Olympic team. Unfortunately, during a subsequent race she broke her arm in 23 places—the injury was so serious that surgeons considered amputation. Instead the doctors repaired the arm, and by 1977 she was back at Badminton, this time on a horse named Tio Pepe. When Tio Pepe broke down in the Badminton steeplechase with injuries to both front legs, Leng once again cursed her luck and considered retirement. Success was waiting for her, though, back home in her barn.

Leng had bought two horses from the same sire, Priceless and Night Cap. A vet told her that Priceless was unsuited to the three day event, but Leng paid no attention. She rode Priceless into the record books, with European Championships in 1981 and 1985, the Badminton title in 1985, and world championships in 1982 and 1986. Priceless also helped Leng to win a team silver and individual bronze medal at the 1984 Olympics in Los Angeles.

Night Cap won his share of three day events as well. On him Leng took the 1984 Burghley title and the 1987 European championship. Recalling her years of success in *Great Horsemen of the World,* Leng said: "Neither Priceless nor Night Cap ever had any trouble whatsoever. And I'm sure it was because they were never pushed, particularly at one day events, and they were never run in bad ground. And they were never run if they had the slightest small problem like a sore knee or a stifle that wasn't quite right."

As the 1988 Olympics approached, Leng found herself astride a new horse, Master Craftsman. She had switched to Master Craftsman after another horse, Murphy Himself, proved to be too strong for her. Master Craftsman lacked experience, but she still managed to finish third in the 1988 Badminton race and to win a qualification for the 1988 Olympic team. What Leng didn't know when she traveled to Seoul was that she had broken her ankle in a fall at Badminton that year. She competed in the Olympics with the bad ankle, winning another team silver and another individual bronze. Only months later, on a visit to America, did she discover the injury. Surgery was required to remove a bone chip.

Throughout her career Leng has been known for the diligent care she lavishes on her horses. She refuses to drug them or to race them on courses

VIRGINIA LENG

English equestrian

Born: February, 1955.

Career Highlights:

- won team gold medal, Junior European championships, 1973
- took first place in European Championships, 1981, 1985, and 1987
- won world championships, 1982 and 1986
- won team silver and individual bronze medal, 1984 Olympic Games, Los Angeles, California
- earned the Badminton title, 1985
- won team silver and individual bronze medals, 1988 Olympic Games, Seoul, South Korea.

that she feels are unsound. Most observers agree that this careful consideration for her mounts has contributed to their longevity and success.

Competitive riding has always been the province of the very rich, but Leng's middle class background never deterred her. Faced with the prospect of giving up her sport, she instead undertook a vigorous campaign to find a corporate sponsor, literally knocking on doors in London and pleading her case. Her future was secured when she convinced the British National Bank to underwrite her expenses. Laughing as she recalled those days, Leng said: "In the end the only reason I succeeded was because the [bank] chairman's wife was fond of horses!"

NANCY LIEBERMAN-CLINE

"I want to stick around long enough to stay embedded in people's minds. You can't force-feed them to remember your accomplishments."

One of the greatest women's basketball players of all time, Nancy Lieberman-Cline never let her gender stand in the way of her success. From 1976, when she made the U.S. Olympic basketball team as a high school student, to 1992, when she narrowly missed another Olympic appearance, Lieberman-Cline was *the* name in women's basketball, the star who drew raves from even casual fans of the game. Lieberman-Cline became a true pioneer in the 1980s when she spent two seasons with the otherwise all-male United States Basketball League as a member of the Springfield Fame. She was also the first woman ever to earn a million dollars as a basketball player—and she did it without leaving the United States.

Looking back over her career in 1991, Lieberman-Cline said that she wanted to "change people's perceptions about women's basketball." She added: "I was good enough to play with the guys and start for the team; no other woman had ever done that. I think my playing in the men's league stretched the horizons for women in the future."

Born in Brooklyn, New York, in 1958, Nancy Lieberman tells of her struggle to assert herself as a youngster. "I came from nothing," she recalled in *Women's Sports + Fitness*. "I was always told I wouldn't make anything of myself. My brother was an A student—he was going to be a doctor. I was just an athlete. I had to learn to depend on me. So I took on an arrogant attitude—not to hurt people, but just to keep striving."

Nancy often argued with her mother about the amount of time she spent on the basketball court. She could not be restrained from the game she loved, however. In the summertime when her high school team wasn't practicing, she would take the A-train to Harlem and join in playground games with the "guys." Her heroes were New York Knicks legend Walt Frazier and boxing champion Muhammad Ali.

"I'm going to make history," Lieberman used to announce in her quarrels with her mother. And that's just what she did. At the age of 17 she became the youngest basketball player, male or female, ever to make the Olympic team—she had not even finished high school. She was part of a U.S. squad that won a silver medal in the first women's basketball tournament ever played as part of the Olympic Games. In college at Old Dominion she won All-America honors three times and led her team to two national championships.

Lieberman-Cline was just one of many athletes who lost an opportunity to shine when the U.S. boycotted the 1980 Olympic Games. In fact, her days as an amateur were numbered. In 1980 an American women's professional basketball league, the WBL, opened up business, and Lieberman-Cline was the top recruit. As a star player, she earned the kind of salary that kept her home in America rather than hopping around Europe in the professional leagues there. When the WBL folded, she moved on to the Women's American Basketball League (WABL), where, as a top star again, she inked a three-year, $60,000-per-year contract with the Dallas Diamonds. The Diamonds folded in 1985 after a year of play but still made good on the contract.

Ironically, Lieberman-Cline made headlines in the 1980s less for her considerable basketball prowess than for her association with tennis star Martina Navratilova. The two athletes met in 1981 when Navratilova was struggling on the tennis tour and Lieberman-Cline was out of work because the WBL had folded. Lieberman-Cline moved in with Navratilova and became the tennis great's personal trainer, helping Martina to improve her game. As *Women's Sports + Fitness* notes, Lieberman-Cline "received worldwide attention as . . . 'the woman who turned Martina's career around.'"

Such accolades might be enough for some people, but Lieberman-Cline wanted more. "I was losing my identity," she told *Sports Illustrated.* "I don't want to be remembered as Martina's coach. I want to be remembered as a great basketball player." Lieberman-Cline has always denied that her relationship with Navratilova went beyond the bounds of close friendship.

Lieberman-Cline got a chance to prove her mettle in 1986. That year, the fledgling United States Basketball League drafted her to the Springfield Fame, an all-male team of NBA hopefuls. While some coaches groused that her presence in the league was "a publicity gimmick," Lieberman-Cline threw her svelte, five-foot-ten-inch body into league games, playing against six-foot-six-inch, 200-plus pound men. Nor was she given a free ride. One observer noted that the men seemed to play harder when she was in the game—so she wouldn't embarrass them.

Her time in the USBL was a career milestone for Lieberman-Cline, and it was also a milestone for women in sports. A few other women players had received tryout nods from NBA teams—most notably Ann Meyers with the Indiana Pacers—but no woman had ever played regularly in a men's professional league before. Not only did Lieberman-Cline play, but she earned

NANCY LIEBERMAN-CLINE

American basketball player

Born: 1958 in Brooklyn, New York.

Education: Attended Old Dominion.

Career Highlights:

- became the youngest basketball player, male or female, ever to make the Olympic team; helped the team win silver medal, 1976 Olympic Games, Montreal, Canada

- led college team to two national championships

- played for two professional women's leagues—the Women's Basketball League and the Women's American Basketball League—between 1980 and 1985

- drafted by United States Basketball League to the Springfield Fame, an all-male team of NBA hopefuls, 1986.

Awards: Named All-American three times in college.

top-scale salary, adding to a bank account that ran to seven figures with endorsement contracts, personal appearance fees, movie and video contracts, and ownership of sporting goods stores.

After two years with the USBL, Lieberman-Cline joined the Washington Generals, a traveling team that plays against the Harlem Globetrotters. She soon found that she didn't like choreographed games and comic play. "The tour was exhausting and my skills got sloppy," she recalled in *Women's Sports + Fitness.* "But since there was no professional women's league, I thought it was my only chance to make basketball my career."

When the U.S. women's basketball team began offering substantial stipends to its players, Lieberman-Cline rejoined it. She played with the team through 1991, looking forward to the 1992 Olympics, but she was passed over in the Olympics year in favor of younger players. She retired from basketball in 1992, the first American woman ever to make a million dollars as a basketball star.

Lieberman-Cline might have played her whole professional career in Europe, where top women players can earn six figure salaries for a season. She stayed in America, she told *Women's Sports + Fitness,* "because I felt my roots were here." This decision makes her singular life history even more phenomenal. Lieberman-Cline dared to try her skills against bigger, stronger men. She proved that women could compete in male leagues. And in the process, she made herself rich and famous. "I'm a role model, and I take that role seriously," she concluded in *Women's Sports + Fitness.* "I want to show little girls I can be an athlete and still be a lady."

REBECCA
LOBO

The most successful collegiate basketball player of recent years, Rebecca Lobo has been showered with every award imaginable, and then some: Associated Press Female Athlete of 1995, Naismith Award-winner, Honda-Broderick Cup recipient, Academic *and* Athletic All-American, NCAA Woman of the Year, Women's Sports Foundation Team Sportswoman of the Year, ESPY's Outstanding Female Athlete. The numerous honors pay tribute to Lobo's contributions to the University of Connecticut women's basketball team, which completed a 35-0 season and won the NCAA championship in 1995. For her part, the likable and modest Lobo finished her college career in 1995 as UConn's all-time leading rebounder (1,268) and shot-blocker (396), while ranking second in scoring (2,133 points) and third in games played (126).

Asked about her fantastic college career, the dean's list student joked: "My college memories are all good except for getting my nose busted a couple times."

Lobo, who joined the U.S. national team in 1995, has been praised as one of the best all-around basketball players to emerge from the university ranks in quite some time. As Ross Atkin put it in the *Christian Science Monitor*, the Massachusetts native's "ability, intelligence, and solid-citizen character make her a role model as well as a worthy ambassador for women's basketball, which is hot." Character is important, but it does not necessarily win basketball games. Lobo also shows consummate skills in scoring, shot blocking, ball handling, and team strategy.

She was born and raised in Southwick, Massachusetts, the daughter of a five-foot-eleven-inch mother and a six-foot-six-inch father. Lobo's mother, RuthAnn, played old-style six-player basketball in high school, and she encouraged all of her children to excel in the sport as well. Rebecca grew up playing two-on-one in her back yard with sister Rachel—also a collegiate star—and brother Jason, who topped out near seven feet tall. "Jason would beat us," Rebecca recalled in a *Boston Globe* profile. "He would intercept our passes because he had that reach. The only way to score against Jason is to take a hook

BASKETBALL PLAYER

"When I first started playing basketball, I never thought any of this was possible. Even when I first came to UConn, it was still all a dream. To win the national championship and seeing all the stuff that goes with it has been unbelievable."

Basketball powerhouse Rebecca Lobo led her UConn team to the NCAA championship in 1995 after an undefeated regular season. (AP/Wide World Photos)

shot." Not surprisingly, ambidextrous hook shots are one of Lobo's specialties today.

As a fourth grader, Lobo played point guard for the local junior high school team. In fifth grade she started for an all-boys team. She made her high school varsity team as a freshman and scored 35 points in her debut. Those points were the first installment in what would become a state high school scoring record of 2,596—which would have been higher had Lobo's coach not yanked her frequently when the team was assured a victory. While Lobo played for Southwick High School, the team earned a 61-1 Bi-County League record and went 76-11 overall.

College recruiters called Lobo in droves. High profile coaches like Stanford's Tara VanDerveer made personal visits and attended Lobo's field hockey games. Among the schools that courted Lobo were Stanford, Virginia, Boston College, and Notre Dame. In the end Lobo decided to stay close to home. She entered the University of Connecticut in the autumn of 1991.

REBECCA LOBO

American basketball player

Born: Southwick, Massachusetts

Education: Attended University of Connecticut, 1991–95.

Career Highlights:

- led UConn Huskies to a 35-0 season and the NCAA championship, 1995
- ranked as UConn's all-time best rebounder (1,268) and shot-blocker (396); ranked second in scoring (2,133 points) and third in games played (126)
- joined the U.S. national team in 1995.

Awards: Named Associated Press Female Athlete of 1995; won Naismith Award and Honda-Broderick Cup, 1995; named Academic *and* Athletic All-American; named NCAA Woman of the Year, 1995; deemed Women's Sports Foundation Team Sportswoman of the Year, 1995; won ESPY awards for Outstanding Female Athlete and Performer of the Year (in the women's basketball category), 1996.

Lobo's debut with UConn was anything but encouraging. As her coach Geno Auriemma put it, she played "bad enough for two people." In a contest against the University of California, she scored just 10 points on 3-of-12 shooting and fouled out in 26 minutes. "I didn't have a clue what college basketball was all about," Lobo admitted in the *Washington Post*. "I knew it couldn't get any worse. I knew it would get better, but I didn't think it would get this good."

With Lobo as the key player, UConn did not just settle for "good." *Great* is more like it. Lobo was selected first team All-America as a junior and senior, and her team made the East Regional finals in 1994 before being beaten by North Carolina. In 1994–95, UConn was undefeated through its regular season and in the NCAA playoffs as well, emerging as national champion with a record-breaking 35-0 year. After that dismal start as a freshman, Lobo played spectacular basketball for the team, working through two broken noses and a broken pinky finger.

At the height of her success in 1994, Lobo discovered that her mother had breast cancer. The news threw the UConn star into an emotional turmoil, but her mother urged her to "take care of your business and I'll take care of mine." While her mother underwent debilitating chemotherapy treatments, Lobo turned in a stellar 1993–94 year and, when she was named Big East Player of the Year, she dedicated the award to her mother. "If my career has helped my mom, that's great," Lobo said. "But she has inspired me a lot more. When I see what she has gone through, in a strange way, it has helped me concentrate on what's important."

Having won the national championship in her senior year, Lobo moved on after graduating to the U.S. women's national team, in preparation for the 1996 Olympics. There she joined a nucleus of seasoned veterans and women who had been making six-figure salaries playing professionally in

Europe. Far from being daunted by her new team status, Lobo has relished the challenges of playing at the next level. "On this team, almost everyone was a Player of the Year. It's like starting over again, having to prove yourself," she said.

Lobo has entered high-profile basketball at a good time. A surge in popularity for women's sports has led to better product endorsement contracts, better salaries for playing with Team USA, and the distinct possibility of playing professionally in America, rather than Europe. In the meantime, Lobo has written an autobiography, *The Home Team,* for publication in 1996. "It's been weird," she told the *Boston Globe.* "Going from a student-athlete last year to where I see myself as just a basketball player right now. And who knows what's going to happen . . . after the Olympics?" Lobo added that fame hadn't changed her or her dreams. "I feel I'm still the same person I always was," she concluded. "And my family and friends still treat me the same way."

NANCY
LOPEZ

Nancy Lopez is professional golf's modern superstar. She became an instant celebrity in 1978 when she won eight tournaments—a record five in a row—as a rookie on the Ladies' Professional Golf Association (LPGA) tour. Since then she has consistently been one of the finest golfers on the women's tour and has earned a place in the LPGA Hall of Fame. Married and the mother of three children, Lopez has won at least one tournament every year since 1978, except in 1986 when pregnancy limited her schedule. She has won more than 45 tournaments and earned close to $4 million, and her talent and engaging personality have helped make women's golf almost as popular as the men's tour.

Lopez was born January 6, 1957, in Torrance, California. Her father, Domingo, owned an auto repair shop, and her mother, Marina, was a housewife. The youngest of two daughters, Nancy is of Mexican descent.

The whole Lopez family took up golf in 1965 as exercise for Marina Lopez. Nancy's father shortened the shaft of an old golf club so she could play along, and she quickly learned the finer points of the game. Convinced that she could become a prodigy, her father coached her, and at the age of nine she won her first pee-wee golf tournament by 110 strokes over her nearest opponent. By the age of 11 she was a better golfer than either of her parents. The family passed up buying a new house and washing machine to save money to help finance Lopez's golfing. There were some chores, like washing dishes, that she didn't have to do because they might injure her hands.

In high school Lopez led her otherwise all-male golf team to the state championship. By that time she was a nationally ranked amateur with a number of important championships to her credit. At 12 she won her first of two United States Golf Association (USGA) junior girls championships. In 1975, when she was a senior in high school, she entered the U.S. Women's Open and finished second against some of the best golfers in the world. The following year she went to the University of Tulsa on a golf scholarship.

During her freshman year at Tulsa, Lopez won the Association of Intercollegiate Athletics for Women (AIAW) golf championship, was named

GOLFER

"All the glamor, fame, signing autographs and admiration doesn't mean anything if you don't have anything at home."

Three-time winner of the Vare Trophy, Nancy Lopez was an overnight sensation on the LPGA tour after joining in 1978. (UPI/Bettmann)

All-American, and was the university's female athlete of the year. She turned professional after her sophomore year. "I felt there was no other place to go," she told the *New York Times*. "I needed to go forward and set other goals, reach the highest point of my whole career."

Lopez joined the LPGA tour in 1978. She won eight tournaments that first year, becoming an instant sensation. Her record-breaking five-tournament winning streak included victories at the Greater Baltimore Classic, the LPGA championship, the Nabisco Dinah Shore, the U.S. Women's Open, the du Maurier Classic in Canada, and the Bakers Trust Classic, which she won in a come-from-behind finish. By the end of her rookie season she had won $200,000 and was the spokesperson for several golf products. She was named LPGA Rookie of the Year and Player of the Year, and she also won the Vare Trophy, given to the player with the best scoring average for the season.

Lopez's sudden stardom brought a badly needed surge of interest to the LPGA tour. Fans mobbed her during tournaments and even yelled at her from car windows as she walked the streets. "Nancy didn't just arrive on the tour, she burst upon it," wrote Rhonda Glenn in *The Illustrated History of Women's Golf*. ". . . It's difficult to comprehend the impact of a single individual on an entire sport. Miss Lopez had more pure charisma than any player since the Babe, and the game to go with it."

Nor did the effervescent Lopez prove to be a flash in the pan. In 1979 she won nine of 19 tournaments—an amazing record that one *Sports Illustrated* reporter called "one of the most dominating sports performances in half a century." For the second straight year she was named LPGA Player of the Year and won the Vare Trophy. Rarely has any athlete dominated a sport through two seasons like Lopez did in women's golf during 1978 and 1979.

A troubled marriage almost forced Lopez off the tour in 1981, even though she continued to perform well. Realizing that her husband was trying to get her to quit, Lopez left him. Shortly after that she married baseball player Ray Knight, who encouraged her involvement with professional golf. The couple have had three children, and Lopez tries to structure her golfing schedule around the needs of her family.

In 1985 Lopez won her third Player of the Year award and her third Vare Trophy as she set a season scoring average record (since broken by Beth Daniel) and won five tournaments, including the LPGA championship. At the Henredon Classic she finished 20 under par, a record that still stands. After taking off most of 1986 to have her second child, she returned to the tour in 1987 and earned her 35th LPGA career victory at the Sarasota Classic. That victory qualified her for the LPGA Hall of Fame, and she was inducted in July of 1987 as the Hall's 11th member. The LPGA Hall has the most difficult en-

NANCY LOPEZ

American golfer

Born: January 6, 1957 in Torrance, California.

Education: Attended University of Tulsa on a golf scholarship.

Career Highlights:

- led otherwise all-male high school golf team to the state championship

- entered the U.S. Women's Open as a senior in high school, finishing in second place, 1975

- won the Association of Intercollegiate Athletics for Women (AIAW) golf championship, 1976

- won eight tournaments—a record five in a row—as a rookie on the LPGA tour, 1978

- won LPGA championship in 1978, 1985, and 1989.

Awards: Named All-American and University of Tulsa's female athlete of the year, 1976; named LPGA Rookie of the Year, 1978; won twin honors of LPGA Player of the Year and Vare Trophy, 1978, 1979, and 1985; inducted into LPGA Hall of Fame, 1987.

try requirements of any sports Hall of Fame, requiring 30 tournament victories, two of them major titles.

Lopez continued her dominance in 1988, winning three tournaments and passing the $2 million mark in earnings. She won another LPGA championship in 1989, earning five birdies in the last eight holes to win by three strokes. The birth of her third child in 1991 caused her to cut back on her golf schedule. She no longer found it possible to bring her young family with her when she traveled, so she tried not to leave home for more than 10 days at a time. (Her husband's involvement with major league baseball means he must travel frequently as well.)

"Being home is a time you can really enjoy sharing things," Lopez told *Golf* magazine. "I'm fortunate enough to say that I could stop [playing golf] right now—I have all the money I'll ever need and enjoy what I have." She added: "I relish my time at home. It's almost sacred to me."

This does not mean we have seen the last of Nancy Lopez. She still is a force in the LPGA and remains one of the most popular individual golfers—male or female—of all time. Golf experts have said that Lopez does not have a good swing, but it seems to work for her. At five-feet-seven inches and 135 pounds, she is not one of the women's tour's bigger players, but she is able to hit the ball as far as anyone. She is an excellent putter, a talent she attributes to hours of practice. Lopez plays well under pressure, especially in close tournaments. "When I get really psyched up . . . I can do anything," she told the *New York Times*. More importantly, she tries not to forget that golf is a game to be enjoyed. "I'm very confident in myself and I love what I'm doing," she observed in *Newsday*. "I'm very relaxed when I'm playing because it's not a job. It's a game."

DONNA
LOPIANO

Donna Lopiano had a dream. She wanted to pitch for the New York Yankees. Like any youngster, she worked hard to fulfill her dream. Every day, from the time she was five until the time she was 11, she threw 500 pitches against the wall behind her parents' house. She developed a whole arsenal of pitches—including a blazing fastball. Then she tried out for Little League.

She was chosen ahead of all the boys in her neighborhood. But when she showed up at the first practice to claim her uniform, a burly parent thrust a rule book in her face, opened to the page that said "girls are not allowed in Little League." Sobbing, she ran home.

"I wasn't allowed to pursue my dream," Lopiano says. "And I suspect that's why I'm doing what I'm doing today, to help little girls behind me."

Lopiano is executive director of the Women's Sports Foundation, an organization that promotes awareness and opportunity for female athletes of all ages. The foundation was begun in 1974 by Billie Jean King and has since attracted the membership of all sorts of women athletes, from casual joggers to Olympians. It provides support groups for women, gives annual awards to outstanding sportswomen, and organizes grass-roots efforts to build the involvement of women in sports. It is safe to say that in Donna Lopiano, the Women's Sports Foundation has found an ideal executive director.

Her long-ago rejection by the local Little League team helped to fan Lopiano's competitive fire. The daughter of restaurant owners Tom and Jo Lopiano, she excelled in a variety of sports, including field hockey, volleyball, and basketball. She never lost that fascination with baseball, however, and when she was 16 her parents more or less bribed a local scout to take their daughter to Stratford, Connecticut, for a tryout with the legendary Raybestos Brakettes softball team. The scout's skepticism lasted only as long as it took to drive from Lopiano's native Stamford to nearby Stratford. There Lopiano practically breezed onto the team without breaking a sweat.

Arguably the best women's fast-pitch softball team of all time, the Brakettes have played all over the country and all over the world, winning

"I'm in the business I'm in now because no kid should be told they can't pursue their dreams."

305

Donna Lopiano, right, holds a news conference upon accepting the post of executive director of the Women's Sports Foundation. Race car driver Lyn St. James, then president of WSF, sits next to her. (AP/Wide World Photos)

fistfuls of national championships and fielding a veritable "Who's Who" of top players. Lopiano played for the Brakettes for nine years as a pitcher and infielder. While she was with them, the Brakettes won six national championships and she was a three-time MVP at the national tournament. She was enshrined in the National Softball Hall of Fame in 1983.

During her years as a Raybestos Brakette, Lopiano graduated from high school, earned a bachelor's degree from Southern Connecticut State University, and completed her master's and doctorate degrees in physical education at the University of Southern California. "No question I stayed in sports because I had been denied the chance to play Little League," she told *Sports Illustrated.* "I always regretted that I never got a chance to see how good I could have been at pitching a baseball."

Lopiano coached basketball, volleyball, and softball at Brooklyn College from 1971 until 1975. Then, armed with her Ph.D. and no small

DONNA LOPIANO

American softball player

Born: C. 1947.

Education: Earned bachelor's degree from Southern Connecticut State University; completed master's and doctorate degrees in physical education at the University of Southern California.

Career Highlights:
- played for Raybestos Brakettes, the best women's fast-pitch softball team of all time, for nine years; helped team win six national championships

- coached basketball, volleyball, and softball at Brooklyn College, 1971–75
- took the position of athletic director for women at the University of Texas at Austin, 1975
- accepted position of executive director, Women's Sports Foundation, 1992.

Awards: Named three-time MVP at the national softball tournament; named American Softball Association All-American nine times; inducted into the National Softball Hall of Fame, 1983.

amount of *chutzpah,* she took the position of athletic director for women at the University of Texas at Austin. UT was a typical institution in that its women's athletic programs lagged far behind the men's programs in staffing, funding, and participation. Lopiano dug in her heels, made her demands, and turned the Lady Longhorns athletic program into "what may be the gemstone of all collegiate programs, male or female," to quote *Sports Illustrated* correspondent Alexander Wolff.

Consider the facts: under Lopiano's guidance, the University of Texas at Austin's athletic program for women began with an annual budget of $57,000 and soared to a $4 million-a-year operation. The well-supported and well-coached teams produced 18 national championships in such sports as basketball, cross-country, indoor track, outdoor track, swimming, and volleyball. The school hosted 314 All-Americans (an average of 21 per year) and 14 Olympians, including five gold medalists. Its basketball coach, Jody Conradt, has won more games than any other women's basketball coach, active or retired.

Lopiano was also admired for her insistence that the UT women athletes earn good grades and finish college. Fully 91 percent of her student athletes earned their bachelor's degrees—a statistic that is the envy of many a male athletic director. Furthermore, the city and the university alumni embraced these strong women's teams wholeheartedly. Lady Longhorn basketball games often drew larger audiences than their male counterparts, and the women athletes became heroes and role models in the community. When she left the university in 1992 to take the helm at the Women's Sports Foundation, Lopiano said of her years in Austin: "Being in a place like that was a gift. I never got a 'no' at Texas."

She still doesn't like to hear the word "no." Since joining the Women's Sports Foundation, Lopiano has been a crusader for gender equity in sports.

She has toured the country to speak on the embattled Title IX legislation that mandates equal opportunities for women in collegiate athletics. She also hopes to use the foundation's resources to fuel a grass-roots effort to encourage young women to participate in sports—and to instruct parents and siblings in the fine art of encouraging young women to compete. "Boys grow up learning what it is to be a member of a team," she told the *St. Paul Pioneer Press*. "That prepares them for work in the corporate world. Girls don't get that opportunity and as women they don't understand what it is to be part of a team. We want parents to realize the tremendous disadvantage to their daughters who don't play sports."

Lopiano has grand plans to increase the membership, the visibility, and the endowment of the Women's Sports Foundation. She is the same poised and demanding individual that she was when she arrived at the University of Texas at the age of 28. Today she says this about opponents of Title IX: "You learn that if you keep at it, eventually your detractors retire or die."

She might never have pitched for the Yankees, but she can still hurl a mean fastball.

WENDY LUCERO-SCHAYES

Wendy Lucero-Schayes wanted to participate in the Olympics. But first she had to find the right sport. She tried gymnastics and figure skating—rejecting both because she couldn't afford the coaching fees—and then found springboard diving. Her dream of making the Olympics came true in 1988, one of the high points of a career that included nine national titles and three U.S. Olympic Festival medals over a period of ten years.

A native of Denver, Colorado, Wendy Lucero was born June 26, 1963, to Spanish immigrants Shirley and Don Lucero. As a youngster Wendy followed her older sister to athletic events and competed with her wherever possible. Her sister was two years older and generally won every sibling competition, but Wendy persisted. Always being the runner-up "kept me in a 'trying to achieve mode,'" she explained. "I would always strive to be the best I could be because I wanted to grasp what my sister was attaining—but I wanted it now, even though I was two years younger."

Eventually Lucero-Schayes did close the gap between herself and her sister. Then she set about finding new challenges in sports. From age nine onwards, she dreamed of being in the Olympics, but late entry into gymnastic and skating lessons put her at a disadvantage in those sports. Her father was an electrician, and the family could not afford the high fees for elite-level skating or gymnastics classes. Instead, Lucero-Schayes returned to springboard diving, a sport she had tried as a pre-teen. Her gymnastics training served her well, and she quickly became very competitive in springboard events. She placed fourth in her state's championships as a sophomore and came in second as a senior.

Lucero-Schayes began competing in national events as a high school student, placing sixth in the three-meter diving event at the Junior Olympic Championships when she was a senior. An Academic All-American, she won a full scholarship to the University of Nebraska, where she won the 1985 NCAA championship on the one-meter springboard and placed first at the 1984 and 1985 Phillips 66 Outdoor Championships. She earned a bachelor's degree in television sales and management in 1986 and sought work as a pro-

DIVER

"The success I've had in sports overcoming those people who didn't think that I could [succeed] has made me like myself better and find out, 'Yeah, I am capable, and I'm not going to let them determine what I can do.' Hopefully I can share that with others."

Wendy Lucero-Schayes was national diving champ several times in the late 1980s and early 1990s, and was twice named female diver of the year. (Courtesy of Wendy Lucero-Schayes)

duction assistant for televised sporting events. She also found work as a free-lance sportscaster for NBC, ABC, and ESPN and hosted a talk show, "Focus Colorado," in her hometown of Denver.

Lucero-Schayes moved from the one-meter springboard to the three-meter springboard in preparation for the 1988 Olympics. Her rigorous training began paying off in 1987 when she won gold medals at the U.S. Olympic Festival and the American Cup II event. That same year she added a bronze medal at the McDonald's International. Still she felt she could do better, and she switched coaches and tried new training techniques.

Strongly motivated to win an Olympic berth because her mother was ill with cancer, Lucero-Schayes achieved her goal in 1988 with a second-place finish at the Olympic Trials. In Seoul she finished sixth in the three-meter springboard event, a respectable showing that enhanced her profile in the Hispanic community in particular. She returned to Denver and continued her

WENDY LUCERO-SCHAYES

American diver

Born: June 26, 1963 in Denver, Colorado.

Education: Won full scholarship to University of Nebraska; earned bachelor's degree in television sales and management, 1986.

Career Highlights:

- placed first at Phillips 66 Outdoor Championships, 1984 and 1985

- won NCAA championship on one-meter springboard, 1985

- won gold medals at the U.S. Olympic Festival, 1987, 1989, and 1990

- won gold medal, American Cup II event, 1987

- earned bronze medal at the McDonald's International, 1987

- won national championships in one-meter and three-meter events, 1989 and 1990

- won one-meter and three-meter events in the national indoor championships; placed first in the one meter and second in the three meter in the outdoor championships, 1991

- took a silver medal at the world championship and Alamo International competitions, 1991.

Awards: Voted U.S. Female Diving Athlete of the Year, 1990 and 1991.

work in communications, meeting her husband, basketball player Dan Schayes, at a charity event.

Lucero-Schayes had her best years as a diver following the 1988 Olympics. She won Olympic Festival titles in 1989 and 1990 and took the national championships in the one-meter and three-meter events those same years. In 1991 she won both springboard events in the national indoor championships, placed first in the one meter and second in the three meter outdoors, and took a silver medal at the world championship and Alamo International competitions. For her efforts she was voted U.S. Female Diving Athlete of the Year in both 1990 and 1991.

A severe intestinal infection hampered Lucero-Schayes's training in preparation for the 1992 Olympics, and she finished a disappointing third in the Trials, just missing a chance to go to Barcelona. Although Lucero-Schayes was disappointed at missing an opportunity to participate in an Olympics held in the country of her ancestors, she had no real regrets about her career. "Diving has been wonderful to me," she said. "Not only did it pay for a college education, but I was able to travel around the world, nothing that my parents were ever financially capable of doing." She added that the rewards of diving included "camaraderie, getting to create friendships with [athletes from] other countries."

Her exposure as a world-class athlete has helped Lucero-Schayes in her broadcasting career as well. She enjoys working in front of a camera *and* speaking to audiences on a variety of motivational themes. "I always felt that communications—whether radio and television, or through newspapers and journalism—it's going to shape our world, it is the up-and-coming future," she said. "I really believe that instead of being on the other side just watching it happen, I want to be involved with helping in a positive way."

VICKIE MANOLO DRAVES

In the 1948 Olympics, Vickie Draves won gold medals in the 10-meter platform and 3-meter springboard diving events, becoming the first woman to win both events at the same Games.

American women have traditionally performed well in Olympic diving events. Victoria Manolo Draves was no exception to that rule. Competing as Vickie Draves, she was the first woman to win gold medals in both the ten-meter platform and the three-meter springboard events. The former national champion accomplished this feat at the 1948 Olympics, using her subsequent celebrity as an entree into exhibition shows in America and Europe.

Victoria Manolo was born on December 31, 1924, in San Francisco, California. Both of her parents were immigrants, her father from the Philippines and her mother from England. While a high school student, Manolo became interested in diving and swimming. She practiced in downtown San Francisco at the Fairmount Hotel and the Crystal Bath Plunge, both of which had public pools with diving boards. She was already a gifted diver when she caught the attention of Phil Patterson, a well-known coach of an amateur swimming and diving team.

After graduating from high school in 1938, Manolo briefly attended San Francisco State junior college, but she ultimately withdrew when World War II broke out. She then began competing in earnest on the amateur diving circuit. In 1941 Jack Lavery, who was associated with the Fairmount Swim Club, took an interest in Manolo (who was forced to compete under the name Taylor, her mother's maiden name, in an effort to disguise her Filipino heritage). Lavery sent a picture of her to Sammy Lee, then one of the finest divers in America. Lee saw in the picture that Manolo had a lot of potential and became interested in her career.

In 1943 Lee, who by that time had become a national diving champion, saw Manolo compete for the first time. He later recalled in an interview that he was stunned by her natural abilities, especially the way she naturally straightened her back just prior to hitting the water—something Lee described as normally requiring a great deal of coaching and practice. After watching her dive, Lee introduced himself and told her that she would become a champion diver.

Manolo reached the nationals in 1944, attending the championships in Shakemack, Indiana. That year's competition was fierce, and she placed in the top four in her two events, the ten-meter platform and the three-meter springboard. The following year Manolo continued diving at the same level of competition, and Lee, again taking an interest in her career, told her that she should consider finding a better, more consistent coach. He suggested Lyle Draves, who was coaching some of the world's best divers at that time at the Athens Swim Club in Oakland, California. In 1945 Manolo began working with Draves, and at that year's national championships placed in the top four again.

In 1946 Manolo and Draves were married. At that year's national championship, competing as Vickie Draves, she won the ten-meter platform competition, her first national championship and the first time she had beaten her arch rival, Zoen Olsen.

Draves qualified for the 1948 Olympics after finishing second to Olsen at the qualifying trials. The story has it that the rivalry between Olsen and Draves heated up at the Summer Games when, over dinner prior to the competition, Olsen vowed to win the gold in both the platform and three-meter springboard events. Draves quietly decided to prove Olsen wrong. It was she who took the gold in both events, becoming the first woman to win both diving events at the same Olympics.

Vickie Draves was the darling of the 1948 Olympics, and when she returned to the United States she was treated like a celebrity. In 1949 she was invited to the Philippines to be honored there. She then appeared around the country in various aquacades and exhibitions. In 1952 she went to Europe and performed with swimmer-turned-movie-star Buster Crabbe's traveling aquacade.

Vickie Draves (Courtesy of International Swimming Hall of Fame)

Victoria Manolo Draves dropped out of international competition after the 1948 Olympics. When her days of touring with the aquacades ended in the early 1950s she settled down and raised a family of four children. She has been inducted into the International Swimming Hall of Fame in Fort Lauderdale, Florida.

VICKIE MANOLO DRAVES

American diver

Born: December 31, 1924 in San Francisco, California.

Education: Briefly attended San Francisco State junior college.

Career Highlights:

- won the ten-meter platform competition, national championship, 1946

- earned gold medals in 10-meter platform and three-meter springboard events, becoming the first woman to win both diving events at the same Games, 1948 Olympic Games, London, England.

Awards: Inducted into the International Swimming Hall of Fame in Fort Lauderdale, Florida.

ANGEL
MARTINO

Swimming is a sport that requires physical *and* mental toughness. Just ask Angel Martino. In 1988 Martino—then known as Angel Meyers—became the first American woman to swim the 100-meter freestyle in less than 55 seconds. She qualified for the U.S. Olympic team, but just two weeks before her planned arrival in Seoul, she was kicked off the team because her blood tested positive for a banned substance. Martino steadfastly maintains she never used performance-enhancing drugs, that the birth control pills she was taking at the time probably skewed the test results. No matter: after preparing for a lifetime, she missed the Olympics.

"A lot of people might have quit after that, thinking, 'What's the use?' " Angel's husband, Mike Martino, told *Swimming World*. "Angel came back with twice the fury."

Twice the fury was all it took. At the 1992 Olympics in Barcelona, Martino won a bronze medal in the 50-meter freestyle and a gold in the 400-meter freestyle relay. Even more remarkably, she has continued to improve her times since and is still competing at an age when most sprint swimmers have called it quits.

Born Angel Meyers, the swimmer was raised in tiny Americus, Georgia, population 16,000. Both of her parents had been competitive swimmers, and when they arrived in Americus they were shocked to find the town had no swim team. They founded one, with Angel and her two siblings as the first members. "The pool was only 16 yards, but that's really all I needed to work on my strokes and develop a feel for the water," Martino explained in *Swimming World*. "That pool was my 'home away from home' four days a week."

Martino was an excellent athlete. Her parents recognized her potential and worked with her to bring it to fruition. The only significant challenge to swimming for her was cheerleading. At one point in high school she literally had to choose between the two when her cheerleading coach complained about her devotion to the pool. Angel was tempted to choose cheering, but her parents convinced her otherwise—and saved her career.

SWIMMER

"I'm taking things as they come. I used to look too far ahead, but I believe that put too much pressure on me. I'm happy with what I'm doing and am only really worried about enjoying the sport."

Angel Martino gives a weary smile upon winning the gold medal in the 100-meter freestyle event at the 1995 Pan Am Games. (AP/Wide World Photos)

Although she was among the top-ranked swimmers in her state during high school, Martino was not able to attract any scholarship offers from the major colleges. Instead she attended Furman University in South Carolina, an NCAA Division II school. There, in the 1986 NCAA Division II championships, she finished first in the 50-yard freestyle, 100-yard freestyle, 100-yard fly, and 200-yard individual medley, setting national Division II records in both 100-yard events. She was named Division II Swimmer of the Year.

Also while at Furman, Angel met fellow swimmer Mike Martino. They began to train together with an eye toward the 1988 Olympics, and eventually their relationship led to marriage. In the meantime they both suffered through Angel's expulsion from the 1988 Olympic team and the inevitable damage it did to her reputation.

Angel felt the only way to prove that she did not rely on drugs to win races was to return to the competitive arena and continue to race. She proved

ANGEL MARTINO

American swimmer

Born: 1967.

Education: Attended Furman University in South Carolina.

Career Highlights:
- became the first American woman to swim the 100-meter freestyle in less than 55 seconds, 1988
- won bronze medal in the 50-meter freestyle and gold in the 400-meter freestyle relay, 1992 Olympic Games, Barcelona, Spain
- finished first in the 50-yard freestyle, 100-yard freestyle, 100-yard fly, and 200-yard individual medley, setting national Division II records in both 100-yard events, NCAA Division II championships, 1986
- set a world record in the 100-meter backstroke, Short Course World Championships, 1993
- won a gold medal, 100-meter freestyle, Pan American Games, 1995

Awards: She was named Division II Swimmer of the Year, 1986.

herself again and again, including at the 1992 Summer Games. Uncertain about her future after those Olympics, she decided to press on, and in 1993 she set a world record in the 100-meter backstroke at the Short Course World Championships.

With her husband's help Martino has continued to train and swim well into her late 20s. Sometimes her opponents are more than a dozen years her junior, but she is undaunted by this new generation of competition. In 1995 she won a gold medal in the 100-meter freestyle at the Pan Am Games, and in 1996, at the ripe old age of 28, she confounded expectations by qualifying for four Olympic events. In Atlanta, Martino will compete in the 100-meter butterfly, the 50- and 100-meter freestyle, and as part of the 4 × 100-meter freestyle relay.

Martino admitted in *Women's Sports + Fitness* that her own brush with drug testing has made her more skeptical about others' positive tests. "Because of what happened to me, I'm not going to automatically assume that someone is guilty," she said. On the other hand, with 20/20 hindsight, she is able to conclude: "If I'd gone to the '88 Olympics, I would have quit swimming after those Games. Now I'm doing what I love to do and still having fun."

LESLIE
MARX

"The part I like best is trying to understand your opponent. You have to figure out what they're going to do next. . . .
Then you have to think about how you want to counter that. The strategic part is the most challenging."

Some might call it a marriage of convenience.

When U.S. fencers—and marriage partners—Leslie and Michael Marx need workout partners, they look no further than across the dinner table. It's Marx vs. Marx, shades of *A Day at the Races,* only the barbs are exchanged at the tip of an épée. "At home, sometimes we will practice against each other," champion fencer Leslie Marx told *USA Today.* And, as might be expected, sometimes things get a little personal. That can happen when both a marriage and an Olympic medal are at stake.

"That time comes when we're practicing something, and he has to correct me," Leslie said. "It's hard to take correction. It's irrational, but I feel like he doesn't like me, he doesn't love me anymore. But he's just trying to make me better."

Even a great performer can always improve, but Leslie Marx has already made her mark in the world of competitive fencing. Ranked number one in the U.S. in épée—the descendent of the dueling sword—in 1995, she is a two-time national champion, the 1995 Pan American Games gold medalist, and a performer to watch at the 1996 Olympics.

A native of Houston, Texas, Leslie was a freshman at Duke University when she chose fencing over volleyball, racquetball, and tennis as a physical education elective. She showed such promise in class that she was recruited out by Duke fencing coach Alex Beguinet, who later introduced her to Michael. Leslie spent her junior year practicing fencing with the Duke varsity, then earned Academic All-American honors as valedictorian of her senior class.

Both Marxes won national championships in June of 1993. Leslie won in épée, a contest of skill in which fencers score by recording electronic "touches" on opponents. The épée is wired with a spring-loaded tip that completes an electrical circuit when depressed to 750 grams of pressure or more. Closing the circuit causes the machine to light. Unlike the foil, where the target area is comprised only by the torso, the target area in the épée is the en-

LESLIE MARX

American fencer

Born: Houston, Texas.

Education: Graduated valedictorian of her senior class, Duke University.

Career Highlights:
- won national championship *twice* in épée
- ranked number one in the U.S. in épée, 1995
- earned gold medal, Pan American Games, 1995.

tire body. "The blade is a bit different than others," Leslie said. "So are the rules. But mainly, it's the target area."

Leslie, with her slim, five-foot-11-inch frame, is more suited for épée than foil, she says. "I'm tall and not fast enough for the foil. My height helps in épée, and I've had a lot of success in it."

Leslie Marx has said that she was drawn to fencing because it seemed more "brainy" than other sports. (Indeed, the title of a recent *Cosmopolitan* magazine article called fencing "The sexy, cerebral sport.") "The part I like best is trying to understand your opponent," said Leslie, who teaches business at the W. E. Simon School of Business at the University of Rochester. "You have to figure out what they're going to do next. Why are they closer to you? Why are they farther away? Then you have to think about how you want to counter that. The strategic part is the most challenging."

Both of the Marx fencers are hoping for Olympic medals in 1996. If Leslie were to win one, she would make history as the first American woman ever to win a fencing medal at the Olympics. If both she and her husband were to win, perhaps those private practice sessions might become safer and more harmonious—just a little Marx family fun.

JILL MATTHEWS

BOXER

"When I fight in the Golden Gloves, the girl in front of me is going to pay for everything in my life: That I didn't make it as a gymnast the way I wanted to, that my parents separated, that any problem I had I was told to keep down. . . ."

Ladies and gentlemen . . . in this corner, wearing the red satin trunks and weighing in at 106 pounds, *Jill Matthews!*

Boxing may have seemed like the very last sport that women would ever try. The idea of getting into a ring and punching an opponent's face to a pulp flies against every stereotype of femininity ever devised. That is exactly why Jill Matthews entered the sport. "If it's typical, if it's normal, I'm not interested," the native New Yorker told *Live* magazine. "It has to be a total challenge, for the body and for the spirit."

Matthews came up a champion flyweight in the first-ever Golden Gloves tournament for women in 1995. The Golden Gloves tournament is one of the most prestigious in amateur boxing and often marks its victors as boxing's future stars. For the attractive and personable Matthews, the Golden Gloves crown was more than just a way to get her picture in the newspaper: it was a vindication for years of struggle as an athlete. "I was beginning to think that I would never make my mark and then boom: people were telling me that I could make history," she said.

Matthews, 32, was born and raised in New York. Her working-class Jewish parents encouraged her to stand up for herself in the tough inner city schools she attended, and at home she had to hold her own against an older brother. Still she was not exactly a street brawler. She was in fact a talented gymnast who spent hours each day working on routines and dreaming of the Olympics. She was good enough in gymnastics to win an athletic scholarship to Southern Connecticut State University, but she has said she failed to make the top tier in the sport because she lacked the "self-confidence" and "composure" of the sport's champions.

After quitting gymnastics, Matthews returned to Manhattan and worked as a hairdresser while attending college part time. She also performed in a punk rock band that was popular on the New York club scene. Realizing that she was losing her physical conditioning, she searched for a new exercise program that would appeal to her competitive spirit. She found her niche at

320

JILL MATTHEWS

American boxer

Born: C. 1963 in New York, New York.

Education: Attended Southern Connecticut State University and Hunter College.

Career Highlights:
- became flyweight champion in first-ever Golden Gloves tournament for women, 1995
- turned pro in 1995, winning $400 in one of her first pro match-ups.

the Wall Street Boxing Club, where she began working out just because she liked the atmosphere.

When the promoters of the Golden Gloves event announced that they would include women on the card for the first time in 1995, Matthews was intrigued. Her friends at the boxing club encouraged her to try her luck. After all, they told her, no other fighter would have more experience than she did. Having trained seriously for "only about three months," Matthews entered the event and won both her preliminary bout and her final match by knockouts. In the final she met Dee Hamaguchi, a Yale graduate with a black belt in judo. Hamaguchi was no match for Matthews, who came out swinging like a fiend and knocked her opponent down in the first ten seconds. The fight lasted one minute and 11 seconds.

Surrounded by reporters after having won, Matthews joked: "Tyson! Now I want Tyson!" In all seriousness, however, she announced that she would turn professional and fight a limited number of bouts each year.

Matthews's first pro match later in 1995 was an eye-opener—or should we say an eye-*closer*. Facing Anissa Zammarron of Austin, Texas, she was declared the loser in the second round by a technical knockout. One of Zammarron's first moves had opened a huge cut above Matthews's eye that required seven stitches. Plagued by the bloody cut, Matthews could not outmaneuver her more experienced opponent. Matthews attributed her loss to the fact that she was not used to fighting without the protective head gear that amateurs use. She vowed to return to the ring and prove herself among the pros just as she had with the amateurs. Her first pro bout brought her $400, from which she had to pay her cornermen and trainers. She later confessed to *Live* magazine that she netted "about $15."

Matthews did not enter boxing to make any kind of feminist point. She happens to have found a sport that answers both her physical and emotional needs. A self-described "psycho" who calls herself the "Zion Lion" when she fights, Matthews told the New York *Daily News:* "Making my opponent fall is like no other feeling in the world. It's sensual, a turn-on, pushing yourself, being ripped and pumped, hyper, aggressive, bright red, on fire, waiting to attack, makes every sweaty, down-and-dirty pore in my body come alive. It fills a craving, a void. . . . I love it!"

Mike Tyson had better watch out.

PAT & KELLY
McCORMICK

It's an age-old question: which is more important, heredity or environment? Do some athletes achieve greatness because they have inherited strength or competitive spirit from their parents? Or are they nurtured to the highest levels by encouraging family members and coaches? In the McCormick family, both elements seem to have been in place. Pat McCormick was one of the most successful Olympic divers of all time, winning springboard and platform gold medals in 1952 *and* 1956. Twenty-eight years later, her daughter Kelly, then 24, won the silver medal in the springboard competition at the Los Angeles Games. Diving, you might say, is the true calling of this dynamic mother-daughter duo.

Pat McCormick was years ahead of her time. She perfected dives seldom attempted by men—dives outlawed by the Olympic committee before her appearance at the 1952 Helsinki Games as too dangerous for women. An oft-told tale features McCormick visiting a doctor. After examining her accumulation of cracked bones and scars from practicing 100 dives a day six days a week, he remarked: "I've seen worse casualty cases, but only where a building caved in."

It has also been said that if Pat McCormick had competed in front of today's amassed media, America would have done a half-gainer over her. As it was, when McCormick returned home from the Helsinki Games, a puzzled neighbor asked her if she had been away on vacation. Part of this lack of notoriety was McCormick's doing, of course. She never particularly courted the spotlight, although after her second double gold-medal showing at the 1956 Olympics she was named Associated Press Athlete of the Year and Sullivan Award winner. By the time her daughter Kelly was born she had been inducted into the International Swimming Hall of Fame.

Born in 1960, Kelly McCormick showed the same free spirit her mother had—pumping herself up with a boom box in rooms between dives during competitions and once evaluating her performance this way: "If you land on your head 10 times, you should be happy." She began diving

"My mother showed me her medal when I was a little girl. I made a bet with her that someday I'd make an Olympic team and win."

—Kelly McCormick Robertson

323

One half of the dynamic mother-daughter diving duo, Pat McCormick does a backward somersault into the water in 1953. (Archive Photos)

PAT & KELLY McCORMICK

American divers

Born: Kelly was born in 1960.

Career Highlights:

- Pat won springboard and platform gold medals, 1952 Olympic Games, Helsinki, Finland
- Pat again won springboard and platform gold medals, 1956 Olympic Games, Melbourne, Australia
- Kelly won silver medal in springboard event, 1984 Olympic Games, Los Angeles, California
- Kelly again medaled in springboard diving, winning a bronze medal, 1988 Olympic Games, Seoul, South Korea.

Awards: Pat was named AP Athlete of the Year and was given the Sullivan Award, 1956; she was later inducted into the International Swimming Hall of Fame.

as a youngster because she wanted medals of her own. "My mother showed me her medal when I was a little girl," Kelly told *Sports Illustrated* before the 1984 Summer Games. "I made a bet with her that someday I'd make an Olympic team and win. The bet's for a Porsche and either an ocelot or a cheetah."

Kelly got the car, but not the cat. She finished just three points shy of a springboard gold medal at the Los Angeles Olympics, coming home with the silver instead. What might have been a high point of her career was dimmed somewhat by the media pressure to match or better her mother's performances, not taking into consideration the changes the sport and its competitors had undergone since the 1950s.

In fact, Kelly's style, which emphasized her gymnastic ability, was described as "eerily similar" to her mother's. Genes? Training? The latter must be given its due, because Kelly studied gymnastics for eight years before giving it up because she "couldn't stand being cooped up indoors." In diving competition she showed her mother's stunning grace and strength, but unlike her parent, she was plagued by a lack of consistency during her career.

Her accomplishments *are* "eerily similar" to her mother's, however. After winning the springboard silver medal in 1984, she continued to compete, returning to the Olympics in 1988 for a bronze in the same event. Both McCormicks thus enjoyed the same Olympic exposure and nearly the same results. Toward the end of her career, Kelly answered questions about following in her mother's shadow by admitting the pressure to achieve had been great. "It's a relief to me [the Olympics are] over," she said. But [my mother] told me that she's really proud of me and that she loves me."

Kelly McCormick is remembered by others for more than her diving. When a teammate clinched an Olympic berth then cried, wishing that her father, who had died a few months earlier, had been there to see her, Kelly stopped her interview with a reporter, turned away and assured her friend. "He's here," Kelly whispered. "You know that."

Now married, Kelly McCormick Robertson has retired from competitive diving and is a coach in Washington State. She's keeping her Olympic medals polished, to show to her own children.

TAMARA
McKINNEY

Her name is legend in the sport of Alpine skiing: Tamara McKinney, the winningest World Cup skier America has ever produced—male or female. Over a career that spanned the 1980s, McKinney won 18 World Cup races and competed in two Winter Olympics. In her early years in the sport, the five-foot-four-inch, 115-pound McKinney was considered too petite to be a serious contender in the slalom and giant slalom races that were her specialty. She put the doubters to rest with her unprecedented string of victories, many of them achieved in the wake of injuries and personal tragedy.

You might say McKinney had little choice but to become a skier. She was born in 1962 on a horse-breeding farm in Kentucky, the daughter of veteran steeplechase rider Rigan McKinney. Tamara's mother, Frances, was a ski instructor who poured all of her energies into teaching seven children how to navigate the slopes. *Sports Illustrated* correspondent William Oscar Johnson wrote: "Like the proverbial show business babies who sleep in trunks backstage, Tamara as an infant napped in a suitcase that her mother carried to weekend races in which her other offspring were competing." Not surprisingly, Tamara was on skis before she could walk properly.

The family obsession with skiing led to a somewhat rootless lifestyle. In the wintertime, Frances and her children would live in Nevada and travel from ski race to ski race. Tamara and her siblings were home-schooled by Frances, who used the same correspondence course she had been taught with as a child. In 1983, Frances McKinney told *Sports Illustrated:* "We lived in some pretty awful places just so we could ski, whatever there was for rent. Sometimes there was no hot water or heat or anything."

The dedication paid off. Tamara, her older brother Steve, and her older sister Sheila all qualified for the U.S. national team as teenagers. For many years Steve was the best-known McKinney. He held the world downhill speed record for eight years and also became the first skier to hit 200 kilometers-per-hour (124 m.p.h.) in a speed competition called the Flying Kilometer.

SKIER

"Skiing is so great. I can go up on a mountain, by myself, away from the whole world, and be really free. . . . I like it up on a mountain where I'm my own best judge."

Tamara McKinney catches air during the women's combined competition at the World Alpine Championship, 1989. (UPI/Corbis-Bettmann)

Sheila McKinney's experience was quite different. A promising skier, she lost a ski during a downhill race in Lake Tahoe, Nevada, and crashed head-first into a wooden pole. The concussion she sustained was so serious she could neither walk nor talk normally for a year. That accident was traumatic for Tamara, too. "I was a forerunner in the race," she explained in *Sports Illustrated,* "and I didn't know that Sheila almost died on the course. If there hadn't been a neurosurgeon right there on the hill, she might not have made it. I was 14 then, and it was my first year on the U.S. team. It was hard because I had to go to the races alone. Sheila was unconscious, and Mom stayed with her. I had something like 12 races in two weeks and I did really poorly. That's the only time I doubted whether I wanted to keep on being a ski racer."

The doubts were put to rest when McKinney joined the World Cup circuit full-time when she was 15. At her first major European event she finished an astonishing third, bringing an avalanche of publicity down upon herself. Shy by nature, McKinney was flustered when the American media began portraying her as the new hope for U.S. skiing. She either fell or was disqualified from her next nine races. She rebounded after a short layoff and began to live up to all of that media hype.

In 1981 McKinney won three races and took the World Cup giant slalom title. In 1982, skiing with a fractured hand, she finished in the top four in seven of the 12 races she entered. The next year she became the first American woman to win the overall World Cup title, the biggest prize in Alpine skiing.

McKinney had high hopes for her performance in the 1984 Winter Games in Sarajevo, Yugoslavia. She was not terribly disappointed with her fourth-place showing in the giant slalom, but then she failed to finish the slalom event. Still she held her own in a sport that has long been dominated by Europeans. She won bronze medals in the combined events at the 1985 *and* 1987 world championships, and in between took first place in quite a number of World Cup races.

The tragic deaths of her father in 1981, her mother in 1988, and her older brother McLane the same year might have sent McKinney into an early retirement. She grieved deeply for her mother in particular and was occasionally brought to tears when reporters hounded her to talk about the loss. Somehow she managed to find strength from the slopes. After a broken leg hampered her performance in the 1988 Olympics, she returned to World Cup prominence in 1989 with a vengeance.

The 1989 world championship Alpine races were held in Vail, Colorado. There McKinney—no longer the teenaged wonder, but a full-fledged star—won the gold medal in women's combined, beating the favored Vreni

TAMARA McKINNEY

American skier

Born: 1962 in Kentucky.

Career Highlights:

- finished third in her first major European event
- won three races and took World Cup giant slalom title, 1981
- finished in top four in seven of 12 races she entered, 1982
- became first American woman to win overall World Cup title, the biggest prize in Alpine skiing, 1983
- won bronze medals in combined events, world championships, 1985 and 1987
- took first place in several World Cup races, 1986
- won the gold medal in women's combined event, world championship Alpine races, 1989.

Schneider. Asked how she felt as the scores proved she had won, McKinney gazed at reporters for a moment, at a loss for words. Finally, all she could say was "Yahoo!"

McKinney's skiing career ended as the 1990s began. The timing had been just right for her, though. In the early 1980s, athletic equipment companies had subsidized skiers by paying sums directly to the U.S. national team, from which each skier earned her share. That system alone is estimated to have netted McKinney a six-figure salary each year, in addition to her prize money. As the rules for amateur competition relaxed, her "salary" jumped even more. In retirement she will have sufficient funds to indulge herself in her other love, equestrian sports.

McKinney will never be far from the slopes, however. She told *Sports Illustrated:* "Skiing is so great. I can go up on a mountain, by myself, away from the whole world, and be really free. . . . I like it up on a mountain where I'm my own best judge."

RACHEL
McLISH

Rachel Livia Elizondo McLish is the woman credited with bringing glamor to women's bodybuilding. She burst into the headlines when she won the 1980 U.S. women's bodybuilding championship and the prestigious Ms. Olympia titles in 1980 and 1982. Also the 1982 world champion, McLish quit competing when the use of steroids became a factor in the sport. She chose instead to crusade against drug abuse of any kind, in the process enhancing her own fame. Today, through lines of workout clothing, videos, and personal appearances, McLish remains dedicated to promoting healthy physical fitness among women.

Born in 1958 in Harlingen, Texas, to Rafael and Rachel Elizondo, McLish first became interested in fitness through the study of ballet and by watching her father lift weights. Even as a child she was fascinated by the strength and grace of the human form. Her own childhood discoveries set the foundation that would later enable her to encourage women to appreciate feminine muscularity as a new physical ideal.

During her high school years McLish won a spot on the cheerleading team and found herself forced to choose between cheering and ballet. She opted for cheerleading. The immediate gratification of popularity and a full social schedule overshadowed her childhood dream of becoming a professional dancer. By the time she enrolled at Pan American University in Texas, she regretted giving up dance and feared that, at age 17, she was too old to pursue it again.

McLish missed the physically active lifestyle she had known all her life and decided to pursue her other love—working with weights. At the time, weight training wasn't very popular with the general public, and exercise clubs were scarce. McLish eventually found a spa called the Shape Center and fell in love with the atmosphere. Unfortunately, as an impoverished college student putting herself through school, she couldn't afford the steep membership dues. Instead, she applied for and was offered a job at the spa. She started by teaching exercise classes and eventually became a manager.

In 1978 McLish earned a degree in health and physical education and formed a partnership to build the Sport Palace, the first and largest health club facility in South Texas. The club was so successful that it eventually expanded to Corpus Christi and Brownsville. In 1980 McLish read about the first U.S. women's

"The point of physical fitness is not narcissism or egotism. It's well-being. Most people have no idea what it's like to feel good all over. All the time. . . . The ultimate rush is the feeling you can get from intelligent exercise. It's addictive. In the best way."

*Rachel McLish displays the winning form that led to her first **Ms.** Olympia title.* (AP/Wide World Photos)

RACHEL McLISH

American bodybuilder

Born: 1958 in Harlingen, Texas.

Education: Attended Pan American University in Texas, earning a degree in health and physical education, 1978.

Career Highlights:
- won the inaugural U.S. women's bodybuilding championship, 1980
- earned Ms. Olympia titles, 1980 and 1982
- won world championship, 1982.

bodybuilding championship being held in Atlantic City, New Jersey. She entered for two reasons: to promote her fitness centers and to serve as a positive "feminine" example of a bodybuilder. She walked away with the title.

As the very first American female bodybuilding champion, Rachel McLish was hailed as a new role model. She appeared on magazine covers and television programs, traveled extensively, and lectured on diet, physiology, and beauty. Her prestige was enhanced when she won the Ms. Olympia titles in 1980 and 1982, as well as the 1982 world championship. When the emphasis in bodybuilding shifted from overall muscle tone to muscular development, however, McLish decided to stop competing.

Her short time at the top paid off in spades. McLish accepted a part in the documentary *Pumping Iron II: The Women* and a starring role in the CBS prime-time television special *Women of the 21st Century*. She made her feature film debut in 1992 in *Aces: Iron Eagle III,* opposite Academy Award-winner Louis Gossett, Jr. McLish might have had more roles in films, but she has always been selective about the parts she takes, refusing any that she feels are demeaning to women.

Other avenues brought McLish even more success. Her two fitness books, *Flex Appeal* and *Perfect Parts,* addressed all aspects of health and fitness, including psychological conditioning, dietary responsibility, nutrition, and sports medicine. In 1990 she introduced a line of activewear fashions in partnership with K-Mart. The line proved quite successful, accounting for 28 percent of total sales of sportswear in the United States in 1991.

Married briefly to her college sweetheart John McLish in the early 1980s, Rachel McLish remarried in 1990. Her husband, Ron Samuels, is an artists' manager and film producer in Los Angeles.

Through her campaign against steroid abuse and her blend of femininity and muscle tone, McLish has helped to make weight training and body shaping one of the fastest growing women's exercise activities. The former Ms. Olympia outlined her philosophy in an interview with the *Los Angeles Times.* "The point of physical fitness is not narcissism or egotism," she said. "It's well-being. Most people have no idea what it's like to feel good all over. All the time. People unfortunately take drugs to do it part of the time. But the ultimate rush is the feeling you can get from intelligent exercise. It's addictive. In the best way."

ANN
MEYERS

*"The better female
players today can
play year-round
now against the
best. International
basketball, sports
festivals, summer
camps. . . . In the
past, girls didn't
grow up playing
basketball. Now
they can."*

Triumph and tragedy—Ann Meyers has seen it all. She is the best
known member of the first generation of high-profile women's basketball players, a sports pioneer with a stunning resume of athletic "firsts." Among them:
first high school player to make the U.S. national women's basketball team;
member of first women's Olympic basketball team (silver medalist); first four-
time All-American at UCLA; first woman to sign a contract with a men's NBA
team. More recently she has been among the first in a group of women broad-
casters for network and cable television.

Yet another of her honors holds even deeper meaning for Meyers.
When she was inducted into the Basketball Hall of Fame in 1993, she became
half of the first Hall of Fame marriage. Her husband, Don Drysdale, was a
member of the Baseball Hall of Fame who pitched for the Los Angeles Dodgers.
Of all her many accomplishments, this one means the most to Meyers—her
husband died shortly after her Hall of Fame induction.

Ann Meyers was born in California and was the sixth of 11 siblings
in her family. She idolized her older brother, Dave, and sought to be a great
athlete like he was. Meyers was successful, but that success had its price. "I
got teased a lot. I was a tomboy. I didn't fit in with the girls," she recalled in
the *Orange County Register*. "I always had short hair. Long hair didn't go in
sports for me. The boys didn't really accept me. Yet the guys liked me because
I was a ballplayer. I was caught in the middle." She added: "I came home a
lot from school crying."

In elementary school Meyers was allowed to play on boys' teams—but
only after her parents went before the school board to plead her case. In junior high and high school she had to settle for women's teams, and she excelled in every sport she entered. She earned varsity letters in seven sports during her high school years—field hockey, badminton, tennis, softball, volleyball,
track and field, and basketball. Basketball was her best sport even then. She
was named to the U.S. national team while still in high school and participated
in the 1976 Olympic Games, where the U.S. women won a silver medal.

Basketball Hall of Famer Ann Meyers is a groundbreaking athlete and broadcaster with a stunning list of achievements. (AP/Wide World Photos)

Athletic scholarships for women were few and far between in the mid-1970s, but Meyers got one. UCLA made her the first-ever female recipient of a full athletic scholarship, and she rewarded the university's faith in her by winning All-American honors all four years, leading the Bruins to a national championship, and being awarded the prestigious Broderick Cup in 1978.

Meyers had attended UCLA because her brother Dave did. After graduating she wanted to follow in his footsteps again—into the NBA. At least one team, the Indiana Pacers, took her seriously. In 1979 the Pacers signed Meyers to a $50,000 no-cut contract and gave her a three-day tryout with the team. She didn't make the team, but she joined its broadcasting crew, paving the way for her future career in that field. While she was not the first female athlete to be given a tryout with an NBA team, she was the first to sign a contract—and very few women have followed in her footsteps.

In 1980 Meyers spent a season with the now-defunct Women's Basketball League, where she was named Most Valuable Player. When that

ANN MEYERS

American basketball player

Born: 1955 in California.

Education: Attended University of California, Los Angeles on full athletic scholarship—the first ever offered to a woman by UCLA.

Career Highlights:
- named to the U.S. national team while still in high school
- participated on the U.S. women's team, which won a silver medal, 1976 Olympic Games, Montreal, Canada
- led the UCLA Bruins to a national championship
- signed by the Indiana Pacers to a $50,000 no-cut contract and given a three-day tryout with the team, 1979
- spent a season with the now-defunct Women's Basketball League, 1980

Awards: Won All-American honors all four years of college, awarded the Broderick Cup, 1978; inducted into the Basketball Hall of Fame, 1993.

---

league folded, she expanded her broadcasting duties, performing color analysis and play-by-play announcing for NCAA playoff games, women's basketball, and NCAA Division II men's basketball. Her primary employer was CBS.

Meyers was competing in a televised women's "Superstars" competition in 1979 when she met famed Dodger pitcher and fellow broadcaster Don Drysdale. Although 20 years her senior, Drysdale began pursuing Meyers very seriously. For a young woman who had often been shunned by eligible bachelors, the attention from such an eminent athlete was heartening. They were married in 1986, two years after Drysdale was inducted into the Baseball Hall of Fame.

The Meyers-Drysdale household was a busy and productive one, with Don working as an announcer for the Dodgers and Ann continuing with her broadcasting of women's sports and NCAA games. The couple had three children—Don Jr., Darren, and Drew Ann. In May of 1993, Ann Meyers was inducted into the Basketball Hall of Fame as her husband and young children looked on. Two months later, Don Drysdale died suddenly of a heart attack after broadcasting a baseball game from Montreal.

Life has offered many challenges for Meyers since she became a widow. She has continued her broadcasting career but has also dedicated herself to keeping her husband's memory vivid for her children. It is not uncommon to see Meyers at Dodger Stadium before home games, introducing her children to players who knew their father both on and off the field.

Meyers credits her late husband as a driving force in her own career, even though he is no longer offering day-to-day encouragement. "Don would have been the first one to kick me in the backside to keep going," she told the *New York Daily News*. "You just don't quit when you've worked this hard." She added: "Because he's not here, and from what I learned from him, he's made me stand on my two feet. I'm forced to make decisions now that maybe

Don would've made or we would've made together. Now, I've got to make those decisions. They're difficult sometimes, but it makes you stronger because you have no one to rely on."

Although her days as an athlete are over now, Meyers can still see the benefits she has reaped from her pioneering career. "I think sports helped me," she explained in the *Orange County Register*. "You don't win every game. There are a lot of defeats in sports. It teaches you to maybe be a little stronger in life after sports." Noting that most people only compete in sports through their 20s—and then live to be 70 or 80, Meyers commented that a continued interest in sports helps people keep their "edge" in later years. "You have to have something in your life," she said. "You have to have that edge. You have to have a challenge to get up each morning and want to keep going."

CHERYL
MILLER

"I feel grateful that I grew up when I did. So many great Black athletes paved the way for me. . . . They pushed, they persevered, and whether they knew it or not, they were opening doors that will never be closed again."

One of the best basketball players of all time, Cheryl Miller was a four-time All-American who led her University of Southern California team to successive NCAA championships in 1983 and 1984. She went on to anchor the U.S. Olympic team that captured the 1984 gold medal in women's basketball. Charismatic and outspoken, Miller has parlayed her athletic triumphs into a successful broadcasting career as a television basketball announcer for ABC-TV. Also a successful college basketball coach, she was voted into the Basketball Hall of Fame in 1995.

Miller was born and raised in Riverside, California, the third of five children born to Saul and Carrie Miller. Her father was a stern taskmaster with many talents, including music and sports. Her mother played on an all-black basketball team. Miller's father had seen his share of racial injustices, and he encouraged his children to be top performers in the classroom and the gymnasium. "[Dad] told us that if a White coach had to choose between a Black athlete and a White athlete of similar skills, he would choose the White athlete. Every time." Miller wrote in *Ebony*. "The moral therefore was that it was not enough for us to be good—we had to be flat out better. He instilled that in all of us from the beginning, and that attitude rubbed off on all of us. A lot of people look at my brother [NBA star] Reggie [Miller] and myself and think that we are cocky and arrogant, and maybe we are but only in the sense that we believe in ourselves and our talent."

Miller learned basketball by playing pickup games with her brothers in the family back yard. By the time she was 11, she was better than any of the other local girls, so she pleaded with a boys' coach to let her try out for his team. After trouncing his son in an "audition," she was still refused a place on the squad. Bitterly disappointed, she vowed never to play basketball again. Her father told her to try out for the women's team and be the very best player on it, instead.

In high school, the six-foot-two-inch Miller towered over her opponents in both stature and talent. Through four years of varsity play, she scored a total of 3,405 points for an overall average of nearly 37 points per game. In

Cheryl Miller takes a shot during a 1984 Olympic game between the U.S. and Australia. (AP/Wide World Photos)

CHERYL MILLER

American basketball player

Born: 1964 in Riverside, California.

Education: Graduated from University of Southern California with a degree in communications.

Career Highlights:

- led her high school team to four consecutive state titles, averaging nearly 37 points per game

- led her University of Southern California team to successive NCAA championships, 1983 and 1984

- played for a team representing the U.S. in the World University Games, where her 37 points in the finals helped the U.S. team bring home the championship, 1983

- anchored the U.S. Olympic team, helping to capture a gold medal in women's basketball, 1984 Olympic Games, Los Angeles, California.

Awards: Named four-time All-American; given Final Four Most Valuable Player honors after tournaments, 1983 and 1984; named National Player of the Year by *Sports Illustrated,* 1985; voted into the Basketball Hall of Fame, 1995.

one 1982 game she scored 105 points, a California high school record. The Riverside High School team rode Miller's coattails to four consecutive state titles, compiling a four-year record of 132 wins and only four losses.

Miller's high school feats made her the most heavily recruited female athlete of her day. Out of over 250 scholarship offers, she chose to attend USC, which already had a strong women's basketball team. Miller was nearly as dominant at USC as she had been at Riverside. Joining a squad that included such talented players as the McGee twins, Pam and Paula, Miller led USC to back-to-back NCAA titles, picking up Final Four Most Valuable Player honors after both tournaments. She also developed a reputation as a show-off and trash-talker. By the time her college career had ended, Miller had broken the NCAA women's career records for scoring, free throws, and steals, and was named All-American each of her four years.

At the same time, Miller was also tearing up courts in international competition. In 1983 she played for teams representing the U.S. in the Pan American Games and the World University Games, where her 37 points in the finals helped the U.S. team bring home the championship.

Miller's popularity reached its peak in 1984 when she was the standout player for the U.S. Olympic team. Her gold medal performance at the Olympics was so compelling that for a short time afterward she enjoyed superstar status on a par with many NBA greats. In 1985 *Sports Illustrated* named her National Player of the Year. She became an international celebrity, gracing magazine covers, meeting heads of state, and making television appearances varying from interviews with Barbara Walters to guest spots on the television drama *Cagney and Lacey.*

Despite a college career averaging 23 points and 11.9 rebounds per game—and an Olympic medal—Miller could not hope to reap the financial rewards of professional play that her male counterparts enjoyed in the NBA. After graduating from USC with a degree in communications, she was offered jobs playing basketball with the Harlem Globetrotters and in a European women's league. Neither of these options appealed to her, however. She preferred to concentrate on the U.S. national team, and she was deeply disappointed when an injury forced her off the team prior to the 1988 Games.

Retiring from basketball in 1988, Miller served as a part-time assistant basketball coach at her *alma mater* and worked as a college basketball commentator with ABC-TV. In 1993 she was hired by USC as head coach of the women's basketball team. By replacing head coach Marianne Stanley—who had sued USC for sex discrimination over discrepancies in salary between male and female coaches—Miller embroiled herself in a controversy. Some of her fellow female coaches publicly criticized her for accepting the job at USC, but she silenced her critics by leading the Women of Troy to the Mideast regional finals of the NCAA tournament in 1994.

In February of 1995 Miller was one of seven players inducted into the Basketball Hall of Fame. Reflecting on her success, the former Olympic star told the *Los Angeles Times:* "I wasn't the greatest athlete and I couldn't jump out of the gym and I wasn't an extraordinary ball handler. I was just someone who loved the game so very much and had a passion for sport and life." The second half of that statement, at least, rings true.

SHANNON MILLER

"Other people may not have had high expectations for me, but I had high expectations for myself."

At four-feet-10 inches and 86 pounds, Shannon Miller may look fragile. Looks can be deceiving, though. Miller made history in 1992 by winning five Olympic gymnastics medals—the most ever won by an American. The following year she reached the top of her sport with the 1993 and 1994 World Gymnastics Championships women's all-around gold medals. Miller has overcome a number of obstacles in her rise to gymnastics prominence, among them the usual round of injuries and a prolonged battle with shyness. She has emerged as a fierce and determined competitor and has remained at or near the top in world and national rankings ever since the Barcelona Olympics.

Shannon Miller was born March 10, 1977, in Rolla, Missouri, but she grew up in Edmond, Oklahoma. Her father, Ron, is a college professor, and her mother, Claudia, is the vice president of a bank. Shannon began gymnastics when she was five, after receiving a special Christmas gift in 1982. "My parents bought my sister and me a trampoline for Christmas," she recalled in *Sports Illustrated for Kids*. "When we started bouncing on it and trying flips, [my parents] freaked out. They thought we would get hurt. So they signed us up for gymnastics classes."

Miller showed great promise as a gymnast, but she was very shy. Her timidity hurt her in competitions, where judges grade on both technical maneuvers and the ability to entertain. Miller, a perfectionist, often became frustrated when she didn't do a routine perfectly. Many times she broke into tears at the end of a performance.

When she was nine, Miller trained for two weeks at a gymnastics camp in what was then the Soviet Union. It was there that her current coach, Steve Nunno, first noticed her. "Shannon was trying so hard and getting extremely frustrated," Nunno observed in the *Sporting News*. "I felt, There's a kid I can help if I can channel that frustration into a positive energy." Nunno, also from Oklahoma, began training Miller at his Oklahoma City gym.

It wasn't long before Miller began to attract attention. She finished second in the all-around and third in the balance beam at the 1988 Junior Pan

Shannon Miller flies over the uneven bars on her way to a bronze, one of five medals she won at the 1992 Olympic Games. (Reuters/Corbis-Bettmann)

American Games, and she finished sixth in the all-around competition at the 1989 International Junior Gymnastics Competition. At the U.S. Olympic Festival in 1989, she won the uneven bars and finished third in the all-around. She made the senior U.S. national gymnastics team in 1990 at the ripe old age of 13.

Miller was a strong factor in the American team's silver medal victory at the 1992 World Gymnastics Championships. Just a few weeks later, her dreams of Olympic competition were almost ended when she fell and dislocated her elbow. She was given a choice of wearing a cast for six weeks and letting the injury heal naturally (which would force her to miss the Olympics), or having surgery to fix the problem. She chose surgery and returned to competition at the U.S. national championships just a month after going under the knife. Amazingly, she won the balance beam competition and finished third in the vault.

TWISTS AND TURNS

A gymnastics competition is made up of four events: the balance beam, floor exercise, uneven bars, and vault. In the balance beam competition, a gymnast must do flips, spins, and other complicated moves on a four-inch-wide beam. During the floor exercise, gymnasts combine difficult twisting jumps with graceful dance movements. In the most dangerous event, the uneven bars, gymnasts swing quickly, moving from bar to bar in quick maneuvers. Finally, in the vault, competitors run and jump off a springboard, twist and turn in the air, bounce off the horse, and then land. Shannon Miller's two favored events are the balance beam and the uneven bars.

Miller announced her presence at the 1992 U.S. Olympic gymnastics trials when she upset Kim Zmeskal and finished in first place. Her stunned coach told the *Sporting News:* "Two months ago, she's in the hospital facing surgery, and asking me if she'll be ready. It's unbelievable that she won." At the 1992 Olympics Miller walked away with a fistful of medals—a silver in the all-around, bronze medals in team competition, uneven bars, and floor exercise, and a silver medal in the balance beam. Her performance was the best by an American since Mary Lou Retton had won an all-around gold in the Soviet-boycotted 1984 Summer Games. "Other people may not have had high expectations for me," Miller told *Sports Illustrated*, "but I had high expectations for myself."

Those high expectations were rewarded again when Miller won all-around gold medals in the 1993 and 1994 world championships. In 1993 she won a tight all-around competition against Romania's Gina Gogean, then qualified for the finals in all four individual events. Fighting an upset stomach, she won individual gold medals in the uneven bars and the floor exercise. The next year she repeated as all-around world champion and won an individual gold medal in the balance beam. All told, through 1994 Miller had won seven world championship medals—more than any other American gymnast, male or female.

Miller's biggest American rival for many years was Kim Zmeskal. Today it is Dominique Dawes who often vies with her for top honors at na-

SHANNON MILLER

American gymnast

Born: March 10, 1977 in Rolla, Missouri.

Education: Graduated from Edmond North High School in 1994 with a 4.0 grade point average.

Career Highlights:
- won uneven bars and finished third in all-around competition, U.S. Olympic Festival, 1989
- won balance beam competition and finished third in vault, U.S. national championships, 1992
- helped to achieve U.S. team's silver medal victory, World Gymnastics Championships, 1992
- won five gymnastics medals—silver in the all-around, bronze medals in team competition, uneven bars, and floor exercise, and a silver medal in the balance beam, 1992 Olympic Games, Barcelona, Spain
- won all-around competition, and individual gold medals in the uneven bars and the floor exercise, World Gymnastics Championships, 1993
- repeated as all-around world champion and won an individual gold medal in the balance beam, World Gymnastics Championships, 1994.

tional and international meets. The gymnast told the *Sporting News* that she does not see her sport as a challenge between rivals. Competitions, she said, "are about each of us going out there and doing our best, not beating one another."

Miller graduated from Edmond North High School in 1994, where she was a 4.0 student and a member of both the Oklahoma Honor Society and the National Honor Society. Her academic standing is doubly impressive in that she also trained for gymnastics at the pace of 48 hours a week. "I don't know if I'd be making straight A's if it weren't for the discipline I got from gymnastics," she told *Sports Illustrated.* Describing herself as an ordinary teen who likes to watch television and play with her dog, Miller notes that she has reached the top in gymnastics because she enjoys competing. "It's hard to think of gymnastics as fun when you're working out eight hours a day," she said. "But when you get into a competition, you know you're having fun. I work hard here [in the gym] because that's where I want to be."

DOMINIQUE
MOCEANU

"I want people to remember me for being happy and for my smile."

Her facial features remind people of Nadia Comaneci, who captured the hearts of the world in 1976. Her expressiveness evokes images of Mary Lou Retton, the similarly seductive star of the 1984 Olympics in Los Angeles. Her father, Dumitru, was a member of the Romanian junior gymnastics team as a youngster, until his mother made him give up the sport to concentrate on his schoolwork. Dumitru planned from her birth to make his daughter the best in the world.

The movie folks in Hollywood are hoping Dominique Moceanu vaults to the top in gymnastics.

Moceanu's life is the stuff dreams are made of. Her parents escaped from the Iron Curtain before she was born and almost literally dedicated their lives to her success. She has been trained by the finest gymnastics coaches in the world and has met and befriended her idol, Nadia Comaneci. Not bad for a girl who has yet to see high school.

Dominique Moceanu was born—where else?—in Hollywood, California, on September 30, 1981. Her father had defected from Romania in 1979 and her mother in 1980. Little Dominique was just three years old when her father contacted legendary gymnastics coach Bela Karolyi in Houston and asked him to work with the child. Karolyi urged a little patience—about six years' worth.

"I told him to let the kid grow up," Karolyi recalled in the *Baltimore Sun*.

When Moceanu said she was ready at age nine—specifically to train with Karolyi—dad, daughter, and mom moved lock, stock, and barrel to Houston. The result? Moceanu has emerged as one of the most promising gymnasts in America. She will likely be a star at the 1996 Olympics, and beyond.

Moceanu showed her mettle at the 1995 Visa Challenge at George Mason University in Virginia, placing first overall while competing against former champions Svetlana Boguinskaia, Kim Zmeskal, and Dominique Dawes, not to mention top gymnasts from Belarus and China. In a review of that competition, *Sports Illustrated's* E. M. Swift wrote: "Dominique performs older than

Gymnastics wunderkind Dominique Moceanu performs a floor routine during the 1994 U.S. championships. (AP/Wide World Photos)

DOMINIQUE MOCEANU

American gymnast

Born: September 30, 1981 in Hollywood, California.

Career Highlights:
• won U.S. junior national championship, 1994

• placed first overall, Visa Challenge at George Mason University in Virginia, 1995.

she looks. Her hand movements on the beam, for example, are not those of a 13-year-old. The way she carries her head, her facial expressions, her swagger, if you will, all conspire to convince us there is an older person inside that tiny body. And as she proved . . . while pretending to play *Let's Twist Again* on the piano during her winning floor exercise routine, she knows how to perform for the crowd."

Gymnastics contributor Dwight Normile gave a more technical evaluation: "Moceanu smiled through four spectacular events with difficulty and amplitude to match. She . . . sailed three releases on bars, railed balance beam and airmailed her tumbling on floor. Anyone struggling to master a front-full on floor might study Moceanu's technique. She twists late, then pops an effortless front layout. . . . She bounded two feet in the air on landing." Normile concluded: "For sure, Moceanu is Bela Karolyi's ace right now, and he knows how to mold a winner."

From her base at Karolyi's gym in Houston, Moceanu has benefitted from the best coaching *and* from the example of Karolyi's other students. Former Karolyi medalist Nadia Comaneci has a special bond with the young gymnast because of Moceanu's Romanian heritage. Zmeskal and Boguinskaia have also strongly influenced the young athlete. "Svetlana's so elegant and expressive [and] Kim's so powerful," Moceanu said. "I try to take that with me."

In *Sports Illustrated,* Karolyi compared his budding star with Mary Lou Retton. "She's an outgoing kid, like Mary Lou," Karolyi said. "She's not a hidden personality. She can laugh one minute and cry the next—an open book. This is a good kind to coach." Karolyi added that Moceanu's youth is a plus as she enters senior national competition from her position as 1994 U.S. junior national champion. "This is a good age," he said. "At 13, they don't get psycho yet over the pressure."

Surrounded by all the best in family, coaches, and mentors, Dominique Moceanu may never "get psycho over the pressure." She's the genuine article. "I want people to remember me for being happy and for my smile," she told *Sports Illustrated.* "I don't fake smile."

Get those cameras rolling.

PATTY
MOISE

Many people follow in their parents' footsteps career-wise. Patty Moise certainly did—her father's passion just happened to be NASCAR racing. Today a full-time driver on NASCAR's Grand National level, Moise is proving that even stock car racing can be a "family affair." In fact, she has further driven home the point by marrying fellow racer Elton Sawyer and competing with him on the circuit.

Moise has turned in three full-time seasons and a number of part-time seasons in her two decades of road and track racing. While she has yet to win a race at the Grand National level, she has been able to attract sponsorship based on her experience and, yes, her gender. As for the way she is treated on the track, Moise told the *Philadelphia Daily News:* "There has been no open hostility. . . . The men treat me just like they treat each other. Which is to say not always good." She added: "There are some people I have more trouble racing around than others, but the same could be said of the other drivers out there. I look at myself as another racer—not a woman racer, but another racer."

A native of Jacksonville, Florida, Moise began racing in 1981 under the watchful eye of her father, veteran stock car driver Milton Moise. According to Milton, his daughter had always loved speed, to the point that the family had its auto insurance cancelled because of her crashes and tickets. Moving into racing was a logical step for Patty, but she faced a prolonged fight for recognition and the level of sponsorship required to mount a winning team.

Moise actually found that the business degree she had earned from Jacksonville University prepared her well for a future with the NASCAR circuits. She discovered that 40 percent of spectators at NASCAR events were women, and she used this fact and other data to sell herself to sponsors. "Being a woman has distinguished me from the crowd," she admitted in the *Philadelphia Daily News.* "A woman stock car racer is something different. Lots of times, it has helped me through the door, but in order to keep the sponsorship, there have to be results."

STOCK CAR
RACER

"Being a woman has distinguished me from the crowd. A woman stock car racer is something different. Lots of times, it has helped me through the door, but in order to keep the sponsorship, there have to be results."

Patty Moise climbs out of her stock car after becoming the first woman to qualify for pole position in the ARCA 200 race, 1989. (UPI/Corbis-Bettmann)

Moise spent her first five years as a road racer and then switched to oval tracks in 1988. Her first three NASCAR seasons she managed only a part-time schedule, but in 1990 she persuaded Simpsonville car builder and team owner Mike Laughlin to use her as his driver the whole year. At the time she told reporters: "When you run just 12 or 13 races a year, you really just want to finish races; you don't want to get in there and get your car all torn up. . . . Now I'm a little more willing to stick my nose in there. And if you race every weekend, you don't mind sticking it in there. If you get into somebody, you're better at handling it."

After meeting with little success that first full-time season, Moise dropped back to part-time and ran fewer than 20 races over the next three seasons. She did not give up, however. Having married fellow driver Elton Sawyer, she worked with him to advance both of their careers. As luck would have it, they both attracted sponsorship for full-time racing in 1994 on the Grand National level, and often they found themselves racing against each

PATTY MOISE

American stock car racer

Born: Jacksonville, Florida.

Education: Earned business degree from Jacksonville University.

Career Highlights:
- attracted sponsorship for full-time racing on the Grand National level, 1994

- founded and operated (with husband Elton Sawyer) Busch Grand National team, with Moise as the full-time driver
- broke the women's one-lap, closed-course speed record by driving 217.498 m.p.h.
- racked up 74-plus career starts, the most by any female driver in the Grand National series.

other in events. The press made much of this NASCAR "first." As for Moise, when asked how it felt to be competing against her husband in such a dangerous sport, she answered simply, "He's just another car."

In 1996 Moise and Sawyer were able to make their dreams come true. With the support of The Dial Corporation, they founded and operated their very own Busch Grand National team, with Moise as the full-time driver. Moise, who once broke the women's one-lap, closed-course speed record by driving 217.498 m.p.h., says she likes the idea that she will call the shots and be in charge of the team, after having had to satisfy other owners for so many years. As for Sawyer, he is frankly awed by his wife's success in NASCAR racing. "If I had to go through what the women who are competitive in racing have had to go through, I'd go get me a regular job," Sawyer said in the *Miami Herald.* "No matter what they do, it's not 100 percent right. If Patty has a strong race, compliments are hedged and a common reaction is, 'Man, what an awesome car.'"

Moise, whose 74-plus career starts are the most by any female driver in the Grand National series, says she has no plans to quit racing any time soon. She told the *Charlotte Observer:* "It's a much better view inside the car looking out the windshield than it is watching others go around."

SHIRLEY MULDOWNEY

DRAG RACER

"I do not want to lose, either for myself, or for my crew—they work so hard to make me do as well as I do. I want to win to 'get even.' Call me anything you want, but winning says it all."

Shirley Muldowney is the kind of woman who won't take "no" for an answer when she wants something. What she wanted was to compete in dragster races, those quarter-mile, hell-on-wheels automotive sprints in specially built hot rods. Muldowney was the pioneering woman who bucked the male dominance of drag racing. Almost universally hated by her male opponents, she excelled in the sport, becoming one of the few racers to win the National Hot Rod Association's top-fuel world championship three times. Her lifestyle and accomplishments were featured in a Hollywood film, *Heart Like a Wheel,* and she is still one of the best-known stars in the drag racing business.

Muldowney was born in 1940 in Burlington, Vermont, the daughter of Tex Rock—real name Belgium Roque—and Mae Roque. A boxer, taxi driver, and occasional violin player, Tex began teaching Shirley to drive at age 12 by sitting her on his lap in the family Chevy. Within two years, Shirley was drag racing down Depot Road in Schenectady, New York, late at night. "My first car was a 1951 Mercury," Muldowney told *Ms.* magazine. "All souped up, lots of carburetors—it was a street-racing machine. I raced on the back streets when the police weren't looking."

At fifteen Shirley dropped out of school and married her sweetheart, auto mechanic Jack Muldowney. The two of them became known as the fastest, most daring drag racers in middle New York. When Shirley Muldowney turned 19, she decided she was ready for real competition. She and Jack began racing professionally, with Jack tooling up the cars and heading the pit crew, and Shirley driving. In those days Shirley was regularly booed by spectators, who saw no room for a woman in hot rodding. She responded by dressing in pink, painting her cars pink, and flaunting her femininity. "I always knew this wouldn't be an easy profession," she told the *New York Times.* "But the attitudes against me didn't bother me. Trying to hold on to a 1,700-pound car with a 2,000-horsepower engine is hard work, and anyone that says different is out of his mind."

352　　GREAT WOMEN IN SPORTS

Shirley Muldowney was the first woman to be licensed by the National Hot Rod Association to drive a top-gas dragster; she went on to win 17 NHRA titles. (UPI/Corbis-Bettmann)

In 1965 Muldowney became the first woman ever licensed by the National Hot Rod Association (NHRA) to operate a top-gas dragster. Although initially considered mainly a curiosity and gate attraction on the drag racing circuit, she quickly proved she had the talent and guts to excel. She won several regional titles in the early 1970s and appeared headed toward national stardom. A divorce in 1972 slowed her progress somewhat, and then in 1973 she suffered a serious crash—her fourth—that left her with second degree burns to her face and eyelids.

Muldowney was no quitter, and after her accident she decided to move up from funny cars to top-fuel racers. She received a license to operate a top-fuel machine—a stiletto-shaped, 24-foot car that rockets down quarter mile strips in less than six seconds, reaching speeds of 250 miles per hour. Such racers boast 2,500 horsepower and require a parachute to slow down.

On the top-fuel dragster circuit, Muldowney won 17 NHRA titles, more than any driver except her arch rival, Don Garlits. She won the association's top-fuel championship three times, in 1977, 1980, and 1982. Despite her spectacular record, Muldowney struggled in her career. In 1980, one of her best years, she netted only $5,000 after expenses. The male racers—including Garlits—usually made a special point of trying to beat her, and she had a very hard time finding corporate sponsors for her trademark pink cars.

All that changed in 1983, when Twentieth Century-Fox released *Heart Like a Wheel,* a film based on Muldowney's life. A critically acclaimed drama, the movie served to introduce Muldowney to a public that had never seen a drag race before. Suddenly she was a celebrity, with women seeking her advice on the sport and men giving her the grudging respect she deserved.

The year after *Heart Like a Wheel* was released, Muldowney suffered the most serious accident of her career. On June 29, 1984, in Montreal, an inner tube snapped and wrapped around the front wheel spindle of Muldowney's racer during a qualifying race. The wheels locked and the car hit a culvert and disintegrated. Muldowney sustained a severed right thumb, a partially severed foot, fractured pelvis, three fractures between the ankle and knee of the right leg, compound fractures of both ankles, torn cartilage in her left knee, two broken fingers, and neck injuries. "When I woke up in the intensive care unit," Muldowney told *People,* "I hurt so bad I didn't care whether I'd make it or not." She spent more than four months in the hospital, undergoing six operations at a cost of $150,000. Surprisingly enough, her old nemesis Garlits helped pay the hospital bills.

Did we say the woman was a quitter? Hardly. After a year of recovery and grueling physical therapy, Muldowney returned to competition in January of 1986. Some months later, she turned in the quickest quarter mile

SHIRLEY MULDOWNEY

American drag racer

Born: 1940 in Burlington, Vermont.

Career Highlights:

- became the first woman ever licensed by the National Hot Rod Association (NHRA) to operate a top-gas dragster

- won several regional titles in the early 1970s

- won 17 NHRA titles on the top-fuel dragster circuit, more than any driver except her arch rival, Don Garlits

- won the NHRA's top-fuel championship three times, 1977, 1980, and 1982.

of her life, with a 5.470 elapsed time at the Winternational drag races in Pomona, California. At the time she told *People:* "Driving is a way of life for me, my bread and butter. And I'm not interested in doing anything else right now. I wasn't ready to give up the cockpit. I was forced out of it. The accident took a lot out of me, but it didn't kill my will to win."

She was still at it in 1989, although her place in the standings had slipped considerably and she once again had trouble nailing corporate sponsorships. Walking with a pronounced limp due to an ankle fusion in the wake of her 1984 crash, she still made the rounds on the circuit, most of the time failing to advance out of the qualifying heats. Ironically, as she entered middle age, she found help from Don Garlits, who had retired from racing after an accident of his own. In the latter years of her career, Muldowney worked closely with Garlits and her second husband, Rahn Tobler. They supervised the mechanical details and the pit crew for her million-dollar dragster, offering racing tips and moral support as well.

Although Muldowney was the first woman on the drag racing circuit, other women have followed in her wake. Muldowney is proud of the fact that she paved the way for these women. "I'm a bit of a toughie, and I had to be in the early days or I would not have survived," she told *Sports Illustrated.* "I like to think I made it easier for other ladies."

LENDA
MURRAY

"At first they didn't want us to be attorneys and didn't want us to be doctors. Now they don't want to see us with muscle. Women will have to determine how they will be perceived."

The Ms. Olympia title—the pinnacle of women's bodybuilding—has belonged to Lenda Murray since 1990. A five-time Ms. Olympia winner between 1990 and 1995, Murray is the undisputed champion of the demanding sport of women's professional bodybuilding. Her successful run as Ms. Olympia is the result of relentless training, natural talent, and a winning personality—all essentials in such a subjective competition as bodybuilding.

Murray never expected to become world famous. She began working out in 1984 with the goal of reducing her hips and toning her figure. At the suggestion of some fellow athletes at her gym she began sculpting her muscles in the classic fashion of modern bodybuilders, and she won the very first professional competition she entered, the 1990 Ms. Olympia contest. Murray explained in *Jet* magazine that while she must prepare "150 percent" for competitions because she is black, her genetic background has helped her to achieve the spectacular musculature for which she is famous. "I see a lot of girlfriends walking around Detroit with my body," the Motor City native said.

The second oldest of six daughters born to Darcelious and Louvelle Murray, Lenda Murray grew up in Detroit. She was an active and athletic youngster who especially enjoyed cheerleading and track-and-field events. Murray attended Henry Ford High School and Western Michigan University, where she performed as a cheerleader and ran in track meets. She majored in political science, intending to become a lawyer. After graduating from college, however, she won a position as a cheerleader for the Michigan Panthers, a team with the United States Football League. She worked with the Panthers for two years and then was invited to try out for the Dallas Cowboy cheerleaders—the best-known cheering squad in the world. She auditioned for the group and made the next-to-last cut before she decided she might need to slenderize her thighs a bit.

Murray was not overweight, but she was not svelte like a model, either. She discovered that the more she exercised, the larger her thighs became. In 1984 she joined a Detroit-area health club called the Power House Gym,

Bodybuilder extraordinaire Lenda Murray has won the Ms. Olympia crown five times since 1990. (© Bill Dobbins)

and there she met some male bodybuilders who correctly identified her as a "natural" for the sport. She began to look at her thighs in a whole new light—and to train for bodybuilding competition. Her decision puzzled her conventional parents, who were somewhat alarmed by the changes to their daughter's physique. "My parents didn't understand it at first," the athlete remembered in the *Detroit Free Press*. "But when I started having some success they realized it was a good thing for me because I'm always busy. . . . They respect all the dedication it takes."

In 1989 Murray decided to go pro, and she entered her first Ms. Olympia event in 1990. The most important and most highly publicized yearly event in the sport, the Ms. Olympia competition has been called "the Super Bowl of women's bodybuilding." Over its first ten years of existence, the competition was dominated by one woman—six-time Ms. Olympia titleholder Cory Everson. Everson retired in 1989, having become world famous and quite wealthy. Murray stepped in to take her place.

In the early days of women's professional bodybuilding, drug use was unregulated and competitors used anabolic steroids at will. By 1990, however, the Montreal-based International Federation of Body Builders had implemented drug testing prior to all sanctioned events. This suited Murray fine, because she did not use steroids. Her spectacular muscles were sculpted by disciplined weight training and a diet that can best be described as gastronomic torture—high protein, low fat meals that quickly become monotonous. "The diet's the toughest part for me," Murray admitted in the *Detroit Free Press*. "I remember thinking in August when I started, 'I'll still be eating this when there's snow on the ground.'"

In order to prepare for the yearly Ms. Olympia title, Murray works out regularly for two to four hours a day. Three months prior to the competition, she begins eight-hour-a-day workouts, six days a week, with a diet that becomes progressively more protein-based as the weeks pass. A typical day's menu might include five rations of skinless turkey breast or fish with rice or a plain baked potato. The potatoes and rice are eliminated four weeks before the competition. All-day workouts focus one day on the upper body and one day on the lower, alternating through six days.

The results of these draconian training measures are the kind of high-definition muscles, streaked with stark veins, that have come to typify world class bodybuilders. Murray noted in the *Detroit Free Press* that the restricted diet and constant exercise "brings you to an incredibly low body fat content and brings up the definition in the muscles."

Judging a bodybuilding competition is a highly subjective matter. While judges definitely look for symmetry and muscle dimension, they also—

LENDA MURRAY

American bodybuilder

Born: Detroit, Michigan.

Education: Graduated from Western Michigan University with a major in political science.

Career Highlights:
- dominated Ms. Olympia competition, winning the title every year between 1990 and 1995.

sometimes unconsciously, sometimes deliberately—factor in such intangibles as beauty, personality, and charisma. For Murray the personality part of the equation came easily, and each subsequent Ms. Olympia title has carried her more into the limelight. Today she is a confident, poised spokesperson for her sport and herself. She told *USA Today:* "I don't think people realize how popular this sport is all over the world." In addition to frequent trips abroad, Murray also spends time in Los Angeles, filming segments of *Muscle Magazine* for ESPN, producing workout videos, and promoting a personal line of workout clothing.

Murray's immediate goal is to win seven consecutive Ms. Olympia crowns, thereby breaking Everson's record. While she can still draw comments from strangers about her unusually muscular frame, she perceives a change in American attitudes toward well-muscled women. "There's definitely a craze, a lot of people starting to realize what weight training does for the physique," she said in the *Chicago Tribune.* In the future, she added, "I see a very muscular woman being able to walk into a restaurant and people not thinking that's something that's totally weird." As for herself, Murray is supremely happy—and wealthy. She estimates that she earns about $300,000 per year—enough to make even a solid month of nothing but skinless white meat palatable. Murray concluded in *Jet* magazine: "I made a decision that I want to be a body builder. I can look in the mirror and I like my body. I'm doing what I want to do."

MARTINA
NAVRATILOVA

TENNIS PLAYER

*"I didn't think I'd
care so much about
how well I played
this year. But I can
feel everybody wants
me to win so badly.
I'm the home team
everywhere."*

—*Navratilova, about her final season,
1994*

One of the world's most successful, colorful, and controversial athletes, Martina Navratilova was *the* tennis player of the 1980s. For 20 years—
from 1974 until 1994—Navratilova was a fearsome presence on the tennis
court, winning singles and doubles matches alike by virtue of her powerful
athleticism and brilliant tactics. The Czechoslovakian native defected to
America in 1975, seeking freedom to orchestrate her own career. Over the
next two decades she would emerge as the best-paid, and arguably the most
famous, female athlete in the world.

Navratilova's records are numerous. She has won more singles and
doubles tournaments than any other woman. Her nine Wimbledon singles victories are the best showing ever for a woman in that prestigious event, and
her 54 total Grand Slam titles (including singles, doubles, and mixed doubles)
trails only the legendary Margaret Smith Court, who won 62. Not only did
Navratilova win big—and often—she provided tennis with one of its greatest
rivalries as she and Chris Evert squared off against one another year after year.
For ten years Evert and Navratilova battled each other for the number one
world ranking, meeting 14 times in the finals of Grand Slam tournaments. It
was there, perhaps, that Navratilova showed her true genius—she won ten of
the 14 Grand Slam finals in which she faced Evert.

Navratilova was born on October 18, 1956, in Prague, Czechoslovakia,
and was raised in the suburb of Revnice by her mother and stepfather. (Her real
father committed suicide when she was very young.) As a lean, athletic child,
Navratilova excelled in many sports, including hockey and skiing. She thought
nothing of competing against boys. "I'm not very psychologically oriented and I
have no idea how I was affected by my real father's abandonment, the secrets and
the suicide, or my feeling about being a misfit, a skinny little tomboy with short
hair," she wrote in her autobiography, *Martina.* "In Czechoslovakia, nobody ever
put me down for running around with boys, playing ice hockey and soccer."

Navratilova's parents were tennis administrators for the Czechoslovakian government, and her grandmother had been on the Czech national

One of the greatest tennis players of all time, Martina Navratilova is shown here executing a forehand shot during the 1988 U.S. Open.

(UPI/Bettmann)

tennis team prior to World War II. It was only natural, then, that the active youngster would gravitate to tennis and begin to take it seriously. She began as most children do, whacking a ball against a wall with a cut-down racket while her parents played on the court. As she grew, her stepfather coached her. She reached the semifinals in the first tournament she entered, at the age of 8. At 14 she won her first national tournament, and at 16 she was the top-ranked female tennis player in Czechoslovakia.

Navratilova's tennis skills enabled her to tour foreign countries, including the United States. She made her first visit to America in 1973, falling in love with junk food, especially pancakes, pizzas, and hamburgers. Quickly gaining 20 pounds, she found her play slowed somewhat, and she lost her first-ever match against Chris Evert when the two met in Akron, Ohio. The next year, having overcome the weight gain, Navratilova began beating the best players in the world, including Smith Court in the quarterfinals of the 1974 Australian Open.

The young tennis star began to feel increasingly stifled by the Czechoslovakian government's management of her career. She defected to the United States at the 1975 U.S. Open, shortly before her 19th birthday. "Politics had nothing to do with my decision," she said. "It was strictly a tennis matter." Navratilova felt she had to defect in order to develop as a tennis player and as a person, but the decision was a painful one. She knew it would be years before she would be able to see her parents and younger sister again, because she could not return to Czechoslovakia and they could not leave the country. Still she held by her decision. "I realized I would never have the . . . freedom to play the best tennis as long as I was under [government] control," she told *Sport* magazine.

Navratilova consistently won singles tournaments over the next few years and by 1977 was the number three player in the world. But she had not been able to win any of the Grand Slam tournaments—the Australian Open, French Open, Wimbledon, or the U.S. Open. In 1975 she reached the finals of the French Open and Australian Open, and in 1976 she lost in the semifinals at Wimbledon to Evert. Her first Grand Slam victory, ironically enough, was a doubles win at Wimbledon—with Evert as her partner.

Having adjusted to life in the West by 1978, Navratilova began to challenge for the number one ranking. Her first Wimbledon singles victory came that year, in a tough match against Evert. In 1979 she won the singles and doubles tournament at Wimbledon, and in 1980 she led the women's tour in money winnings.

On July 21, 1981, Navratilova became an American citizen. She was no ordinary taxpayer. From 1982 until 1987 she was the top-ranked women's tennis player in the world and a regular winner of Grand Slam and other tournaments. She won the Wimbledon singles championship in 1982, 1983, 1984, 1985, 1986, and 1987; the Australian Open in 1981, 1983, and 1985; the French Open in 1982 and 1984; and the U.S. Open in 1983, 1984, 1986, and 1987. Her doubles victories—most often paired with Pam Shriver—were just as frequent. At one point in 1984, Navratilova had a winning streak of 74 matches.

For Navratilova, success meant hard work and plenty of it. She ate a special diet and trained hard—lifting weights, running sprints, and studying every aspect of the game. She asked for and accepted advice from coaches and other players, and she was one of the first athletes to employ a full-time personal trainer. Her physique stood in contrast to that of many American female athletes of the past who tried to maintain the unlikely combination of so-called "classic" femininity and the necessary muscle tone and conditioning. When the press began to speculate about her sexual orientation, she made little effort to hide the fact that she was homosexual. "I never thought there was anything strange about being gay," she remarked in her autobiography. "Even when I thought about it, I never panicked and thought, Oh, I'm strange, I'm weird, what do I do now?"

In 1986 Navratilova came back to her home country for the first time since her 1975 defection, returning as a member of the U.S. Federation Cup team that eventually defeated Czechoslovakia. Her return was a major media event, and as she played well and won, she became a favorite of the fans. She was showered with flowers on the court, and crowds clamored for her autograph. Reluctant to respond at first, Navratilova finally loosened up and blew kisses to the crowd. "The whole experience was beyond my wildest dreams," she said later.

The superbly conditioned Navratilova once claimed that she planned on playing professionally until she turned 40, or beyond. As newcomers such as Steffi Graf and Monica Seles began to challenge her top ranking, however, she faced the fact that she was slowing down. Graf, who won all four Grand Slam tournaments in 1988, defeated Navratilova in the finals at Wimbledon that year. Although Navratilova held on until 1994, she won only one more Grand Slam event, the 1990 Wimbledon. She retired in November of 1994.

One of the wealthiest women in sports, Navratilova lives in Aspen, Colorado, where she donates her time and money to charitable causes. Named Female Athlete of the Decade for the 1980s by *National Sports Review,* United Press International, and the Associated Press, she personified tennis greatness—and unbridled athleticism. "Navratilova has turned into far more than

MARTINA NAVRATILOVA

Czechoslovakian-born American tennis player

Born: October 18, 1956 in Prague, Czechoslovakia.

Career Highlights:
- triumphed at Wimbledon with singles victories in 1978–79, 1982–87, 1990; doubles in 1976, 1979, 1981–84, 1986; and mixed doubles in 1985
- won Australian Open singles, 1981, 1983, and 1985; doubles, 1980, 1982–85, 1987–89
- won French Open singles crown in 1982 and 1984; doubles in 1975, 1982, 1984–88; mixed doubles in 1974 and 1985

- took U.S. Open singles championship in 1983–84, 1986, and 1987; doubles in 1977–78, 1980, 1983–84, 1986–87, 1989–90; and mixed doubles in 1985 and 1987.
- compiled 54 total Grand Slam titles, including singles, doubles, and mixed doubles (second best Grand Slam record ever).

Awards: Named Female Athlete of the Decade by *National Sports Review,* United Press International, and the Associated Press, 1980s.

merely one of us," Curry Kirkpatrick wrote in *Newsweek.* "She is mentor, conscience, role model, our own World Icon. The best female athlete of all time, arguably. Grand-slam tennis champion, certainly. Above all, grande dame in humanity."

PAULA
NEWBY-FRASER

The very name of the race—"Ironman Triathlon"—evokes images of macho bravado. The demands of the race—a 2.4-mile swim, 112-mile bike race, and 26.2-mile marathon—defy the endurance of any athlete, male or female. Amazingly enough, Paula Newby-Fraser has made the women's Ironman Triathlon her signature event and is not only the world record holder but also one of the best triathletes of either gender. Newby-Fraser has won the Gatorade Ironman Triathlon no less than seven times. She has more victories in the grueling event than any other competitor, placing her firmly on top in triathlon racing since 1988.

Known affectionately in the pages of *Women's Sports + Fitness* as "the Queen of Multisport" and "the Empress of Endurance," Newby-Fraser came to her sport in a rather roundabout way. She was born in Harare, Zimbabwe, in 1962 and was the youngest of two children. While she was still young, her family moved to Durban, South Africa, where her father owned the second-largest industrial paint company in the country. Growing up in a privileged class, Paula was given ballet lessons and swimming classes. She was so good in the latter sport that she earned a national ranking in South Africa while still in high school.

In a classic case of teen athletic burnout, Newby-Fraser decided not to pursue either swimming or ballet in college. She attended the local university in her home town and "pretty much gave up physical activity altogether and gained a lot of weight," she told *Women's Sports + Fitness*. She added: "I just had such an overdose of physical activity as a young child, that it was almost a relief when I got to college and could hang out with friends and party."

Newby-Fraser graduated from college in 1984 and took a full-time job. Bothered by the weight she had gained, she decided to start jogging. That led to aerobics classes and weight lifting a few mornings each week. "Toward the end of '84, I noticed a 'thing' called triathlons," Newby-Fraser recalled. "The biggest race of the year was held in my hometown. It was almost an

"I've gained a lot of inner strength from winning. I have no fear of losing. The thing that drives me in long races is crossing the finish line first, knowing that the hard work has paid off. I'm the queen of delayed gratification."

Ironman-length race and the winners were sent to Hawaii. [I] went up to watch the big race, and I thought, 'This is ludicrous! These people are out here so long.' But [my boyfriend] said, 'Let's try one of these.'"

Newby-Fraser and her boyfriend bought bikes and began riding and running every day. Late in January of 1985—just eight weeks after purchasing the bike—she entered her first triathlon. She won hands down and set a new women's course record. More amazingly, she finished in the top 10 overall. Three months later she won the national Ironman Triathlon in the women's division and earned a free trip to Hawaii to compete in the annual Ironman Triathlon there—considered the event's top race.

Because her experience in Ironman events was so slim, Newby-Fraser trained very casually for her first major Ironman Triathlon. "I'd never biked 112 miles in one week, never mind in one day, and I'd never run a marathon," she admitted. ". . . I just wanted to finish the race." When she arrived in Hawaii and began some training runs there, she was overwhelmed by the heat and the sunburn she sustained on her bike rides. Nevertheless, she persisted, and to her surprise she finished third in her first-ever world class Ironman race.

"It was a turning point for me," Newby-Fraser recalled of that victory. "I was looking at girls who were professional triathletes and made money out of the sport. I finished only five or six minutes behind the winner and I'd never done those distances before." She realized that she could win the event if she just trained seriously, so with her parents' blessing she moved to Southern California and began racing regularly. In her first year of American triathlon competition she won $25,000.

Soon after arriving in California, Newby-Fraser met triathlete Paul Huddle. He agreed to help her increase her training load in preparation for the Ironman distance. His encouragement and suggestions paid off—Newby-Fraser finished second in the 1986 Hawaii Ironman Triathlon, placing behind Patricia Puntous. Puntous was later disqualified for drafting on her bike, and Newby-Fraser was named the winner. She took home $17,000 in prize money and rapidly scooped up more from endorsement contracts and sponsorships.

Newby-Fraser finished third in the 1987 Hawaii Ironman and third in the 1987 Ironman world championships. After that, however, the race pretty much belonged to her. Over the next eight years, she won the women's Hawaii Ironman Triathlon seven times, breaking records in the bike course and the marathon. In 1988 she finished the entire race with a time of 9.01.01, 11th overall. She shaved another five minutes off this phenomenal time in 1992, setting a women's course record of 8.55.28 that has yet to be broken. The following year she won the event after having taken six months off with a stress fracture to the ankle. Through 1995 she had won 21 major ultra-distance races.

PAULA NEWBY-FRASER

Zimbabwean-born triathlete

Born: 1962 in Harare, Zimbabwe.

Career Highlights:
- won the national Ironman Triathlon in the women's division, South Africa, 1985
- finished third in her first-ever world class Ironman race, 1985
- finished second in the Hawaii Ironman Triathlon (the winner was later disqualified for drafting on her bike, and Newby-Fraser was named the winner), 1986

- finished third in the Hawaii Ironman and the Ironman world championships, 1987
- won the women's Hawaii Ironman Triathlon seven times over the next eight years, breaking records in the bike course and the marathon.

Awards: Named Professional Athlete of the Year by the Women's Sports Foundation, 1990.

Needless to say, her domination of the Ironman Triathlon brought Newby-Fraser a great deal of publicity, especially in track and field circles. As early as 1990 she was named Professional Athlete of the Year by the Women's Sports Foundation, beating out the likes of Steffi Graf and Beth Daniel. As the 1990s progressed and her winning continued, she received book offers and became a spokesperson for women's fitness.

Newby-Fraser won her seventh Hawaii Ironman in 1994 and soon after announced that she would be paring down her racing schedule. She said the 1995 Hawaii Ironman would be her last, and indeed it nearly did her in. Leading handily as the race neared its end, she was overcome by dehydration and exhaustion and collapsed just 200 feet from the finish line. When she was finally able to drag herself to the finish 22 minutes later, she still earned fourth place.

The Ironman Triathlon will be an Olympic event for the first time in 1996. Despite her years of success in the event, Newby-Fraser has no solid plans to compete. "I didn't get into triathlons to do it for God and country, and the Olympics wasn't even a consideration then," she said. "Perhaps if I were 15 years younger it would be different, but I can't speculate about that." As for her professional career, Newby-Fraser feels she has reached the end of the line. "I have perhaps two more years of racing in me," she told *Women's Sports + Fitness* in 1995. She added: "I'll be more involved in the periphery of the sport—being a spokesperson for the Ironman, for instance. . . . And I'll do more writing."

Future Olympic champions will have to work very hard to best this outstanding endurance athlete.

MARGARET OSBORNE DUPONT

A superior all-around player, Margaret Osborne duPont played well into her forties, and was inducted into the Tennis Hall of Fame in 1967

Margaret Osborne duPont was one of the best all-around tennis players America has ever produced. In the course of a 20-year career on the courts, she won 37 major tournaments, placing her fourth on the all-time win list behind Margaret Smith Court (62), Martina Navratilova (54), and Billie Jean King (39). Osborne duPont was an effective singles player who won the French championship in 1946 and 1949, Wimbledon in 1947, and the U.S. championship in 1948, 1949, and 1950. Her success in singles matches was more than augmented by her fantastic performance in doubles and mixed doubles play. Teamed with Louise Brough she won a record 21 major doubles tournaments, including 13 at Forest Hills.

Margaret Evelyn Osborne was born March 4, 1918, in Joseph, Oregon. She grew up in San Francisco, where her interest in tennis was fanned by her parents. In the days of her youth, tennis was one of the few sports considered suitable for young ladies—such pastimes as softball, track and field, and basketball were deemed "unfeminine," especially in the pages of the press. Osborne began competing on the tennis circuit as a teen and by 1938, when she turned 20, she was ranked seventh in the nation. Remarkably, she went on to be ranked in the national top ten 14 times over the next 20 years, hitting number one in 1948 and holding the top notch until 1950.

At the height of her career, Margaret Osborne married William duPont in 1947. Marriage and even the birth of a son failed to slow her down at all. She won Wimbledon in 1947 and the U.S. championship in 1948, 1949, and 1950. Having found a perfect doubles partner in Louise Brough, she became the right court member of one of the most successful women's doubles teams in history. Brough and Osborne duPont won the Wimbledon doubles crown five times and took the U.S. doubles championship 12 times in 14 appearances.

Great friends off the court, Osborne duPont and Brough only became fierce toward each other when they met in singles competition. Their rivalry produced some exciting tennis finals, including the 1949 Wimbledon, which

A powerful singles player, Margaret Osborne duPont also had stunning success in doubles competitions. (UPI/Bettmann)

MARGARET OSBORNE DUPONT

American tennis player

Born: March 4, 1918 in Joseph, Oregon.

Career Highlights:

- won French Open singles competitions, 1946 and 1949; doubles in 1946, 1947, and 1949
- triumphed in Wimbledon singles in 1947; doubles in 1946, 1948–50, and 1954; mixed doubles in 1962
- won the U.S. Open singles, 1948–50; doubles, 1941–50, 1955-57; and mixed doubles, 1943–46, 1950, 1956, 1958–60
- won 37 major tournaments including singles, doubles, and mixed doubles, placing fourth on the all-time win list.

Awards: Inducted into the Tennis Hall of Fame in 1967.

Brough won 10-8, 1-6, 10-8, and the 1948 Forest Hills, where Osborne duPont triumphed 4-6, 6-4, 15-13. As the scores suggest, the two women were so well-matched that their singles showdowns often stretched to record numbers of games.

A full 31 of Osborne duPont's major titles came from doubles and mixed doubles play, 20 of them with Brough. Her other partners included Sarah Palfrey Fabyan, Bill Talbert, Ken McGregor, Ken Rosewall, and Neale Fraser. Her success with doubles helped to prolong Osborne duPont's career. She was still playing and winning—mostly doubles and mixed doubles—when she turned 40 in 1958. That same year she was ranked fifth in the nation.

Osborne duPont won her last major title with Neale Fraser in 1960 at the U.S. championships for mixed doubles. Two years later she ended her career with victories in the Wightman Cup, a British-U.S. series in which she had remained unbeaten through 10 singles and nine doubles appearances. She was captain of the U.S. Wightman Cup team nine times, out of which the team brought home the Cup on eight occasions.

One of the few competitors ever to win major tournament victories after having had a child, Margaret Osborne duPont was inducted into the Tennis Hall of Fame in 1967.

SONIA
O'SULLIVAN

Beloved on two shores, Sonia O'Sullivan is a middle distance runner to be watched in the next few years. O'Sullivan was named 1995 Woman Athlete of the Year by *Track and Field News* in honor of her string of victories in mile and 5000-meter races during the 1995 track season. The 26-year-old native of County Cork, Ireland, is poised to win big as the Olympics roll around in 1996.

O'Sullivan came to running in a rather unique way. The oldest of three children of a chemical factory foreman and a housewife, she grew up in Cobh, Ireland, an island town off the mainland of County Cork. She began racing at age 12 but quit soon after, figuring she could never be as good as some of the other members of the local track club. What saved her as an athlete was the distance between her house and her school.

"Where I went to school was really close to where I lived," she told *Track and Field News*. "I probably shouldn't have had to run to school, but I did. Because it was so close, you kind of assumed you were always going to be on time so then you kind of left it to the last minute to leave all the time and always ended up being late, so I had to run. It was less than half a mile, 400 meters or something. You'd see me tearing across the road."

With such a dependable training schedule, O'Sullivan's return to competitive racing was only a matter of time. She re-discovered the sport in high school and began working out every day after classes. "I used to finish school at 4:00 in the evening, and I would get changed immediately and go for a run about 4:30 or so, sometimes with some of the fellows from the local club, a lot of the time by myself," she said. As she improved, she discovered that her running talent could lead to travel and the chance to see the world beyond her small island town.

O'Sullivan won an athletic scholarship to Villanova University outside of Philadelphia in 1987. She arrived in America with high hopes but then suffered under the pressures of school work, culture shock, and the expectations for her success. "I was injured quite a lot," she recalled. "I felt I kind of

"I always think the more I race, the more confident I get and I just run better and better each race."

371

Sonia O'Sullivan celebrates her victory in the 3,000-meter race at the European Athletics championships in 1994. (AP/Wide World Photos)

owed something to the school because they'd given me so much—the scholarship—and I wanted to be running with the team. Because I was injured, I tried too hard to come back but I kept getting injured. Once I kind of relaxed about the whole thing, things started to come together." Since completing her degree, O'Sullivan maintains a residence near Philadelphia.

The injuries did not shut O'Sullivan down completely in college. She was a two-time NCAA 3000-meter champion, and she also began making her mark in the longer distances. After graduating from Villanova, she decided to train full time and devote herself completely to her sport—even though such a thing was almost unheard-of in provincial Ireland. She adopted a constant training regimen that could vary in its elements but had to be performed every day. Layoffs were infrequent and brief. In order to be able to train year-round, she was known to travel to Australia when the weather was bad in Ireland and America.

O'Sullivan emerged in 1995 as a runner with not only physical stamina but also an ability to psyche out her opposition in the mental chess game

SONIA O'SULLIVAN

Irish track & field athlete

Born: C. 1969 in Cobh, Ireland.

Education: Won an athletic scholarship to Villanova University, outside of Philadelphia, starting in 1987.

Career Highlights:
- became two-time NCAA 3000-meter champion
- won an important mile race in Cologne, Germany, over defending world champion Hassiba Boulmerka
- won 3,000-meter race, European Athletics championships, 1994
- beat top-ranked 5000-meter runner and world record holder Fernanda Ribeiro four times, clocking a 14.41.30 time that ranks third in history.

Awards: Named 1995 Woman Athlete of the Year by *Track and Field News*.

that is middle distance running. She won an important mile race in Cologne, Germany, over defending world champion Hassiba Boulmerka. She also beat top-ranked 5000-meter runner and world record holder Fernanda Ribeiro four times, on one occasion clocking a 14.41.30 time that ranks third in history.

The affable Irishwoman believes that her best times lie ahead of her. Running is her life, and it is an enjoyable if hectic existence. O'Sullivan told *Track and Field News* that she likes the training aspect of her work as much as the winning. "I think the buildup is the most satisfying part, knowing that you're ready to win the race," she said. "The hardest part is to go out there and do what you know you can do."

JULIE PARISIEN

SKIER

"The chairlift was like our baby-sitter. I started skiing when I was two, and I hated it. What I loved was the lodge, video games and hot chocolate."

Julie Parisien is battling for recognition in a sport that has never been kind to Americans—downhill ski racing. A member of the women's pro ski tour since 1994, Parisien is a two-time Olympian and the 1993 slalom silver medalist at the world championships. At one time ranked number one in the world in slalom, Parisien is "a hard core athlete, with disciplined, determined workout habits to match," to quote *Skiing* magazine.

Discipline was not always a part of Parisien's makeup. She grew up in a skiing family, following her older brother Rob and younger sister Anna—who have both been ski team members—onto the slopes. Recalling her early years in *Sports Illustrated,* Parisien said: "The chairlift was like our baby-sitter. I started skiing when I was two, and I *hated* it. What I loved was the lodge, video games and hot chocolate." Strange words from a woman who now trains for her sport eleven months of the year.

Parisien was born in Quebec but raised in Auburn and Sugarloaf, Maine. It was the family's move to Sugarloaf that sparked the 10-year-old Parisien's interest in competitive skiing. As her skills grew, she was accepted to Burke Mountain Academy in Vermont, and she made the junior team as a teenager. "Even at that age I needed competition," she recalled in *Sports Illustrated*. "I adored it. It forced me to learn about myself, to improve myself."

Parisien moved slowly but steadily through the national team ranks, graduating to the top in 1991. In March of that year, she announced her arrival by winning the Waterville giant slalom, the first U.S. World Cup win in four years. The next year she scored top-six finishes in seven major events, including a slalom win at Sundsvall, Sweden, as well as two top-five finishes (fourth in slalom, fifth in giant slalom), at the Albertville Olympics.

Her 1992 Olympic appearance was particularly frustrating for Parisien, and her showing there helped to contribute to her slip from number one to number seven in the world slalom standings. After leading the Olympic slalom event after the first run, she played it conservative, coming up short in her quest for even the bronze medal by 5/100 of a second. She also missed

Julie Parisien attacks the slalom course at the 1993 World Alpine Championships to win a silver medal. (AP/Wide World Photos)

JULIE PARISIEN

Canadian-born American skier

Born: C. 1971 in Quebec, Canada.

Career Highlights:
- won silver medal at the world championships, 1993
- won the Waterville giant slalom, the first U.S. World Cup win in four years, 1991
- finished second overall in rookie year on the women's pro ski tour, 1994.

Awards: Named Rookie of the Year after first year on the women's pro ski tour, 1994.

the bronze medal in the giant slalom by 41/100 of a second. "Fourth place is the worst place in the Olympics," the skier fumed in *Sports Illustrated.* "It sucks."

In 1993 Parisien struggled. Injuries she had sustained to her wrist and mouth bothered her (she has four false teeth, the result of a collision on the ski slope). She also had to battle a migraine condition that caused changes in vision and debilitating headaches. Worse, her older brother, J. P., died in a car crash. Parisien had been quite fond of her sibling and mourned his loss deeply. These serious setbacks notwithstanding, she still finished 27th in the overall World Cup standings—better than any other American that year.

After appearing in the 1994 Winter Games, Parisien turned professional and joined the women's pro ski tour. There she continued her comeback, winning Rookie of the Year honors and finishing second overall. Paul Major, Parisien's coach at the 1992 Olympics, told *Skiing* magazine that the Vermont-based skier could very well re-write the record books some day. "Julie could set the pace for the entire world," Major claimed. "She has that kind of potential. She has the potential to take the whole sport of women's skiing a little higher."

DENISE
PARKER

Shortly after Denise Parker returned from the Seoul Olympics in 1988, the state of Utah lowered the age requirement for a bow-hunting license from the age of 16 to 14. The state didn't do that in *honor* of Parker, who'd been the youngest American competitor at the 1988 Olympics, placing 21st overall and sharing in a team bronze medal. Utah did it *for* her. And while state officials explained the details of the change to the assembled media, Parker—one of the best American archers ever—stepped out into the wild and felled a 14-point buck from 35 yards. She was only 14 at the time.

Parker has competed in two Olympics and was the winner of five medals—four gold, one silver—at the 1995 Pan American Games. She has held the U.S. national indoor archery title for seven out of the last eight years and plans to compete in her third Olympiad in 1996. As a 19-year-old, Parker finished fifth in Barcelona, where she won two matches in the Olympic round before losing by two points, on the last arrow, in the quarterfinal. The U.S. archery team finished fifth.

Born December 12, 1973, Parker was just ten years old when her stepfather, Earl, asked her if she wanted to accompany him to an archery range a few miles from home in South Jordan, Utah. At the time Denise was a confirmed tomboy who played soccer, basketball, and softball against male or female opponents. She also enjoyed working in a crew for her stepfather at motorcycle races. On that fateful afternoon, however, Denise—whose natural father had died of cancer when she was three—trailed after Earl to the archery range.

A few years later, she was flying to Japan to tape a TV show called *Super Kids of the World*, appearing on the cover of *Parade* magazine, and shooting an arrow through a Lifesaver on *The Tonight Show*. In a sport where age and strength are an asset, the slight teenager had become a phenomenon.

Earl Parker, who admits, "I'm kind of a stickler about doing things right," vividly remembers the early practice sessions in the family back yard. Sometimes he and Denise would shoot to see who had to do the dishes.

ARCHER

"If you don't have the ability to learn in this sport, you'll fall behind. Denise is a good observer. She can suffer a failure, go back to the barn, work it out and come back stronger."

—Ed Eliason, veteran of U.S. archery teams

Denise Parker aims for a bull's-eye during the 1987 Pan American Games. (UPI/Corbis-Bettmann)

"Shoot six to ten arrows, then pull them out of the target and go back and shoot again," he told the *Deseret News*. "I imagine it got pretty boring for her. But she didn't want to stop. She wanted to shoot more."

Denise added: "For me to have fun I have to be good."

Initially, the plans were for Denise, a fourth grader during the 1984 Olympics in Los Angeles, to work up to the 1992 Olympics in Barcelona. But then came the 1987 U.S. indoor championships, where Denise, though competing in the junior division, shot at the same distance as the senior women and tallied the highest score of the tournament. "It was there," she recalled, "that I decided I wanted to be in the Olympics."

Parker subsequently placed fifth in the 1987 Olympic Festival, then burst onto the scene for good at the Pan Am Games in Indianapolis, where she won the individual gold medal and helped the U.S. squad to the team gold. All of a sudden, she was years ahead of schedule and headed for Seoul.

DENISE PARKER

American archer

Born: December 12, 1973.

Career Highlights:

- won individual gold medal and helped U.S. win team gold medal, Pan American Games, 1987
- played for U.S. team, helping to win team bronze medal, 1988 Olympic Games, Seoul, South Korea
- earned four gold medals and one silver, Pan American Games, 1995
- held the U.S. national indoor archery title for seven out of the last eight years.

"I didn't expect to do so well early," Parker admitted. "I guess the practice and stuff just caught up." Said her father: "Denise was just born that way, with talent. We just helped her develop it. She's competitive and she has this special talent that you can explain something to her and she can visualize it. You can say, 'You're doing this wrong. I want you to do it this way,' and she does it."

Not that everything came naturally. Parker, who also excelled in basketball and golf, put in hours and hours of practice, did special exercises to counter tendinitis in her shoulder, and worked with a psychologist to improve her concentration.

New York Times reporter William C. Rhoden pinpointed Parker's strengths in his coverage of the Indianapolis Pan Am Games. Rhoden wrote: "What makes Parker's early success especially impressive is that it comes in a sport that demands rigorous concentration and steel-nerve discipline. Archers must hold their bows steady and straight, ignoring rain, searing heat, or any other distraction that may interfere with shooting the most efficient shot."

Ed Eliason, a grizzled veteran of U.S. archery teams, observed of Parker: "If you don't have the ability to learn in this sport, you'll fall behind. Denise is a good observer. She can suffer a failure, go back to the barn, work it out and come back stronger."

The best news is that the U.S. can count on Parker for years to come. Archers outlast most other Olympic competitors, and if they can continue to be injury-free, they can reap huge amounts of experience in international competition. Once a 14-year-old *wunderkind* who just wanted to qualify for a bow-hunting license, Denise Parker is today a seasoned veteran of archery competitions who has literally traveled around the world to participate in events.

Asked if she ever planned to retire, Parker simply said: "Archery is a lifetime sport. That's how I think of it."

And she has plenty of life to live.

MARY PIERCE

"Before, when people talked about me, it was always, 'Mary Pierce, look what her dad did to her.' All along, I was hoping and waiting for the day when people would just say, 'There's Mary Pierce, look what she did on the tennis court.'"

Mary Pierce is really enjoying professional tennis these days. It wasn't always that way for the engaging Pierce, winner of the 1995 Australian Open and a solid contender on the women's tour. For years the victim of a domineering and abusive father, Pierce has blossomed as a player since she gained freedom from her father's coaching. Where once she was tense and tentative on the court, she is now more relaxed and able to focus on the game. That newfound confidence has led to better play for the up-and-coming Pierce, who won her first Grand Slam event in 1995.

Let's call Jim Pierce the classic tennis father. Overbearing parents are nothing new to sports—many athletes, both male and female, have been pushed too hard by fathers with high hopes. But few parents have exceeded Jim Pierce in overblown zeal for a daughter's career. As *Redbook* correspondent Suzanne Gerber put it, "Jim Pierce's harsh treatment of Mary was well known to other players and coaches, and to many fans." Only when Mary became old enough to assert herself seriously did her extraordinary life story begin to unfold the way she wanted it to.

Mary Caroline Pierce was born in January of 1975 in Montreal, Canada. Her mother, Yannick, was of French origin and had been a graduate student in the United States when she met Jim Pierce, an itinerant construction worker and jewelry salesman. Shortly after Mary was born, the Pierces moved to Hollywood, Florida. There, at the age of 10, Mary began to play tennis. Within her first month she had taught herself enough to beat all of her friends.

Jim Pierce decided to give his daughter private lessons, and as she learned the sport he immersed himself in it too. Before long he took over her coaching duties himself, imposing a strict diet and exercise program on his daughter and working her long hours in practice sessions. By the time Mary was 12, she was ranked second in the nation among 12-and-under girls. She turned pro in 1989, soon after her 14th birthday.

Trouble among the Pierces was evident as early as 1990, when *Sports Illustrated* did a feature on the young tennis prodigy. The magazine revealed

Mary Pierce battles with Natalie Baudone during a first-round match of the 1993 U.S. Open. (Reuters/Bettmann)

MARY PIERCE

Canadian-born American tennis player

Born: January, 1975 in Montreal, Canada.

Career Highlights:
- advanced to the finals of the French Open, 1994

- ranked as one of top five women's players in the world, 1995

- won first Grand Slam singles competition, Australian Open, 1995.

---

that Mary, then ranked 186th in the world, was almost literally living in the family's car as Jim, Yannick, and the two Pierce children traveled from tournament to tournament. Coaches came and went, often quickly quarreling with Mary's father. Even the U.S. Tennis Association tried to intervene on Mary's behalf and find her a training base, only to be thwarted by the overzealous Jim. Even worse, the magazine revealed instances of Jim's verbal abuse of his daughter when she lost her matches. And at one point he was ejected from a tournament for yelling "Beat the bitch!" in reference to Mary's opponent.

Matters reached a head in 1993 at the French Open. While sizing up her competition from the stands, Mary began talking and joking with her cousin. Her father became so enraged that he threw the cousin to the ground and caught him in a choke hold. The attack was sufficiently violent that Mary's cousin was forced to seek medical treatment—and Jim was once again barred from attending tournaments. This was the last straw for Mary. She fired her father and sought a new coach—Nick Bollettieri, who has worked with Andre Agassi, Boris Becker, and Monica Seles.

For a time Jim Pierce followed his estranged daughter around, driving her to hire a bodyguard and seek a restraining order against him. Eventually father and daughter re-established minimal contact, but not to the point where Jim was allowed any involvement with Mary's tennis. With Bollettieri's help, Mary ended a 19-match losing streak against Top Ten competitors and advanced to the finals of the French Open in June 1994—beating top-ranked Steffi Graf in the process. Just six months later, in January of 1995, Mary won her first Grand Slam singles tournament, the Australian Open. Asked to describe how the victory felt, she told *Redbook* magazine: "I think *fun* is the main word. My life off the court has changed. I'm feeling good inside, so I guess it shows on the outside too."

Ironically, as the spotlight has moved from Mary Pierce's family struggle to her achievements in tennis, she has insisted that her father's influence was actually a benefit to her career. "It's too bad nobody ever brings up what my father has done for me on the plus side," she said in *Tennis* magazine. "There's a lot there that doesn't come up, because the media focuses on certain things and exaggerates or enlarges them. But there *were* positives mixed in with the negatives. After all, my father trained me, and here I am. He gave me a good work ethic that I think I've kept. He was always very tough on me—often he was too tough. But one of the few justifiable reasons for his behavior was that he wanted to make me mentally tougher. That has helped me, it's undeniable."

Since she's just 21 years old now, Mary has years ahead to prove her point.

MEREDITH
RAINEY

"Running is fun for me because I know I can be better. Also, it's fun because it's not a life-or-death thing for me. It's an option. I'm doing it because I want to."

Meredith Rainey skipped running track from seventh grade right through high school. She attended Harvard University, that bastion of academia, and graduated *cum laude*. Hardly the suggested training schedule for an Olympic athlete, but Rainey has nonetheless appeared in two Olympics, where she was a featured performer in the grueling 800-meter race. Rainey's career is a case of talent and desire overcoming a wealth of obstacles, from the demands of an Ivy League education to the dislocation of training three thousand miles from home. She will be an athlete to watch probably through the year 2000.

Born October 15, 1968, in New York City, Rainey grew up in the Crown Heights section of Brooklyn. Hers was a family of educated and socially conscious parents and grandparents—her maternal great-grandfather had been burnt out of his house in Charleston, South Carolina, for daring to stand up to white people, and her grandmother was a respected civic leader in Brooklyn. The younger daughter of a school teacher and a police officer, Rainey attended private schools and began running track at age eight for the Atoms Track Club.

At 12 Rainey abandoned track completely. Although she had been a winning sprinter, athletics never presented themselves as a high priority in her household—a premium was placed on education and getting into a top-ranked college. Rainey certainly accomplished that goal. She was accepted at Harvard University and enrolled in the autumn of 1986. In November of her freshman year she sought out the Harvard track coach and returned to competition. "I felt like I was coming home," she recalled in a June 1993 *Runner's World* profile.

Despite the demands of her Harvard studies, Rainey soon excelled on the Ivy League track circuit. She began with the 400-meter race and then moved up to the 800 with gratifying results. In her junior year she won the event at the National Collegiate Athletic Association Championships—the first time an Ivy League woman had ever won a national collegiate track title. As

Meredith Rainey runs her specialty, the 800-meter race, at the 1995 Pan American Games. (© Al Bello/Allsport Photography USA Inc.)

a Harvard senior she not only turned in an honors thesis on the history of inner city settlement houses, she also won the 800-meter race at the U.S. Nationals.

Rainey graduated from Harvard in 1990 and developed a two-year plan that would take her to the Olympics. She finished third at the 1992 Olympic trials and qualified for the U.S. team, but her experience in Barcelona was a great disappointment—she placed third in the first heat she ran and thus did not even qualify for the semifinals. "After working so hard to get there, having my whole Olympic experience amount to 2 minutes was a real emotional letdown," she admitted in *Runner's World.* "At the Trials, finishing third was as good as finishing first. In the Olympics, finishing third in my heat was as bad as finishing last."

In the wake of the 1992 Olympics, Rainey sought the help of coach Brooks Johnson, a former Olympic track coach and currently the director of track and field at Cal Poly, San Luis Obispo. Working with Brooks meant that

MEREDITH RAINEY

American track & field athlete

Born: October 15, 1968 in New York, New York.

Education: Attended Harvard University, graduating *cum laude in 1990.*

Career Highlights:
- won the 800-meter race at the NCAA Championships—the first time an Ivy League woman had ever won a national collegiate track title, 1989

- won the 800-meter race at the U.S. Nationals, 1990

- finished third at the 1992 Olympic trials, qualifying for the U.S. team

- won the 800-meter race at the U.S. nationals with a time of 2:00.07, 1995.

Rainey would have to leave New York City and live in California—a major sacrifice for someone who describes herself as an "East Coast person." Rainey spent two years in California with Johnson and still structures her workouts around his suggestions. For his part, coach Johnson told *Runner's World* that Rainey has championship potential. "Meredith has the bloodlines of a true thoroughbred," he said. "She comes from one of the more accomplished, committed black families in America. She's very cerebral, but she doesn't trip herself up by the wrong kind of thinking. As far as running goes, she has done her studying and knows what's out there in terms of talent. She knows that hers is at the very top level. If she hadn't come to that assessment, she would have already taken her honors degree from Harvard and be well on her way in a career in public policy."

The career in public policy will have to wait. Now training primarily in Silver Spring, Maryland, with frequent visits to San Luis Obispo, Rainey has consistently improved her times in the 800-meter event. She was the 1995 U.S. champion with a time of 2:00.07 in preparation for the 1996 Summer Games in Atlanta. Rainey plans to continue her track career at least until the 2000 Olympics and then return to her scholarly pursuits. "I just don't think it takes a narrow-minded athlete to win," she explained in *Runner's World.* "It's the narrow-minded people who most often burn out. Running is fun for me because I know I can be better. Also, it's fun because it's not a life-or-death thing for me. It's an option. I'm doing it because I want to."

MARY LOU
RETTON

A 1993 national poll ranked Mary Lou Retton as one of the most popular female athletes in America (sharing top honors with Dorothy Hamill). This might not be so remarkable if Retton had won a medal at the 1992 Olympics, but in fact it had been almost ten years since the vaulting wonder from West Virginia had brought home Olympic gold in gymnastics. Perhaps because of her All-American looks and high spirits—as well as her perfect ten performance—Retton left an indelible mark on sports fans. Gold medals are one thing, but having your picture on the Wheaties box *really* puts you on the map.

Retton was just a four-foot-nine-inch 16-year-old when she won the all-around gold medal in gymnastics at the 1984 Summer Olympic Games. Her performance proved to the world that the United States was a gymnastic force to be reckoned with. She also proved to admiring fans everywhere that a gymnast need not be needle thin and wisp light. Some observers likened her muscular, solid body more to that of a linebacker than to the lithe creatures usually seen passing between the uneven bars. Yet her decisive, powerful, and daring delivery in the end proved no less graceful than any the world has ever seen.

Retton was born January 24, 1968, in Fairmont, West Virginia, a small coal mining town. She was the youngest of five children. Her father was a former New York Yankees farm team shortstop who owned a coal transportation equipment business. Mary Lou began acrobatic and ballet classes at the age of four because she was "very hyper." Sports provided exactly the outlet she needed for her energy, and by the age of seven she was training seriously in gymnastics. In 1976, when she watched Nadia Comaneci stun the world at the Olympics, she began to lay plans for her own Olympic future.

The opportunity to become a world-class gymnast simply didn't exist in Fairmont. Retton and her family realized that she would have to live away from home in order to train at a first-class facility. In 1983 she left West Virginia to move in with a family who had another gymnast in the

GYMNAST

"You give up your childhood. You miss proms and games and high school events, and people say it's awful. . . . I say it was a good trade. You miss something, but I think I gained more than I lost."

387

Mary Lou Retton took home five medals from the 1984 Olympics, including the all-around gold medal. (Archive Photos/Popperfoto)

same school as the one Retton chose to attend—Bela Karolyi's World Gymnastics. The Houston school, undoubtedly the best known in the country, is run by Karolyi, a Romanian coach who was then renowned for training Comaneci.

Of her decision to leave home Retton told *Time* magazine: "I knew that if I wanted to have a chance at a medal in the Olympics, I was not going to do it if I stayed at home. And I had worked all of those long, hard years."

For his part, Karolyi had spotted Retton's potential as early as 1982. He was thrilled to be able to work with her. "Nadia was a great champion, but Mary Lou is bigger," he told *Newsweek.* "She's got the psychological power to go through the most difficult moments without falling apart." Retton's other strong suit was her ability to play to the crowd, to make eye contact with an audience and communicate her own high spirits.

Retton scored her first major victory in the 1982 McDonald's American Cup competition. In February of 1983 she won the Caesars Palace Invitational all-around medal. After that competition, a *Harper's* contributor observed that Retton had "such a boxy, compact body that some coaches feel that she won't grow gracefully in the sport."

No comment could have been further from the truth. Under Karolyi's tutelage Retton honed her artistry and polished her considerable talents. Just six weeks before the 1984 Olympics she suffered a knee injury that required arthroscopic surgery, but she had recovered completely by the time she reached Los Angeles. Even before the competition began she won the hearts of America with her friendly, down-home personality, her rural, middle-class upbringing, and her teenaged bravado.

Retton's chief competitor at the Olympics was Romanian Ecaterina Szabo, the reigning world champion and pre-Olympic favorite. Indeed, Szabo appeared destined to dominate the 1984 Summer Games when she won individual gold medals in the floor exercise, balance beam, and the vault, and the team gymnastics title as well. In the all-around competition, Szabo scored a perfect 10 on the balance beam, and going into the last phase of the competition—the vault—she had a slender lead over Retton. Mary Lou knew she had to make a perfect 10 on her vault in order to edge Szabo out for the all-around gold.

The "boxy" Retton made it look easy. Given two chances to score a 10 on her vault, she got the score on her first attempt. She could have stopped then and there and headed off for her medal, but as the partisan Los Angeles crowd cheered her on, she vaulted again—and earned another perfect score. Retton won the all-around gold medal, as well as silver medals in team and vault and bronze medals in uneven bars and floor exercise. Hers was one of America's best showings ever in gymnastics.

"Mary Lou has two great qualities that put her where she is," Don Peters, the U.S. women's team coach, told the *New York Times*. "First, physically, she is the most powerful gymnast who ever competed in the sport, and she takes great advantage of that in her tumbling and her vaulting. . . . Second, she's one hell of a competitor. As the pressure gets greater, Mary Lou gets greater."

America fell head over heels for Mary Lou Retton. *Sports Illustrated* named her 1984 Sportswoman of the Year. Her smiling face graced the front of the Wheaties box—an honor almost always reserved for male athletes. And she showed her success was no fluke when she toured 28 cities, appearing in parades, shows, and special events. For years following her Olympic appearance she was one of the most visible—and most popular—athletes in the nation.

MARY LOU RETTON

American gymnast

Born: January 24, 1968 in Fairmont, West Virginia.

Career Highlights:

• won the McDonald's American Cup competition, 1982

• won the Caesars Palace Invitational all-around medal, 1983

• won the all-around gold medal in gymnastics as well as silver medals in team and vault and bronze medals in uneven bars and floor exercise, 1984 Olympic Games, Los Angeles, California.

Awards: Named Sportswoman of the Year by *Sports Illustrated*, 1984.

That popularity has not faded as the years progress. Retton is still a sought-after commodity for product endorsements and gymnastic exhibitions. Married and living in Houston, Texas, she had her first child in 1995. Retton has worked as a television commentator, most notably for the Olympics and for a show entitled *American Sportswomen*. She also tours the country to give motivational speeches. "I tell people how to leave the comfort zone and meet life's challenges," she told *People*.

No one could be more qualified on that subject than you, Mary Lou.

MANON
RHEAUME

Can women play professional hockey in the men's leagues? Manon Rheaume is answering that question in the affirmative, playing goalie for the Atlanta Knights, a minor league franchise in the National Hockey League. Rheaume (pronounced *Ray-ohm*) is a French Canadian player and the first woman ever to play in an NHL game. Given a tryout for the Tampa Bay Lightning in 1992, she is signed to a contract with that team through 1996. For Rheaume, playing against men is not the goal *per se*. She just wants to compete at the level where her skills will be tested. "I'm happy to be with Atlanta because I have a good chance to get experience, to learn more," she said. "I didn't try to be the first woman to do this, I just want to play."

Rheaume was born and raised in Lac Beauport, a suburb of Quebec City in Canada. She learned to skate soon after learning to walk and was quite good at it by age four. Her father, Pierre, flooded the back yard so Manon and her brothers, Martin and Pascal, could skate there. Pierre also ran the town's outdoor ice rink and coached a boy's hockey team. Through her early years Manon spent hours watching her brothers practice hockey on the rink. Then they would come home and practice some more—and she joined in.

One day when Rheaume was five, her father found himself short a goalie for a local tournament. She volunteered her services. Rheaume told *People:* "I said to my father, 'I would like to be your goalie.' He laughed. But then he said, 'Why not? You take shots from your brothers at home.'"

The minute she tried her skills in real competition, Rheaume was hooked. For a time she mixed hockey with other activities such as ballet and skiing. But she loved the sport so much that it soon consumed all of her spare time. "I didn't just play hockey," she said in *People.* "It was my passion."

Her ability landed her on boys' teams all through school and the youth leagues. After high school she made Canada's Junior B league and even played briefly on the Junior A level—the level just below the NHL. With women's teams she was nothing less than a star. As the goaltender for the Canadian

"The players are bigger, the speed is faster, and the shot is harder. It's a big difference."

—Manon Rheaume, on life in the NHL

Manon Rheaume (left) is one of many women who play ice hockey, but she became the only woman to be signed to play on an NHL team when the Tampa Bay Lightning hired her in 1992. (© S. Halleran/Allsport Photography USA Inc.)

national women's team she helped to win a gold medal at the 1992 women's world championships in Finland. Rheaume gave up just two goals in three games in the world championship tournament.

Rheaume found that her stint in the Junior A league gave her a hint as to what she would be up against in big-time hockey. "Some players tried to make me afraid with some very high shots," she admitted in *People*. One of those shots shattered her face mask and caused a three-inch gash above her eyebrow. "The blood started running," she said. "But I continued to play. I didn't want anyone to say I stopped because I was a girl."

Critics charge that Rheaume was given a tryout for the NHL expansion Tampa Bay Lightning *because* she was a girl. Many so-called hockey purists saw Rheaume's audition for the team as a cheap publicity ploy. *Sports Illustrated* correspondent E. M. Swift called the action "manipulative and sexist, a desperate attempt to sell a bad hockey team to an uninitiated Southern city." Such grumbling notwithstanding, Rheaume comported herself bravely in her Tampa Bay tryout, giving up two goals and making seven saves in the first period of an exhibition contest. Tampa Bay general manager Phil Esposito signed her to a three-year contract and sent her to the minors in Atlanta.

Esposito too faced charges that Rheaume's inclusion in the NHL was a mere stunt to generate ticket sales. "I'd be a liar to say I wasn't using this for publicity," he admitted in *People*. "But I don't care if she is a woman. If there were a horse with skates and it could stop a puck, I'd put it in there."

It's safe to say that Manon Rheaume can stop a puck. Goaltending is one area of hockey that relies less on strength than on reflexes and timing. However, strength is still important, and at five-foot-six and just 135 pounds Rheaume is quite small by NHL standards. In order to improve her upper body conditioning, she has employed a personal trainer and lifts weights to beef up her shoulders and arms. As for being checked, both legally and illegally, she spends little time worrying about what an opponent might try. "I don't think about getting hurt when I'm on the ice," she claimed in *Women's Sports + Fitness*. "It wouldn't be good for a figure skater to think about getting hurt if she misses a move. I just think about doing my job. If I were afraid, I wouldn't have come to the tryout."

Rheaume's dark-eyed beauty led the staff of *Playboy* to offer her $50,000 for a photo shoot. She turned them down flat. At least for her, a place in the NHL farm system is much more than just a chance for cheap headlines. It's the opportunity to play hockey at its highest level and to test her mettle against stronger, faster, and more aggressive opponents. Rheaume notes that among her fellow players, at least, she gets the respect she deserves. "They play against me like they play against another goaltender," she said in *Women's Sports + Fitness*. "They try . . . to make me afraid. I have to deal with this; they do this with other goaltenders. If I have a chance to play, I'm going to play."

WOMEN ON ICE

Manon Rheaume is not the only woman who plays ice hockey, though she does seem to be getting all the publicity. For the 1994–95 season, U.S.A. Hockey, the governing body for hockey in the States, registered 322 girls' ice hockey teams, and that does not include high school and college teams. The U.S. Women's National Team, playing in the first-ever women's world tournament in 1990, took home a silver medal. They repeated their top-tiered performance at the 1992 worlds. Any lingering doubts about whether women can play hockey should be removed when women's ice hockey becomes a full medal sport at either the 1998 or 2002 Winter Olympics.

MANON RHEAUME

Canadian hockey player

Born: C. 1972 in Lac Beauport, a suburb of Quebec City, Canada.

Career Highlights:
- tended goal for the Canadian national women's team, helping to win a gold medal, women's world championships, 1992

- became first woman ever to play in an NHL game after being signed to a contract with the Tampa Bay Lightning, 1992.

LIBBY
RIDDLES

The year was 1985, and two women were trying to win the honor of being the first female winner of the Iditarod Trail sled dog race. Libby Riddles was the long shot candidate. In her previous races she had finished no higher than 18th, while her rival, Susan Butcher, had finished second twice. The Iditarod is a race in which anything can happen, however, and 1985 proved to be Riddles's year. She and her team of dogs—all of whom she had raised herself—won the grueling 18-day event. And so it was Libby Riddles, and not Susan Butcher, who became the first woman to win the Iditarod.

Riddles was born and raised in St. Cloud, Minnesota. She grew up loving animals, dreaming of being a cowgirl or running a farm. At the age of 16 she was introduced to another possibility by a boyfriend named Dewey Halverson. Halverson had been to Alaska, and he wanted to live there and raise sled dogs. His stories of the wild northern country thrilled Riddles. They decided to go north together.

Although she was a teenager at the time, Riddles was realistic and mature for her age. She did not just run off to Alaska, but rather finished her high school studies in an accelerated course and worked a part-time job in order to save enough for a plane ticket and expenses. When she arrived in Alaska, she moved in with Halverson in a cabin near Anchorage, where she helped him train sled dogs for racing. What she thought might be an ideal existence became frustrating. "I learned real quick it's not much fun to help somebody else drive dogs," she explained in *Women's Sports + Fitness*. "I wanted to do it myself."

Her chance came not with Halverson but with another boyfriend, Joe Garnie. Riddles met Garnie during the 1981 Iditarod, and soon afterwards she moved to his remote northern village of Teller (population 250). Theirs was hardly a life of luxury. They shared a small trailer without a bathroom, heated only by an oil stove. Fishing and hunting helped to provide their food. Their dogs, descended from a tough line of part-hound, part-huskie ancestors, helped them to perform the heavy chores. "We're actually living the lifestyle," Riddles

"If I had to treat all my dogs like soldiers, it would just take the fun out of it. I feel like I'm a real expert at keeping my dogs happy. But when things get serious, they listen to me, too. You've got to be strict with them."

395

Libby Riddles, shown here at the start of the 1995 Iditarod, became the first woman to win Alaska's "last great race" in 1985. (Archive Photos)

told *Women's Sports + Fitness.* "I think that's part of the reason Joe and I have done well in the racing business. The dogs kinda know that they're being used for an actual purpose, rather than by some guy who's just running a 40-mile loop every night. We haul fish with the dogs, haul firewood with 'em. We'll go up the beach and haul walrus with 'em. It gives the dogs a more versatile outlook on life."

In 1985 Riddles was one of 61 entrants (56 men, five women) in the annual 1,172-mile Iditarod race. Unable to attract sponsors to offset the estimated $7,000 cost for one race, she sewed fur hats for sale and gave sled dog exhibitions to tourists. Additional money was raised from bingo games in Teller. Riddles started in Anchorage at the 42nd position, armed with a sled full of dog food, dried moose meat, and "Eskimo ice cream"—a concoction of grated reindeer fat mixed with seal oil, salmonberries and sugar.

The 1985 Iditarod was run in some of the worst weather the racers had ever seen. Heavy snows forced a three-day halt at midpoint, and at times

LIBBY RIDDLES

American dogsledder

Born: April 1, 1956 in St. Cloud, Minnesota.

Career Highlights:
• became the first woman to win the Iditarod, 1985.

Awards: Received the humanitarian award, given to the Iditarod musher who takes best care of his or her dogs, 1985; named Women's Sports Foundation Pro Sportswoman of the Year, 1985.

the temperature plunged to -50 degrees. Riddles had her share of troubles during the two-and-a-half week run. Early in the race her dogs ran away with the sled, and she had to walk some distance before discovering that they had been stopped by another musher. A few days later some of her animals came down with a virus that affected their appetites and energy levels. She was very careful not to work the dogs too hard, and she massaged their feet with oil frequently to prevent skin lesions.

With her dogs recovered and running strong toward the end of the race, Riddles made her move. At Unalakleet, some 270 miles from the finish line at Nome, she shortened her break time and headed out of town ahead of the other racers. She did the same thing at the next point, Shaktoolik, despite being told that a severe ground blizzard was brewing. Riddles took off straight into the blizzard, but after three hours of running into the wind her dogs were exhausted. She spent the next 12 hours huddled in her sleeping bag on the sled, while her dogs slept in the snow. The blizzard was still raging when they woke up, but the rest stop had revived the dogs. They ran strong after that, in first place, all the way to Nome.

Riddles finished the race in 18 days, 20 minutes, and 17 seconds, a full two hours before her nearest competitor. She became the first woman ever to win the Iditarod and, as an added bonus, she received the year's humanitarian award, given to the musher who takes best care of his or her dogs. As for Susan Butcher, she had to drop out of the race at an early stage when her dogs tangled with a moose and got stomped, two of them fatally.

With typical candor, Riddles downplayed the significance of her first-ever victory. "I want to be thought of as a racer first," she told the crowd. Then, expressing her frustration at the financial sacrifices she had to make to get into the Iditarod, she added: "To all those who didn't sponsor me, thanks for keeping me tough!"

Riddles told *Women's Sports + Fitness* that the secret to her success was the special relationship she formed with her dogs. "When I'm out there racing, I'm racing as much as anybody to win," she said. "But I'm also out there because I enjoy being with my dogs and I love what I'm doing." Smiling, she concluded: "What I like about my dogs is they tend to be more personable and have a little bit better manners than others. Just the weather up here really toughens the dogs' mental attitude. It toughens up the drivers, too."

CATHY
RIGBY

Before Cathy Rigby came along, American women gymnasts were regularly overshadowed by their European counterparts. Rigby became America's first serious medal contender in gymnastics, and in two Olympic appearances and several World Cup events, she emerged as a top performer *and* a media darling. If those years were fraught with anguish for Rigby, she never showed it. She appeared to be a happy, sprightly athlete that all America could love.

Reality was a bit darker for the two-time Olympian. During her gymnastic career and afterwards, Rigby struggled with an eating disorder and with feelings of inadequacy. When she finished 10th at the 1972 Olympics she was crushed. "I began to think, 'Did I fail everyone?'" she explained in *People* magazine. "And when you're scared to death like that, you put a veil across everything. Pretty soon you just become an image of what you think you should be."

Cathy Rigby was born December 12, 1952, in Long Beach, California. She was a sickly infant who only weighed four pounds at birth, but as she grew she proved to be a strong and daring child. She climbed furniture fearlessly and played active games with her two brothers and two sisters. At eight she began ballet lessons, and at ten she decided she wanted to try gymnastics. Enrolled in a local tumbling class, she soon caught the eye of Bud Marquette, gymnastics coach of the Southern California Acro Team (SCAT). Marquette persuaded the Rigbys to allow Cathy to join his troupe, and at 11 her gymnastics career began.

Rigby told *People* that she was often caught in a power struggle between her coach and her father, who differed on the course her training should take. The friction spilled over into her home life, and she found an escape in her sport. "Gymnastics was a way to be away from home," she recalled, "but it too had its problems." One of those problems was keeping her weight down. When she jumped from 95 to 105 pounds at 16, Rigby panicked. Desperate to lose weight, she followed another gymnast's advice and began engaging in the practices that lead to bulimia.

GYMNAST

"In high school I never went to the prom because I was too consumed with gymnastics. Also, with my hair in pigtails and looking about 10, I wasn't exactly date material."

Cathy Rigby practices her scissors split in 1970. (UPI/Bettmann Newsphotos)

Few people were aware that Rigby's life was anything but perfect. While other girls her age sat in high schools all day, she traveled the world giving gymnastics exhibitions with the SCAT team. At 15 she qualified for the U.S. Olympic team and went to Mexico City, where she placed 16th. In the 1970 world championships in Yugoslavia she became the first American to win a medal—silver for the balance beam—in international competition. She placed first in the all-around at the 1971 World Cup gymnastics championships in Miami.

With her face on the cover of America's most popular magazines and her lifestyle the subject of television profiles, Rigby became America's first marquee gymnast. She embraced the role gracefully, hiding her troubles from all but her closest confidantes. Expectations were high that Rigby would win several medals at the 1972 Olympics, but in the Olympic trials she injured her foot. She missed training for several weeks and was no match for Russia's Olga Korbut at the Munich Games. Rigby finished 10th.

CATHY RIGBY

American gymnast

Born: December 12, 1952 in Long Beach, California.

Career Highlights:

- began touring and performing gymnastics exhibitions at age 11 with the Southern California Acro Team (SCAT), 1963

- became the first American to win a medal—silver for the balance beam—in international competition, world championships, 1970

- placed first in the all-around at the World Cup gymnastics championships, 1971.

Her Olympic disappointment did little to erode Rigby's popularity in America. Although she retired from competition after the 1972 Summer Games, she stayed in the public eye as a television commentator for gymnastics events and a motivational speaker. She founded her own gymnastics academy in California, married, and had two sons.

Inevitably the hidden turmoil in her life became overwhelming. The bulimia followed her into adulthood, at times imperiling her health. Her first marriage failed. With the help of her second husband, she began to address her health issues and finally learned to eat right and to be comfortable with a healthy weight. Subsequently she had two more children, both daughters.

Rigby has had an interesting career since leaving gymnastics. In addition to her television work, she has toured in theatrical productions, most notably *Peter Pan*. The first time she appeared in *Peter Pan* she lip-synched the songs. Now she does her own singing, after having taken voice and acting lessons. Reflecting on her theatrical career, Rigby told *People:* "Having started from scratch in gymnastics, I knew I could get better [at singing] if I just worked at it. It's that athlete's obsessiveness—the need to prove yourself and work harder than anybody else."

SHAWNA
ROBINSON

"I've never wanted to flaunt the woman thing. I just want to be thought of as being a good driver, not a good female driver."

Shawna Robinson has spent more than a decade immersed in the macho world of NASCAR racing. The whole time she has had to race against men—a women's sports car tour simply doesn't exist. This has proved both a challenge and a frustration to Robinson, who is the first woman ever to win a major NASCAR race. Often working without adequate sponsorship, driving against competitors who may or may not be deliberately trying to sabotage her chances, Robinson has never given up her quest for respect as a stock car driver. "I've never wanted to flaunt the woman thing," she told *Sports Illustrated*. "I just want to be thought of as being a good driver, not a good female driver."

Driving was all Robinson ever wanted to do. Her father, Richard Robinson, was an amateur racer and sponsor of diesel truck races in the Midwest. Growing up in Iowa, Robinson and her four siblings raced everything they could lay their hands on: minibikes, snowmobiles, motorcycles, and—when they became old enough to get licenses—cars. When Robinson was 18 her father taught her how to drive the big diesel trucks he raced on weekends. The five-foot six-inch, 110-pound Shawna thought nothing of piloting the 14,000-pound truck cabs in short-track events. Despite a wealth of obstacles—especially male racers who resented her—she became the first woman ever to win a big truck race.

In 1988 Robinson moved from diesel trucks to Dash division NASCAR racing. It was quite a step from a truck to a four-cylinder subcompact car, but Robinson made the adjustment easily. In June of 1988 she made history when she won the AC Delco 100 NASCAR race in Asheville, North Carolina. She was the first woman ever to win a major NASCAR event. Named Most Popular Driver in the Dash division later in 1988, she was on hand when her winning Pontiac Sunbird was donated to the International Motorsports Hall of Fame.

If Robinson expected smooth sailing through the various stock car divisions, she soon discovered that her success would have to be fought for every step of the way. Like other female drivers on the circuit, she has strug-

Shawna Robinson keeps track of her competitors' times before qualification runs for a 1992 Grand National race. (UPI/Corbis-Bettmann)

SHAWNA ROBINSON

American stock car racer

Born: C. 1965.

Career Highlights:

- made history by winning the AC Delco 100 NASCAR race in the Dash division; became first woman ever to win a major NASCAR event, 1988
- rose from the Dash division into the Grand National category, where competitors drive full-size, eight-cylinder cars that can reach speeds of 200 miles per hour

- became first woman ever to win the pole position at a Grand National NASCAR race; in qualifying for the Busch Light 300 she set a Grand National track record lap speed of 174.330 miles per hour, 1994.

Awards: Named Most Popular Driver in the Dash division; named Rookie of the Year; invited to donate her winning Pontiac Sunbird to the International Motorsports Hall of Fame, 1988.

gled to land serious sponsors or to find a team that will accept her as a full-time driver. Nevertheless, in less than a decade she has risen from the Dash division into the Grand National category, where competitors drive full-size, eight-cylinder cars that can reach speeds of 200 miles per hour.

In 1994 Robinson became the first woman ever to win the pole position at a Grand National NASCAR race. She qualified for the Busch Light 300 in Atlanta by setting a Grand National track record lap speed of 174.330 miles per hour. That speed gave Robinson the best position for the prestigious race, and she fully expected to run well and make history again. Instead, in the very first lap, fellow racer Mike Wallace pulled alongside her and caused her car to broadside yet another racer's vehicle. Both cars were severely damaged, but Robinson was able to get hers back into the race. She completed 63 laps before radiator damage forced her into the pits permanently.

Robinson declined to speculate on the reason for Wallace's dangerous actions. Other male racers suggested that he might have set out to thwart her deliberately, because she was a woman. Robinson was certainly disappointed at the outcome of her first pole position race. "How many fans were taking bets, 'Is the girl going to crash on the first lap?'" she asked rhetorically in *Sports Illustrated.* "By starting on the pole and racing well, I hoped I could have changed those attitudes."

Time is still on Robinson's side, however. Still in her early 30s, she can conceivably race for another decade. More women are appearing in the ranks of NASCAR driving, and sources estimate that as much as 40 percent of the NASCAR fan base is female. Robinson is fueled by the love of her sport as well as the ambition to make a mark for women on the Grand National circuit. "Years from now," she concluded in *People,* "I don't want to be someone people will say about, 'Whatever happened to her?'"

WILMA
RUDOLPH

Wilma Rudolph made history at the 1960 Summer Olympics in Rome, when she became the first American woman to win three gold medals in track and field competition. Rudolph's brilliant accomplishments were all the more remarkable because she came from modest circumstances and endured a childhood of sickness and disability. Her confidence may have flagged at times as a youngster weighed down with leg braces and special shoes, but through the efforts of her devoted family—and her own steely determination to strengthen herself—she rose to Olympic glory. Her victories in Rome helped to set the stage for a life dedicated to the principles and practices that helped her to succeed.

The deck seemed completely stacked against Rudolph when she was born. Her father had 11 children by a first marriage and eight more with Wilma's mother, of which Wilma was the fifth. At birth she weighed only four-and-a-half pounds. While she was still an infant the family moved to Clarksville, Tennessee, where her father worked as a railroad porter and her mother cleaned houses six days a week.

At the age of four, Rudolph contracted polio. The disease weakened her and made her vulnerable to pneumonia and scarlet fever. She survived the potentially deadly illnesses, but she lost the use of her left leg. A specialist in Nashville showed the family how to massage the limb, and Wilma's older siblings pitched in their services to help their sister regain strength. Still, she needed leg braces, and she absolutely hated them.

After five years of treatment, Rudolph one day stunned her doctors when she removed the braces and walked by herself. She had been practicing—with the help of her siblings—for quite some time. Soon she was able to walk even better with the help of a supportive shoe. This she wore until she was 11. After that, she not only left braces and orthopedic shoes behind, she confounded every prediction that she would be a disabled adult. "By the time I was 12," she told the *Chicago Tribune*, "I was challenging every boy in our neighborhood at running, jumping, everything."

TRACK & FIELD
ATHLETE

"The triumph can't be had without the struggle. And I know what struggle is. I have spent a lifetime trying to share what it has meant to be a woman first in the world of sports so that other young women have a chance to reach their dreams."

At the 1960 Olympics, Wilma Rudolph became the first American woman to win three gold medals in track and field competition. (Archive Photos/David Lees)

Rudolph had to plead for a chance to play high school basketball, and she was only given a place on the team because the coach wanted her older sister to play. Nevertheless, she soon blossomed into a fine basketball player. As a sophomore she scored 803 points in 25 games, a new state record for girls' basketball. She also started running in track meets and found that her greatest strengths lay in the sprint. She was only 14 when she attracted the attention of Ed Temple, the women's track coach at Tennessee State University. Temple told her she had the potential to become a great runner, so she trained with him during her summer recesses from school.

The Olympic Games were a far-off dream to a young black woman in Tennessee. Rudolph was a teenager before she even learned what the Olympics were. She caught on fast, though. In four seasons of high school track, she never lost a race. At the tender age of 16 she qualified for the Summer Olympics in Melbourne, Australia, and came home with a bronze medal in the 4 × 100-meter relay. Rudolph recalled in the *Chicago Tribune:* "I remember going back to my high school this particular day with the bronze medal and all the kids that I disliked so much or I thought I disliked . . . put up this big huge banner: 'Welcome Home Wilma.' And I forgave them right then and there. . . . They passed my bronze medal around so that everybody could touch, feel and see what an Olympic medal is like. When I got it back, there were handprints all over it. I took it and I started shining it up. I discovered that bronze doesn't shine. So, I decided, I'm going to try this one more time. I'm going to go for the gold."

She got her chance in Rome four years later, and she won all three of her gold medals in dramatic fashion. In both the 100-meter dash and the 200-meter dash, she finished at least three yards in front of her closest competitor. She tied the world record in the 100 meter and set a new Olympic record in the 200. Rudolph also brought her 4 × 100-meter relay team from behind to win another gold medal. The French called her "La Gazelle."

Wilma Rudolph became an instant celebrity in Europe and America. Mobs gathered wherever she was scheduled to run. She was given ticker tape parades, an official invitation to the White House by president John F. Kennedy, and a dizzying round of dinners, awards, and television appearances. The praise had a hollow ring, however, since she received little, if anything, in the way of monetary rewards. Years later, Rudolph told *Ebony:* "You become world famous and you sit with kings and queens, and then your first job is just a job. You can't go back to living the way you did before because you've been taken out of one setting and shown the other. That becomes a struggle and makes *you* struggle."

WILMA RUDOLPH

American track & field athlete

Born: June 23, 1940 in St. Bethlehem, Tennessee.

Died: November 12, 1994 in Nashville, Tennessee.

Education: Attended Tennessee State University, graduating in 1963.

Career Highlights:

• won every race she entered in four seasons of high school track

• earned bronze medal as member of 4 × 100-meter relay team, 1956 Olympic Games, Melbourne, Australia

• won three gold medals—in the 100-meter dash, 200-meter dash, and 4 × 100-meter relay—1960 Olympic Games, Rome, Italy.

Awards: Received Sullivan Award, 1961; inducted into United States Olympic Hall of Fame and the National Track and Field Hall of Fame.

Rudolph made one decision that she stuck to firmly: she refused to participate in the 1964 Olympic Games. She felt that she might not be able to duplicate her achievement of 1960 and did not want to appear to be fading. She retired from amateur athletics in 1963, finished her college work, and became a school teacher and athletic coach. She also became a mother, raising four children on her own after being divorced twice.

In the three decades after her retirement, Wilma Rudolph sought to impart the lessons she learned about athletics to other young women. She wrote an autobiography, *Wilma,* that was published in 1977. She lectured in every part of America and even served in 1991 as an ambassador to the European celebration of the dismantling of the Berlin Wall. Rudolph helped to open and run inner city sports clinics and served as a consultant to university track teams. Her own organization, the Wilma Rudolph Foundation, is dedicated to promoting amateur athletics.

"I think the thing that made life good for me is that I never looked back," Rudolph told *Ebony*. "I've always been positive no matter what happened."

Rudolph was honored with membership to the United States Olympic Hall of Fame *and* the National Track and Field Hall of Fame. She spent her later years living in Indianapolis, traveling frequently and becoming well known for her motivational speeches to youngsters. "I love working with kids. It's the motherly instinct in me," she told *Newsday*. In an interview with *Ebony,* Rudolph claimed that her moment of Olympic glory "sort of sent my way all the other positive things and feelings that I've had. That one accomplishment—what happened in 1960—nobody can take away from me. It was something I worked for. It wasn't something somebody handed to me."

Just over a year after being honored as one of "the Great Ones" at the first National Sports Awards in 1993, Wilma Rudolph died of brain cancer in Nashville, Tennessee.

GABRIELA
SABATINI

Argentina's Gabriela Sabatini is one of the few modern tennis players who has effectively challenged the Steffi Graf-Monica Seles juggernaut. The 1990 U.S. Open winner—and former number-one player—Sabatini has been praised for her "complete game" and her serve-and-volley attack. Considered an idol and a role model in her native land, Sabatini has been on the women's professional tour since April of 1985, when she was a not-so-tender 14.

Tennis magazine correspondent Peter Bodo has called Sabatini "one of the most intensely lionized prodigies of the Open era" but adds that the athlete "managed to escape the perils that have caused so many other wunderkinder to burn out and come crashing down to earth. This has been quite an achievement, and it is a tribute to Sabatini's sound sense of self, her fidelity to the game and to her supportive family and professional associates."

Sabatini was born on May 16, 1970, in Buenos Aires, Argentina, the daughter of Osvaldo and Beatriz Sabatini. Her father was an executive with General Motors while she was growing up, but he quit in 1986 to manage his daughter's career. Sabatini began playing tennis when she was six and began taking private lessons the following year. "Tennis was like a toy to me," she recalled in the *New York Times*. "Instead of having dolls, I was playing tennis." She developed rapidly and by the age of 10 was ranked first in her country in the 12-and-under division.

After one year of junior high school, Sabatini moved to Key Biscayne, Florida, in order to continue training with her coach, Patricio Apey. She joined the pro tour in 1985 and announced her presence by beating three top-ranked tennis players at the 1985 Family Circle Magazine Cup in Hilton Head, South Carolina. Shortly after that, she became the youngest semi-finalist in the French Open's history.

In the wake of her first success, Sabatini dropped out of school in order to devote herself totally to tennis. She practiced for hours every day and often late into the night and competed 20 out of 27 weeks on four continents

"I love this sport. I'm happy to be out there. I like to keep trying and I like to work hard. I just don't like to lose."

Gabriela Sabatini hits a return to Anke Huber during the 1995 Advanta Championship. (AP/Wide World Photos)

GABRIELA SABATINI

Argentinean tennis player

Born: May 16, 1970 in Buenos Aires, Argentina.

Career Highlights:
- ranked fifth in the world, 1988
- won silver medal, singles competition, 1988 Olympic Games, Seoul, South Korea
- triumphed in singles competition, U.S. Open, 1990
- won Virginia Slims Championship, 1995.

Awards: Named Rookie of the Year by *Tennis* magazine, 1985.

---

with the tour. In 1985 she was named Rookie of the Year by *Tennis* magazine, and by 1988 she was ranked fifth in the world.

Her top ranking brought Sabatini into an unusual relationship with Steffi Graf. While often faced with the daunting task of trying to beat Graf in singles competition, Sabatini frequently paired with Graf for doubles play. She had more success *with* Graf than against her, but she did defeat Graf in the 1988 Virginia Slims tournament. In 1991, as part of a coaching change and psychological makeover, Sabatini chose to end her doubles relationship with Graf.

Sabatini made her best showing in 1990 when she won the U.S. Open and ascended briefly to the top ranking. By April of the next year she had earned $4 million—the fifth highest total on the women's tour. Product endorsements, including one for a perfume named after her, added to her total. Even so, the pressure of the tour had begun to take its toll. Her new coach, Carlos Kirmayr, told the *Washington Post* that Sabatini needed to broaden her horizons if she hoped to continue playing top-ranked tennis. "It had reached a point where she was thinking about her job all the time," he told the *Washington Post*. "It is impossible to act and work like a professional when you live your job 24 hours a day."

Bothered by tendinitis beginning in 1992, Sabatini slipped in the rankings and did not win a major tournament for the next two-and-a-half years. Observers maintained that one of her problems was an ineffective serve, "a liability in the era of bangers and powerful big rackets," to quote *Sports Illustrated* correspondent Sally Jenkins. Sabatini was urged to take a sabbatical from her sport in order to rest and regroup, but she felt she ought to work through her problems on the court. By 1995 she had rebounded, winning the Virginia Slims Championship in a tournament that included a decisive first-round defeat of Martina Navratilova.

"Sabatini has been a reliable, conscientious, gracious veteran of the tour for 10 years now," Bodo wrote in *Tennis*. "When the competitive spark is in her eye, she's a fetching advertisement for the game." Sabatini sees no reason to curb her devotion to the tour or her obsessive interest in tennis. She thinks about the game all the time because she is thrilled to be involved with it professionally. "I love this sport," she said. "I'm happy to be out there. I like to keep trying and I like to work hard. I just don't like to lose."

ARANTXA SANCHEZ VICARIO

Arantxa Sanchez Vicario is a complete tennis player, comfortable in both singles and doubles competition. Ranked number one worldwide in both singles *and* doubles in 1995, Sanchez Vicario has been a virtual regular in Grand Slam finals for quite some time. In 1994 alone she won both the French Open and the U.S. Open singles championships, and in 1995 she was a finalist in three of the four Grand Slam events. Sanchez Vicario is a fierce competitor on the court and a bubbly and energetic person in her private life. The native of Barcelona is the first Spanish player, male or female, to hold the number one ranking in the open era.

Arantxa (pronounced ah-RAHN-cha) Sanchez was born December 18, 1971, in Barcelona, Spain. She was named after Saint Aranzazu, the patron saint of the Basque region of Spain. Her father, Emilio, is an engineer, and her mother, Marisa, is a teacher. Arantxa began playing tennis when she was two years old, literally toddling around the court and getting in everyone's way. A scaled-down tennis racket became her favorite toy, and she spent hours hitting balls against a wall. At the age of eight she began wearing the ball holder she has made famous. It clips on the back of her skirt and holds an extra ball when she serves.

Sanchez Vicario began practicing at the Club Real de Tenis, close to her home. The club has clay courts, which is still the athlete's favorite surface on which to play. She was the number-one ranked female player in Spain by the age of 13, and she turned professional at the age of 14 in 1986.

At the end of her first year as a professional, Sanchez Vicario was ranked 124th in the world. That soon changed when she advanced to the quarterfinals at the 1987 French Open in a performance so strong that she was named Most Impressive Newcomer by the Women's Tennis Association. In 1988 she defeated the legendary Chris Evert in straight sets in the third round of the French Open, and she won her first singles tournament, the Belgium Open, by defeating Raffaella Reggi, 6-0, 7-5, in the final. By the end of 1988 Sanchez Vicario was number 18 in the world.

TENNIS PLAYER

"She's feisty and fiery and laughs back at the public when she misses an easy shot. But beneath all the fun and the giggles, she's a lion."

—Tennis commentator Ted Tinling

413

Sanchez Vicario faced the challenge of her life in 1989 when she advanced to the finals of the French Open and met the heavily favored Steffi Graf. At the time Graf had won five straight Grand Slam singles titles and 117 of her previous 121 matches. Sanchez Vicario was not intimidated. In the French Open final, she won the first set, lost the second, and was trailing in the third. In an amazing turnaround, Sanchez Vicario won 16 of the last 19 points, took the last four games of the third set, and won the championship, 7-6, 3-6, 7-5. In her fractured English, she told *Sports Illustrated:* "I am very joyed. I am so excited to win Steffi." She added: "Everybody else lose to Steffi in their head before they step on court. I say, 'I beat her. It is possible, no?' They say, 'Arantxa, you crazy.' I say, 'No, it is all in the mentality. I come to play her, not pray to her.'"

With her French Open victory, Sanchez Vicario became the first Spanish woman to win a Grand Slam singles tournament. She was also the youngest player at the time to win the French Open. Sanchez Vicario became a hero in Spain, and she and her family met privately with King Juan Carlos and Queen Sofia. Nor was her performance in France a fluke. Later in 1989 she reached the singles quarterfinals at both Wimbledon and the U.S. Open. She finished the year as the sixth-ranked player in the world.

With her newfound success, Arantxa Sanchez decided to add her mother's maiden name—Vicario—to her own. She has been a presence in both singles and doubles competition ever since. In 1990 she won two singles and four doubles tournaments but failed to defend her French Open crown. The following year she made the French Open finals again, beating Graf in the semifinals. This time her finals opponent was Monica Seles, then the top-ranked player in the world. Seles beat Sanchez Vicario 6-3, 6-4.

One of Sanchez Vicario's biggest disappointments occurred at the 1992 Olympic Games. The Summer Games were held in her hometown of Barcelona, and the tennis matches were attended by the king and queen of Spain. Playing in doubles with countrywoman Conchita Martinez, Sanchez Vicario won a silver medal when she and Martinez were beaten in the finals by the American team of Fernandez and Fernandez (Gigi and Mary Joe).

That doubles loss—however embarrassing before the hometown crowd—was more than offset by Sanchez Vicario's performance on the pro tour. There she burned the opposition down. With partner Jana Novotna, she won ten women's doubles tournaments, including the Australian Open in 1992. Sanchez Vicario also won the Australian Open mixed doubles tournament with her partner, Todd Woodbridge of Australia, in 1993. More important, she took both the French Open and the U.S. Open singles titles the following year, and she made the final round at the Australian Open. Not surprisingly, she was accorded the number one world ranking on February 6, 1995.

ARANTXA SANCHEZ VICARIO

Spanish tennis player

Born: December 18, 1971 in Barcelona, Spain.

Career Highlights:
- won French Open singles competition, 1989 and 1994
- won silver medal (playing Conchita Martinez) in doubles and bronze medal in singles, 1992 Olympic Games, Barcelona, Spain
- won Australian Open doubles competition (with Jana Novotna), 1992 and 1995; mixed doubles (with Todd Woodbridge), 1993
- won U.S. Open singles championship, 1994; doubles competition, 1993 and 1994
- took Wimbledon top honors in doubles (with Jana Novotna), 1995
- ranked number one worldwide in singles and doubles, 1995.

Awards: Named Most Impressive Newcomer by the Women's Tennis Association, 1987.

Today Sanchez Vicario looks like someone who can "win Steffi"—and anyone else for that matter. In defense of her top ranking in 1995, she made the singles finals of the Australian Open (losing to Mary Pierce), the French Open (losing to Graf), and Wimbledon (losing again to Graf). In doubles competition she and Novotna won Wimbledon and the Australian Open, among other tournaments.

Sanchez Vicario is looking forward to yet another Olympic appearance in 1996, as well as further victories as a singles and doubles competitor. Her career earnings of almost $10 million rank third in the history of women's pro tennis. "In Spanish, *crac* is like a boom! It means big champion," she told *Sports Illustrated.* "My brother Emilio tell the newspapers, 'Arantxa is Crac!'"

Say it again, Emilio. Arantxa *is* crac.

SUMMER SANDERS

SWIMMER

"Once, I swam because it was habit, it was something I'd always done. Now, it's my risk and my decision, and that makes life a lot more interesting."

One of the most visible and popular athletes from the 1992 Olympics, Summer Sanders holds American swimming records in the 200- and 400-meter individual medleys. She is an eight-time United States national champion and the winner of four medals in Barcelona.

On March 16, 1992, Leigh Montville wrote in *Sports Illustrated*: "Summer Sanders. Could there be a name that is more American? More golden?" The swimmer received her unusual first name in an odd way. Her parents' first child was due on June 21, the first day of summer. They decided to use the name "Summer" because of the date. However, the baby that arrived on June 21 was a boy. He earned the name Trevor, and Summer got the original name even though she was born in October of 1972. Sanders once joked about the whole scenario in *Sports Illustrated*. "The first question always is, 'Were your parents hippies?' The answer is no. The second question always is, 'Do you come from California?' The answer is yes. The third question always is, 'What's your brother's name? Winter?' I hate the third question. It's so stupid."

When Sanders was a toddler, her father had a swimming pool built in the family's back yard. Little Summer did not seem interested in learning to swim at all, and her worried parents hovered around her whenever she went near the pool. Then one day, when their backs were turned, she leaped in and swam with her older brother. At three she could swim a standard 25-yard lap, and at four she was winning races against seven-year-olds. At the tender age of 15 she earned times in the 200- and 400-meter individual medleys and the 100- and 200-meter breaststrokes that won her the opportunity to swim in the 1988 Olympic qualifying meet.

Everyone—including Sanders—was astonished by her performance at the 1988 Olympic trials. She qualified for the finals in the 400-meter individual medley (she finished eighth), and she missed making the Olympic team by a mere .27 second in the 200-meter individual medley. She had never before even qualified for a national final. Elated by her strong showing, Sanders returned home to Roseville, California, determined to make the 1992 Olympic team.

Summer Sanders cheers upon winning the gold medal in the 200-meter breaststroke at the 1990 Goodwill Games. (UPI/Corbis-Bettmann)

An honors student in high school, Sanders won an athletic scholarship to Stanford University. She was named NCAA Swimmer of the Year in both 1991 and 1992, even though she relinquished her NCAA eligibility to pursue endorsement opportunities as the 1992 Olympics approached. At the Olympic trials in March of 1992, she established herself as the ascendant star in women's swimming, winning the 200- and 400-meter individual medleys and the 200-meter butterfly, and finishing second in the 100-meter butterfly. In all, she qualified for five Olympic events and was considered a serious contender in all of them. "This is the payoff for all the tears, the pain, the frustration," she told *Sports Illustrated.* "You work so hard. You sit in a little room and wait for your coach to come in with the workout cards, these blue cards that tell what you have to do, and you're scared about what the cards will say. You see the cards, and you know the pain that is in them. You need the payoff somewhere."

Sanders's "payoff" at the Olympics in Barcelona was spectacular. The 19-year-old with the odd name became an American hero of the Summer

SUMMER SANDERS

American swimmer

Born: October 1972.

Education: Won an athletic scholarship to Stanford University.

Career Highlights:
- won U.S. national championship eight times

- earned a gold medal in the 200-meter butterfly, another gold in the 400-meter medley relay preliminaries, a silver in the 200-meter individual medley, and a bronze in the 400-meter individual medley, 1992 Olympic Games, Barcelona, Spain.

Awards: Named NCAA Swimmer of the Year in both 1991 and 1992.

Games, earning the gold medal in the 200-meter butterfly, another gold in the 400-meter medley relay preliminaries, a silver in the 200-meter individual medley, and a bronze in the 400-meter individual medley. Sanders was the first woman swimmer since 1976 to compete in four individual events and the first since 1984 to win four medals at one Olympiad. Asked to describe her feelings as she accepted her awards, Sanders admitted in an August 10, 1992, *Sports Illustrated* piece: "I just want to sit down and relax. I want to enjoy the feeling that nobody expects me to do anything great tomorrow."

Pretty and engaging, Sanders found that her Olympic fame opened many doors in the public arena. She won lucrative product endorsements and appeared as a guest star on her favorite daytime drama, *All My Children*. She also became an MTV host and earned still more money as a motivational speaker. As for her swimming, however, she was never able to better her times from the summer of 1992. She announced her retirement in January of 1994.

After a 17-month hiatus Sanders returned to competitive swimming in April of 1995 when she was accepted to the United States Swimming Resident National Team. She joined the team in Colorado Springs and was dismayed to find that the coach, Jonty Skinner, had reserved a separate lane of the pool for her to use. She was "segregated" because she could not keep up with the other swimmers, and Skinner did not want her to become discouraged. Over a period of weeks she performed the most demanding workouts that Skinner could devise, and by June she was allowed to join the group. In her first competition, the Charlotte Ultraswim on June 18, 1995, she finished seventh in the 100-meter butterfly, in a tie for sixth in the 200-meter butterfly, and fifth in the 200-meter individual medley.

Sanders faced a considerable challenge in her attempt to make the 1996 Olympic team. She had to compete against younger rivals who have been swimming consistently over the past two years. She had to guard against injuries and ignore the evidence that women's swimming is a sport best performed by teenagers. On the other hand, Sanders knew how it felt to be the best and to win gold medals and national championships. Unfortunately, that knowledge was not enough. In the Olympic trials in March 1996, Sanders failed to qualify for the Summer Games in Atlanta.

GINA
SATRIANO

"I love baseball because it's not a game about size or strength. And I love the challenge."

Gina Satriano was the first girl ever to play in a boys' Little League in California. She was a pioneer then, and she remains a pioneer today as one of the stars of the Colorado Silver Bullets women's professional baseball team. For Satriano, a deputy district attorney for Los Angeles, the dream of playing real baseball against male opponents is one for which no sacrifice is too great. As a member of the first Silver Bullets roster she took an unpaid leave of absence from her job to travel with the team for the summer. The following season she did the same thing again. "We're making history wherever we go," she told the *New York Times* of her baseball team. ". . . And I love the challenge."

The daughter of Tom "Satch" Satriano, a former infielder for the California Angels and the Oakland Athletics, Gina Satriano grew up playing backyard baseball with her dad. She just loved the game, and her father took care to instruct her in the proper way to hit and field. In 1973, when Satriano was seven, she decided she wanted to play in the local Little League alongside the boys. It had never been done before. She was refused a tryout until her mother, Sherry, threatened to file a lawsuit.

Satriano won a spot on a Little League roster, but the fight had only just begun. Her family received hate mail and threatening phone calls in the middle of the night. Someone burned down a tree in the Satrianos' front yard. Young Gina played on.

High school was another matter. School officials simply would not let Satriano try out for the baseball team, so she gave in and switched to softball. She returned to hardball in college, becoming the only female member of the University of California at Davis varsity team. She was eager to begin the season there, when suddenly she was told she lacked the ability to compete with the men. Once again she felt victimized by sexism, but she made no official protest. Instead she concentrated on her studies, earning grades good enough to qualify her for law school at Pepperdine University.

Satriano had landed a well-paid and interesting job in criminal law as deputy district attorney for the City of Los Angeles when, in 1994, she

GINA SATRIANO

American baseball player

Born: C. 1966.

Education: Attended University of California at Davis for undergraduate studies and Pepperdine University for law school.

Career Highlights:

• tried out for and won a position on the fledgling Colorado Silver Bullets, a professional women's baseball team, 1994

• earned a position on Silver Bullets in the team's second season, 1995.

heard that a professional women's baseball team was forming. She decided to try out, even if it meant taking a leave of absence from her $52,000-a-year job. "My gut took only half a minute to decide," she told *Newsweek* on May 9, 1994. "I can be a lawyer for the rest of my life, but I can't do baseball forever."

More than 1,300 women tried out for 24 spots on the fledgling Colorado Silver Bullets baseball team. Satriano was one of the lucky 24 who survived the final cut. Throughout the summer of 1994 she traveled with the team and was one of its pitchers, compiling a 6.06 earned run average through 22 games and an 0-3 won-loss record.

The competition for roster space on the Silver Bullets was even greater in the spring of 1995, but Satriano once again made the team. She told the press that she realizes she can't play forever—that her employers in Los Angeles would not be that patient—but that she wanted to enjoy the sport for another season or two. She explained in a September 4, 1994, *New York Times* profile that the lessons she was learning on the baseball diamond were proving helpful to her in the courtroom, where she prosecutes criminal cases. What had she learned from baseball? "The ability to perform under pressure and to maintain a level of mental toughness and quickness," she said. "And not being intimidated by criticism, which comes not just from playing baseball, but mainly from being a woman in a man's world."

VRENI SCHNEIDER

SKIER

"When she sees snow, she wants to ski— day and night if possible. Other racers must force themselves to ski, but she enjoys it and that's the difference."

—Jan Tischhauser, one of Schneider's coaches

Seven women have won two Olympic gold medals in Alpine skiing, including Hanni Wenzel and Petra Kronberger. But no other woman has duplicated Vreni Schneider's feat—she has won three golds and five medals overall in three Winter Olympics appearances. In eight seasons of World Cup racing between 1984 and 1992, Schneider won 38 World Cup races, making her the winningest skier of her generation and the heiress apparent to such legendary stars as Annemarie Moser-Proell, Maria Wallise, and Michela Figini. Unlike her predecessors, however, Schneider was able to capitalize on her wholesome, small-town image to enhance her stardom and increase her bank account.

Schneider was born in 1966 in the picturesque Swiss village of Elm, population 800. Her father, Kaspar, owned a shoe repair shop in the town. Schneider first strapped on skis at the age of three, taking her chances on the ski slopes of a nearby resort. She loved the sport so much that she began racing as a first grader. Rarely did she lose. In the country where skiing is an all-consuming pastime, Schneider advanced through the national team ranks as if she walked on water. One of her coaches, Jan Tischhauser, told *Sports Illustrated* that the secret to Schneider's vast success was simple: "When she sees snow, she wants to ski—day and night if possible." The coach added: "Other racers must force themselves to ski, but she *enjoys* it and that's the difference."

Schneider announced her presence to the world at the 1988 Winter Olympics, where she torched the rest of the field in slalom and giant slalom for two gold medals. In the opening technical event, the giant slalom, she was sitting in fifth place after the first run. On her second run she showed the greatest skiers in the world why she owns the giant slalom event—in races that are often won by tenths or even hundredths of a second, Schneider won by a whole second. In slalom, where she wasn't favored to medal, Schneider again put down a second run that was nothing short of breathtaking. Styled "the most brilliant single effort of the Alpine in women's Olympic history,"

Vreni Schneider attacks a gate in a giant slalom race in Waterville, New Hampshire, 1986. (UPI/Corbis-Bettmann)

VRENI SCHNEIDER

Swiss skier

Born: 1966 in Elm, Switzerland.

Career Highlights:

- won two gold medals, in slalom and giant slalom, 1988 Olympic Games, Calgary, Canada
- won the World Cup overall title and set a record with 14 World Cup wins, 1989
- took a silver medal in the combined, a bronze medal in the giant slalom, and a gold in the slalom, 1994 Olympic Games, Lillehammer, Norway
- won 38 World Cup races between 1984 and 1992, making her the winningest skier of her generation.

Schneider floored those in attendance by clocking a run that gave her the gold by an amazing 1.68 seconds.

The following ski season, Schneider had her best year ever, winning the World Cup overall title and in the process setting a record with 14 wins. She continued to be a dominant force in her sport into the early 1990s and was favored to win a medal at the 1992 Games in Albertville. Instead she was bitterly disappointed at those Winter Games when she fell in the giant slalom and managed only a seventh place finish in the slalom.

By the time the 1994 Olympics rolled around, Schneider was a *grande dame* in skiing, 29 and possessing an arsenal of trophies, medals, and championships. She was not finished, though. At Lillehammer she took a silver medal in the combined, a bronze medal in the giant slalom, and a gold in the slalom. Once again her slalom victory was a come-from-behind classic. Schneider stood in fifth place after the first run, .68 of a second behind the leader, 18-year-old Katja Koren of Slovenia. Undaunted, Schneider attacked the course with such blistering determination that she surged into first place with the fastest time of the day. "I went so hard I was unprepared when the finish line came up," she told the *New York Times*. "Before I knew it, the race was over." She collected a third gold medal for an Alpine skiing event, an unprecedented accomplishment.

When not competing on the world tour, Schneider continues to live in Elm, where she owns a sporting goods store. Reporters both here and abroad have described the Swiss skier as modest and engaging, a good role model both on and off the slopes.

BRIANA
SCURRY

America has never won an Olympic medal in soccer, but that may be about to change. Now the women will be playing, and where the American women go, hopes ride high. Briana Scurry will be part of Team U.S.A. in the debut Olympics for women's soccer. To her has fallen the important task of guarding the goal as the U.S. women set out to do what the men have never done—claim a medal.

Scurry is a recent addition to the U.S. women's team, having begun her international career in 1994. Prior to joining the American team, the Minnesota native played at the University of Massachusetts, which lost only three times during her tenure there. During her years at Massachusetts Scurry posted 37 shutouts in 65 games for a goals-against average of 0.56. She was named 1993 National Goalkeeper of the Year for leading her team to the NCAA semifinals. In her senior season she started all 23 games and recorded 15 shutouts and an 0.48 goals-against average.

The U.S. women's soccer coach, Anson Dorrance, caught Scurry in action in 1992 and began following her career with the idea that she might make a good addition to the national team. Dorrance let Scurry's college coach know that she was being scouted, and Scurry was quite surprised to hear it. "I really never had any aspirations to play on the national team," she told *USA Today*. "When my coach at UMass informed me that I had the potential, I didn't believe him."

Her doubts notwithstanding, Scurry joined the U.S. women's soccer team in March of 1994. She was quickly pressed into action when veteran goalie Sue Harvey sustained a serious back injury. Scurry lost little time in establishing herself. She was named Most Valuable Player at the 1994 Chiquita Cup, where the United States destroyed arch-rival Norway 4-1. Scurry also starred for the United States at the 1994 tournament to determine qualifiers for the 1995 world championships in Sweden. At the championship, only the second women's world tournament ever, Scurry continued to defend well, but a single goal she yielded to the Norwegians was enough to allow the

"I really never had any aspirations to play on the national team. When my coach at UMass informed me that I had the potential, I didn't believe him."

Briana Scurry guards her team's goal during the 1994 Chiquita Cup; afterward, she was named MVP. (© Simon Bruty/Allsport Photography USA Inc.)

Scandinavians to avenge their Chiquita Cup defeat and end the U.S. team's hopes at the semifinal stage.

All told, Scurry played 15 of 23 games in 1995, posting an enviable 11-2-2 record and recording the most shutouts in a single season in the history of the women's national team—11. Her first year with Team USA was equally promising, as she earned seven shutouts in 12 starts.

The 1996 Olympics offer Scurry and her teammates a chance to prove that they can once again take the top ranking as they did in 1991 at the first-ever women's world championships. The team has been practicing together consistently for two years, giving newcomers like Scurry a chance to work together with veterans such as Michelle Akers and Mia Hamm. Scurry has also received a salary, housing, and bonuses from U.S. Soccer, enabling her to stay in America with the team rather than taking a position within a European league.

BRIANA SCURRY

American soccer player

Born: September 7, 1971 in Minneapolis, Minnesota.

Education: Attended the University of Massachusetts.

Career Highlights:
- posted 37 shutouts in 65 games for a goals-against average of 0.56 during her college career
- joined the U.S. women's soccer team, 1994
- played 15 of 23 games on the women's national team, posting an enviable 11-2-2 record and recording the most shutouts (11) in a single season in the history of the women's national team, 1995.

Awards: Named National Goalkeeper of the Year for NCAA play, 1993; named Most Valuable Player at the Chiquita Cup, 1994.

If Scurry harbors any lingering doubts, they tend to center around her lack of experience in international play. "My biggest need is reading the game," she admitted in *USA Today*. "I haven't had a lot of opportunity to do that. . . . I want to bring my goalkeeping up a level so I have to make fewer diving saves."

It's a safe bet she'll do just that.

MONICA SELES

"I didn't want to go into the history books 20 years from now and have people read, 'She was a great grunter, a great giggler and had a lot of hair.'"

Monica Seles is such a fierce competitor that even a bizarre assault in 1993 could not put a dent in her fabulous tennis career. Once the top-ranked women's tennis player in the world—and undoubtedly a candidate for that honor in the future—Seles is a former teen prodigy who hits the ball as hard as any woman in history. Famous for the grunts and squeals she makes when she swings, she has won a number of tennis's Grand Slam tournaments, including the Australian Open, the U.S. Open, and the French Open. She is such a great athlete that even being stabbed in the back by a crazed fan has not crushed her fighting spirit.

Seles was born December 2, 1973, in Novi Sad, Yugoslavia. Her father, Karolj, was a cartoonist and film director, and her mother, Esther, was a computer programmer. Seles began playing tennis with her brother, Zoltan, at the age of six. Her father taught her the unique style she uses today, hitting both her backhand and forehand with a two-handed grip. To encourage his daughter to hit the ball hard, Seles's dad drew cartoon characters on the balls for her to smash. His teaching style worked wonders. "Because he used cartoons and lots of humor, I always enjoyed practicing," Seles told *World Tennis*.

With her father as coach, Seles won the Yugoslav 12-and-under girls championship when she was nine years old and the European 12-and-under championship when she was only 10. In 1985, when she was 12, she was named Yugoslavia's sportswoman of the year. Playing in a tournament in Florida, Seles caught the attention of Nick Bollettieri, coach of many champion players, including Andre Agassi. Bollettieri offered Seles a scholarship to play at his tennis academy in Bradenton, Florida. She went to live there at the age of 12, and her parents soon quit their jobs and followed, renting a small flat in Bradenton.

Seles developed her game at the academy, and soon the other girls were refusing to play against her because she was so good. Bollettieri had her practice with the boys, including Jim Courier. "Nick ordered me to hit with

Monica Seles shows off her Australian Open trophy and souvenir koala after defeating Mary Joe Fernandez, 1992. (Reuters/Bettmann)

Monica one day," Courier recalled in *Sports Illustrated*. "First ball, *whap!* she smacks a winner. Next, *whap!* winner. . . . After fifteen minutes I walked off. I told Nick, never again." Seles also managed to earn straight A's in school.

Feeling that she was ready, Seles turned professional in February 1989. She reached the semifinals of her first professional tournament and defeated top-seeded Chris Evert to win her first title in her second tournament. (Evert got revenge at the U.S. Open that year, beating Seles 6-0, 6-2.) Seles reached the semifinals of the 1989 French Open, where she lost in three sets to number one-ranked Steffi Graf. That match was the beginning of a rivalry that has continued to this day, with several bizarre twists and turns.

Seles became a star in 1990. She won the Italian Open, beating Martina Navratilova, and the German Open, where she defeated Graf. More important, she won her first Grand Slam title, the French Open, defeating Graf 7-6, 6-4 in the final. The victory made Seles the youngest player in this century to win a Grand Slam final. Later that year she became the youngest player to win the Virginia Slims Championship, her first of three consecutive singles titles in that tournament.

From October 3, 1990, to March 18, 1992, Seles reached the finals of every tournament she entered—21 straight. "Clearly, Seles looms as the single greatest threat to Graf," wrote Steve Fink in *World Tennis*. "The lefty, with two-fisted strokes off both sides, overflows with confidence and a sense of limitless possibilities. Her ground game is devastatingly potent and her will to win is almost tangible."

Monica the grunter—whose laugh has been compared to Woody Woodpecker's—won the French Open in 1990, 1991, and 1992, the Australian Open in 1991 and 1992, and the U.S. Open in 1991 and 1992. She is the first woman to win three consecutive French Opens since Hilde Sperling in 1935–37. She missed Wimbledon due to a leg injury in 1991 and lost to Graf in the finals the following year, after officials warned her not to grunt too loudly.

Clearly the phenomenon from Yugoslavia was the tennis player of the moment. Seles moved to the top in the world rankings on March 11, 1991, and defended her status through 1992 and the beginning of 1993. As if to prove her supremacy, she beat Graf in the 1993 Australian Open and won two of the first four tournaments in which she appeared. Then tragedy struck.

On April 30, 1993, at a tournament in Hamburg, Germany, Seles was stabbed in the back as she rested between games. Her attacker, a 38-year-old unemployed German named Guenter Parche, told the police that he was a fan

MONICA SELES

Yugoslav-born tennis player

Born: December 2, 1973 in Novi Sad, Serbia.

Career Highlights:
- won the Italian Open and the German Open, 1990
- took the Virginia Slims Championship, 1990, 1991, and 1992
- earned the French Open crown in 1990, 1991, and 1992
- triumphed in the Australian Open in 1991, 1992, 1993, and 1996
- won the U.S. Open in 1991 and 1992.

of Graf and had attacked Seles because he wanted Graf to be the number one player again. Graf was terribly upset about the assault and was one of the first people to visit Seles at the hospital.

Because Seles would not testify against her assailant, he received only probation. International efforts to have him re-tried were to no avail. As she recuperated from the attack, Seles was faced with the knowledge that her attacker was roaming free, possibly still intent on causing her harm. She had to overcome not only the physical disability but enormous psychological damage as well. "The one place I felt safe was a tennis court," she told *Sports Illustrated* in 1995. "That's the place where I'd have no worries, whatever was going on in my private life or in my school. I felt comfortable. And now, this is the place I feel least safe."

The fight had not gone out of Monica Seles, though. She returned to professional tennis in 1995 and—despite some nagging injuries—won the 1996 Australian Open by beating Anke Huber in straight sets. In the wake of the victory, Seles told reporters that she plans to undertake a new conditioning program and forge ahead, with her eye on that top ranking.

Fans the world over are pulling for her.

MARGARET
SMITH COURT

TENNIS PLAYER

*Margaret Smith
Court was such a
dominating player
that her chief rival,
Billie Jean King, gave
her a nickname:
"The Arm."*

Step aside, Martina and Steffi. A quiet lady from Australia has you both beaten—and the best male players as well. Margaret Smith Court won more major championships during her 18-year tennis career than any other player, male or female. She literally dwarfs the competition. Between 1960 and 1975 she won 62 major titles in singles, doubles, and mixed doubles, including a Grand Slam (the Australian Open, the French Open, Wimbledon, and the U.S. Open) in 1970. Her nearest rival, Martina Navratilova, won 54 tournaments and never compiled a Grand Slam year. A natural lefthander who learned to play the game from the right, Smith Court dominated tennis through the 1960s and 1970s, fending off rivals such as Billie Jean King, Chris Evert, and Rosemary Casals.

Margaret Smith was born July 16, 1942, in the country town of Albury, Victoria, Australia. Her father worked in a cheese and butter processing plant, and unlike many parents of sporting children, was not interested in tennis. Nor were any of her three siblings drawn to the game. Margaret learned to love the sport herself by sneaking through a hole in the fence at a local country club and playing when the courts were free. She was thrown out of the club so many times between the ages of eight and ten that finally the club owner decided to give her a membership and treat her to lessons. The owner, Wally Rutter, had no children of his own, and he and his wife unofficially adopted Margaret and lavished the expensive coaching upon her that her parents could never afford.

As a teen Smith moved to Melbourne, where she continued her lessons at a club owned by former world champion Frank Sedgman. In order to defray the expenses of her training, she worked as a receptionist in Sedgman's office. Her progress was rapid, and at the age of 18 in 1960 she won her first of *seven* consecutive Australian Open championships. All told, she would win the Australian Open 11 times.

The young Margaret Smith joined the international tour in 1961 after her second Australian Open victory. Despite suffering from nervousness

Margaret Smith Court beats Billie Jean King to become the Wimbledon singles champion in 1970. (AP/Wide World Photos)

on court and shyness off it, she won the Kent All-Comers Championship, and reached the semifinals in the Italian Open and the quarterfinals at Wimbledon and the French Open. It was an inauspicious beginning to a fantastic career.

In 1962 Smith decided to travel independently of the Australian national team. Her newfound independence increased her confidence, and she picked up—in addition to another Australian Open singles victory—the French and American championships. Seeded first at Wimbledon, she drew another young up-and-comer, Billie Jean King, in the first round and lost in a tough match. Nevertheless, she finished the year ranked first internationally.

A Wimbledon win was not long in coming. In 1963 Smith drew Billie Jean King as an opponent in England not in the first round but in the finals. This time Smith won the match, confirming her top ranking.

Her nervousness returned the following year, compounded by boredom with the constant practicing and travel. Despite winning the 1965 U.S. Open and reaching the finals at Wimbledon in 1966, she decided to retire. She told reporters she felt she had missed some of the fun of being a teenager, and she wanted to make up for it. She returned to Western Australia and opened a boutique, and in October of 1967 she married Barry Court, a wealthy wool broker. He encouraged Margaret to return to the tour, and she did so in 1968, this time traveling with her spouse. It didn't take her long to make up for lost time.

Smith Court won every Grand Slam tournament *but* Wimbledon in 1969, but she will be best remembered for her 1970 season. That year she completed the Grand Slam. At Wimbledon that year, nursing a sprained ankle, she met King in the finals again. The two women slugged it out for hours in one of the best Wimbledon finals matches ever played. In a record-setting 46 games, Smith Court finally defeated King 14-12, 11-9. Smith Court's 1970 Grand Slam was the second by a woman in the history of tennis.

Pregnancy cut short Smith Court's 1971 season, but she returned in time to win six tournaments in 1972 for $22,662 in prize money. As she regained her form she went on to win 16 of 18 tournaments she appeared in, adding almost another $40,000 to her earnings. Then came possibly her most embarrassing moment as a tennis pro. Answering a challenge by the bragging Bobby Riggs, she agreed to play a singles match against him and donate the proceeds to charity. Riggs capitalized on Smith Court's well-known jitters and beat her in straight sets. That fiasco was the only dim spot in an otherwise brilliant 1973 season, in which Smith Court won 18 of 25 tournaments, including the Australian, French, and U.S. Opens.

Smith Court was ranked number one seven times between 1962 and 1973. She won her first major championship in 1960 and her last, the U.S.

MARGARET SMITH COURT

Australian tennis player

Born: July 16, 1942 in Albury, Victoria, Australia

Career Highlights:

• won Australian singles competitions, 1960–66, 1969–71, and 1973; doubles, 1961–63, 1965, 1969–71, and 1973; and mixed doubles, 1963 and 1964

• triumphed in French Open singles competitions, 1962, 1964, 1969, 1970, and 1973; doubles, 1964–66 and 1973; and mixed doubles, 1963–65 and 1969

• took U.S. Open championship in singles, 1962, 1965, 1969, 1970, and 1973; doubles, 1963, 1968, 1970, 1973, and 1975; and mixed doubles, 1961–65, 1969, 1970, and 1972

• won Wimbledon singles, 1963, 1965, and 1970; doubles, 1964 and 1969; and mixed doubles, 1963, 1965, 1966, 1968, and 1975

• won 62 major titles in all (including singles, doubles, and mixed doubles)—more than any other tennis player, male or female.

Awards: Inducted into the Tennis Hall of Fame, 1979.

Open doubles, in 1975. Although she continued to play until 1977, her advancing age and the rigors of caring for young children—she eventually had three—caused her to seek retirement. She was inducted into the Tennis Hall of Fame in 1979.

We can only wonder what kind of wealth Margaret Smith Court might have amassed had she played in more recent years. Her entire career earnings, spanning the amateur and Open eras, has been estimated at $550,000. By contrast, Steffi Graf won $877,724 for the four Grand Slam tournaments she won in 1988. This disparity in no way diminishes Smith Court's contributions to tennis. She was one of the greatest champions of all time.

ANNIE
SMITH PECK

*A worldclass
mountain climber
and explorer, Annie
Smith Peck climbed
Mount Huascarán,
the second tallest
peak in South
America, at the
age of 58.*

Annie Smith Peck's 40-year career as a traveler and record-setting mountain climber began as a hobby and continued to within a year of her death at the age of 85. She climbed mountains throughout the world, and a peak in Peru was even named after her. Born in Providence, Rhode Island, on October 19, 1850, Peck came from a prominent New England family; her father was a successful lawyer. After working for a time as a teacher she attended the University of Michigan. In 1885 she became the first woman to be admitted to the American School of Classical Studies in Athens.

Following her studies in Europe, Peck tried to earn her living by giving lectures on Greek archaeology. When this occupation proved unrewarding financially, she decided to switch to giving lectures on her hobby—mountain-climbing. In 1895 she became the third woman to climb the Matterhorn in the Swiss Alps, then she went on to climb other mountains in the Alps as well as Mount Shasta in California and Mount Orizaba, at 18,700 feet the highest mountain in Mexico. Buoyed by her success, Peck resolved to climb a mountain that had never been scaled and that was higher than any man had ever climbed.

For this feat Peck chose Mount Illampu, which rises to 21,276 feet north of La Paz in Bolivia, and which at that time was thought to be the highest mountain in South America. Traveling to La Paz in July of 1903, Peck hired two professional guides and arranged for an American professor of geology to accompany her. The guides proved unreliable and the professor, who was not interested in the climb, became ill along the way. They were able to reach only 15,350 feet before turning back. Peck then went to Peru to climb El Misti, a 19,199-foot peak.

Depressed by her failure on Mount Illampu, Peck returned to New York, determined to try again. Within a year she had obtained financial support for another expedition to Illampu. She departed on June 21, 1904, taking with her a snowsuit made out of animal skins that explorer Robert Edwin Peary had brought back from the Arctic and that was donated to

During her lifetime, Annie Smith Peck, shown here in 1923, was considered the world's foremost woman mountain climber. (UPI/Bettmann)

her by the American Museum of Natural History. Her male companion was an Austrian who had volunteered for the trip—Peck always thought she needed to be accompanied by a man, although they invariably turned out to be unsuitable as partners. Climbing Illampu for the second time, she reached 18,000 feet before the pleas of the Austrian and her local guides forced her to turn back.

Not one to give up, Peck traveled to Mount Huascarán in the Andes north of Lima in Peru. She had heard that Huascarán might be even taller than Illampu, and that was correct, though at 22,205 feet it is actually the second-tallest mountain in South America, only 440 feet lower than Mount Aconcagua. Journeying to the city of Yungay at the foot of the mountain, she was accompanied by a young American miner she had met in Yungay as well as some men from Yungay. Almost at the outset she and the miner quarreled about the best way to make the climb, so they ended up taking separate routes. Peck was able to make it to a narrow ledge at 19,000 feet overlooking the glacier that divided the mountain into two peaks, only to descend just in time to miss being buried by an avalanche. After dismissing the miner, she tried climbing up another face of the mountain with the local guides but she was forced to turn back.

Peck was broke when she returned to New York. She was able to go back to Huascarán only because a magazine had given her a $600 advance to write a story about her climbing experiences. Traveling to Peru in 1906, she tried twice more—unsuccessfully—to conquer Huascarán with a local companion she called "E—," who turned out to be even more useless than her previous partners. When she arrived in New York after her failed attempts, she found that the magazine loved her stories and was willing to sponsor another expedition.

Peck went back to Yungay in 1908, meeting two Swiss guides, Rudolf and Gabriel, whom she had hired for the trip. On this attempt Peck managed to climb to the top of Huascarán, but only with great difficulty. She and her guides lost most of their equipment, including the Peary snowsuit, and they were frequently in danger of sliding down the mountain. At the last minute, just as they were about to scale the summit, Rudolf ran ahead of Peck and reached the peak before her. On the trip back down the mountain Rudolf lost his mittens and suffered frostbite; he would later have part of one hand, including a finger, and half of one foot amputated.

At the age of 58 Peck had finally conquered Huascarán. Once she had reached the top she tried to determine the mountain's height, but that was impossible under prevailing conditions. Estimates indicated that it reached 24,000 feet. If so, then Peck had set a world record. However, her great rival,

ANNIE SMITH PECK

American mountain climber

Born: October 19, 1850 in Providence, Rhode Island.

Died: July 18, 1935 in New York.

Education: Attended the University of Michigan; became the first woman to be admitted to the American School of Classical Studies in Athens, 1885.

Career Highlights:
• became the third woman to climb the Matterhorn in the Swiss Alps, 1895

• climbed Mount Orizaba, at 18,700 feet the highest mountain in Mexico

• conquered Mount Huascaran (21,812 feet), setting a record for the highest climb in the Western Hemisphere, 1908

• climbed Mount Coropuna in Peru (21,079 feet).

Awards: Given a medal (for climbing Huascarán) by the Peruvian government, which named the peak she had climbed Cumbre Ana Peck.

Fanny Bullock Workman, refused to concede that Peck had beaten her because Workman had climbed to 23,300 feet in the Himalayas.

Workman went so far as to hire a team of American engineers to travel to Peru and measure Huascarán. They found that the peak Peck had climbed was the lower of the two, measuring "only" 21,812 feet. Peck had therefore set a record for the highest climb in the Western Hemisphere but not in the world. The record was to last for 26 years. Peck was given a medal by the Peruvian government, and the peak she had climbed was named Cumbre Aña Peck.

When Peck returned to the United States she wrote about her experiences in a book, *A Search for the Apex of America,* which was published in 1911. She went on to climb Mount Coropuna in Peru (21,079 feet); on the peak she hung a banner that read "Votes for Women." Continuing to travel extensively in South America, Peck wrote a guidebook and a statistical handbook on the continent. During 1929 and 1930 she made a tour of the whole continent, using all the commercial airlines that were then in operation and writing a book about her trip.

In January 1935 Peck started out on a trip around the world. She got only as far as Athens where, in February, she became tired while climbing the Acropolis (she was 84 years old). She returned to New York and died there on July 18, 1935.

KAREN SMYERS

*"All athletes are
mentally tough in
their own way. I'm
not unique. I'd rather
do the Ironman than
be one of those
golfers standing over
the ball, trying to
make a clutch putt."*

If the computer consulting firm she worked for hadn't closed shop in 1989, Karen Smyers might have spent her life tapping away at a keyboard. Instead, Smyers is a world-renowned triathlete and the winner of the 1995 Ironman Triathlon held in Kailua-Kona, Hawaii. A former sprint distance world triathlon champion, Smyers also won five consecutive national championships at the Olympic triathlon distance (one-mile swim, 25-mile bike ride, and 6.2-mile run). While the Ironman pays better prize money—and punishes its entrants accordingly—Smyers has continued to compete at the shorter distances in order to raise public awareness of the sport. "For every one Ironman, there are 50 shorter races that are so much more suitable for most people," she told the *Los Angeles Times*.

Karen Smyers grew up in Weathersfield, Connecticut, one of a family of eight siblings. All of her brothers and sisters were interested in sports. Karen's favorite in high school was competitive swimming. She continued swimming during college at Princeton University, where she earned a degree in economics.

It was during her university years that Smyers began to sour on swimming. She had been training four to five hours a day, and she felt her body was telling her to quit. "I burned out on swimming after college at Princeton," she said in the *San Jose Mercury News*, "but I wanted to keep competing at something, and I figured triathlon would be the best choice."

Smyers entered her first triathlon in 1984, riding the same old bicycle she used to commute to work. She quickly realized that she would have to buy better equipment if she wanted to be competitive. When the Bud Light Series triathlon came to Boston that same year, she entered as an amateur with a better bike, and—surprising everyone—finished first in her division and second overall. Had she entered as a pro, she would have won $500. "It was the last race I entered as an amateur," Smyers told the *Boston Globe*.

For some time after turning professional, Smyers kept her job at a computer consulting firm and trained and competed in her spare time. When the firm closed, she decided to become a full-time triathlete. She specialized in the shorter distances: sprint, which is a 1/2-mile swim, 15-mile bike ride, and 3 1/2-mile run, or Olympic and international distances, which were longer but still far short of the grueling Ironman Triathlon.

Smyers won a world triathlon championship in 1990 and five consecutive national championships beginning that same year. In 1992, after a particularly busy and successful season, she was named Triathlete of the Year by *Triathlete* magazine—an honor she termed "the ultimate." Nor did she miss the salary her day job with the computer company had brought. Between her prize money and her endorsement contracts with shoe, sportswear, and bike companies, she has begun earning a six-figure salary.

Inevitably, the Ironman Triathlon beckoned. Smyers had avoided that strength-sapping race for years, feeling that the rigors of training for it would wear her out. Finally, when her husband, Michael King, announced that he was entering the Hawaii endurance contest as an amateur in 1994, Smyers followed his lead and entered as a professional. "I hate to burst anyone's bubble, but I'm no bionic woman," she told the *Boston Globe* at the time. "You don't have to be Superwoman to do this. All you have to be is balanced. And you can't have a weakness."

Smyers finished fourth in her first Ironman Triathlon. Her time was the fastest ever among women for a debut participant. In 1995 she returned to Kailua-Kona, and this time she won the event after perennial champion Paula Newby-Fraser collapsed short of the finish line. Her victory in the 1995 Ironman has established Smyers as a dominant force in the triathlon at any distance—and a model of physical endurance for the growing number of women who are competing in triathlons.

Sadly, the women's triathlon will not be added to the Olympics until the year 2000. By then Smyers plans to be retired and raising children. Years ago she expressed great interest in being an Olympian, but she is not disappointed that the chance may have passed her by. "The Olympics are clearly a big step for the sport," she commented in the *Boston Globe*. "Maybe it will help initiate some junior programs, or more involvement in the college and high school level."

As for Smyers, she plans to continue competing in triathlons—including the Ironman—for a few more years. Asked in the *Globe* if participating in such a grueling competition required extra toughness, Smyers had this to say: "All athletes are mentally tough in their own way. I'm not unique. I'd rather do the Ironman than be one of those golfers standing over the ball, trying to make a clutch putt."

KAREN SMYERS

American triathlete

Education: Attended Princeton University, where she earned a degree in economics.

Career Highlights:
- won the world triathlon championship in 1990
- won five consecutive national championships at the Olympic triathlon distance (one-mile swim, 25-mile bike ride, and 6.2-mile run), 1990–94

- won the 1995 Ironman Triathlon.

Awards: Named Triathlete of the Year by *Triathlete* magazine, 1992.

Not many people would choose to swim 2.4 miles, bike 112 miles and run 26.2 miles rather than amble across a perfect lawn and gently sink a ball into a hole. Perhaps Smyers is tougher than she thinks.

ANNIKA
SORENSTAM

Annika Sorenstam has been hailed as one of the strongest in the next generation of LPGA members. In only her second year with the LPGA tour, the Swedish-born Sorenstam won the 1995 U.S. Women's Open Championship, fighting off the likes of Pat Bradley, Betsy King, and Meg Mallon in the process. The Women's Open was Sorenstam's first American pro tournament victory and a stunning way to serve notice of her arrival in the LPGA. Later in 1995, the 24-year-old former NCAA champion was named LPGA Player of the Year.

Sorenstam is one of a group of Swedes who have moved into the LPGA after touring successfully in Europe. She follows in the footsteps of Liselotte Neumann, the 1988 Women's Open winner, and Helen Alfredsson, who won the 1993 Nabisco Dinah Shore Open tournament. Like Neumann and Alfredsson, Sorenstam was named Rookie of the Year after her first season with the LPGA in 1994. And following in *her* footsteps is her younger sister Charlotta, the 1993 NCAA golf champion.

To Americans raised in sunny climates, this "Swedish invasion" in golf seems astounding. Sweden's image is one of snowdrifts and ski champions, not a good location for sports that have to be played outside in nice weather. Asked in the *Los Angeles Times* how she possibly trained for the success she has achieved, Sorenstam set the record straight. "You have to understand, in the southern part of the country, we do not get snow," she said. "If we do, it goes away almost immediately. It is in the north part of the country where the conditions are extreme. We can play golf seven months a year. Some play it all year."

Sorenstam told *Golf* magazine: "Sports has always been a big thing at home." Both of her parents loved to compete at the club level, and they played basketball and handball, ran track and field events, and golfed whenever possible. Sorenstam herself liked tennis. She began playing tournaments at the tender age of five, but by the time she reached her teens she found her skills had reached a plateau. Enter golf, which she had been playing on the side since

GOLFER

"She's real shy, a nice person, and pretty humble, [but] very driven, very focused about what she wants to accomplish—to be the best. She doesn't let anything get in the way of that."

—Leta Lindley, Sorenstam's teammate and roommate at the University of Arizona

ANNIKA SORENSTAM

Swedish golfer

Born: October 9, 1970 in Stockholm, Sweden.

Education: Attended University of Arizona, 1990–92.

Career Highlights:
- won the NCAA golf championship, 1991
- won the 1995 U.S. Women's Open Championship.

Awards: Named College Player of the Year, 1991; named European Women's Tour Rookie of the Year, 1993; named LPGA Rookie of the Year, 1994; named LPGA Player of the Year and won the Vare Trophy for lowest scoring average, 1995; received the ESPY Award for women's golf, 1996.

she was 12. Sorenstam decided to switch her priorities and, immersing herself in golf training, she qualified for the Swedish junior national team at 16.

She was sure she had made the right decision when she watched Neumann win the U.S. Women's Open in 1988. "It was a delayed telecast, but I remember staying up all night to watch it," Sorenstam recalled in *Golf* magazine. "I did think, `Yeah, that could be me someday.'"

In 1990 Sorenstam became a student-athlete at the University of Arizona. Part of the school's appeal was the climate, but the hot, sunny weather still took some getting used to. "It was quite a cultural shock coming from Sweden to the Arizona desert," she admitted in *USA Today*. "I didn't even know what the desert was like, but I knew I wanted to play golf and I knew I could play there all winter."

As a college freshman Sorenstam won the NCAA golf championship and was named College Player of the Year. She spent only two years in Tucson before deciding to go professional. Her decision was based on her dissatisfaction with the Arizona program. "The Swedish system is different," she explained in *Golf*. "The philosophy is that people are like plants. Some need space, some grow close together. You need to find your way."

Sorenstam returned to Europe and qualified for the European Women's Tour in 1993. After being named Rookie of the Year on that tour, she qualified for the LPGA in 1994. Some top-notch players struggle for years in the LPGA before finding success. Sorenstam was different. In 1994 she was named LPGA Rookie of the Year. The following season she placed in the top ten in seven of 11 tournaments *before* winning the Women's Open. She also shot a phenomenal 22 under par, including all four rounds in the 60s on a par 73 layout, at the OVB Damen Open in Salzburg, Austria.

Late in 1995 Sorenstam was named LPGA Player of the Year and winner of the Vare Trophy for lowest scoring average. She has quickly moved into a top money-winning position on the tour, and a contract with Callaway Golf brings her additional income. Her Women's Open championship notwithstanding, Sorenstam feels she has room for improvement. She predicts that she will get stronger in the coming years.

Described as "sweet and shy," Sorenstam lives in San Diego when she is not touring Europe, Australia, or America to play golf. She is a quiet-living woman who enjoys listening to music, cooking, and staying at home with her fiance, David Esch. One of three Swedes who have won LPGA Rookie of the Year awards in the last eight years, Sorenstam predicted that a new era of European domination of the LPGA is on the horizon. "I don't know why we're so successful, other than it's more acceptable for Europeans to come to America and play," she said in *USA Today*. "I think more Europeans will come over every year to play professional golf."

If they're as good as Annika Sorenstam, the Americans had better watch out.

LYN
ST. JAMES

RACE CAR DRIVER

"All the good things in my life have happened because of racing. It helped me develop an identity. I've learned a lot about myself, about how to stretch my limits."

Theoretically, race car driving should be a sport where women could easily compete with men on a full footing. In reality, the "good ol' boy" network is nowhere more firmly entrenched than on the car racing circuits. This fact has never deterred Lyn St. James, who in 1992 became the second woman ever to race in the Indianapolis 500. St. James finished a respectable 11th in the 1992 Indy and won Rookie of the Year honors—a significant accomplishment for a woman in her forties. She is also the first woman ever to win a professional road race driving solo *and* the first woman ever to exceed 200 miles per hour on an oval track.

A dangerous obsession? Most certainly, but St. James is a seasoned professional who has the training, the physical stamina, and the financial support to keep herself and her vehicles on top of the game. "You wear the car," she explained in *Lear's* magazine. "Every fiber of your body is with that car. Everything gets transmitted up through the tires, through the suspension and the seat into your body. It's a very sensitive, precise experience. . . . It's driving by the seat of your pants."

St. James was born Evelyn Cornwall on March 13, 1947. (She changed her name to race professionally, inspired by television actress Susan St. James.) An only child, she grew up in Willoughby, Ohio, where her father was a sheet metal worker. St. James's mother was crippled as a child, and her only way of getting around was in a car. "A car gave my mother power and mobility," St. James told *Sports Illustrated*. "She would talk about the car as if it were human."

In the very proper 1950s and early 1960s, St. James was educated at an all-girls school near Cleveland. She played sports there but was more committed to the piano—she had begun playing at age six. "My mom raised me to be well educated and refined," St. James recalled in *Lear's*. "She felt the piano would help me learn to be a lady and give me something I could always fall back on. Race-car driving was not what she had in mind."

Nor did St. James have race cars in mind at the outset of her career. She earned a piano-teaching certificate from the St. Louis Institute of Music

Lyn St. James chats with Hall of Fame golfer Carol Mann, right, after a two-mile run at the Texas World Speedway in which St. James averaged more than 221 mph. (AP/Wide World Photos)

and then took a job as a secretary, teaching piano lessons on the side. To any outside observer, she was just another young American woman—one who happened to like to drive fast.

In fact, the seeds of her future stardom had been sown in high school, when she went to the drag races one night with her friends. After her friend had lost his heat, she made a remark. He challenged her: "If you think you can do any better, go ahead." She did, and won. "I'll never forget it," St. James admitted of her first taste of the sport. "Of course, when I got home my mom said, 'You did *what?*' I still don't think [my parents] get why I'm doing this."

After marrying John Carusso, who also loved racing, St. James and her husband began competing in local Sports Car Club of America (SCCA) races. In her debut race, St. James spun out and wound up in a pond at Palm Beach International Raceway. She soon learned the ropes, however, and in 1976 and 1977 she won the SCCA Florida Regional Championship. The following year she advanced all the way to the SCCA Runoffs in Atlanta—amateur racing's national championship. There she ran out of luck when her engine blew up.

St. James told *People* that her experience at the Runoffs served to challenge her further. Looking around at the other competitors—actor Paul Newman among them—she realized that they had spare cars and top-notch equipment. "That's when I said to myself, 'I'm going to *prepare* to win,'" she said. "I'm going to get sponsors, and I'm going to be a professional race-car driver."

That is how Evelyn Cornwall became Lyn St. James, professional road racer. In her first season as a pro she won the Top Woman Driver award in the International Motor Sports Association Kelly American Challenge series. In 1981 she talked Ford Motor Company into sponsoring her, and she became part of the company's motorsports program. She traveled across the country acting as a products spokesperson for Ford as well as racing for them.

In 1985 St. James became the first woman ever to win a solo North American professional road race when she finished first at Watkins Glen, New York. Since then she has achieved many firsts. She was the first woman to average more than 200 miles per hour on an oval track, at Alabama's Talladega Superspeedway in 1985. She later set a second speed record there in 1988.

JANET GUTHRIE

The first woman driver to race in the Indianapolis 500 was Janet Guthrie. Guthrie was initially dismissed as a publicity seeker, and her detractors claimed that women were too weak to drive race cars. In 1976, Guthrie qualified for the Indy 500, but the owner of the car withdrew his support at the last minute. In 1977, she again qualified for the race, but was able to complete only 27 laps before car troubles sidelined her. Finally, in 1978, she was able to thumb her nose at the people who said women weren't strong enough to handle Indy cars. She qualified for the Indy 500 and finished impressively in ninth place. When asked whether a woman can compete with men in the demanding Indy races, Janet Guthrie's standard reply is "I drive the car. I don't carry it."

LYN ST. JAMES

American race car driver

Born: March 13, 1947.

Career Highlights:

- won the SCCA (Sports Car Club of America) Florida Regional Championship, 1976 and 1977
- finished first at Watkins Glen, New York, becoming the first woman ever to win a solo North American professional road race, 1985
- became the first woman to average more than 200 miles per hour on an oval track, at Alabama's Talladega Superspeedway, 1985
- won, along with male teammates, the GTO class of the famed Daytona 24 Hours marathon, 1987 and 1990
- finished in 11th place in the Indianapolis 500, becoming the second woman ever to participate in that race (the first was Janet Guthrie in 1976), 1992.

Awards: Won the Top Woman Driver award in the International Motor Sports Association Kelly American Challenge series in her first season as a pro; won Rookie of the Year honors after racing in the Indy 500, 1992.

Along with her male teammates, she won the GTO class of the famed Daytona 24 Hours marathon in 1987 and 1990.

St. James moved to Indy cars in 1988, in time becoming the first woman ever to compete full-time on the Indy professional circuit. Her status in the sport was threatened in 1991 when Ford pulled out of its sponsorship, but early in 1992 she earned the backing of J.C. Penney, Agency Rent-A-Car, Goodyear, and Danskin. She found out only weeks before qualifying that she was set to race at the famous "Brickyard" in Speedway, Indiana. Her car cost nearly a million dollars.

Becoming only the second female driver ever to qualify for the Indianapolis 500 (the first was Janet Guthrie in 1976), St. James finished her debut Indy in 11th place for Rookie of the Year honors. The next year, 1993, she qualified again but finished 25th in a field of 33 when her engine stopped running. St. James told *Lear's:* "I realized that what really attracted me to racing, aside from my fascination with cars, is the fact that you wear a helmet and now you're invisible. Because I was always very self-conscious. I never thought I was pretty. Never felt my appearance was a statement. I had to find someplace else for that part of me, and it was when I put that helmet on. Then, I'm not judged by how I look or how nicely I smile. It's just me and the race car. As I developed over the years and won races and drove faster cars, I started developing more confidence as a person, more clarity and definition in my life."

For years St. James has been active with the Women's Sports Foundation, serving as its president in 1990. Her book, *Lyn St. James' Car Owner's Manual,* is particularly addressed to women and covers the subjects of maintenance, repairs, and purchasing a new car. She has also served as director of consumer relations for the Car Care Council, a trade group that addresses safety and maintenance concerns on behalf of car and truck owners. She has visited the White House five times.

Recently St. James has set a new goal for herself. With her second husband, Roger Lessman, she hopes to set a new world land-speed record on Oregon's famed Bonneville Salt Flats. In order to challenge for the record, St. James will have to power a vehicle to an amazing 450 miles per hour. Asked how it would feel to drive a car almost as fast as a 747 jet flies, St. James told *Lear's:* "That's cool. Once you're up over two hundred, it all looks the same anyway."

Whatever car she wears, Lyn St. James wears it well.

PICABO
STREET

With a name like Picabo ("peek-a-boo"), you've got to be good at something. Picabo Street isn't just good, she's great. Her career as a downhill and slalom skier has taken off recently, beginning with a silver medal in the 1994 Olympics and cresting with the 1995 World Cup downhill title. Street is the first American ever to win a downhill season championship, and—with fellow team member Hilary Lindh—she has established a solid American presence on the downhill tour. And, as her name might suggest, she's a "personality kid" who enjoys her celebrity status and speaks her mind freely. "I *like* sharing my feelings," she says. "I want everyone to enjoy my success with me."

Picabo's life has been unconventional since the day she was born, at home, in a tiny Idaho town. Her birth certificate listed her as Baby Girl, and as far as she knows that is the only name she had until she was three. Her parents, Stubby and Dee Street, were "classic flower children," to quote *Skiing for Women,* and they raised Picabo and her brother Baba in Triumph, Idaho, population 50. The Street family grew vegetables, raised pigs and chickens, and had no television in the home. Stubby and Dee liked to take epic cross-country journeys in their car, bringing the children along for the ride.

One of these vacation trips brought Picabo her name. When her parents discovered that she would need a real name for the passport they had to buy to visit Mexico, Stubby and Dee named their daughter Picabo. The name came from a town in Idaho that is in turn taken from a Native American word for "shining waters." Today its very hippy authenticity is part of Picabo's maverick image.

Growing up in tiny Triumph, Idaho, Picabo had no girlfriends. Instead she played with the boys, taking great pride in beating them at their games. "We'd play football, basketball, and soccer," she recalled in *Skiing for Women.* "Not only did I want to be as good as the boys, I wanted to be *better.*" She also showed an early flair for ski racing and was named to the U.S. Ski Team as a teen. In 1988, at the age of 16, she won the national junior downhill and super G titles.

SKIER

"*Sports are an avenue to be happy with myself. And that's why I do the media I do. It's important for girls to see bigger women with strong opinions, who are also sensitive and vulnerable. I want to tell them, 'You can be a strong athlete and still be feminine.'*"

451

Picabo Street soars through the air during the combined downhill race at the 1994 Winter Olympics. (Reuters/Mike Blake/Archive Photos)

The word "discipline" was hardly in Picabo's vocabulary in those days. Fellow team members remember her as rowdy and fun-loving on tour, but her coaches were frustrated by her training habits and lackadaisical attitude. "The pattern with Picabo was the phenomenon of the wunderkind," coach Paul Major told *Sports Illustrated* late in 1995. "Picabo burst onto the ski team with natural talent. She threw herself down the hill. No obstacles. But she relied on natural talent to keep her on the team. She didn't know the stakes had been raised. She didn't push herself. She was rebelling, asking why should she conform."

In July of 1990, Picabo was kicked off the U.S. team when she arrived at training camp out of shape and unmotivated. At first she didn't tell her parents what had happened—they were living in Hawaii at the time. Later, when Stubby found out about her expulsion, he challenged Picabo to come to Hawaii and get herself into shape. She accepted the challenge, and later that same year she won the overall title on the junior North American circuit. In 1991 Major invited her back.

With a little more maturity on her side, Picabo emerged as a serious downhill contender. She was a 21-year-old B-team member in 1992–93 when she stunned everyone by winning a silver medal in the downhill combined at the world championships in Morioka, Japan. She also finished 10th in the downhill. Then she garnered another second place at the season finale World Cup downhill in Lillehammer, Norway. Street had come of age too late for the 1992 Olympics (where Lindh took a silver in downhill), but she seemed poised to make a big impression in 1994.

That she did, winning the Olympic silver medal in downhill with typical Picabo verve. America suddenly discovered its sassy new skiing star, who preferred playing "peekaboo" with Elmo

KATJA SEIZINGER

Picabo Street's closest competitor in the downhill circuit is Katja Seizinger. Hailing from Eberbach, Germany, Seizinger has been a dominant force in women's alpine skiing since the early 1990s. When she was only 19 years old, she won a bronze medal in the super-G at the 1992 Winter Olympics in Albertville, France. She came within 20 points of winning the 1993 overall World Cup title; during that season she collected six World Cup victories, winning both the downhill and super-G titles. And to prove that she wasn't a flash-in-the-pan competitor, Seizinger took home gold in the downhill event from the 1994 Olympics in Lillehammer. And she shows no sign of slowing down.

on *Sesame Street* to sitting down on the staid talk shows. Picabo's engaging personality helped to fuel her celebrity, and in 1995 she became the first and only woman to sign with the new Nike Sports Management Group, an agency whose client list includes Deion Sanders, Ken Griffey, Jr., Scottie Pippen, and Alonzo Mourning. A Nike executive said at the time: "We think she has the potential to be as large as any female athlete out there."

Winning is the key, however, and Picabo has shown that her Olympic success was no mere fluke. In 1995 she became the first American woman

PICABO STREET

American skier

Born: C. 1972 in Triumph, Idaho.

Career Highlights:

- won the national junior downhill and super G titles, 1988
- won a silver medal in the downhill combined at the world championships, 1993
- garnered a second place at the season finale World Cup downhill, 1993
- earned a silver medal, 1994 Olympic Games, Lillehammer, Norway
- won World Cup downhill title, becoming the first American ever to win a downhill season championship, 1995.

---

ever to win the World Cup title when she finished first in six of nine downhill races. An early victory in the 1995–96 season brought her a sixth consecutive victory on the tour. "I love what I'm doing," she told *Skiing for Women.* "For so many ski racers, competition becomes a job. If it does, you'll never be great at it. For me, the World Cup circuit is so much fun; I love the day-in and day-out—seeing everyone go through changes, going through changes myself, making new friends, learning new languages."

In her spare time, Picabo likes to hang out with her friend and fellow ski racer Alberto Tomba, whose oversized personality matches her own. Picabo has met President Clinton and Donald Trump; she has appeared on *American Gladiators* (she won); and she has received thousands of fan letters, some of them merely addressed to "Picabo Street, Somewhere in Idaho." The letters manage to find her even though she recently bought a home in Portland, Oregon.

Picabo has some goals that she has yet to achieve: she wants to win a gold medal at the 1998 Olympics, and she wants to compete in multiple events, including slalom and giant slalom. Don't look for her to become a proper conformist, however. "I get to stretch the rules because I am special," she boasted in *Sports Illustrated.* "Not because I wanted to be special. I've shown that on the mountain. Rules are obstacles, things that get in the way of where I want to go."

VIVIAN
STRINGER

In 1995 Rutgers University's women's basketball team moved into the Big East with a brand new coach, C. Vivian Stringer. Stringer, whose coaching record prior to Rutgers was a fabulous 520-135 over 23 seasons, became the best-paid women's coach in the country. Reports from Rutgers indicate that her base pay of $150,000 can, with incentives and special services, reach as much as $300,000 per year. Her base pay alone is more than the Rutgers football or men's basketball coaches earn.

Few college coaches are more deserving of the national spotlight. A widowed mother of three, Stringer has made a success of balancing family and work, handling the pressures of winning basketball, and raising a disabled child. She is the first women's coach in the country to guide two different college teams to the NCAA Final Four (Cheyney State in 1982, University of Iowa in 1993) and the genius behind the "Venus Flytrap" half-court defense. As columnist Bill Lyon of the *Philadelphia Inquirer* observed: "Vivian Stringer possesses an extraordinary basketball mind. Beyond that, she embodies all that we say we want in our coaches and educators. Those who are exposed to her influence invariably grow. They are taught—and encouraged—to think."

Stringer's early years infused her with the iron will that has served her so well in adulthood. She was born in 1948 in Edenborn, a small town in western Pennsylvania. Growing up there in the last years of segregation, she found few opportunities to indulge her love of sports. In high school she became the first black member of the cheerleading squad—choosing cheerleading only because the school had no women's basketball or track teams.

As an undergraduate at nearby Slippery Rock University, Stringer made up for lost time. She played basketball, field hockey, softball, and tennis, performing so well that she made the school's athletic Hall of Fame. Also while at Slippery Rock, she met and married a gymnast named Bill Stringer. Together Vivian and Bill took jobs at the historically black Cheyney State University in 1971—Bill as a teacher of exercise physiology, Vivian as a volunteer basketball coach.

BASKETBALL COACH

"Vivian Stringer possesses an extraordinary basketball mind. Beyond that, she embodies all that we say we want in our coaches and educators. Those who are exposed to her influence invariably grow. They are taught—and encouraged—to think."

—*columnist Bill Lyon*, Philadelphia Inquirer

455

VIVIAN STRINGER

American basketball coach

Born: March 16, 1948 in Edenborn, Pennsylvania.

Education: Attended Slippery Rock University in Pennsylvania.

Career Highlights:

- spent 11 seasons as women's basketball coach at Cheyney State University, leading her team to the first Final Four tournament for women in the 1981–82 season
- became head coach of women's basketball at the University of Iowa, 1983

- led the Iowa Hawkeyes to the women's Final Four, 1992–93
- hired to coach Rutgers University's women's basketball team, becoming the best-paid women's coach in the country, 1995.

Awards: Named to Slippery Rock University's athletic Hall of Fame; named Naismith National Coach of the Year and honored by the Smithsonian Institution as a notable black woman in sports, 1993.

Vivian Stringer spent 11 seasons at Cheyney State, sharing the small gymnasium with men's coach John Chaney. Her women's team proved to be the newsmakers, as she developed a winning program with top recruits and innovative playmaking. In 1981–82, when the NCAA finally inaugurated a women's championship tournament, Stringer's Cheyney State team made history by participating in the first Final Four—and the first finals.

The success was bittersweet for Stringer, however. Even as her team was turning in a championship year, her middle child, Janine, contracted a severe case of meningitis that left her wheelchair-bound and helpless. Stringer found herself flying between Final Four practices in Norfolk, Virginia, and hospital visits to Janine in Philadelphia. "The thing about me and Final Fours, I really haven't experienced them," she recalled later in *Newsday.* "I've done it, going through the movements. But in terms of experiencing all the surroundings, the Final Four was like a vacuum."

Stringer left Cheyney State in 1983 to become head coach of women's basketball at the University of Iowa. When Stringer took over the Iowa program, the team was struggling along in the lower ranks of the Big Ten. She soon changed all that. In her first season the team went 17-10. After that, the sky was the limit. The Hawkeyes turned in 10 straight 20-victory seasons, won nine NCAA tournament berths, and took six conference championships.

The highlight of Stringer's years in Iowa came in 1992–93, when she led the Hawkeyes to the women's Final Four. Once again the championship tournament was something of a blur for the coach. Her devoted husband died of a massive heart attack just before the season began, depriving her of her family's true anchor. When her husband died, Stringer told the *Philadelphia Daily News,* "I very seriously thought of not working again. I just felt I couldn't get the energy or enthusiasm to do it. Athletics seems like such a contradiction between life and what happened to my husband. It all seemed like such play. But my sons helped me through that. Basketball kept some semblance of sanity. I wrapped myself up in it."

After the 1992–93 season, Stringer was named Naismith National Coach of the Year and was honored by the Smithsonian Institution as a notable black woman in sports. Then, in 1995, Rutgers called.

Not only did New Jersey's state university offer Stringer the highest salary of any women's basketball coach in the country, the college also reportedly sweetened the deal with incentives that included, among other things, qualified home health care for her disabled daughter. For her part, Stringer chose to move to East Brunswick because she would be closer to her family and to her husband's grave. And then there's the challenge—Rutgers recently entered the Big East, the same conference that includes the 1995 NCAA champion University of Connecticut.

Stringer feels she can lead the Rutgers program to prominence relying on her strengths—recruiting, discipline, and intelligent strategy. She has high expectations for her players. "You can either give a person a fish or teach them to be a fisherman," she explained. "I want [players] to be fishermen. I want them to be students of the game. That's always been a trademark of my teams." Reflecting on her history-making contract, Stringer said: "I don't want to be the big man or big woman on campus. I just want to be a good person and do a good job. . . . But I just love to coach, and I love people."

SHERYL SWOOPES

"If someone had
told me growing
up that basketball
would change my
life, I wouldn't
have believed it.
Basketball is just
what I did for fun."

Sheryl Swoopes may go down in history as the first woman ever to have an athletic shoe named after her. Or, more likely, she may earn a place in the books as one of the finest basketball players—male or female—ever to grace a court. A former NCAA champion and record-breaking scorer, Swoopes is a starter for the U.S. Olympic team and an articulate and engaging spokesperson for her sport. Her signature sneaker, Nike's "Air Swoopes," is just one of many honors that have accrued to her since her college days.

Marsha Sharp, Swoopes's coach at Texas Tech between 1991 and 1993, told *Sports Illustrated* that Sheryl will be the player to watch in years to come. "She'll be a legend in women's basketball, but not just because of her play," Sharp said. "She has a charisma that the crowd loves. You never doubt that she is a team player."

Sheryl Swoopes grew up in Brownsfield, a small town in West Texas. She was not one to let a little thing like her gender get in the way of her sporting activities. "All I ever did in my spare time was play basketball," she recalled in the *Washington Post*. "I played with guys all the time. I've always played with my two older brothers. I guess that's how I developed my game. It helps to play with the guys. They're so much more physical than girls are. Once you go out and you play with guys, and you get in a situation with girls, you think, 'Well, if I scored on that guy, I know I can score on her.'"

Six feet tall and a skilled ball handler, Swoopes was recruited out of high school by coach Jody Conradt at the University of Texas in Austin. Swoopes accepted a scholarship to the school but stayed only four days. She got homesick. She returned to Brownsfield and attended South Plains Junior College, where she was named Junior College Player of the Year. In 1991 she moved on to Texas Tech in Lubbock, less than 40 miles from her home.

The women's basketball program at Texas Tech had long labored in the shadow of the more famous team in Austin. Swoopes changed all that. In 1993 she led the Lady Rangers to the NCAA Final Four and, once there, gave notice that a star had arrived. In the semifinal game against Vanderbilt, she

As a star player for the Texas Tech Lady Rangers, Sheryl Swoopes scored more points in an NCAA final (47) than any other player, male or female, in NCAA history. (Courtesy of Walt McAlexander)

SHERYL SWOOPES

American basketball player

Education: Attended Texas Tech University.

Career Highlights:
- led the Texas Tech Lady Rangers to the NCAA Final Four, 1993
- scored 47 points in the NCAA championship final, the most ever scored in an NCAA men's or women's championship game

- landed a spot with the U.S. women's basketball team, 1994.

Awards: Named team Sportswoman of the Year by the Women's Sports Foundation, 1993.

---

scored 31 points and grabbed 11 rebounds. That was a mere warmup, however. In the NCAA championship final she scored 47 points, hit four of six three-pointers and was a perfect 11 for 11 on the foul line. Her 47 points were the most ever scored in an NCAA championship game, beating the old record of 44 set by none other than Bill Walton.

Awards and honors were heaped upon Swoopes after that fateful championship. The accolades proved bittersweet, because even the shower of medals and trophies could not provide Swoopes a basketball job in America. She wanted to play professionally, and that meant moving to Italy. "I don't like the idea of leaving the States," she told *Sports Illustrated,* "but it'll give me more international experience."

Just six months after taking the NCAA title, Swoopes found herself in Bari, a town in Southern Italy, on a team whose coach spoke only Italian. The transition from college to this foreign atmosphere was quite difficult, and Swoopes's game suffered. "I didn't catch on at first," she admitted in the *New York Times*. "At home I didn't have to think about practice because, first of all, I could speak English. But I've pretty much started to pick up on the little things—like directions."

Just a few months later Swoopes left Italy after a contract dispute. Without a team to sharpen her skills, she gravitated back to Texas Tech, where she played pickup games and did some volunteer coaching. Her layoff was brief, however. In 1994 she landed a spot with the U.S. women's basketball team. She played in the world basketball championships and the Goodwill Games, aware that her skills had eroded during her hiatus from competition.

A new challenge loomed on the horizon: the 1996 Olympics. With her place on Team U.S.A. secure, Swoopes began practicing in earnest. "The fact that [the Olympics] is here in the U.S. gets me all excited, because my family can come watch me play," she said in *USA Today*. "I've always wanted to play in the Olympics. I can taste it right now."

More than just a gold medal is riding on the 1996 Olympics for the women's basketball team. A good showing will enhance the prospects for a women's professional league here in America. It will also bring untold largesse to star players in the form of product endorsements. Swoopes has already had her share of these, and they've made her a wealthy woman. Nike named a line of basketball shoes "Air Swoopes" in her honor, borrowing a tag line from their other superstar, Michael Jordan. Swoopes has starred in commercials for Nike and other products, and she has become an unofficial spokesperson for the Olympic team.

Swoopes's radiant personality and basketball talent could bring her the level of fame that attends some of the NBA's male players. All of this is a sweet surprise for the small-town Texas girl who has never cared much for being away from home. "If someone had told me growing up that basketball would change my life, I wouldn't have believed it," Swoopes declared in *Newsweek*. "Basketball is just what I did for fun."

DEBI
THOMAS

FIGURE SKATER

She may well be the last of a breed. Debi Thomas, the first African American to win a world championship in singles figure skating, refused to put her life on hold just so she could skate, skate, skate. Balancing her studies at Stanford University and her training and competing as a world-class skater, she won the 1986 world championship and U.S. national championships in 1986 and 1988. Thomas had the distinction of being the only performer to beat Katarina Witt in world competition. More important, she was the first black woman to advance to the top in the figure skating world.

Born in Poughkeepsie, New York, on March 25, 1967, Thomas grew up the youngest of two children in a one-parent family. Her father and mother divorced when she was young, and she lived throughout the year with her mother, Janice Thomas. Janice liked opera, ballet, and ice shows, and she took her children to see them as well. At the age of five Debi became fascinated with skating after watching a clown ice performer named Mr. Frick. She began taking lessons in a class at a local rink, quickly demonstrating a natural talent for the sport.

Thomas won her first competition at the age of nine, with a routine based on music from *Fiddler on the Roof*. Once she won, she was hooked. The following year, 1977, she began training under Scottish coach Alex McGowan, at the Redwood City Ice Lodge. Coach and pupil quickly developed a rapport, although McGowan was at first skeptical about Thomas's chances on the national level. His doubts were erased when, at age 11, Thomas landed her first triple jump. She made the finals in the novice class at 12 and won a silver medal.

That victory sparked a crucial decision. Thomas chose to leave school and study by correspondence so she would have more time to train. She had her eyes on the national junior championship. Nothing worked for her in 1980, however, and instead of advancing to the nationals, she failed even to make the sectional competition. Thomas later told *Time* that this disappointment shaped her whole skating philosophy. "I decided that I wasn't going to

Debi Thomas gives a gold medal performance during the 1986 World Figure Skating Championships. (Reuters/Bettmann Newsphotos)

put the rest of my life on the line in front of some panel of judges who just might not like my yellow dress," she said. She returned to high school in Redwood, California, determined to give equal time to her studies.

Other considerations entered into Thomas's decision. Her family was not wealthy, and the considerable training costs—sometimes as much as $25,000 a year—put a burden on Janice Thomas especially. Often Debi would have to forego training in the summertime so her mother could catch up on the bills. Debi was also famous for making her own costumes, and for using worn-out skates until they crumbled.

Coach McGowan feared that national-level judges would not accept Thomas because she was black. This was not a matter of personal prejudice—the coach feared that the national judges would doubt Thomas's ability to convince the *international* judges. The worries were in vain on all counts. As a pre-med freshman at Stanford University, working on only five weeks' practice, Thomas won the 1986 national championship by landing five triple jumps in her long program. Six months later, she added the world championship to her titles, beating the lithe Katarina Witt in a stunning upset.

Thomas refused to leave college to train full time, and the demands of her class work soon took a toll. In 1987 she tried to repeat her five-week training regime, only to suffer calf pulls in both legs and then tendinitis in her ankles. She lost her national title to Jill Trenary and later lost her world crown to Witt. Only then did Thomas agree to take a year sabbatical from Stanford to prepare for the Olympics. She and her coach moved to the Olympic training facility in Boulder, Colorado, and settled into the six-day-per-week training schedule most skaters follow.

Concerned that she was being beaten by Witt's superior artistry, Thomas sought the advice of ballet star Mikhail Baryshnikov. He sent one of his choreographers, George de la Pena, to assist Thomas in preparing her routines. The artistic improvements helped Thomas to regain her national title in 1988, and she entered the Winter Games as one of the favorites.

The women's figure skating finals at the 1988 Winter Games have been dubbed "the battle of the Carmens." Quite by chance, Thomas and Witt had chosen the same music—based on the opera *Carmen*—for their long programs. Witt skated first, and while her jumps were conservative she did land them all—and her artistry was, as usual, outstanding. Still, Thomas had a good chance going into her routine, if only she could land her more difficult jumps perfectly. Unfortunately, a triple-triple combination early in her program didn't go quite as planned. Thomas landed on two feet out of the second jump, and after that the heart seemed to go out of her performance. Fumbling through two more triple jumps, she eventually had to settle for the bronze medal.

DEBI THOMAS

American figure skater

Born: March 25, 1967 in Poughkeepsie, New York.

Education: Attended Stanford University, earning a bachelor's degree in engineering in 1991; attended medical school at Northwestern University.

Career Highlights:

• won the 1986 world championship, becoming the first African American to win a world championship in singles figure skating

• won U.S. national championship, 1986 and 1988

• garnered bronze medal, 1988 Olympic Games, Calgary, Canada

• earned bronze medal, world championships, 1988.

"The three weeks after the Olympics were probably the hardest of my life," Thomas recalled later in *Sports Illustrated*. "I cried every day." Her disappointing performance at the Winter Games soon gave way to a bronze medal showing at the 1988 world championships. Then, with few regrets, Thomas retired from skating and returned to Stanford.

Most world class skaters go on after the Olympics to forge lucrative careers in ice shows. Thomas chose another path. She earned a bachelor's degree in engineering from Stanford in 1991 and attended medical school at Northwestern University, planning to specialize in orthopedic surgery and sports medicine. Thomas has skated an occasional ice show, and she conducts skating clinics, but she has bigger fish to fry. In 1995 she visited the NASA Space Center in Houston as a possible candidate for the astronaut corps.

While she may not have been the most successful skater in history, Thomas has been refreshing for a number of reasons. As a black woman, she was a figure skating pioneer, winning championships in a sport previously dominated by whites. And as a woman with serious lifelong career goals, she refused to compromise her education for a brief moment of skating fame. She may have won a bronze medal in the Olympics, but she seems poised to win a gold medal in life.

JENNY THOMPSON

SWIMMER

"I like to think of myself as a well-rounded person. I think I would go crazy if I was just thinking about athletics all day long."

Jenny Thompson, an Olympic double gold medalist and the first American woman in 59 years to set a world record in the 100-meter freestyle, is one of the most decorated athletes in the history of the NCAA. She also holds the American records for both the 100-meter freestyle and the 100-yard freestyle. Unlike the majority of Olympic-caliber swimmers, she chose to complete her college education rather than give up her eligibility early in favor of swimming stipends and product endorsements—and thus burned a hole in the NCAA while earning a bachelor's degree. "I like to think of myself as a well-rounded person," Thompson told the *Contra Costa Times* on March 21, 1995. "I think I would go crazy if I was just thinking about athletics all day long."

Although she is no stranger to international competition, one feat has eluded Thompson: she has never won an *individual* gold medal in a world competition. Both of her Olympic golds were awarded for relay work. In individual races, she has been beaten by Chinese swimmers, including Le Jingyi, Zhuang Yong, and Lu Bin. It was Le Jingyi who stole Thompson's world record in the 100-meter freestyle at the 1994 World Championships in Rome. Far from feeling defeated, however, Thompson is on a personal quest to unseat her Chinese rivals, preferably at the 1996 Olympic Games. Since the Chinese program has been tainted by the discovery of ten positive drug tests among their top swimmers, Thompson has made much of the fact that she performs drug-free.

The youngest child and only daughter in her family, Thompson was born in Georgetown, Massachusetts, on February 26, 1973. Growing up with three older brothers, she was more or less forced to assert herself, a practice that she has since adopted in her swimming style. Thompson's parents divorced when she was two, and she grew up in a single-parent household. Her mother worked as a medical technologist, but the family still had to count their pennies at every turn. Thompson recalled in a March 28, 1994, *Sports Illustrated* profile that she and her mother often shared a brown-bag lunch at swim meets while other swim families dined in restaurants. The money saved

Jenny Thompson powers her way to a gold medal as anchor of the 400-meter freestyle relay team during the 1992 Olympics. (AP/Wide World Photos)

on meals helped fund her lessons at the Seacoast Swimming Association in Dover, New Hampshire. Recalling those times in a July 1995 *Swimming World and Junior Swimmer* profile, Thompson admitted: "My mom has a real high credit card bill to this day."

Thompson showed swimming prowess early and continued to improve throughout her high school years. She was world-ranked in the 50-meter freestyle as a 12-year-old. In 1987 she became the youngest U.S. swimming gold medalist ever when she won the 50-meter free at the Pan American Games, and in 1991 she was named Swimmer of the Meet at the High School All-Star meet after winning both the 50-meter and 100-meter freestyle.

Thompson accepted a scholarship to Stanford University and there began an amateur career that has never been equalled in NCAA swimming history. In four years with Stanford, she won an unprecedented 19 NCAA titles (individual and relay) and led her university's celebrated team to four consecutive national championships. She also excelled at Pan Pacific meets, in

JENNY THOMPSON

American swimmer

Born: February 26, 1973 in Georgetown, Massachusetts.

Education: Attended Stanford University on scholarship, earning a degree in human biology, 1991–95.

Career Highlights:
- won the 50-meter freestyle event at the Pan American Games, becoming the youngest U.S. swimming gold medalist ever, 1987
- set a new world record in the 100-meter freestyle, U.S. Olympic Trials, 1992
- earned two gold medals, in the 400-meter freestyle relay and the 400-meter medley relay, and a silver in the 100-meter freestyle, 1992 Olympic Games, Barcelona, Spain

- won six gold medals at the Pan Pacific meets, five U.S. national titles, and five NCAA titles, 1993
- won two gold medals, national championships, 1994
- won three individual events (100-yard butterfly, 100-yard freestyle, and 200-yard individual medley) and anchored two winning relay teams, NCAA Championships, 1995
- won an unprecedented 19 NCAA titles (individual and relay) in four years with Stanford, and led her team to four consecutive national championships.

Awards: Named U.S. Swimming's "Swimmer of the Year," 1993.

1993 alone winning six gold medals at that event. She was named United States Swimming "Swimmer of the Year" in 1993 after taking five U.S. national titles, five NCAA titles, and the six Pan Pac gold medals.

The determined Thompson accomplished all her victories between 1991 and 1995 within the NCAA's stringent guidelines for practice time and personal behavior. She set a high priority upon earning her college degree—and keeping her swimming in proper perspective. "I wanted to experience college like it's supposed to be experienced, for the full period of time. I didn't want to give any of it up," she explained in the *Contra Costa Times*. In 1995 Thompson earned her degree in human biology. She plans to attend graduate school in the public health field.

Thompson's 1992 posting of a 54.48 time in the 100-meter freestyle at the U.S. Olympic trials set a new world record that held for three years. She was also a highly visible member of the 1992 U.S. Olympic Team. At the Summer Games in Barcelona she earned two gold medals, in the 400-meter freestyle relay and the 400-meter medley relay, and a silver in the 100-meter freestyle. In the ensuing years she has become a vocal champion of drug testing for Olympic athletes. As she told *Sports Illustrated,* "I want the play in my pool to be fair."

Thompson broke her arm in May of 1994 but returned to win two gold medals in the national championships in August of that year. At the 1994 World Championships she saw her 100-meter freestyle record fall, but undaunted she surged through 1995, winning three individual events (100-yard butterfly, 100-yard freestyle, and 200-yard individual medley) and anchoring two winning relay teams at the 1995 NCAA Championships. Richard Quick, who coached Thompson at Stanford and who will also head the coaching duties for the 1996 women's Olympic swimming team, told *Swimming World and Junior Swimmer* that his star athlete has been galvanized by the competition she is facing on the international front. "I think Jenny could be a successful athlete in another sport if she had chosen to," he said. "She's a very powerful woman. She's improved through the years because she's willing to work on her weaknesses and takes to coaching very well." He added: "The world record was Jenny's greatest accomplishment. The greatest frustration is I feel like cheaters took it away. I don't think there is any question about it. I think Jenny is going to swim better than she ever has in Atlanta. She will swim her lifetime best performances. Her goal is to win the races, regardless of what happens with the Chinese."

Outside of the pool, Thompson is as down-to-earth and easygoing as any native of rural New England. Friends joke about her collection of flags and clothing featuring the American flag pattern. Lea Loveless, Thompson's teammate at Stanford, told *Swimming World and Junior Swimmer* that the preference for red, white, and blue "is not just an Olympic thing. You could say [Jenny's] model is Wonder Woman." Like her comic book heroine, Thompson is dreaming of victory over a set of international foes. She says she is ready to win. "I compare (Barcelona) to my first Olympic Trials in 1988 when I choked as a nervous 15-year-old," she concluded in *Swimming World and Junior Swimmer*. "But I came back in the 1992 Olympic Trials with much more confidence. So I look at the Olympics as a learning experience, and I know what to do in Atlanta."

GWEN TORRENCE

TRACK & FIELD ATHLETE

"I always feel, not that I'm the best but certainly one of the best. But I still have to train as hard as ever, because nothing is guaranteed in this sport."

"Everyone wants to be the world's fastest woman," Gwen Torrence once told *Sports Illustrated*. Everyone might want the title, but Torrence has a better chance than most of winning it. An Olympic medalist and 1995 national champion in both the 100-meter and 200-meter sprints, Torrence has forged an amazing—and at times controversial—career in track and field. Formerly an unmotivated trainer with an affection for soap operas and junk food, Torrence has more recently dedicated herself thoroughly to her sport and has seen her determination pay off in major victories.

The 1996 Summer Olympic games are practically being played in Torrence's back yard. She was born in Atlanta on June 12, 1965, and she still lives in nearby Lithonia, Georgia. One of five children born into a working-class family, she was seven years younger than her nearest sibling and was thus doted upon by her older brothers and sisters. Her family lived in a housing project when she was a baby, but by the time she was ready for school they had moved to a better home in Decatur, a suburb of Atlanta. There she attended Columbia High School and found the eye of physical education teacher Ray Bonner.

Bonner had to do quite a bit of coaxing to get Torrence to run. When he finally convinced her, she refused to wear athletic shorts or running shoes. "I felt [spikes] were too hot for my skinny little legs," she explained in a 1988 *Sports Illustrated* profile.

Thus, during a gym class when she was in tenth grade, Torrence set an unofficial state record in the 220-yard dash while wearing low-heeled patent leather pumps. After that, Bonner insisted that she train properly in the right clothing and shoes. He told her that God would be angry with her if she wasted such natural talent.

The lecture worked. Despite embarrassment about her "skinny little legs," Torrence became a high school All American and three-time state champion at the 100- and 200-meter distances. She took double gold medals in those events at the TAC Junior Olympics during her senior year of high school,

Gwen Torrence finishes first in a 200-meter heat at the 1992 Olympics; she went on to win a gold medal in the final of that event. (AP/Wide World Photos)

and in 1984 she qualified for the U.S. Olympic trials. At 19 she had such misgivings about her ability to make the Olympic team that she refused to participate in the trials. Her time was yet to come.

Torrence attended the University of Georgia on an athletic scholarship and began her college career in the controversial developmental studies program, a remedial course of study. She was given four quarters to move out of that program and into the standard university curriculum, and she did so, eventually earning dean's list grades.

The athlete often cites 1986 as the turning point in her running career. That year she beat 1984 Olympic gold medalist Evelyn Ashford in the 55-meter dash at the Millrose Games. Her winning time of 6.57 seconds was a meet record. In 1987 she won NCAA championships at 55, 100, and 200 meters, and she also took gold medals in the 100- and 200-meter races at the World University Games in Zagreb, Yugoslavia.

Torrence attended her first Olympic Games in 1988. In Seoul she finished fifth in the 100-meter finals and sixth in the 200-meter finals. For a time she thought that was the closest she would ever get to an Olympic medal. She became pregnant in 1989 and suffered complications that kept her bedridden for three months. She lost the muscle tone, strength, and stamina that are essential parts of any world class athlete's arsenal. After her son was born late in 1989, she realized how much conditioning she had lost. "I had to learn how to run all over again," she recalled in *Women's Sports + Fitness*.

Through all of 1990 Torrence didn't win a single race. She realized, however, that her layoff from running had filled her with new determination and the will to train. Gradually she regained her form, and in 1991 she finished second in both the 100- and 200-meter races at the world championships. The only woman who beat her, Katrin Krabbe of Germany, later tested positive for the banned drug clenbuterol.

Torrence's performance at the 1992 Olympics is remembered less for her success there than for a remark she made that caused a scandal. After finishing a disappointing fourth in the 100-meter sprint final, she commented that she thought three other performers in that race had been using performance-enhancing drugs. When the remark was repeated in the press, some observers dismissed her accusations as a case of "sour grapes." The controversy would not die, however. Even though Torrence did not "name names," the other runners in the race complained loudly about the remark, and she later issued a formal apology. Then, while being hounded by press and public, she went out and won the Olympic gold medal in the 200-meter sprint, took another gold in the 4 × 100-meter relay, and a silver in the 4 × 400-meter relay.

GWEN TORRENCE

American track & field athlete

Born: June 12, 1965 in Atlanta, Georgia.

Education: Attended the University of Georgia on an athletic scholarship.

Career Highlights:

- beat 1984 Olympic gold medalist Evelyn Ashford to win the 55-meter dash at the Millrose Games, 1986
- won NCAA championships at 55, 100, and 200 meters, 1987
- took gold medals in the 100- and 200-meter races at the World University Games, 1987
- finished second in 100- and 200-meter races at the world championships, 1991
- won gold medals in the 200-meter sprint and the 4 × 100-meter relay, and a silver in the 4 × 400-meter relay, 1992 Olympic Games, Barcelona, Spain
- won the 100- and the 200-meter sprints, U.S. outdoor championships, 1995.

The days of controversy are behind Torrence now, and as a defending Olympic champion she has been methodically preparing for the 1996 Summer Games. She has suffered injuries to her right hamstring and knee, but she ran through the pain at the 1995 U.S. outdoor championships and won both the 100- and the 200-meter sprints. She plans to keep a light schedule of competitions until just prior to the Olympic trials in order to minimize her risks for further injury.

Married and the mother of a son named Manley Waller, Jr., Torrence is an athlete who chooses to speak her mind. The fact that the 1996 Olympics are being held in her home town she regards as nothing less than Divine Providence. "The Games' being here [in Atlanta] are a gift from God," she commented in a 1994 issue of *Track & Field News*. "He didn't like what happened to me in '92, so He's trying to make up for that by bringing the Games here." She added: "Now I just have to make that team. There are three spots to be earned and I always feel, not that I'm *the* best but certainly *one* of the best. But I still have to train as hard as ever, because nothing is guaranteed in this sport."

CATHY
TURNER

"They say I'm too aggressive. They're not used to someone fighting for the turns the way I do. What it really is, I just popped into their sport and beat them all, and they're pissed."

—Turner, in response to her opponents' claims that she skated unfairly in the 1994 Olympics

Cathy Turner's speed skating career was in turns colorful and controversial. A specialist in short-track speed racing, she won gold medals in two Olympiads—1992 and 1994—but particularly in the latter Winter Games was plagued by charges of "dirty skating." Turner, a former recording artist, singer, and songwriter, declared that she had done nothing illegal to win her medals. "I'm a competitor. I had to fight," she explained in the *New York Times*. "I couldn't just let people in. I'm not a dirty skater. I'm an aggressive skater."

Part of Turner's problem lay in the very nature of short-track speed skating. Unlike long-track skating, where entrants compete against the clock, short-track skating pits a pack of skaters against each other over 500-meter and 1,000-meter distances. As the skaters jockey for position, spills are commonplace. Some may be deliberate, but most are purely the consequence of too many fast-moving people in close proximity to one another.

In her defense, Turner maintained that the accusations leveled against her were a matter of "sour grapes" on the part of her principal opponents. After all, Turner had been completely out of the sport for eight years before returning to compete in the 1992 Olympics. As "Nikki Newland" she had attempted to be a professional recording artist, writing her own songs (including the memorable "Sexy, Kinky Tomboy" and a sports theme number, "Born to Be Champions"). She had also been in and out of several colleges and had been treated for severe depression. Thus Turner was more than a dark horse when she returned to the short track—she was supposed to be "over the hill" and unprepared for world-class competition. Instead she emerged a champion. Twice.

Her long hiatus from speed skating was, Turner contended, the result of being pushed too hard too young by a domineering father. She began skating at age six and quickly showed talent. Her father, a telephone repairman, could not afford the expensive coaching that speed skating demands, so he oversaw his daughter's training and conditioning regimen. In 1979, when she was 16, Turner became the national short-track champion. A year later she had moved out of her parents' home and quit skating altogether.

Cathy Turner catches her breath after being disqualified in the semifinal of the 1,000-meter short track event of the 1994 Olympics. (AP/Wide World Photos)

"I never really knew who I was," Turner recalled in the *New York Times*. "I always had to be the best. My father was 'Cathy's father.' We even had a boat named 'Cathy's Father.' In that mindset, I kind of lost a dad. My skating, my success was his daughter, not me."

Taking the stage name Nikki Newland, Turner embarked upon a music career, performing with a series of bands and then moving into the studio to record songs and commercial jingles. This too proved to be a difficult undertaking, and by 1987 Turner was forced to seek professional treatment for a deep depression. "I could have cared less if I lived or died," she told the *New York Times*.

In the summer of 1988, Turner read a newspaper article about a former speed skating acquaintance who had won an Olympic medal as a cyclist. The article galvanized Turner's resolve to return to competitive skating. She returned to the ice at Northern Michigan University, where she earned a bachelor's degree in computer science while training as a short-track speed skater.

CATHY TURNER

American speedskater

Born: C. 1963.

Education: Attended Northern Michigan University, where she earned a bachelor's degree in computer science.

Career Highlights:
- became the national short-track champion, 1979
- won a gold medal in the 500-meter race and a silver in the 3,000-meter relay, 1992 Olympic Games, Albertville, France
- won a gold medal in the 500-meter short-track race and a bronze in the 3,000-meter relay, 1994 Olympic Games, Lillehammer, Norway.

For the next three years she worked diligently, aided by a sports psychologist who encouraged her to compete for her own satisfaction, not to please others.

Short-track skating became an Olympic event at the 1992 Winter Games, and Turner was there for the U.S. She won two medals in Albertville—the gold medal in the 500-meter race and a silver in the 3,000-meter relay. At first Turner thought this fabulous achievement would jump-start her singing career. But the expected movie and recording deals failed to materialize, and she found herself skating with the Ice Capades. Even that fizzled after a year, so she returned to speed skating in preparation for the 1994 Games.

Turner returned to medal form at the 1994 Olympics, winning another gold in the 500-meter short-track race and a bronze in the 3,000-meter relay. Her gold medal victory was marred by the complaints of her competitors, however. Silver medalist Zhang Yanmei of China accused Turner of grabbing her leg and throwing her off balance. Canadian skater Nathalie Lambert claimed Turner knocked her down in a qualifying heat. "We thought [Turner] had cleaned up her act, but, obviously, when you get to the Olympics, there's a lot of pressure," Lambert complained in the *New York Times*. "She should have been disqualified. But the problem is, Cathy Turner never gets disqualified. Somebody must like her. She's made my last two years totally wasted. In the garbage. I'm very angry with Cathy Turner."

For her part, Turner insisted that she had skated aggressively, but fairly—and that the other skaters only complained because they had lost. "It's nothing new, it is an ongoing thing," she told *Sports Illustrated*. "They say I'm too aggressive. They're not used to someone fighting for the turns the way I do. What it really is, I just popped into their sport and beat them all, and they're pissed."

Fast as she "popped in," Turner popped out again. Married to a veterinarian and comfortable in her home in Hilton, New York, she retired before the 1994 world championships. "I have a husband and a life," she concluded in *Sports Illustrated*. "I'm going home."

And she's taking those four medals with her.

REBECCA
TWIGG

CYCLIST

Rebecca Twigg has been around for a long time, and she's not about to quit now. The six-time world champion in the 3,000-meter individual pursuit bike race, Twigg is as strong at 32 as she was at 20. Her most recent victory in the 3,000 meter came in November of 1995 in Bogota, Colombia, where her time of 3:36.081 earned her a new world record. A cycling champion in the 1980s, Twigg came out of retirement before the 1992 Olympics to win a bronze medal, beating a field of younger women in the process. Now, age and injuries notwithstanding, she plans to compete in Atlanta.

Los Angeles, 1984: Olympic cycling history was made, and Twigg was there. Nipped at the line by teammate Connie Carpenter, she locked a second-place finish in the first Olympic women's road race—the only distaff cycling event that year.

The 1988 Summer Games added women's track cycling events—in which Twigg had won her world championships—but illness, crashes, and fatigue prevented her from qualifying for the U.S. team that year. Disenchanted with her sport at the age of 25, she retired from competitive cycling. Or so she thought.

Settling into a nine-to-five routine as a computer programmer, Twigg reduced her exercise schedule to aerobics and occasional bike rides for pleasure. Then came the news that a women's 3,000-meter individual pursuit race—Twigg's best event—would be added to the program at the 1992 Olympics in Barcelona. Twigg leaped out of retirement and called her former coach, Eddie Borysewicz.

Borysewicz was not at all skeptical about Twigg's chances. "She's a lady that if she likes, she can do," he explained in the *Olympian*. "There are not many like her. Every 50 years there's born one. Age is no main factor. Mind, dedication, health are main factors. And she can do it, no problem."

Well, maybe a *little* problem. Having been off the bike for three years, Twigg discovered she had the legs of a tourist. Her spin was gone, her muscles were leaden. But mind, dedication, and health she had, and after a month

"She's a lady that if she likes, she can do. There are not many like her. Every 50 years there's born one. Age is no main factor. Mind, dedication, health are main factors. And she can do it, no problem."

—Eddie Borysewicz, Twigg's coach

477

Rebecca Twigg raises her arms in victory after the individual road race event of the 1987 Pan Am Games. (UPI/Corbis-Bettmann)

REBECCA TWIGG

American cyclist

Career Highlights:

- won world championship in the 3,000-meter individual pursuit bike race six times

- earned silver medal in women's individual road race, 1984 Olympic Games, Los Angeles, California

- won a bronze medal in the 3,000-meter individual pursuit race, 1992 Olympic Games, Barcelona, Spain.

and a half of serious training, she began to recover her racing form. "It's hard to say what's age and what's just being away from [racing]," she admitted in *Women's Sports + Fitness*. "It takes longer to recover from workouts and races."

At Barcelona, spectators who didn't know Twigg's history would never have guessed that she had been "retired" for three years. She collected a bronze medal in the first Olympic women's pursuit. Next stop: the world championships in Hamar, Norway, where she picked up her fourth 3,000-meter individual pursuit gold. This she did with a certain panache, posting a record time of 3:37.347, almost .8 of a second faster than the previous world record. Added to the mix were a dozen or so miscellaneous victories scattered through the year.

Has she slowed down since? Not a chance. At the 1995 world championships in Bogota, she competed with a brand-new metal plate in her shoulder. She broke her collarbone just two weeks before the event and decided to opt for a surgical fix so she wouldn't miss the race. "After four days I started to feel better," she told *USA Today* of her surgery. "Then I caught a cold. I figured it just wasn't meant to be, but I decided to go to worlds anyway and just try my best."

The best is hard to beat. Twigg shaved almost a full second off her previous world record and took her sixth world championship. Twigg was thrilled that the painful injury had not slowed her down. "I didn't know what I could do until I was put in that situation," she explained. "A good attitude helped. I still kept trying, I still had a chance to do something."

If her chances extend into 1996, Twigg will return to her third Summer Olympics, almost a decade after she decided to quit her sport. Twigg has even higher aspirations, though. She thinks she might like to race at the 2000 Summer Games in Sydney, Australia. What gives her the ambition to compete against riders half her age? "I've never been to Australia," she says.

WYOMIA TYUS

As the 1968 Olympics rolled around, race relations in America were so polarized that some black militants encouraged black athletes to boycott the Games. Each black athlete had to make an individual decision, but none was affected more deeply by the controversy than Wyomia Tyus. A world champion sprinter, Tyus had won the gold medal in the 100-meter dash at the 1964 Summer Games. She was favored to win again, and if she did, she would become the first athlete, male or female, to take the same individual sprint gold medal in consecutive Olympics.

Tyus chose to go, but she showed her support for the boycott by wearing black clothing—even when she accepted that history-making gold medal. For indeed she did win the 100-meter sprint again, and she took a second gold as anchor for the 400-meter relay team. A member of the Olympic Hall of Fame, she is considered one of the fastest women in the history of track and field events.

Tyus was born August 29, 1945, in Griffin, Georgia. Her father, Willie Tyus, worked in a dairy, and her mother, Marie, was a laundress. Tyus was the youngest of four children and the only girl. She learned sports in order to keep up with her brothers and then played women's basketball and ran track in high school. Her first love was basketball, and only after she came to the attention of Tennessee State University track coach Ed Temple did she begin to pursue running seriously. After Tyus won a Georgia high school championship in the sprint, Temple invited her to participate in the Tennessee State Track and Field Clinic. This she did for two consecutive summers, and after graduating from high school she entered Tennessee State as a recreation major.

Tyus established herself as the sprinter to beat as early as 1962, when she won the 50-yard, 75-yard, *and* 100-yard dashes at the Amateur Athletic Union (AAU) Girls' National Championships. At the time she had yet to enter college. As an undergraduate she continued her winning ways, concentrating on the 70-yard and 100-meter dashes. Having won the 100-meter sprint at the National AAU Women's outdoor championships in 1964, she was se-

Wyomia Tyus wins a qualifying heat for the 100-meter dash prior to winning the gold medal in that event at the 1968 Olympics. (AP/Wide World Photos)

lected to the U.S. Olympic team. In Tokyo at the Summer Games that year, she established a new Olympic record and won the gold medal in her signature event. She also took home a silver medal for the 400-meter relay.

Tyus became the world record holder in the 100-meter dash in 1965 and generally defended her record from all comers. She gained significant recognition for her accomplishments, and in 1966 she and her teammate Edith McGuire, along with coach Temple, were named goodwill ambassadors to Ethiopia, Kenya, Uganda, and Malawi. Their travels in those countries included track clinics and demonstrations aimed at teaching athletes in those nations how to better compete in the world arena.

The troubled racial climate at home left black athletes like Tyus in a quandary in 1968. Should they compete in the Olympics, representing a country they felt to be racist and unfair to people of African descent? Or should they stay home in protest, letting the hated Soviet Union swallow up all the gold medals? In the end Tyus decided to compete. She was not as daring as

WYOMIA TYUS

American track & field athlete

Born: August 29, 1945 in Griffin, Georgia.

Education: Attended Tennessee State University, graduating in 1968.

Career Highlights:

- won the Amateur Athletic Union (AAU) National Championships ten times
- established a new Olympic record and won the gold medal in the 100-meter sprint; also took home a silver medal for the 4 × 100-meter relay, 1964 Olympic Games, Tokyo, Japan

- became the world record holder in the 100-meter dash, 1965
- won gold medals for the 100-meter sprint and as anchor for the 4 × 100-meter relay team, 1968 Olympic Games, Mexico City, Mexico.

Awards: named a goodwill ambassador to Ethiopia, Kenya, Uganda, and Malawi, 1966; inducted into the Tennessee Sports Hall of Fame, the Georgia Athletic Hall of Fame, the Women's Sports Foundation Hall of Fame, the Black Athletes Hall of Fame, and the Olympic Hall of Fame.

American athletes Tommy Smith and John Carlos who, when receiving Olympic medals for their track victories, raised their hands in the "black power" salute and bowed their heads. Still she made a quiet protest of her own. "I wore dark shorts after winning my gold medal," she recalled, ". . . and dedicated my medal to [Smith and Carlos] for what they did."

With her consecutive Olympic victories in the 100-meter dash, as well as her relay silver from 1964 and gold from 1968, Tyus established herself as the fastest woman of her time. She graduated from Tennessee State in 1968 and retired from amateur sports following the Olympics. "After the Olympics I did not even run across the street," she joked. Tyus married Art Simburg and moved to Los Angeles, California, where she became the mother of two children, a daughter named Simone and a son, Tyus Tillman.

In another era Wyomia Tyus would have had it all: the Nike contracts, the workout videos, the lucrative fees for making personal appearances. Those perks were simply not available to athletes—especially black women athletes—in the late 1960s. Instead she performed as a track professional for the International Track Association, becoming the leading money winner on the tour and winning all 22 races in 1974. After retiring from that circuit she taught physical education in junior and senior high school, coached at Beverly Hills High School, and acted as a consultant to the Olympic Experience Group.

Tyus has continued to be active as a supporter of women's athletic efforts. She has served on the advisory board of the Women's Sports Foundation and has participated in the Colgate-Palmolive Help Young America campaign. She has also lent her talents to the U.S. Olympic Committee and the Black Studies Center at the University of California, Los Angeles. In addition to the Olympic Hall of Fame, she has been inducted into the Tennessee

Sports Hall of Fame, the Georgia Athletic Hall of Fame, the Women's Sports Foundation Hall of Fame, and the Black Athletes Hall of Fame.

In his memoirs, Ed Temple noted of his former star that she was "ten times AAU National Champion and All-American Athlete in both indoor and outdoor competition, and five times world record holder in 50, 60, 70, and 100-yard dashes and meter sprint." She is equally noteworthy for her grace under pressure and her ability to translate track championships into learning experiences for a new generation of women runners.

AMY
VAN DYKEN

SWIMMER

"This is something I've dreamt about for a long, long time. I try not to think about how fast it's happened, how far I've come, because if I think about it, I might not believe it's really happening."

—Van Dyken, on her success as a worldclass swimmer, 1994

It's hard enough to be an Olympic swimmer if you're in the peak of health. For Amy Van Dyken, the road to greatness has been tougher yet. Van Dyken's lifelong battle with asthma has not stopped her from being one of the fastest sprint swimmers in the nation. In fact, the disabling disease is indirectly responsible for her prowess as a swimmer—she began swimming to strengthen her lungs.

Today Van Dyken is a two-time U.S. national champion in the 50-meter freestyle sprint. She holds the U.S. record in that event, and in 1995 she broke the short-course world record in the 50-meter butterfly as well. All of this is a miracle to Van Dyken, who as a child could hardly mount a flight of stairs without collapsing. "With my medical condition, people thought I would never compete at this level," she said.

Van Dyken was born February 15, 1973, in Englewood, Colorado. At the age of 10 months she developed a severe case of asthma. One of her doctors told the *Rocky Mountain News* that hers was "the worst case of asthma I ever saw." Thin and sickly, Van Dyken missed many of childhood's pleasures because allergies aggravated her asthma. "Kids used to laugh at me," she recalled in the *Gazette Telegraph*. "They'd have their little necklaces hanging around their necks. I'd have my inhaler. I couldn't go to the zoo. I couldn't play basketball. I couldn't even play tag. I had a hard time laughing at a joke."

When Van Dyken was six, her doctor suggested that she take up swimming to improve her lung capacity. She was hardly an overnight sensation when she hit the pool. She literally could not swim the length of an Olympic-sized pool until she was 12, and she often finished last in age-group meets even when she was entered against much younger children. Somehow Van Dyken never gave up trying, though, and when she turned 13 she started to improve. Her first blue ribbon in a local swim meet was a prize sweeter than any Olympic medal.

Van Dyken attended Cherry Creek High School, where she became state champion and record-holder in the 50-meter fly and the 100-yard fly. Twice she was named Colorado Swimmer of the Year. Recruited heavily throughout

AMY VAN DYKEN

American swimmer

Born: February 15, 1973 in Englewood, Colorado.

Education: Attended University of Arizona, 1992–94; transferred to Colorado State University.

Career Highlights:
- won a silver medal in the 50-yard freestyle, NCAA championships, 1993

- won a gold medal in the NCAA championships, 1994

- earned a bronze medal in the 50-yard freestyle, world championships, 1994.

Awards: Named NCAA Swimmer of the Year, 1994; designated *Swimming World* magazine's Swimmer of the Year, 1995.

---

the West, she chose to attend the University of Arizona. While there, in 1993, she won a silver medal in the 50-yard freestyle at the NCAA championships.

Van Dyken was not satisfied with her progress in Tucson, however. In 1994 she decided to transfer to a college closer to home, Colorado State University. "I'd been at Arizona two years, and I hadn't seen much improvement," she explained in the *Rocky Mountain News*. "That would be disheartening for anybody. My feeling was, 'If I can't reach the level I want to be at, why continue?'" Her new coach at Colorado State, John Mattos, structured a conditioning program to accommodate Van Dyken's asthma, and she quickly made the improvements she had been seeking. Her gold medal performance at the 1994 NCAA championships in the 50-yard freestyle set American and U.S. Open records. Later that same year she earned a bronze medal in the same event at the world championships. She was named 1994 NCAA Swimmer of the Year.

In 1995 *Swimming World* magazine designated Van Dyken its Swimmer of the Year after she broke her own 50-meter freestyle records at the Pan Pacific swim meet. At six feet tall and 150 pounds, Van Dyken is strong enough and certainly determined enough to pursue an Olympic medal—or medals—in the short distance sprints. Ironically, some of the medicines she could take to improve her asthma are banned by the International Olympic Committee. Van Dyken must make do with less effective medications and sheer iron will. "It's kind of hard for me right now," she admitted in the *Gazette Telegraph*. "I want to breathe, but I also want to compete. I've got to find that happy medium." She seemed to have found that medium at the Olympic trials in March 1996. Van Dyken not only qualified for the team, she came in first in both the 50- and 100-meter freestyle races.

Few people ever mean it when they say they want something "worse than breath itself." For Van Dyken that may very well be the case. She wants an Olympic medal, and she won't let her medical condition ruin her chances. She declared: "When you're standing up on the medal stand and the national anthem is playing. . . . Oh yeah, I'd give up breathing for that."

ERIKA VON HEILAND

*"Erika's probably the
fastest player we
have in the women's
events. If Erika is on,
she can be
competitive
internationally."*

—U.S. Badminton coach Vicki Toutz

Erika von Heiland is nothing if not persistent. When the U.S. badminton team yanked her funding prior to the 1992 Olympics, she borrowed money on her credit cards in order to continue pursuing a spot at Barcelona. That decision was quite a gamble, but the enterprising von Heiland came up a winner—after months of uncertainty and confusion with the intricacies of national rankings in badminton, she emerged as the top women's singles player in the nation. She got her chance to go to Barcelona and has been securely on the U.S. team ever since.

Von Heiland, a native of the Philippines who lives in Anaheim, California, is one of the best women's badminton players in the world. Her resume includes appearances at the 1989, 1991, and 1993 world badminton championships and a silver medal in singles at the 1991 Pan American Games. More recently she won a bronze medal in doubles play with Linda French at the 1995 Pan Am Games. A 1994 *magna cum laude* criminal justice graduate of Arizona State University, she has been following dual career paths in badminton and private detective work.

Von Heiland was born December 24, 1965, in the Philippines and grew up there as a promising athlete. Her game was tennis, and she was good enough to qualify for the Philippine national junior team. "I was ranked 10th in the country in tennis and wasn't good enough to cut it," she said in the *Los Angeles Times*. "One day, a bunch of my friends got me to get on the badminton court."

By the time von Heiland tried her hand at badminton, she was a relatively ancient 17. She picked up the game quickly, however, soon qualifying for the Philippine national team. For the next two years she represented the Philippines at international tournaments. Then she emigrated to the United States with an eye toward a bigger and better-funded national badminton team.

Injuries almost ended her career before she could establish herself in America. Von Heiland endured three years of inactivity due to knee injuries—a cartilage tear in the right knee and a dislocated left kneecap. "The doctors

ERIKA VON HEILAND

American (born in Philippines) badminton player

Born: December 24, 1965 in Angeles City, Philippines.

Education: Graduated *magna cum laude* with a criminal justice degree from Arizona State University, 1994.

Career Highlights:

- won a silver medal in singles, Pan American Games, 1991

- won a bronze medal in doubles play with Linda French, Pan Am Games, 1995.

told me that my chances of competing again were very, very slim," she recalled in the *Los Angeles Times*. "I was told my playing days were over. I needed to do something with a goal at the end, so I started to body build."

Von Heiland was considering entering bodybuilding competitions, but a visit to her former home changed her mind. Back in the Philippines, the same friends who had encouraged her to play badminton in the first place urged her to try it again. When she discovered she could play without pain, she returned to America and resumed her badminton career. She qualified for the U.S. national team in 1989, won an athletic scholarship to Arizona State University, and represented the U.S. at the world badminton singles competition in 1989.

In January of 1991, U.S. Badminton officials chose von Heiland as one of its athletes to participate in Olympic qualifying tournaments around the world—18 months, 23 countries—with no guarantee that she would make the final 40-player international Olympic singles pool. Von Heiland took a leave of absence from college, but after a year on the badminton circuit, her chances of reaching the Olympics looked so poor that she lost her funding. U.S. Badminton, she told the *Times,* "decided to put all their energies and finances into the doubles players for one of the 56 doubles slots, which is very understandable."

Von Heiland accepted the ruling body's decision, but she was determined not to let 12 grueling months of competition go to waste. She took out a loan from her bank and borrowed against her credit cards to raise the money she needed to support herself through the final six months of Olympic qualifying tournaments. When the complicated computer-ranking system finally spilled its results prior to the 1992 Summer Games, she stood right at the top among the American women. She won a singles slot in Barcelona, but was deeply disappointed by a first-round loss to Denyse Julien of Canada.

The loss in Barcelona has only whetted von Heiland's appetite for more Olympic competition, either as a singles player or a doubles partner. She is still among the top five American women in the fast-paced sport, and an appearance in Atlanta is a distinct possibility. U.S. coach Vicki Toutz told the *Olympic Factbook:* "Erika's probably the fastest player we have in the women's events. If Erika is on, she can be competitive internationally."

After years spent pursuing a tennis career, von Heiland is comfortable and confident that she has found her niche in badminton. "There is a big difference between tennis and badminton," she explained in the *Los Angeles Times.* "The hand-eye coordination is the same, but badminton is in the wrist and tennis is in the arm." For Erika von Heiland, badminton is more than in the wrist—it's in the cards.

GRETE
WAITZ

In 1991 *Runner's World* magazine named its "female runner of the quarter century": Grete Waitz. The Norwegian dynamo was chosen for the honor by a panel of international running experts, all of whom were well aware of her stellar career as a marathon and middle distance runner. At one time or another, Waitz has held world records in the 3,000 meter, the 8 kilometer, the 10 kilometer, the 15 kilometer, the 10 mile, and the marathon. She was the first woman to run a marathon in under two and a half hours and the first female world champion at the marathon distance. As Peter Gambaccini noted in *Runner's World,* Waitz "almost singlehandedly . . . set the standard for women's distance running as the sport began to proliferate on American roads. The public came to view her triumphs as givens even before the races were run."

Born Grete Andersen in the suburbs of Oslo, Norway, Waitz preferred running with her older brothers to practicing the piano that her mother had bought for her. While still a young teen she began rising before dawn to run. She just couldn't get enough of the sport. She was 16 when she won Norway's junior championships at 400 and 800 meters. The following year she ran the 800 in the European championships and became Norway's national 800- and 1,500-meter champion. She also competed in the 1972 Olympics in the 1,500-meter event.

Waitz only seemed to get stronger as she got older. She moved from the shorter distance races into longer events, setting a world record at 3,000 meters in 1975. She also won world cross-country titles in 1978, 1979, 1981, and 1983. In those days before shoe sponsors and government subsidies, she worked as a schoolteacher to support herself, training during her spare time.

Waitz's introduction to the marathon has become a legend in running circles. In 1978 she was persuaded to try the New York City Marathon by her husband, Jack Waitz. She agreed to do it only because she thought it might be nice to visit America. Waitz had literally never run a marathon before, and the 26.2-mile distance was further incomprehensible to her because

"To suddenly be a hero on a world basis was hard for me to understand. God gave me a gift. I got the chance to use it. I felt uncomfortable with the credit."

Grete Waitz crosses the finish line first among women for the eighth time in the 1986 New York City Marathon. (AP/Wide World Photos)

she was used to gauging distance by kilometers. Winding her way through New York's five boroughs, suffering from dehydration and muscle cramps, she kept looking for the finish line in vain. When she finally found it, she had done nothing less than claim victory and set a new women's world record for the marathon (2:32.30), crushing the old record by two minutes.

No one needed to explain the significance of this victory to Waitz. If she had broken the world record while being completely untrained at the marathon distance, what might happen if she *trained* for the event? The world would soon find out.

Waitz went on to win eight more New York City Marathons and 13 of 19 official marathons she entered between 1978 and 1988. She set world records in the event in 1978, 1979, 1980, and 1983. Her personal best of 2:24.54 is a time any male runner would envy. At the first-ever running of the world marathon championships in 1983 she was, little surprise, the winner. She defeated the field of women runners by a three-minute margin.

Favored to win the gold medal at the 1984 Olympic Games—where the marathon was included for the first time—Waitz endured a disappointment when she was beaten by Joan Benoit Samuelson. Nevertheless, Waitz did earn the silver medal, a significant victory for a country the size of Norway.

Waitz was a champion at the dawn of America's fascination with running, and she was surprised at the level of celebrity she attained. "To suddenly be a hero on a world basis was hard for me to understand," she told *Runner's World*. "God gave me a gift. I got the chance to use it. I felt uncomfortable with the credit. I didn't think I deserved what people were saying. My talent is just more visible than theirs."

 ## LAST BUT NOT LEAST

While Grete Waitz has officially retired from running, she continues to be involved with the running community as a sort of unofficial ambassador. At the 1995 New York City Marathon, Waitz greeted the last of some 29,700 competitors at the finish line: a woman who calls herself "the world's slowest woman runner." Zoe Koplowitz has completed the New York marathon eight times—on crutches. Koplowitz, 46, suffers from multiple sclerosis. She completed the 1995 marathon, walking with the aid of her aluminum crutches, in twenty-six hours.

That visible talent lasted well into the 1980s, long enough to establish Waitz as not only a champion marathoner but also a comfortable spokesperson for running, health, and fitness. She inaugurated a Grete Waitz Run of five kilometers in her hometown of Oslo in 1983, and 3,000 runners turned out to participate. Just a decade later, the same event drew 40,000 Norwegians, many of whom had taken up running in response to Waitz's example. "We want to show the world we are a healthy nation," Waitz explained in the *Saturday Evening Post*. "We're encouraging people to build simple physical activity into their daily lives."

GRETE WAITZ

Norwegian distance runner

Born: October 1, 1953 in Oslo, Norway.

Career Highlights:

- set a world record in the 3,000 meters, 1975

- won world cross-country titles, 1978, 1979, 1981, and 1983

- won nine New York City Marathons

- set world records in the marathon in 1978, 1979, 1980, and 1983

- won the first-ever world marathon championships, 1983

- earned a silver medal in the marathon, 1984 Olympic Games, Los Angeles, California.

Awards: Named by *Runner's World* magazine "female runner of the quarter century," 1991; inducted into Women's Sports Foundation Hall of Fame, 1995.

Waitz and her husband divide their time between homes in Oslo and Gainesville, Florida. Although a string of injuries ended her marathon career in 1991, Waitz continues to participate in distance events in a symbolic way. She accompanied her former coach, Fred Lebow, in the 1992 New York City Marathon, as Lebow ran the course after having been treated for cancer. In 1993 she was seen at the race's finish line embracing Zoe Koplowitz, a runner with multiple sclerosis.

The legendary Grete Waitz may have retired, but she has certainly not given up running. "It's part of my life," she told the *Saturday Evening Post.* Then she added: "The difference is now I take it nice and easy. . . . I only run six to eight miles a day."

ORA WASHINGTON

It is tempting to speculate about how famous Ora Washington might have become had she arrived on the scene after the days of segregation. Considered a pioneer and an inspiration for black American athletes every-where, Washington excelled in tennis and basketball at a time when black women could only play other black women—never whites. She was the singles champion of the all-black American Tennis Association (ATA) every year between 1929 and 1935, and again in 1937. She was also a member of the championship ATA women's doubles team for seven years in a row.

At the same time that Washington was dominating the ATA, Helen Wills, a white player, was winning consecutive championships in the United States Lawn Tennis Association. Wills's accomplishments were well documented in the newspapers at the time, but she would never accept the challenge of meeting Ora Washington in a singles match. Nor would the posh clubs where Wills played admit Washington so she could compete. None of this diminishes Washington's achievements by any means. It is rather a sad commentary on a dark period in our nation's history.

Washington, who was born in the Germantown section of Philadelphia in 1898, took up tennis at the urging of friends after her sister died. It was thought that the healthy activity would help the grieving girl to reconcile herself to the loss. Washington's gift for tennis was soon obvious. At Baltimore's Druid Hill Park in 1924 she won her first national championship, beating Dorothy Radcliffe. For the next 12 years Washington was nearly undefeated among players of the ATA and the African American National Tennis Organization.

Washington held the ATA singles championship for eight years, seven of them consecutive through the 1930s. Her approach was unorthodox—she gripped the racket halfway up the handle and rarely took a full swing, and she did not believe in warm-ups. "I'd rather play from scratch and warm up as I went along," she was fond of saying. Despite her eccentricities, she so thoroughly dominated her tennis leagues that some years she was never defeated at all.

TENNIS & BASKETBALL PLAYER

"Courage and determination were the biggest assets I had."

ORA WASHINGTON

American tennis & basketball player

Born: 1898 in Philadelphia.

Died: 1971.

Career Highlights:

• won singles championship of the all-black American Tennis Association (ATA), 1924, 1929–35, and 1937

• played as member of the championship ATA women's doubles team for seven years in a row

• held position of star center for the *Philadelphia Tribune* girls basketball squad for 18 years.

Washington retired from the ATA not once but twice. On the occasion of her first retirement she was coaxed back into play by a competitor, Flora Lomax of Detroit, who, upon winning the women's singles title, urged Washington to try to regain it. Washington rose to the challenge and defeated Lomax in a special match. Her second retirement occurred after a tennis official complained that her continued presence in the ATA had "killed the spirit" of young hopefuls who preferred not to meet her on the court.

At the same time that she was winning her tennis championships, Washington was also making a mark in women's basketball. She was the star center for the *Philadelphia Tribune* girls squad for 18 years and for awhile was top scorer. She played as well for the Germantown Hornets, serving as team captain for the 1929–30 season. It was with the *Philadelphia Tribune* team that she got the headlines, however. Playing by "boys' rules"—threesomes for offense and defense at opposite ends of the court—she and her teammates toured the country, presenting clinics and demonstrations and playing against any team that cared to challenge them. In *The Negro in Sports,* Edwin Bancroft Henderson states that this phenomenal team lost only six games in nine years while literally traveling thousands of miles and criss-crossing dozens of states.

Washington's success came many decades before black American athletes could hope to profit financially from their sports. Nevertheless, her fighting spirit and more than 200 trophies prepared her well to work hard and prosper in the business world. By 1961 she was owner of an apartment building she had purchased with earnings from work in domestic service. More important, she was well known for conducting free training sessions and coaching youngsters at the community tennis courts in Germantown. She died in 1971.

In their book *Black Champions Challenge American Sports,* Wally Jones and Jim Washington quote historian Malcolm Poindexter on Ora Washington's contributions to sports. Poindexter observed: "If history were able to repeat itself and the tennis world could have seen fit to drop its racial behavior 40 years ago, Philadelphia would probably have the distinction of honoring Miss Ora Washington as the holder of the national women's singles title and the woman who held it longer than any other in American history."

PAULA
WEISHOFF

VOLLEYBALL
PLAYER

"She was an intimidating player and a physically imposing athlete. Her power made her a feared player. . . . She could do it all."

—Chuck Erbe, former USC coach

Paula Weishoff has been around volleyball for a long time. And she has never lacked for work. Far from it. Weishoff has two Olympic medals to her credit—a silver from 1984, a bronze from 1992—and has multiple Most Valuable Player honors for the U.S. national team *and* for teams in the Italian professional league. For nearly a decade the intimidating six-foot-one-inch middle blocker has divided her time between stints with the U.S. team, the professional beach volleyball tour, and the European professional circuit. She is happy anywhere she plays.

A native of Torrance, California, Weishoff always stood out as an athlete . . . a *tall* athlete. She had reached six feet by eighth grade. "I was always at the end of the line because I was always the tallest and my name is Weishoff," she joked in the *Los Angeles Times*. "In my eighth grade class picture I scrunched down so that I wouldn't stick out. It was hard growing up."

Finding volleyball helped ease those growth pains. Weishoff began playing volleyball as a freshman at West Torrance High, and by her senior year, 1978, she had helped her team to reach the semifinals of the Southern Section playoffs. She was named Southern Section 3-A Division volleyball player of the year. Weishoff had higher aspirations, however. Recruited heavily, she chose to attend the University of Southern California.

During her freshman year at USC, Weishoff led the Trojans to a 46-4 season and the national championship. Individual honors included Association of Intercollegiate Athletics Women's Player of the Year. Nevertheless she left college after one year to join the national team. "The main reason I went to USC was to train for the Olympics," she noted in the *Los Angeles Times*. "The only thing I regret is not finishing school. Now the national team has a good program. Players have a chance to finish school."

The Olympics beckoned. Weishoff had already earned All-America and Most Valuable Player citations at the 1980 U.S. Junior Olympics. The national team welcomed her steely presence. She announced that presence by starring on the bronze medal-winning American team at the 1982 world cham-

Paula Weishoff scores a point over her Japanese opponents during a goodwill match in 1981. (AP/Wide World Photos)

pionships. Then, in the 1984 Olympics, she took command. Team U.S.A. won the silver medal, and Weishoff was awarded U.S. Most Valuable Player. "[Paula] was at her best every night," assistant coach Greg Giovanazzi told the *Los Angeles Times*. "She was the only one who played great every single night. It was hard for us to imagine someone can play that consistently at a level like that with so much pressure and competition."

Shortly after the Olympics, Weishoff took her skills to Italy and joined the women's professional league there. "I went to Europe because there were no leagues here," she said later. Unlike many American athletes who join foreign tours, Weishoff found that she loved living abroad. She made friends in Italy, settled down, and pretty much ruled out returning to America to play volleyball.

A change in rules made it possible for Weishoff to rejoin the U.S. national team even though she was a professional, and sure enough the team called prior to the 1992 Olympics. She accepted the challenge, for awhile jet-

PAULA WEISHOFF

American volleyball player

Born: C. 1962 in Torrance, California.

Education: Attended the University of Southern California for one year, 1978–79.

Career Highlights:

- led the USC Trojans to a 46-4 season and the national championship, 1979
- starred on the bronze medal–winning American team, world championships, 1982
- led U.S. team to a silver medal, 1984 Olympic Games, Los Angeles, California
- helped U.S. team win a bronze medal, 1992 Olympic Games, Barcelona, Spain.

Awards: Awarded U.S. Most Valuable Player, 1984 Olympics; received Outstanding Player of the 1992 Olympics citation.

ting between practices in San Diego and games in Milan for her former team. At the 1992 Summer Games she turned in a fine performance, compiling 96 kills and nine blocks in six matches as the Americans took the bronze medal. This time her personal honors included an Outstanding Player of the 1992 Olympics citation. Then it was back to work in the pro ranks—beach volleyball in 1993, team volleyball in Italy, Brazil, and Japan.

Weishoff has once again joined Team U.S.A. in preparation for the 1996 Summer Games. At 34 she will be the oldest and most experienced member of the roster, perhaps a step slower than she was in 1984 but far wiser and more skilled at the nuances of the game. U.S. volleyball coach Terry Liskevych has called Weishoff one of the "mainstays" of his team and a "big factor" in the U.S.'s success. "She's a great athlete," Liskevych told the *Los Angeles Times.* "She's technically very sound, and she plays with a lot of aggressiveness. . . . She's going to get a lot of balls set to her."

HANNI
WENZEL

When people talk of Alpine skiing powerhouses, their attention naturally wanders to places like Austria, Switzerland, Sweden, and Norway. So it was no wonder that in 1980 at the Winter Olympics in Lake Placid, New York, people had a hard time pronouncing Liechtenstein (lick-ten-shtine). What they didn't have a hard time pronouncing, though, was the tiny country's most famous athlete—Hanni Wenzel.

Bottom line: at the 1980 Games, Wenzel matched the greatest Olympic skiing performance ever put forth by a woman. Her gold medal sweep in slalom and giant slalom, coupled with her silver in downhill, duplicated West German Rosi Mittermaier's near-perfect Alpine sweep in the 1976 Olympics.

The giant slalom was not supposed to be Wenzel's strongest event. Although she had finished in the top 10 in every giant slalom race that season, Wenzel did not seem to have what it would take to put together a medal-winning performance. Opinions changed, though, when she won the last World Cup giant slalom before the Olympics by over five seconds—an absolutely astounding lead in a sport often hinging on the blink of an eye.

The other technical event at the 1980 Olympics, slalom, was dominated during the year by the Austrians. They had finished 1-2-3 in the previous World Cup season. In the 1980 season, no fewer than six skiers had won in the eight races. An Austrian 20-year-old was to be on the Olympic victory stand twice, and so was Wenzel. The bronze medalist in 1976 in the slalom, Wenzel tore through the tough course at Lake Placid to win by a second and a half.

The big race of the 1980 Winter Games was Wenzel's weakest event, the downhill. None of the pre-Olympic publications counted her even near medal contention. So when the times were put into the books, James Major, former World Cup editor for *Skiing* magazine put it this way: "[Austrian star] Anne-Marie Moser's gold was the victory of the favorite, Wenzel's silver the upset, and [Swiss racer] Marie-Theres Nadig's bronze a defeat."

That Olympic year was a very special one for Wenzel. Not only did she match the greatest Olympic skiing achievement ever by a woman, she also

SKIER

Hanni Wenzel dominated alpine skiing in 1980, earning two gold medals and one silver at the Winter Olympics, as well as winning the World Cup overall title.

HANNI WENZEL

Liechtenstein skier

Born: C. 1957.

Career Highlights:

- earned bronze medal in the slalom, 1976 Olympic Games, Innsbruck, Austria

- won World Cup overall title, 1980
- won gold medals in slalom and giant slalom, and a silver medal in downhill, 1980 Olympic Games, Lake Placid, New York.

won the World Cup overall title. And she got to share in the celebration with her brother Andreas, who also medaled at the 1980 Games (silver in giant slalom) and won the men's World Cup overall title. For a tiny country like Liechtenstein, the tandem Wenzel victories were like a feast after a very long famine.

JOYCE WETHERED

She was an unlikely champion: shy and uncomfortable in crowds, completely focused on her own game to the exclusion of all else, and content to retire early and play only for fun. Nevertheless, Joyce Wethered left her mark on women's golf and still stands today as one of the mythic champions in the sport. From 1920, when she entered her first English amateur championship almost on a whim, to 1929, when she came out of retirement long enough to win one more British Open, Wethered captivated golf fans all over the world.

Born November 17, 1901, Wethered grew up in a golfing family. Her father was a prosperous English businessman who himself once had a handicap of six, and her older brother Roger won his own share of amateur titles in Great Britain after the First World War. Wethered and her brother began golfing as youngsters during holidays to Scotland. Neither of them had any formal training in the sport, but they attended matches, watched the great players of their era, and then went home and tried to duplicate their swings.

Wethered was a delicate child and very shy. Even though her parents had the means to send her off to school, they chose to keep her home, where she was tutored privately. This suited her fine, and she never dreamed that her quiet life would take a dramatic turn.

It happened in 1920, when she entered the Surrey County amateur golf championship. To her surprise, she advanced to the semifinals in competition with some of Great Britain's finest players. Wethered had little desire for the fame and laurels that go with golfing greatness, but like any sportsman she enjoyed the thrill of a good competition. Thus, when a friend asked her to go with her to the English Ladies' Closed Amateur Golf Championship in June of 1920, Wethered agreed. She entered the competition, along with about 100 other contestants, and—once again to her surprise—advanced through the rounds, beating every opponent she drew.

In her first amateur championship, 19-year-old Joyce Wethered advanced to the final round and found herself pitted against defending cham-

GOLFER

"[I realized] that any disturbing personality must be shut out of my consciousness and that the game must be played against no particular opponent, but with the sole idea of producing the right figures."

Joyce Wethered prepares to make a shot during an exhibition match in New York, 1935. (UPI/Bettmann)

pion Cecil Leitch, a seasoned veteran and a formidable golfer. As the match began, Leitch took a six-stroke lead after 20 holes and seemed on the way to an easy victory. Instead, Wethered composed herself, tied the match with just two holes to go, and engineered a cool, come-from-behind win with an easy putt on the last hole. The gallery was aghast as the unknown teenager left the course, having dethroned a world-renowned champion.

Wethered's legend began then and there. She had sunk the winning putt just as a freight train lumbered by at the edge of the golf course. After the match, reporters asked her why she hadn't waited until the train passed to make her shot. Her reply: "What train?"

Lest anyone think her first British amateur championship was a fluke, Wethered returned to the competition the following year and again drew a final matchup with Leitch. While both golfers played superbly, Wethered seemed only to get stronger as Leitch faltered. A second championship was assured well before the final holes.

Wethered is widely acknowledged to be the best player of her generation. As an amateur she did not compete in America, but she won four British Open amateur championships and five consecutive English ladies' championships between 1920 and 1929. By the mid-1920s she was so well-known that she would be mobbed any time she appeared on a golf course—and the reporters followed her just as they do the stars of today. For a shy woman like Joyce Wethered, this was intolerable. She "retired" from competition in 1926 and returned to a quiet life, appearing only infrequently as a partner for her brother in mixed foursomes.

Only a truly challenging match could draw Wethered out of retirement, and such a match happened along in 1929. That year, officials announced that the British Open Amateur Championship would be played at St. Andrews golf course in Scotland—one of the most difficult courses in the world. The American champion Glenna Collett promised to be there, and golf fans everywhere anticipated a great showdown when Wethered agreed to come out of retirement to participate. Collett and Wethered had already met once, at the 1925 British amateur championship. There Wethered had defeated Collett in an early—but hard-fought—round.

The 1929 British amateur championship is considered one of the great matches in modern sports. Wethered was a near-mythic figure in the United Kingdom, but she had not played a serious competition in three years. Collett, in the meantime, had been touring regularly and winning, too. Their showdown in the final was a real nail-biter. Collett took a six-shot lead in the morning round, but Wethered battled back and went into the lead in the early afternoon. Slowly, however, Collett whittled Wethered's four-shot lead down to

JOYCE WETHERED

English golfer

Born: November 17, 1901 in England.

Career Highlights:

- won her first British national amateur championship, 1920

- won four British Open amateur championships in the 1920s

- won five consecutive English ladies' championships between 1920 and 1929.

---

a mere two shots going into the last three holes. Wethered, the consummate "cool" player, realized she would have to perform superbly in order to maintain her slender lead. She did just that, and as she sunk the winning putt, the crowd erupted into hysteria. Both she and Collett had to be carried from the throng by policemen.

Soon after that memorable victory Wethered lost her amateur status because she began working in the golf department of a noted London store. She made one barnstorming tour of America in 1935, playing exhibitions with Babe Didrickson and Gene Sarazen, but she returned to England as soon as possible and settled back into her quiet life. In 1937 she married Sir John Heathcoat-Amory and moved into his Devonshire manor house. As Lady Heathcoat-Amory she became a noted horticulturist, gradually transforming the acres around her house into a massive flower and shrubbery garden.

Most golf historians consider Wethered the best of her time. She was a cool competitor who had a knack for blocking out everything but her own performance and her objectives in critical matches. She was an excellent putter and was often supremely confident in her ability. In her sporadic decade of competition, 1920–29, she lost only two matches in tournament competition. Such consistency is hard to find in any era.

KATHY
WHITWORTH

One of the most successful and enduring golfers in history, Kathy Whitworth holds the record for most official career victories as a professional, with 88. Whitworth was a popular star performer with the Ladies' Professional Golf Association (LPGA) through the 1960s and 1970s, and she continued to win into the 1980s at a record-breaking pace. Whitworth was the first woman golfer to win a million dollars in purses—a feat that is more remarkable because she played most of her career before the days of big money prizes. She was known as an intense competitor who held herself to impossible standards and then met them, time after time.

Kathrynne Ann Whitworth was born September 27, 1939, in Monahans, Texas, but she grew up in the New Mexico ranching community of Jal. Her father owned a hardware store that catered to the oil and gas industries in and around Jal, and he also served as mayor for three terms. Her mother likewise performed many civic duties, but none of them was more important than nurturing the three Whitworth children.

A natural athlete, Whitworth discovered golf in 1954 at the age of 15. Her first outing at the local country club was not promising, but she became obsessed with the sport and talked her parents into giving her lessons. After working with the professional at the Jal Country Club, she was recommended to Harvey Penick of Austin, Texas. Penick had taught golf greats Betsy Rawls, Ben Crenshaw, and Tom Kite. Whitworth and her mother drove down to Austin from Jal for intensive three-day lessons with Penick, staying at inexpensive hotels and taking notes on paper sacks. Before long, Kathy Whitworth had blossomed.

Just three years after discovering the sport, Whitworth won the 1957 New Mexico Women's Amateur tournament and received an invitation to the prestigious Titleholders championship. She received a golf scholarship to Odessa Junior College in Texas but quit after a year to turn pro. "I couldn't afford to play a lot of amateur golf," she said. "If I was going to learn the game, I was going to have to learn it on the tour."

GOLFER

"All I ever wanted was to be the greatest woman golfer in the world."

505

Kathy Whitworth blasts out of a sand trap onto the 18th green to win the Titleholders tournament, 1966. (AP/Wide World Photos)

Learn it she did, though her early progress was slow. In her second season she earned a respectable $5,000 and was voted LPGA "most improved player." She won her first tournament, the Kelley Girl, in 1962 and went on to win at least one tournament every year for 17 consecutive seasons.

Few players did more to establish the respectability of the LPGA than Whitworth. She was the consummate professional, answering reporters' questions gracefully and performing excellent—if not emotion-free—golf. Whitworth announced her presence in the LPGA in 1965, when she won the first of seven Vare Trophies, given to the player with the best scoring average in any given year. That same year she won her first important tournament, the Titleholders. She repeated as Titleholders champion in 1966 and won her first of three LPGA championships in 1967.

Not only did Whitworth play as a member of the LPGA, she also worked for the organization, serving as its president four times. In the late 1960s and early 1970s she was named LPGA Player of the Year a phenomenal seven times and was leading money winner eight times. Her LPGA championships in 1967, 1971, and 1975 might well have included two more victories, since she was defeated in an 18-hole playoff by Sandra Post in 1968 and lost in sudden death to Shirley Englehorn in 1970. While still an active and winning player, she was inducted into the LPGA Hall of Fame in 1975.

Whitworth's career took a down turn in the late 1970s, and for a time she considered leaving the tour. Then she rebounded, winning the Coca-Cola Classic in 1981 and surpassing Mickey Wright as the winningest woman golfer with a victory at the 1982 Lady Michelob Classic. Still she pressed on, eyeing Sam Snead's record of 84 career victories. She broke that record in 1984 by winning her 85th official LPGA outing, and she went on to garner three more tournament victories.

Newsweek correspondent Pete Axthelm once wrote that Whitworth was "the quiet, gracious lady of sport," adding that her career "helped women's golf to grow into a thriving business." Indeed, Whitworth's career spanned vast changes in the LPGA, from its early years when purses were sparse and players sought the most affordable accommodations, to the days of first-class air travel and four-star hotels. Recalling her early years on the tour, Whitworth said: "We would always have a good time. There wasn't that much money involved. It was just a game back then. After a tournament, everyone kind of celebrated together. Usually, the winner would pay for the drinks because she was the only one who had any money."

Even in her fifties, Whitworth was reluctant to leave the LPGA. She finally retired in favor of seniors tournaments, but she considers golf a "lifetime commitment" that she "loves" to undertake. "Why not continue to do

KATHY WHITWORTH

American golfer

Born: September 27, 1939 in Monahans, Texas.

Education: Received a golf scholarship to Odessa Junior College in Texas, quitting after one year to turn pro.

Career Highlights:

- holds the record for most official career victories as a professional, with 88

- became the first woman golfer to win a million dollars in purses

- won the Titleholders tournament, 1965 and 1966

- won LPGA championships in 1967, 1971, and 1975.

Awards: Won seven Vare Trophies: 1965–67, 1969–72; named Associate Press Athlete of the Year, 1965 and 1967; named LPGA Player of the Year seven times: 1966–69, 1971–73; inducted into the LPGA Hall of Fame, 1975.

what you love to do, if you're successful at it and get some enjoyment out of it?" she asked. "Even if you're not as successful as some people think you should be, who cares?"

No one will ever accuse Kathy Whitworth of not being as good as she could be. She is a golfing great, one of the best, a shining example of tenacity and resolve.

DEENA
WIGGER

Deena Wigger is one of the "comeback kids" of the 1996 Olympics. Wigger, whose shooting resume fairly ripples with gold, silver, and bronze medals earned at various national and international competitions, has had nothing but disappointments where the Olympics have been concerned. She finished ninth in Seoul in 1988 and didn't even qualify for the 1992 Olympic team. Today, having put her sport into perspective, she is a winner again, most recently at the 1995 Pan American Games.

Lones Wigger, a rifle gold medalist at the 1964 and 1972 Olympics, knew early on that his daughter had a golden eye. "The first time we put [Deena] on the sandbag—she laid the rifle on a sandbag to shoot—she took a long time getting set up," he told the *Denver Post*. "She wouldn't shoot the shot until everything was perfect." After Deena, then 12, squeezed off five shots, Lones took a look at the results. "The five-shot group looked like one hole," he said. "That was a pretty good indication that she was going to do well."

Coached by her father, Deena, who was born on August 27, 1966, established a high national ranking as a teenager and qualified for the 1988 Summer Games when she was 22. There she suffered her first major upset, finishing ninth.

"I was real nervous before I went to the '88 Games and I didn't know how to deal with it," Wigger said. "I shot safe. I didn't shoot to win. I was real disappointed and started thinking, 'Here my dad did it so many times and I was too scared to do it.' I started thinking it wasn't natural for me. I didn't shoot (after that) for quite a while."

Wigger, who won a gold medal at the 1983 Pan Am Games and led her college team at Murray State University to the NCAA championships in 1987, analyzed her own shortcomings: "I was in the top two nationally for awhile. It wasn't difficult for me to make a team, to win a medal. But once you get into the leading position, you have more to lose. When you're first starting out, all you can see is what's ahead. You don't look back."

SHOOTER

"It wasn't difficult for me to make a team, to win a medal. But once you get into the leading position, you have more to lose. When you're first starting out, all you can see is what's ahead. You don't look back."

Deena Wigger practices with a .22-caliber rifle in preparation for the 1983 Pan Am Games. (AP/Wide World Photos)

Indeed, shooting is a sport won and lost on mental toughness. The sport doesn't discriminate based on height, power, or weight. Women and men compete side-by-side in collegiate competitions with no discernible differences in their scores. The discipline requires intense concentration, however, and even the competitor's own heartbeat can throw her out of contention. Olympic shooters commonly wear several layers of clothing to insulate their heartbeats.

When Wigger failed to make the 1992 U.S. Olympic team, she kept insulating her heartbeat—but she listened to her heart. She began to question her involvement as a resident athlete at the Olympic Training Center in Colorado Springs, Colorado. "All I did was shoot all the time," she told the *Fort Benning Leader*. "I was shooting seven hours a day and that became my life. Before, I had things going on and my main priority was school. And I think shooting should be a priority, but I don't think it should be the only thing you have going. I think that when that happens and you don't have a good competition, you seem to put all your self-worth into the competition."

DEENA WIGGER

American shooter

Born: August 27, 1966.

Education: Attended Murray State University.

Career Highlights:

• won gold medals, Pan Am Games, 1983 and 1995

• led her college team to the NCAA championships, 1987.

Wigger's self-doubts were magnified by her frustration at not earning any money. "You're almost stagnant for those years when you're training for the Olympics," she said. "It's like you're not making progress in other areas of your life."

The answer for her was an enlistment in the Wyoming Air National Guard in 1994, and active duty in the Air Force in 1995. While in the Air Force she will serve as an assistant coach for the Air Force Academy rifle team, with an eye on training hopefuls for the Olympics. She has said that she may attend officer candidate school or earn a master's degree.

Has the day job helped her regain her shooting edge? Absolutely. She won a second Pan Am Games gold medal in 1995, earning the U.S. a rifle slot at the 1996 Olympics. On her third attempt to ace the Summer Games, Deena Wigger may well be right on target.

ESTHER
WILLIAMS

Esther Williams never won an Olympic medal. She spent only a few years in amateur swimming competition. Nevertheless, she did more to popularize the sport of swimming than any other athlete, male or female, living or dead. Through the 1940s and 1950s, in films that showcased her aquatic ballet talents, Williams *was* American swimming. She made the sport look simultaneously sexy, artistic, and downright fun.

Pure luck and her mother's persistence paved the way for Williams's swimming career. Esther was born in 1923 in Inglewood, California, and was the youngest of five children. Her mother, a teacher and social worker, campaigned successfully to have a municipal playground constructed in the neighborhood. The playground—complete with swimming pool—was located right across the street from the Williams home. Young Esther soon took advantage of its proximity, earning free swimming time by collecting and counting locker room towels.

Williams soon began participating in swim meets, and in her early teens she joined the prestigious Los Angeles Athletic Club. At 17 she achieved national prominence by winning every race she entered at the 1939 Women's Outdoor Swimming Nationals. She took the gold medal in the 100-meter freestyle, won as part of the 300-meter and 800-yard relays, and set a national record for the 100-meter breast stroke. Her performance at the nationals earned her a berth on the 1940 Olympic team, but the 1940 Summer Games were cancelled due to World War II.

In that era many competitors in amateur sports were independently wealthy. While the Williams family was comfortable financially, Esther simply did not find it feasible to continue swimming as an amateur. Uncommonly beautiful and cheerful, she found work modeling sportswear at Magnin's, one of Los Angeles's biggest department stores. Later in 1940 she auditioned for Billy Rose's Aquacade, a traveling swimming show. To her surprise, she was hired not just as a chorus line swimmer but as a star. She spent the following eight months touring with the show, co-starring with another well-known swimmer/actor, Johnny Weissmuller (famed for his work in *Tarzan* movies).

Esther Williams dazzles an audience at the Sahara night club in Las Vegas, 1954. (UPI/Bettmann)

ESTHER WILLIAMS

American swimmer and performer

Born: August 8, 1923 in Inglewood, California.

Career Highlights:
- won gold medals in every race she entered—100-meter freestyle, 300-meter and 800-yard relays, and 100-meter breast stroke—at the Women's Outdoor Swimming Nationals, 1939
- earned a position as performer for Billy Rose's Aquacade, a traveling swimming show, 1940
- made a number of swimming movies for M-G-M, 1940s and 1950s.

When the Aquacade folded in 1941, Williams found herself besieged by Hollywood talent scouts who predicted she would have a brilliant future in films. She found the idea far-fetched. "I can't sing, I can't dance, I can't act," she told the studio heads. Finally she signed a contract with Metro-Goldwyn-Mayer because that studio allowed her a six-month preparation period. She trained in speech and acting, and she took singing and dancing lessons.

All of the formal preparation for film work was fine, but Williams already had the essential talent she would need to become a Hollywood star—she could swim, and swim beautifully. Although she made a number of non-swimming movies for M-G-M in the 1940s and 1950s, it was her swimming films that made her a star. These loosely-plotted but gorgeously photographed musicals—among them *Bathing Beauty* (1944), *Easy to Wed* (1946), *On an Island with You* (1948) and *Million Dollar Mermaid* (1952)—were vastly popular not only in America but also abroad, especially in India and the Middle East. As for Williams's star quality, one *New York Herald Tribune* writer summed it up thus: "Miss Williams is no actress, but she is extraordinarily graceful when she gets in the drink."

Esther Williams's career rose and fell with the popularity of the big-budget Hollywood musical. As the 1960s progressed, she settled down to manage the many businesses and investments she had made with her profits from her films. She lived in California with her third husband, Fernando Lamas, until he died of cancer in 1982.

Williams lent her presence to the nostalgic *That's Entertainment* films, one of which showcased some of her more elaborate water ballets. At the height of her popularity in the late 1940s and early 1950s, she was one of the top earners in Hollywood, but her influence stretches far beyond that. Williams glamorized swimming, especially synchronized swimming, turning an athletic endeavor into an artistic pursuit. She might not have been able to act, dance, or sing very well, but she could swim—and she made the world want to swim along with her.

HELEN
WILLS

In the 1920s, women who wished to compete in the Olympics were labeled "unfeminine" and accused of interfering with manly endeavors. Such sports as running and swimming were considered too strenuous for the delicate female physique, and nasty remarks flew whenever women tried to challenge those assumptions. Helen Wills helped put those unfair stereotypes to an end. A refined, upper class lady who wore eyeshadow during her tennis matches, Wills drew headlines as "Queen Helen," the national tennis champion who made sports an acceptable pastime for American women.

Wills won seven U.S. singles championships between 1923 and 1931 and four doubles titles in the same period. It took her a mere 30 minutes to beat her opponent in the 1924 Olympics for a gold medal. In the days when women's sports were accorded almost no press coverage whatsoever, she brought women's tennis its first high-profile rivalry when she faced off against Helen Jacobs. Before Helen Wills, "nice girls" didn't play sports. After Wills, women played, and won, big time.

Wills was born in Berkeley, California, in 1905. Her father was a prominent and quite wealthy doctor who had strong opinions about the benefits of vigorous exercise. Although young Helen was often discouraged from making friends her own age, she was allowed to play tennis at the fashionable Berkeley Tennis Club. She quickly became so good at the sport that her father arranged for private lessons. Her coaches were amazed at her persistence—stories abound of her practicing a single shot more than a thousand times in one afternoon.

Wills won her first U.S. singles championship in 1923 at the age of 18. The following year, as repeat American champion she was invited to participate in the 1924 Olympics. Reporters dubbed her "Little Miss Poker Face" and "Queen Helen," and sure enough she showed who ruled when she arrived in Paris for the Olympics. She won the gold medal by defeating her opponent in straight sets. She added another gold in doubles play. Smashing the resistance to women in sports, she returned to America a bona fide heroine.

TENNIS PLAYER

Dubbed "Queen Helen" by the press, Helen Wills defied the conventional wisdom of her era, proving that even "nice girls" could play sports—and win.

Helen Wills practices in New York, working toward a successful return to the tennis circuit after back injuries sidelined her for two years. (AP/Wide World Photos)

It would be many years before tennis would return to the Olympics as an official sport. After 1924, the Olympic Committee removed both men's and women's tennis from the roster of sanctioned sports. So for many, many years, Helen Wills's two gold medals gave her Olympic bragging rights in the tennis community.

Another American named Helen rose to challenge Wills as the 1920s ended. Helen Jacobs made no secret of her desire to dethrone the "tennis queen." The two met at the U.S. Championships at Forest Hills, New York, in 1927, where Wills was the defending champion. What the press and public did not know on that occasion was that Wills had suffered a back injury and was trying to play through the pain. She went on with the match, losing the first set 8-6 and winning the second 6-3. Then the pain became so severe that she could no longer answer Jacobs's shots. With Jacobs leading 3-0 in the final set, Wills mumbled some words to the umpire and left the court.

HELEN WILLS

American tennis player

Born: October 6, 1905 in Centreville, California.

Career Highlights:

- won U.S. Open singles championships, 1923–25, 1927–29, and 1931; doubles, 1922, 1924, 1925, and 1928; and mixed doubles, 1924 and 1928
- earned gold medals in singles and doubles competition, 1924 Olympic Games, Paris, France
- won Wimbledon singles titles, 1927–30, 1932, 1933, 1935, and 1938; doubles titles, 1924, 1927, and 1930; and mixed doubles, 1929
- won French Open singles crowns, 1928–30 and 1932; and doubles, 1930 and 1932.

Awards: Inducted into the Tennis Hall of Fame, 1969.

To all outward appearances, Wills had simply quit rather than suffer the inevitable defeat. Only later, when the news of her serious spinal injury finally made it into the papers, did the fans understand what had really happened that day at Forest Hills. Most observers felt Wills would never return to competitive tennis, and indeed for two years she was out of the game. Then, in 1929 she returned—in time to face Helen Jacobs yet again at the Wimbledon finals.

This time Wills was healthy but out of practice in top-level tournament play. Somehow she managed to stay alive, however, and in the final against Jacobs she came from behind to win the match. She later described that victory as one of the most satisfying of her career.

Wills married in the early 1930s and retired from tennis at mid-decade. Her effect on women's sports had been nothing less than phenomenal. Almost singlehandedly she created an interest in women's athletics, while simultaneously providing a role model of the feminine competitor. Her success is significant even judged by today's standards. Judged by the standards of her own era, she was just what the press called her—a queen.

KATARINA WITT

"When you are on the ice and the audience is with you and you can hear the music and express the music, it is so much more than a sport."

A *Sports Illustrated* reporter once described her as "12-car-pile-up-gorgeous," and few would dispute that description of Katarina Witt. One of the most beautiful and engaging performers ever to take the ice, Witt was also one of the most successful skaters in terms of medals and championships. She was the first skater since 1936 to win gold medals in back-to-back Olympics, and her five world championships and six European championships placed her in the company of legendary figure skaters Peggy Fleming and Sonja Henie. Witt's ability to charm an audience was her strongest suit through a long amateur career in which she represented communist East Germany. That same infectious personality has served her well since then as an Emmy Award–winning professional and director of her own ice skating show.

Witt was born December 3, 1965, in Karl-Marx-Stadt, East Germany. At the time of her birth, East Germany was an "Iron Curtain" country, controlled by a communist government. Far from feeling repressed by the regime, Witt has always maintained that she could not have become a skater in America or any other capitalistic nation. Her parents held middle class jobs and could never have afforded to pay for the expensive training, costumes, and travel required of a competitive skater. Witt never had to worry about the cost of anything. The government paid all of her expenses and even provided her with a much-coveted house and car.

Witt's training as a world-class skater began when she was five years old at the Kuechwald rink in her local neighborhood. After begging her parents for lessons, she joined a class that had already made a half-year of progress. "The teacher said I would have to learn as much in half a year as the others learned in a year," she recalled in a book entitled *Great Skates*. "I did that."

At ten Witt caught the eye of noted East German coach Jutta Mueller. Mueller not only took over as Katarina's skating coach, she also sought to control every aspect of the youngster's life. The spirited Witt often chafed under the many rules and regulations, but she remained under Mueller's supervision, skating six hours a day, 11 months out of each year. Off the ice, Mueller

Katarina Witt, two-time Olympic gold medalist, strikes a pose during an exhibition number in Paris, 1988. (AP/Wide World Photos)

worked on Witt's appearance, deciding how she wore her hair and makeup, and what costumes were appropriate for competition. More important, Mueller taught Witt how to use her flirtatious personality to captivate judges and audiences alike.

In 1980, when she was 14, Witt finished tenth in the world championships. She improved quickly after that and, in 1982, won the first of six consecutive European championships. That same year she finished second to American Elaine Zayak at the world championships. By 1984 she was ready and able to claim her share of the skating limelight.

Witt had never won a world championship when she entered the 1984 Olympics in Sarajevo, Yugoslavia. Nevertheless, she was considered a favorite to win a medal at the Winter Games. Her main competition was Rosalind Sumners of the United States. Witt trailed Sumners after the compulsory figures, but she gained ground in the short program and—with a flawlessly skated long routine done to a medley of American show tunes—she won the Olympic gold medal over Sumners by one-tenth of a point.

No figure skater had won back-to-back Olympic gold medals since Sonja Henie did it in the 1930s, but Witt decided to try. She won the European championship in 1984 and 1985 and the world championship in 1985. An upset victory by American Debi Thomas in the 1986 world championships brought Witt just the rivalry she needed to renew her fighting spirit, and she entered the 1988 Olympics in top form.

The competition between Thomas and Witt at the 1988 Olympics in Calgary, Canada, was affectionately known as "the dueling Carmens," since both skaters chose music from the opera *Carmen* for their long programs. Thomas was thought to have an edge in the medal race. She was more athletic, jumped higher, and attempted more difficult moves during her routines. Witt had her own strengths, however—style and artistic interpretation. In the end, her dramatic "dying Carmen" long program, although conservatively skated, brought her a second Olympic gold.

In 1988 Witt won her final world championship and turned professional. She teamed up with 1988 Olympic male gold medalist Brian Boitano and made several television specials with him, including *Canvas of Ice* and *Carmen on Ice*. The latter show brought Witt an Emmy Award in the category of classical music/dance. Witt and Boitano then undertook a live national tour in 1990. It proved so successful that they formed a small ice show under their own direction and named it *Katarina Witt and Brian Boitano—Skating*.

Prior to the 1994 Olympics, a rule change occurred that allowed professional skaters to compete in the Winter Games. Witt jumped at the chance

KATARINA WITT

German figure skater

Born: December 3, 1965 in Karl-Marx-Stadt, East Germany.

Career Highlights:

- won six consecutive European championships, 1982–87
- earned gold medal, 1984 Olympic Games, Sarajevo, Yugoslavia

- won world championships, 1984, 1985, 1987 and 1988
- earned a second consecutive gold medal, 1988 Olympic Games, Calgary, Canada.

Awards: Won an Emmy Award in the category of classical music/dance for the television special *Carmen on Ice,* 1988.

to vie for yet another medal, and although her performance at the 1994 Winter Games was overshadowed by younger performers such as Nancy Kerrigan and Oksana Baiul, she still finished a respectable seventh in the competition. Since then she has enjoyed the busy life of a celebrity, earning money from ice shows and product endorsements in Germany and America.

Witt once said that the secret to her success was that she always chose one man in the audience during competition and then skated for him as if in an act of love. This novel approach might explain part of her vast popularity—after she won her first Olympic gold medal she received 35,000 fan letters, many of which contained marriage proposals. Charm was only one component of her talent, however. While she always observed that competition should be more than "skate-jump, skate-jump, skate-jump," she could skate and jump with the best of them. She simply preferred to let her artistry speak for itself—and it did, making her the most successful and best-known skater of modern times.

HILLARY
WOLF

*"As a little kid I
showed no mercy.
And in judo,
especially in judo,
you need that
confidence, that
meanness, that show
no mercy."*

What happens to little girls who think ballet is boring, and who like to fight? They could go into acting and star in a series of movies, as Hillary Wolf has done. Or they could take up judo and become national champions in their weight class . . . as Hillary Wolf has done. Wolf, who is the top-ranked American woman in her weight class in judo, is a teenager who has successfully mounted a dual career while still in high school. Some fans will recognize her as Macaulay Culkin's older sister in the *Home Alone* movies. Others may get to know her when the Olympics roll around and she is there, taking her opponents to the mat.

Wolf, who lives in Chicago, began her sporting career as many youngsters do, by taking ballet lessons. She quickly decided that she wasn't "doing anything" in dancing class, that the pace was simply too slow for her energy level. Instead she followed her older brother to judo lessons, and there she found a niche. As of 1996 she had been involved in the sport for 11 years.

Judo was a sideline for Wolf throughout much of her childhood and early teens. Interested in acting—although not formally trained—she was able to land roles in almost a dozen feature films. Her first was *A Matter of Principle,* starring Alan Arkin. She has also appeared in several made-for-television movies, including *Big Girls Don't Cry*. Her most memorable part, however, was that of the obnoxious older sister in *Home Alone* and *Home Alone II*. "I've never taken any acting lessons," Wolf explained in *Newsday*. "I never was in a school play. I don't think there's any job that has easier money than acting."

Wolf did not have a chance to utter the immortal Culkin primal scream—"Aaaaaaahhhhhh!"—in *Home Alone*. Her sport gives her ample opportunity to bellow, however, and there she has ascended to the top ranks. In 1995 she won the world junior championship in the 48-kilogram (106-pound) class, after having been a four-time U.S. judo junior national champion. She is the first American ever to capture a gold medal in the world junior judo championships.

HILLARY WOLF

American judoist

Born: C. 1978.

Career Highlights:
- won U.S. judo junior national championship four times
- won the world junior championship in the 48-kilogram (106-pound) class, becoming the first American ever to capture a gold medal in the world junior judo championships, 1995.

As Wolf prepares for competition in the Olympics and in judo's senior ranks, it is safe to say that she made the right career choice back when she was five. "As a little kid I showed no mercy," she said. "And in judo, especially in judo, you need that confidence, that meanness, that show no mercy. . . . It's been like I really wanted to fight."

LYNETTE WOODARD

"Everybody has a talent. Whatever you do, do it to the hilt! . . . Whether somebody encourages you or discourages you. In season, out of season. And wonderful, wonderful things will happen to you. You might play for the Harlem Globetrotters."

Making a living playing basketball has always been hard for American women. Lynette Woodard made a success of it by playing for the Harlem Globetrotters. Woodard joined the Globetrotters—America's premier comic basketball team—in 1985, becoming the first woman to play big-time professional basketball on a men's team. For Woodard, a former gold medal Olympian and basketball coach, the Globetrotters presented the opportunity she had always yearned for: to play side-by-side with men as an equal partner.

A native of Wichita, Kansas, Woodard began her devotion to basketball at a very young age. She and her older brother Darrell played "sockball" at home, sometimes joined by their fireman father. "We'd roll up socks for a ball and shoot off the bedroom door," she recalled in *People*. Although Woodard's parents were not particularly athletic, she had important role models in her extended family. Her cousin, Hubie "Geese" Ausbie, was a member of the Harlem Globetrotters. "Geese showed us how to spin a basketball on our fingers and do all those Globetrotter tricks," Woodard said. "It was a joy to my heart."

Woodard watched her famous cousin both on and off the court, practicing his moves until she could do them as well. She was also a serious student of basketball who grew to the enviable height of five-foot-eleven. While a student at Wichita North High School, she led the women's basketball team to two consecutive state championships with an impressive record of 59 wins and 3 losses. Heavily recruited by college basketball coaches, she decided to stay in state and attend the University of Kansas at Lawrence.

During her four years at UK, Woodard scored 3,649 points, an average of 26.3 points per game and an NCAA women's record. She eventually broke 24 of the 32 records the NCAA kept regarding women's basketball. Not only was she a star on the court, she was also a dedicated student, earning a degree in speech/communications and being named a four-time academic and athletic All American. She was the first UK student ever to have a jersey number retired at the end of her college career.

Lynette Woodard appears in full Harlem Globetrotter regalia after being named the first woman to play on this professional team, 1985. (UPI/Bettmann)

In 1980 Woodard was named to the U.S. national basketball team in preparation for the Summer Olympics. To her great disappointment, then-President Jimmy Carter decided to boycott the Olympics in protest of the Soviet Union's invasion of Afghanistan. Deprived of her opportunity to be an Olympian, Woodard went back to college and graduated in 1981. Then she spent a year in Schio, Italy, where she was the only English-speaking player on a company-sponsored women's league team. Although she received good wages for her participation on the team, Woodard did not lose her amateur status. The team's once-a-week schedule gave her ample spare time.

Like many American women compelled to play basketball abroad, Woodard was very lonely and isolated in Italy. When she arrived she did not know the language, and she was homesick for her family and friends in America. The experience, she told the *New York Times,* "taught me a lot. I had to really search inside. I got a chance to see myself. I had been in a structure all my life, and I was out for the first time, and here I was standing in nowhere land. I think it really helped me grow as a person. I learned to appreciate a lot more things. Even though it was difficult, deep down in my heart I'm really grateful for the experience."

Woodard returned to the United States in 1982 to work at UK as an academic advisor and volunteer assistant basketball coach. She also trained in preparation for the 1984 Olympic team tryouts. During the summers of 1982 and 1983 she traveled all over the world with Team U.S.A., and when the final 1984 Olympic team was chosen she was named its captain. As the leader of perhaps one of the best American women's basketball teams ever assembled, Woodard was instrumental in the Americans' 1984 gold medal victory.

After the Olympics Woodard was literally a woman without a team. Never mind that she had helped bring gold medal glory to America; there was no place for her to play professionally in the United States. Woodard returned to UK as an assistant coach, but a new idea dawned in her head: she asked her cousin Ausbie to inquire about possibilities with the Globetrotters. Just six weeks later she read in the newspaper that the famous comedy team would indeed recruit a female player to help revive sagging ticket sales. Woodard was determined to be that player.

Woodard attended several Globetrotters tryout camps over the summer and early autumn of 1985. She was one of ten finalists, and then was named the newest Globetrotter in October 1985. Team manager Earl Duryea told the *New York Times* that all of the finalists were excellent players, but that Woodard was "a 10 in a group of 9 3/4's."

LYNETTE WOODARD

American basketball player

Born: C. 1959 in Wichita, Kansas.

Education: Attended the University of Kansas at Lawrence, earning a degree in speech/communications and graduating in 1981.

Career Highlights:
- scored 3,649 points during four years of college basketball, an average of 26.3 points per game and an NCAA women's record

- played professional basketball in Italy, 1981–82
- led U.S. team (as captain) to gold medal, 1984 Olympic Games, Los Angeles, California
- played professional basketball with the Globetrotters, 1985–87.

Awards: Named four-time academic and athletic All-American during college; won Wade Trophy, awarded to best woman basketball player in the U.S., 1981.

Woodard was thrilled. "It's a wonderful feeling. I'm so excited I can't hide it," she told *Jet*. "... I'm here and there's a lot of work to be done. I'm just going to blend in and let it flow."

Blend in she did, beginning as a "hopper," or straight ball player who helped the comic players set up their routines. Gradually she was given her own chance to play the comic, and the crowds loved seeing her out there on the court. Her outgoing personality meshed well with the male Globetrotters, and—other than having her own dressing room prior to exhibitions—she was treated as any member of the team. Woodard explained her enthusiasm for the Globetrotters in a *Los Angeles Times* profile. "It's entertainment," she said. "I see laughter and smiles on people's faces. They come in and they're happy. There are so many terrible things happening in the world. You can make people forget about their problems just for a couple hours. That's good. . . . You see those little kids. Those eyes sparkle. And I know their hearts, because that used to be me. They want that autograph."

Woodard spent two seasons traveling with the Globetrotters and then quit the team. Over time she found that the contract she signed was just too binding, leaving her no time to pursue product endorsement deals or other moneymaking opportunities. After leaving the team in 1987 she returned to UK as a basketball coach. She also made some instructional videos and appeared as a motivational speaker.

Before Lynette Woodard, no woman had ever played professional basketball on a day-to-day basis alongside men. She broke a barrier, and the Globetrotters at least have had women performers ever since. As for the future of women's basketball, Woodard told the *New York Times:* "I don't know how long it will take, but a woman will play in the N.B.A. I want people to see me play with the Globetrotters and say a woman could also have the ability to play in the N.B.A."

MICKEY WRIGHT

"I knew if I did it as well as I could, I would win. If I did as well as I could, it would have been better than anybody else did it, and therefore it would win."

When people talk about great golf technique, Mickey Wright's name invariably pops up. Wright was a star of the LPGA tour in the late 1950s and early 1960s, and she helped the fledgling Ladies' Professional Golf Association to increase its stature and popularity. A perfectionist who was often haunted by her anxieties, Wright won more tournaments in a shorter time than any of her contemporaries. She was LPGA champion in 1958, 1960, 1961, and 1963 and is the only woman in golfing history to have held four major American titles at one time.

Born Mary Kathryn Wright in San Diego, California, she was raised under prosperous circumstances in the picturesque California town of La Jolla. Her father, an attorney, perhaps imbued her with some of his competitive spirit—he once rode a horse from the Midwest through the Rocky Mountains all the way to the West Coast. Her grandmother was the first woman pharmacist in Illinois, and her grandfather had been an inventor. Mickey herself was drawn to golf from an early age, and she was given all the lessons and course time she needed to develop. Among the teaching pros who helped to shape her legendary swing were Johnny Bellante, Harry Pressler, and Les Bolstad.

At the age of 13 Wright won her first major victory—the Southern California Girls' Junior championship. Three years later, in 1952, she won the U.S. Girls' Junior championship. She moved on into women's amateur competition the next season, and in 1954 she finished fourth in the U.S. Women's Open. Babe Didrikson Zaharias, the winner of that tournament, quipped to the young Wright: "What are you doing, copying my swing?"

Wright had no need to copy anyone's swing—her own was top rate. She practiced incessantly and—with the help of her coaches—developed one of the best technical swings of any woman golfer in history. In 1955 the exuberant Wright turned professional, joined the LPGA, and announced to the world that she planned to be "the best woman golfer in the world some day." Many teenagers make such lofty predictions, but few actually see them materialize. Wright had the talent and the determination to make her dreams come true.

Mickey Wright birdies her second hole in a row during the Dallas Civitan Open Golf tournament in 1965. (AP/Wide World Photos)

From 1958 through 1964 Wright was *the* woman golfer in America. She won well over 50 tournaments, including four U.S. Women's Open titles, four LPGA championships, the Western Women's Open titles, and two Titleholders victories. In one heady period between 1960 and 1962, she held all four major titles—the Open, the LPGA championship, the Western Open, and the Titleholders—simultaneously. Sadly, her earnings during those years were only a fraction of what they might have been in more recent times.

The most popular golfer on the women's tour, Wright was under enormous pressure to perform, as well as to serve as an LPGA spokesperson. She kept a busy schedule of tournaments and speaking engagements, finding little time to rest and regroup. Inevitably the toll began to tell on her game, and when she injured her wrist just prior to the U.S. Women's Open in 1965, she decided to retire and return to college.

"The main emotion going into any new season was fear," she recalled in *The Illustrated History of Women's Golf.* "Every season, just every season. It was the fear that no matter how good the previous year had been, this year would not be as good, and the pressure to win that first tournament was unbelievable." She continued: "It's really like a monkey on your back. You have to get it off at some point because it really wears you out. If you spend your life trying to impress or please other people, it's a tremendous strain because you can't do it. Nothing is ever enough. I think I spent my whole golf life that way."

The game kept calling Wright, however. She simply could not turn her back on it. She returned to the tour in 1966 and finished second in the LPGA championship. Further wrist and foot injuries eroded her play at the end of the decade, and she retired again in 1971. Even so, she occasionally emerged as a tournament entrant, winning the 1973 Colgate-Dinah Shore championship and participating in the 1979 Coca-Cola Classic. In the 1980s she appeared from time to time in Legends of Golf tournaments. Otherwise she was content to play recreational golf and tend her Florida property with its population of wild shore birds.

Betsy Rawls, tournament director for the LPGA, is one of the many professionals who think Wright may have been the best woman golfer of all time. "She set a standard of shot-making that will probably never be equalled," Rawls told the *Illustrated History of Women's Golf.* "Mickey's swing was as flawless as a golf swing can be—smooth, efficient, powerful, rhythmical, and beautiful. Her shots were something to behold. . . . She contacted the ball at precisely the right point in the arc of the swing and with such clubhead speed that no shot was impossible for her. She was a spectacular golfer to watch."

How great was Wright? She still holds the 18-hole scoring record for two competitive rounds of 62, both shot in the mid-1960s. As for her stellar

MICKEY WRIGHT

American golfer

Born: February 14, 1935 in San Diego, California.

Career Highlights:

- won the LPGA championship in 1958, 1960, 1961, and 1963

- earned U.S. Women's Open titles, 1958, 1959, 1961, and 1964

- won the Western Women's Open title, 1962, 1963, and 1966

- achieved Titleholders victories, 1961 and 1962

- held all four major titles—the Open, the LPGA championship, the Western Open, and the Titleholders—simultaneously, becoming the only woman in golfing history to have done so

- won the Colgate-Dinah Shore championship, 1973.

career with the LPGA, Wright remembers the pressures of the tour as well as the pleasures of her many victories. "The perfectionist bit in golf doesn't have as much to do with doing it perfectly as the total rejection and horror of doing it badly," she said. "And I don't know which comes first, or which is more important. Winning really never crossed my mind that much. It's trite, but I knew if I did it as well as I could, I would win. If I did as well as I could, it would have been better than anybody else did it, and therefore it would win." She added: "I look back on it like it's somebody else. It's like a dream, another life. What amazes me is that I could have done it as long as I did."

KRISTI
YAMAGUCHI

"I've never thought of myself as a Henie or a Heiss. They are legends. But it's an honor that people are talking about me and those things."

At five feet tall and weighing just 93 pounds, Kristi Yamaguchi hardly seems imposing. Tiny as she is, however, she is a giant in the sport of figure skating. The 1992 Olympic gold medalist, Yamaguchi demonstrated her artistry in a spectacular, near-flawless performance that evoked memories of her personal hero, Dorothy Hamill. Yamaguchi's 1991 world championship and 1992 Olympic gold did more than just bring new laurels to these shores, though. Her success was a fabulous achievement for Asian Americans, a minority group that often receives little recognition for athletic achievement in this country.

Yamaguchi is a fourth-generation Japanese American who was born and raised in California. Early in her career, reporters were often surprised that she spoke such good English. In fact, as one of three children of a dentist and a medical secretary, she never spoke anything else.

Both of Yamaguchi's parents were among the 120,000 Japanese Americans who spent time in internment camps during World War II. Jim Yamaguchi was four when his family was taken from its California ranch and sent to a relocation camp in Arizona. For three years he lived behind a fence. Carole Yamaguchi was born in a Colorado camp, even while her father, George Doi, was stationed in Europe with the U.S. Army.

"My grandfather [Doi] didn't talk much about World War II, but he let me know how proud he was to see me make it as an Asian American representing the United States," Yamaguchi told the *Chicago Tribune* in 1992. "My parents let us know how fortunate we are now. Otherwise, they really don't look back on [internment] too much. It was just a time of a lot of fear in the country."

Kristi was born July 12, 1971, with a foot deformity. Both of her feet pointed inward, necessitating plaster casts reinforced with metal bars that forced her feet into the proper position. She learned to walk in the casts as a baby, and when they were removed she had to wear corrective shoes. Carole Yamaguchi told the *San Jose Mercury News:* "It was in part because of that that

Kristi Yamaguchi waves from the winner's podium after winning the gold medal in singles figure skating at the 1992 Olympics in Albertville, France. (Reuters/Bettmann)

KRISTI **YAMAGUCHI**   533

I wanted [Kristi] to get involved in things involving her legs and feet, like dancing and skating. That, and the fact that she really liked skating."

When Kristi was four she watched Dorothy Hamill win a gold medal in the 1976 Olympics. She fell in love with Hamill *and* her sport. "I had my Dorothy doll and I took it with me everywhere," Yamaguchi explained in the *St. Paul Pioneer Press*. By that time Yamaguchi was already taking skating lessons, and she quickly became very serious about them. "When I look back on it, I worked incredibly hard for a little kid," she recalled in the *Mercury News*. "I would not get off the ice until I did some particular move right or until I did something a certain number of times. From the time I was six, I kept bugging my mom, 'Let's go skating, let's go skating.' "

By the time she turned 11, Yamaguchi was one of those skaters who arrived at the rink at 5:00 a.m. and skated for five hours before doing her school work with a private tutor. The few spare hours in the day were devoted to dance lessons or homework—she had very little social life and counted as friends the other skaters she knew. Her equally dedicated mother served as manager, chauffeur, travel agent, music consultant, press spokeswoman, and liaison between coaches and teachers.

In 1982 Yamaguchi's coach, Jim Hulick, paired her with 13-year-old Rudy Galindo. They were a fitting match: both were small and not exceptionally strong, but they had a flair for performance and a strong work ethic. They clicked, and in 1986 they won a bronze medal at the world junior figure skating championships. The next year they took the gold medal. In 1988, their first year competing against adult skaters, they finished fifth at the national championships. They became national champions in 1989, the same year they finished fifth in the worlds.

Hulick's death in 1989 brought new challenges for the Yamaguchi-Galindo partnership. Yamaguchi decided that she wanted to train as a singles skater in Edmonton, Alberta, with Christy Kjarsgaard Ness. That more or less forced Galindo to relocate to Edmonton as well, a development he did not like. Nevertheless, the pair won the 1990 national title and again placed fifth at the world championships. Yamaguchi decided later that year that she wanted to train alone. "I started as a single skater and did pairs just for fun," she explained in the *Detroit Free Press*. "It was clear to me that if I was going to make great improvements in one or the other, I had to drop one."

Free to devote herself to singles programs, Yamaguchi quickly developed into a world champion skater. She had always competed as a solo artist—and had even won a 1989 silver medal at the national championships, behind Jill Trenary. Over the next two years she continued to settle for silver in the nationals, in 1990 behind Trenary and in 1991 behind Tonya Harding.

KRISTI YAMAGUCHI

American figure skater

Born: July 12, 1971 in Hayward, California.

Career Highlights:
- skated with Rudy Galindo, winning a bronze medal in pairs skating at the world junior figure skating championships, 1986; the gold medal at junior worlds, 1987; the gold medal at the national championships, 1989 and 1990

- won silver medal in singles competition, national championships, 1989, 1990, and 1991

- captured gold medal in singles, world championships, 1991

- earned gold medal in singles competition, 1992 Olympic Games, Albertville, France.

Yamaguchi's chances got a boost when compulsory figures were dropped from most competitions. Her talents lay in artistic interpretation rather than technical expertise, and with the new emphasis in that direction she soon ascended new heights.

A new routine based on the Spanish music "Malaguena" worked to near perfection at the 1991 world championships in Munich, Germany, and Yamaguchi broke through her string of second-place finishes to capture the world title. In doing so, she even garnered her first perfect 6.0 mark for artistic impression. Her newfound stardom made her a hero to Asian Americans, and it also made her an odds-on favorite for the 1992 Winter Olympics in Albertville, France.

She did not disappoint. Entering the Olympic Games as the reigning national and world champion, she skated a flawless short program and—despite a fall—took a commanding lead after the long program. Beaming with pride as she received her gold medal, she told the press: "I'm a little surprised everything happened to me so fast. I've dreamed of it ever since I was a little girl and first put a pair of skates on. To think that it came true. . . . *Wow!*"

The "dream come true" has continued for Yamaguchi since she turned professional in September of 1992. She is a sought-after star for product endorsements, and she has appeared in numerous ice shows, both live and for television. Despite the immense demands of business and touring, Yamaguchi says she hasn't changed and that she still absolutely loves to skate. "I'm just an athlete," she said. "It's still funny to have other people fussing over your hair, pretending you're a model for a day. I still feel I'm the same old kid, and someone who still wants to be one."

SHEILA
YOUNG

"My sports have been terrific to me. Sure, I've paid the price— you have to do that to get to the top. But it was worth it. I wouldn't trade places with anybody."

In the days before women got their share of the sports limelight, there was Sheila Young. Young was a world champion cyclist *and* a gold medal Olympic speed skater—the kind of athlete who today could retire on her endorsement contracts alone. In the 1970s, however, Young lived a spartan existence, trained on frozen ponds, and got more recognition in foreign countries than she did at home. Few have equalled her achievements, however. She was a truly great sportswoman.

Born in the Detroit suburb of Birmingham, Michigan, Young entered sports reluctantly. Although she taught herself to ride a two-wheel bike when she was four, she did not care for winter sports and had to be bribed to go skating with her father and siblings. Finally, when she was nine years old, she caught the speed skating bug. Her older sister was also involved in the sport, so they trained together on the frozen lakes and public rinks outside of Detroit.

As she got older, Young got better and better at speed skating. As a junior national champion, she met coach Peter Schotting, who predicted she could be a world champion if she trained with him for just a year. She took the challenge, plunging into a rigorous exercise and conditioning regimen that included hours of skating, running—and cycling. The cycling was necessitated by the change of seasons. Young simply did not have a rink to skate on in the summertime. What she discovered, however, was that she could dominate cycling the same way she was learning to dominate skating.

In 1973 Young accomplished what no other American athlete had ever done before. She won world championships in two completely different sports. She took a gold medal in the 500-meter sprint at the world speed skating championships, and she forged a dramatic victory in cycle track racing later that year in San Sebastian, Spain. In her cycle race, she completed the final race after having suffered a number of serious cuts and lacerations during a qualifying round. The cuts were serious enough to warrant her withdrawal from the race, but she told the doctors: "Paste me together!" and she kept competing. Her reward was a world championship.

Sheila Young skates her way to a silver medal in the 1,500-meter event at the 1976 Winter Olympics. (AP/Wide World Photos)

Young competed in the 1972 Olympics as a sprint skater, failing to win a bronze medal by a mere 8/100 of a second. In 1976 she would not be denied. At the Innsbruck Winter Games she won a gold medal in the 500 meter, a silver in the 1500 meter, and a bronze in the 1000 meter—making her the first American of either gender to win three medals in one Winter Olympics.

Nowadays such a spectacle of athletic superiority would bring fabulous monetary rewards, and fame far and wide. For Young, competing successfully in two different sports required great sacrifices of time and money, with little if any compensation after she won. Her success as a speed skater is even more remarkable given the vast disparity in training facilities and financial subsidies between America and the Soviet Union. The odds were against Young before she even strapped on her skates, but just as in her cycle racing she was not about to be denied.

Still, at times the athlete couldn't help but express some frustration—especially about the fact that in her day cycle racing was not an Olympic sport.

SHEILA YOUNG

American cyclist & speedskater

Born: October 14, 1950 in Birmingham, Michigan.

Career Highlights:

- won world championships in two completely different sports: took a gold medal in the 500-meter sprint at the world speed skating championships, and forged a dramatic victory at cycle track racing world championships, accomplishing what no other American athlete had ever done before, 1973

- won speedskating gold medal in the 500 meter, a silver in the 1500 meter, and a bronze in the 1000 meter, 1976 Olympic Games, Innsbruck, Austria, becoming first American of either gender to win three medals in one Winter Olympics.

In the book *Golden Girls,* she explained her position. "I'm proud of my sports," she said. "I get a lot of recognition in other countries. I wish my sports were bigger here, but not for the glory. I wish they were recognized more because people are missing a chance to see how exciting they are."

The public finally has caught on. Top speed skaters train at state-of-the-art facilities, with stipends from U.S. Skating. If they win they can hope to attract contracts for product endorsements and personal appearances. Women's cycling is now an Olympic sport, giving extra opportunities to female athletes. All of this has come too late for Sheila Young, but it is doubtful that anyone will ever surpass her dual-sport achievements.

"My sports have been terrific to me," Young once said. "Sure, I've paid the price—you have to do that to get to the top. But it was worth it. I wouldn't trade places with anybody."

KIM ZMESKAL

GYMNAST

Her coach called her the "little pumpkin," but there was nothing small about Kim Zmeskal's achievements. Zmeskal did something extraordinary, and all-too-rare for American women: she captured a gold medal in the 1991 world championships all-around competition. The following year, on the eve of the Olympics, she earned individual gold medals in floor exercise and balance beam, beating a well-trained and highly competitive international field. Outgoing and hard-working, Zmeskal has drawn comparisons with Mary Lou Retton because her build is so muscular. Together with teammate Shannon Miller, she has helped bring a new level of respect to the American women's gymnastics team.

Zmeskal was one of the rare and lucky gymnasts who could train without leaving her hometown. Born and raised near Houston, she began tumbling at age six when she followed a friend into the Sundance Athletic Club. The club had recently been bought by gymnastics coach Bela Karolyi, the force behind such legends as Nadia Comaneci and Mary Lou Retton. When Zmeskal became serious about the sport, she found she could spend long hours at the club without sacrificing the normalcy of her home life. That proved to be a big plus for her career.

As a seventh grader, Zmeskal was chosen to be one of "Karolyi's Kids," an honor reserved for a half dozen elite gymnasts being groomed for world competition. Zmeskal, who had never been tagged as a prodigy, was thrilled. She left school and continued her studies through correspondence, while spending as many as eight hours a day training with Karolyi. "All I've missed of my childhood is leaving school," she told *Sports Illustrated* in 1992. "I don't count that as too much of a sacrifice. I can still go back. I've had a pretty good life, knock wood."

Karolyi began to detect the seeds of greatness in the athlete he called "little pumpkin." Sure enough, in the autumn of 1991, the four-foot-seven, 80-pound Zmeskal made history when she won the first gold medal in the gymnastics all-around at the world championships held in Indianapolis.

"I used to dream of the day when I could just flop on the living room couch after school and watch television from 5 to 9 p.m. But now that I can do it, I'm not interested."

Kim Zmeskal performs her floor exercise routine at the 1992 World Gymnastics Championships; she won the gold medal in this event. (AP/Wide World Photos)

Zmeskal also helped the Americans win a team silver medal by turning in a perfect 10 vault late in the team competition. After the event, Karolyi told *Time:* "Kim has an outstanding capability to pull herself together and perform consistently under pressure. You can see on her face that she'll do it, no matter what."

Zmeskal's gold medal performance drew sneers from at least one of her competitors, Svetlana Boguinskaia of the former Soviet Union. Boguinskaia suggested that Zmeskal had only won because she was on her home turf. As if to prove her Soviet counterpart wrong, Zmeskal traveled to Paris in the spring of 1992 and captured two gold medals in individual events, floor exercise and balance beam. The stage was set for a showdown between Zmeskal, the three-time U.S. champion, and Boguinskaia at the 1992 Summer Games.

Both Zmeskal and her coach thought the 1992 Olympics would be Kim's chance to shine. She was known for her mental toughness and admired

KIM ZMESKAL

American gymnast

Born: February 6, 1976 in Houston, Texas.

Career Highlights:
- captured a gold medal in the world championships all-around competition, and helped the Americans win a team silver medal by turning in a perfect-10 vault, 1991

- earned individual gold medals in floor exercise and balance beam, world championships, 1992

- won U.S. championships three times

- earned a bronze medal in team competition, 1992 Olympic Games, Barcelona, Spain.

---

for her healthy-looking, muscular physique. No American had beaten her in years, and she had won the most recent world championship. Boguinskaia, her most serious challenger, was 19, a veritable senior citizen in the gymnastics ranks.

Curiously enough, the Olympics proved Zmeskal's downfall. While teammate Shannon Miller won two silver and two bronze medals, Zmeskal came up nearly empty-handed, earning only a bronze in team competition. In her best event, the balance beam, she fell off during a cartwheel back handspring. She had never missed the move before, even in practice.

"I'd always imagined the Olympics would be the best meet of my whole life. And it wasn't," Zmeskal said in *Sports Illustrated*. ". . . I was worried I'd let everybody down. Bela. The team. The American people. How could I not? The television camera was right in my face." On the other hand, Zmeskal concluded that she was glad to have won a team bronze. "The bronze medal was so cool," she said. "That was the best night of the whole year. It was my best performance."

Shortly after the 1992 Olympics, Zmeskal decided to reduce her training time and enjoy the life of a normal high school junior. She soon discovered that she really hadn't missed much, spending all those hours in the gym. "After two weeks it was already boring," she told *Sports Illustrated*. "I used to dream of the day when I could just flop on the living room couch after school and watch television from 5 to 9 p.m. But now that I can do it, I'm not interested."

The path led back to Karolyi's gym, and Zmeskal is still there, still competing on the national level, and helping to groom the next generation of Olympians. From her own experiences, she told *Sports Illustrated*, "I've learned you don't have to win first place to win. People have been so supportive. It's almost like they feel it's good that someone doesn't always win. This hasn't been bad for me at all, not winning [an Olympic] gold medal. It's almost better."

And her plans for the 1996 Summer Games?

"I'll be there," she said. "In the stands."

INDEX

Bollettieri, Nick 382, 428
Bolstad, Les 528
Bonaly, Surya 32, **52–5**, 285
Bonner, Ray 470
Borysewicz, Eddie 477
Boulmerka, Hassiba 373
Bowdoin College 39, 40
boxing 320–2
Braatz, Kim 93
Bradley, Pat 443
Bredael, Annelies 289
Brennan, Frank 265
Brisco, Valerie **56–9**, 209
Broderick Cup 76, 78, 297, 299, 335, 336
Brooklyn College 306, 307
Brough, Louise 368, 369–70
Brown, Alice 17
Brunet, Pierre 225
Budd Pieterse, Zola **60–3**, 116, 242
Budd, Zola *see* Budd Pieterse, Zola
Bueno, Maria 73, 265
bull riding 244–5
Bullock Workman, Fanny 439
Burke Mountain Academy 374
Burnham, Elizabeth 93
Buser, Martin 67
Butcher, Susan **64–7**, 395, 397
Button, Dick 230

C

California State College, Los Angeles 267
California State University, Northridge 56, 58, 209, 210
Callaghan, Richard 48, 50
Canvas of Ice 520
Capriati, Jennifer **68–71**
Capriati, Stefano 68, 70
Carey, Merritt 13
Carlos, John 482
Carmen on Ice 520, 521
Carroll, Frank 284
Carver, Chris 134
Casals, Rosemary **72–5**, 265, 432
Casals, Rosie *see* Casals, Rosemary
Caulkins, Tracy **76–8**
Cavanagh, Sarah 13
Central Oregon Community College 212, 214
Chadwick-Onyszkiewicz, Alison 47
Chaney, John 456
Chapman College 246, 248
Charles, Lisa 13

Charpia, Billie Jo 93
Chen Lu 54, 285
Cheyney State University 455, 456
Chow, Amy **79–82**
Cinderella . . . Frozen in Time 217
Clark, Mary Ellen **83–6**
Clemson University 160
Cline, Nancy Lieberman *see* Lieberman-Cline, Nancy
Coachman, Alice **87–90**
Cole, Amy 93
College at New Paltz, New York 235
Collett, Glenna 503, 504
Colonial Affair 279, 281, 282
Colorado Silver Bullets **91–4**, 420, 421
Colorado State University 485
Comaneci, Nadia **95–8**, 274, 346, 347, 387, 388
Connecticut Falcons 247–8
Conner, Bart 97, 98
Conradt, Jody **99–101**, 306, 458
Cooksey, Patricia 281, 282
Coombes, Melissa 92, 93, 94
Cornell, Sheila 205
Cornwall, Evelyn *see* St. James, Lyn
Cossaboon, John 219
Coughenour, Cara 93
Courier, Jim 428, 430
Court, Margaret *see* Smith Court, Margaret
Cowgirl Hall of Fame 245
Cox, Lynne **102–5**
Crenshaw, Ben 505
Cress, Missy 93
Crookenden, Ian 73, 74
cross-country skiing 222–4
Croteau, Julie 92, 94
Cumbre Aña Peck 439
cycling 477–9, 536–8

D

Dallas Diamonds 295
Daniel, Beth **106–8**, 260, 303
Dartmouth College 193
Davis, Charlotte 134
Davis, Pamela 93
Dawes, Dominique **109–13**, 345, 346
Decker, Mary *see* Decker Slaney, Mary
Decker Slaney, Mary 60, 62, 63, **114–7**
de la Pena, George 464